Time Out

Sydney

www.timeout.com/sydney

Time Out Digital Ltd
4th Floor
125 Shaftesbury Avenue
London WC2H 8AD
United Kingdom
Tel: +44 (0)20 7813 3000
Fax: +44 (0)20 7813 6001
Email: guides@timeout.com
www.timeout.com

Published by Time Out Digital Ltd, a wholly owned subsidiary
of Time Out Group Ltd. Time Out and the Time Out logo are
trademarks of Time Out Group Ltd.

© **Time Out Group Ltd 2016**
Previous editions 1997, 2000, 2001, 2004, 2006, 2008, 2011.

10 9 8 7 6 5 4 3 2 1

This edition first published in Great Britain in 2016 by Ebury Publishing.
20 Vauxhall Bridge Road, London SW1V 2SA

Ebury Publishing is part of the Penguin Random House group of companies
whose addresses can be found at global.penguinrandomhouse.com

Distributed in the US and Latin America by Publishers Group West
(1-510-809-3700)

For further distribution details, see www.timeout.com.

ISBN: 978-1-84670-984-5

A CIP catalogue record for this book is available from the British Library.

Printed and bound in China by Leo Paper Products Ltd.

Contents

92

Sydney's Top 20	10
Sydney Today	18
Itineraries	24
Diary	28
Sydney's Best	40

Explore 46

Sydney Tours	48
Circular Quay & the Rocks	52
Central Sydney	60
Eastern Suburbs	92
Inner West	118
North Shore	136
Northern Beaches	146
The West	154
The South	160
Sydney's Best Beaches	164

Arts & Entertainment 176

Children	178
Film	181
Gay & Lesbian	190
Nightlife	200
Performing Arts	210

Escapes & Excursions 222

Escapes & Excursions	224

In Context 240

History	242
Architecture	254

160

105

130

Essential Information 264

Hotels	**266**
Getting Around	**282**
Resources A-Z	**287**
Further Reference	**294**
Index	**296**

Maps 300

New South Wales	**302**
Greater Sydney	**303**
Sydney Harbour	**304**
Sydney by Area	**307**
Street Maps	**308**
Street Index	**317**
Sydney Ferries Map	**319**
Sydney Trains Map	**320**

268

Time Out Sydney

Editorial
Editor Phil Bunting
Proofreader John Shandy Watson
Indexer Sophy Leys Johnston

Editorial Director Sarah Guy
Group Finance Manager Margaret Wright

Design
Art Editor Christie Webster
Group Commercial Senior Designer Jason Tansley

Picture Desk
Picture Editor Jael Marschner
Deputy Picture Editor Ben Rowe
Picture Researcher Lizzy Owen

Advertising
Managing Director St John Betteridge

Marketing
Senior Publishing Brand Manager Luthfa Begum
Head of Circulation Dan Collins

Production
Production Controller Katie Mulhern-Bhudia

Time Out Group
Founder Tony Elliott
Executive Chairman Julio Bruno
Chief Executive Officer Noel Penzer
Publisher Alex Batho

Contributors
Sydney's Top 20 Emma Joyce, Emma Dallas. **Sydney Today** Jenny Valentish, Angus Fontaine. **Itineraries** Emma Joyce, Emma Dallas. **Diary** Emma Joyce, Emma Dallas. **Sydney's Best** Emma Joyce Emma Dallas. **Explore** Erin Moy, Freya Herring, Emily Lloyd-Tait, Emma Joyce, Dee Jefferson. **Best Beaches** James Wilkinson, Daniel Winter. **Children** Jenny Valentish, Emma Joyce. **Film** Jenny Valentish, Nick Dent. **Gay & Lesbian** Jenny Valentish, Andrew Georgiou. **Nightlife** Jenny Valentish, Jordan Kretchmer. **Performing Arts** Jenny Valentish, Dee Jefferson. **Escapes & Excursions** James Wilkinson, Daniel Winter. **History** Juliet Rieden, Jenny Valentish. **Architecture** Angus Fontaine, Jenny Valentish. **Hotels** James Wilkinson. **Getting Around, Resources, Further Reference** Nicholas Fonseca.

Maps JS Graphics Ltd (john@jsgraphics.co.uk)

Cover and pull-out map photography Cahir Davitt/AWL Images

Back cover photography Clockwise from top left: Dan Breckwoldt/Shutterstock.com; Courtesy The Langham, Sydney; CoolR/Shutterstock.com; PomInOz/Shutterstock.com; Brett Stevens/Courtesy Bennelong Restaurant

Photography pages 5 (middle left), 20/21, 31, 33, 99, 105, 136/137, 144, 166, 228, 261 (bottom) PomInOz/Shutterstock.com; 7, 138 Aleksandar Todorovic/Shutterstock.com; 10 Kiyoshi Hijiki/Shutterstock.com; 12 (top) Victor Maschek/Shutterstock.com; 12 (bottom) Goran Bogicevic/Shutterstock.com; 13 (bottom), 27, 62, 63, pull-out map AGNSW; 14, 116, 257 © Nicholas Watt courtesy Sydney Living Museums; 16/17 Michael Nicholson; 17, 25, 40/41 (bottom), pull-out map © Brett Stevens; 18/19, 52 Hpeterswald/Wikimedia Commons; 22, 38 Destination NSW; 23 Josef Nalevansky/City of Sydney; 26 (bottom) Hollie Adams; 28/29, 34 (top) Daniel Boud; 30 (top), 35 (top), 205 Eva Rinaldi/Wikimedia Commons; 30 (bottom), 57 Leah-Anne Thompson/Shutterstock.com; 32 Nadezda Zavitaeva/Shutterstock.com; 34 (bottom) © Hamilton Lund; 36 (top) mariematata/Shutterstock.com; 36 (bottom) Prudence Upton; 39 © Hamilton Lund, Sydney Living Museums; 40/41 (top) © Stephen Antonopoulos/Images for Business; 42 (top) Chris Court Photography; 43 (bottom) Jeremyshaw.com.au; 44 (top) Samuel Byrne; 44 (bottom) © Linnet Foto; 44/45, 208 Stuart Scott; 46/47, pull-out map CoolR/Shutterstock.com; 48 Eoghan Lewis; 52/53 Chris Howey/Shutterstock.com; 68, 69 Anliette; 74 Tooykrub/Shutterstock.com; 85 Alan Benson; 86 JAZZDOG/Shutterstock.com; 88 (bottom) Hollie Adams; 102/103, 110 Wiiin/Shutterstock.com; 111 Will Horner; 112, 129, 156, 157 Sardaka/Wikimedia Commons; 117 © James Horan courtesy Sydney Living Museums; 118, 134, 214 (left), 215, 216 © Brett Boardman Photography; 118/119 © Niall MacLeod/CORBIS; 124, 125 jonesphoto.com.au; 128 Maksym Kozlenko/Wikimedia Commons; 133 BenHosking Photo 2011; 135 © Jamie Nimmo; 140/141 Luckies/Shutterstock.com; 146/147 Mandy Zieren; 150 Eden Connell; 154 J Miller; 158 James Horan, Historic Houses Trust of NSW; 168/169 Diliff/Wikimedia Commons; 172 Enoch Lau/Wikimedia Commons; 176/177 Sathit/Shutterstock.com; 179 Alex Proimos/Wikimedia Commons; 180 Australian Reptile Park; 182 (bottom) Greg Corbett; 188 Enzo Amato; 189 Snap Stills/REX Shutterstock; 193 ZAC/Wikimedia Commons; 199 © MediaServicesAP/Demotix/Corbis; 204 Simon_sees/Wikimedia Commons; 212 Irenaeus Herok; 214 Helen White; 217 James Green; 218, 219 Peter Greig; 220 Ken Butti - MEDIAIDEM; 221 Keith Saunders; 229 FotoSleuth/Wikimedia Commons; 242/243 The LIFE Picture Collection/Getty Images; 245, 248, 250 Wikimedia Commons; 246 Conollyb/Wikimedia Commons; 253 Lisa Maree Williams/Getty Images; 258 © Stephen Antonopoulos/Images for Business; 259 Tuangtong Soraprasert/Shutterstock.com; 260 e X p o s e/Shutterstock.com; 261 (top and middle) Hpeterswald/Shutterstock.com; 262 Lebelmont/Shutterstock.com; 274 Autumn Mooney Photography; 278 (middle) True Blue Cockatoo; 286 Jamie Williams/City of Sydney

The following images were supplied by the featured establishments: 5 (middle right and bottom), 15, 24/25, 26 (top), 32/33, 35 (bottom), 42 (bottom), 43 (top), 45, 49, 50/51, 60, 70, 78, 79, 81, 84, 88 (top), 90, 91, 100, 114, 115, 122, 123, 127, 130, 131, 136, 142, 143, 146, 149, 152, 153, 154/155, 160, 181, 182 (top), 183, 185, 186, 190, 191, 192, 194, 195, 197, 198, 200, 202, 203, 207, 233, 238, 264/265, 266, 268, 269, 270, 271, 272, 273, 276, 277, 278 (top and bottom), 280

About the Guide

GETTING AROUND

Each sightseeing chapter contains a street map of the area marked with the locations of sights and museums (❶), restaurants (❶), cafés and bars (❶) and shops (❶). There are also street maps of Sydney at the back of the book, along with an overview map of the city on pages 8-9. In addition, there is a detachable fold-out street map.

THE ESSENTIALS

For practical information, including visas, disabled access, emergency numbers, lost property, websites and local transport, see the Essential Information section. It begins on page 266.

THE LISTINGS

Addresses, phone numbers, websites, transport information, hours and prices are all included in our listings, as are selected other facilities. All were checked and correct at press time. However, business owners can alter their arrangements at any time, and fluctuating economic conditions can cause prices to change rapidly.

The very best venues in the city, the must-sees and must-dos in every category, have been marked with a red star (★). In the sightseeing chapters, we've also marked venues with free admission with a FREE symbol.

PHONE NUMBERS

The area code for Sydney is 02, but you don't need to use this when calling from within Sydney and New South Wales. Just dial the eight-digit number listed in the guide. From outside Australia, dial your country's access code (00 from the UK, 011 from the US) or a + symbol, followed by the Australian country code (61), then 2 for Sydney (dropping the initial zero) and the number. So, to reach the Museum of Sydney, dial + 61 2 9251 5988.

FEEDBACK

We welcome feedback on this guide, both on the venues we've included and on any other locations that you'd like to see featured in future editions. Please email us at guides@timeout.com.

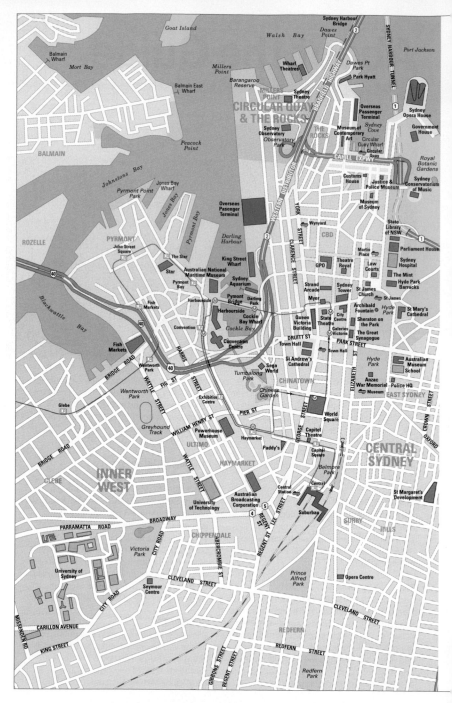

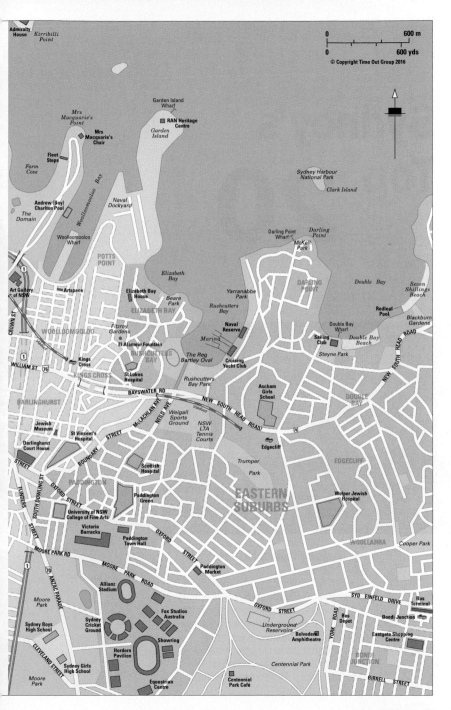

Sydney's Top 20

From iconic buildings to idyllic beaches, we list the city's finest.

1 Sydney Opera House
(page 58)

The Opera House may define Sydney's image internationally, but it only opened in 1973. The building's stunning design, encompassing four major performance halls, has been debated ever since, with interpretations ranging from shells to sails and waves, and even a family of swans. Book a tour and make up your own mind.

2 Bondi to Coogee coastal walk
(page 106)

Make Bondi Beach the start of your day out, but don't stop there. The spectacular Bondi to Coogee coastal walk has cliff-top views with waves crashing far below, trendy beaches such as Tamarama (known to some as Glamarama) and family sands such as Bronte. Watch out for Australia's most scenic cemetery, along with parks, bays and rock pools. After the two-hour walk, you can catch a bus from Coogee back to the city.

3 Royal Botanic Gardens
(page 67)

Wrapped around Sydney Harbour just along from the Opera House, full of majestic trees, spacious lawns, bird-filled ponds, ornamental flowerbeds and even a fernery, the Royal Botanic Gardens is a real oasis. The gardens have more than a million specimens, and there's even a hop-on, hop-off 'trackless train' for the less energetic. Sit beneath the large trees on the gentle hill, have a bite of lunch and take in the beauty of the harbour.

4 Museum of Contemporary Art
(page 58)

Once the offices of the Maritime Services Board, this waterside temple to contemporary art was overhauled and reopened in 2012 with light, airy, uncluttered interiors, more floor space and a boxy new façade. There's more to the place than good looks, though: the rooftop café and sculpture terrace are worth checking out after you've found out what today's leading Aussie artists are getting up to. And the building's original sandstone heart is still there.

5 CBD shopping
(page 69)

The grande dame of Sydney shopping, the 19th-century Queen Victoria Building fills an entire block with its elaborate Romanesque architecture. It's worth a visit even if you spend nothing. The 1892-vintage Strand Arcade also has a certain grandeur (and some of Australia's leading fashion designers), while the more modern Galleries Victoria is home to a mix of boutiques and other retailers, a food hall and the monumental Arthouse Hotel.

6 Hyde Park Barracks
(page 63)

Designed by convict architect Francis Greenway, the Hyde Park Barracks housed 15,000 male convicts between 1819 and 1848. Later, it became a female immigration depot and a government

asylum for infirm, destitute women. Today, you can explore the convict experience, lie in a convict hammock, and discover the daily lives of other occupants at this landmark in the historic Macquarie Street precinct.

7 Climb the Harbour Bridge
(page 48)

You can walk across the Harbour Bridge, catch a train or bus, or drive, but it's much more exhilarating to climb it with BridgeClimb Sydney – over the arc of the 'coat-hanger' that crowns it. All you'll need are sunglasses and comfortable shoes – BridgeClimb provides the rest. When you've ascended the arches and

reached the summit 134 metres above sea level, your climb guide will take the photo that proves your fearlessness.

8 Art Gallery of NSW
(page 63)

Sydney's most important public gallery, showing its artworks in expansive, light-filled spaces against the backdrop of the city and the harbour. There is a good collection of colonial and 19th-century Australian works, a few European old masters, modern and contemporary displays and two floors of Asian art. Check out, too, the galleries celebrating Aboriginal and Torres Strait Islander art.

9 Newtown
(page 132)

Sydney's Inner West boho hub is home to boutiques, vintage clothes stores and bookshops, as well as fine cafés and Thai restaurants. Check out Cream on King for moderately priced retro rags and terrace boutique Pretty Dog for designs crying out to be taken for a whirl around the room (even if you can't afford to take them all home).

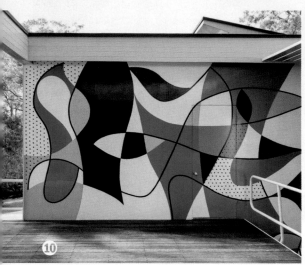

12 Surry Hills
(page 80)

Once the scruffy home to Sydney's rag trade and a former local haunt for sundry nefarious folk, Surry Hills is now Sydney's buzziest and most happening 'burb. Want clothes? Hop along Crown and Bourke Streets or hit the monthly markets for some seriously cool vintage. Hungry? Well, 'Surry', as some locals call it, is brimming with Sydney's most innovative chefs and character-filled restaurants. And if you're thirsty, whether for a classic cocktail or a big bold red, Surry Hills has got you covered with its many pubs and bars. In spring, prepare to bask in the sunshine, beer in hand, as local musicians light up the stage of the one-day Surry Hills Festival.

10 Rose Seidler House
(page 257)

Designed for his parents by young immigrant Harry Seidler – later responsible for some of Sydney skyline's landmark buildings – the house, completed in 1950, overturned almost every convention of suburban home design, architecture, art and technology in a bold vision for a new way of living. Today, still surrounded by bushland with views of Ku-ring-gai Chase National Park, it is one of the finest examples of midcentury modern domestic architecture in Australia.

11 Kings Cross
(page 88)

Anchored by Macleay Street, Potts Point has been described as a little slice of Paris, with tree-lined streets and gorgeous old art deco buildings. Stroll down the road and just around the bend, however, and you can still get a taste of the old Kings Cross: as Sydney's seediest strip (in every sense of the word), it's the red-light area the local worthies have not yet managed to close down.

13 Northern Beaches
(page 146)

Sydney's Northern Beaches stretch invitingly from day-trippers' Manly to millionaires' row Palm Beach, 28 kilometres (17 miles) to the north. You can reach a roll call of stunning beaches by bus or car – Freshwater, South and North Curl Curl, Dee Why, Collaroy, Narrabeen, Mona Vale, Newport, Bilgola, Avalon and Palm Beach itself, famously the location for TV soap *Home and Away*. Don't miss Pittwater, a large inlet that stretches north from Mona Vale on the peninsula's eastern side, dotted with yachts and surrounded by hills of eucalyptus.

14 Rocks pub crawl
(page 54)

Lay the foundations for a boozy day on the Rocks at the Australian Heritage with a Coat of Arms pizza and a bottle of boutique beer, best enjoyed at one of the outdoor tables on Cumberland Street. Then hit the Glenmore's roof for some afternoon brews. Next stop, find a place to prop yourself up at the bar of the Lord Nelson for a house-brewed beer and maybe a meat pie floater. And, for your final hurrah, raise a glass at the venerable Fortune of War, thus completing the ultimate historic Sydney pub crawl.

15 Bennelong
(page 59)

There are four ways to eat here, in this space inside the Opera House sails: executive chef Peter Gilmore's restaurant downstairs; the Cured & Cultured eaterie up a floor; and the bar at the top; or, for $650 per head, the chef's table in the custom-designed kitchen. The geometric arched ceiling is stunning and the harbour views from the bar superb.

16 Taronga Zoo
(page 180)

Set on Sydney Harbour's northern shore and reached by a 12-minute ferry ride from the city, Taronga Zoo is home to 4,000 animals from over 350 Australian and international species, many of them threatened. With keeper talks, shows, tours, events and concerts, there's usually something going down at the zoo. There's even Roar & Snore – billed as Sydney's ultimate sleepover – where you camp overnight in the heart of the zoo and wake up to views of the Opera House and Harbour Bridge.

17 Carriageworks Farmers Market
(page 87)

In just a few short years Carriageworks Farmers Market, formerly Eveleigh Farmers Market and still known by that name to many, has become

19 Cockatoo Island
(page 83)

This one-time convict prison, later Australia's biggest shipyard, is Sydney's version of Alcatraz. Grab a ferry to the UNESCO World Heritage-listed island and enjoy an audio or guided tour recounting the lives of convicts incarcerated in the sandstone jail, or watch volunteers bring the island's shipyard machinery back to life. The Island Bar heaves with revellers in warm-weather months, and there are campsites and other accommodation options.

Sydney's top fresh food and produce market. Join the throngs of hip Inner Westers here on a Saturday morning as producers come from all over the state laden with gorgeous-looking produce. Grab a bite to eat at food stalls run by leading lights of Sydney cuisine, such as Billy Kwong or Bird Cow Fish, or just buy a cup of coffee and take a seat at the sun-exposed Carriageworks wall opposite. Saturday morning bliss.

18 Australian Museum
(page 63)

Established in 1827 with the aim of procuring 'many rare and curious specimens of Natural History', the Australian Museum has grown into an internationally recognised collection of over 18 million cultural and scientific objects that document the biodiversity and geodiversity of the region. As well as significant ethnographic and archaeological materials representing Aboriginal and Torres Strait Islander cultures, the collection encompasses Pacific Islander, Asian, African and American artefacts.

20 Drag shows
(page 194, 195)

This city is world-renowned for its talented drag queens. You'll see plenty of them at Mardi Gras, but for the rest of the year, the best place to find them is on the golden gay mile of Oxford Street in Darlinghurst. There are hourly drag shows on weekend evenings at the Stonewall Hotel, plus regular drag events at the Shift Bar, while megaclub Arq Sydney hosts its own regular drag extravaganzas.

Sydney Today

Still growing.

TEXT: JENNY VALENTISH & ANGUS FONTAINE

It is not possible to compare Sydney with Rome, Athens or even London, her mother city; they are centres of the Old World and Sydney is only three human lifetimes old. Sydney today is a city at a confluence of energies, with tidal flows of money and people shaping its space. Sydney's population is expected to reach five million in 2016; it's the iconic gateway to Australia and a true global city.

This Sydney is different to the one that showed itself off to the world with the 'best ever' Olympics in 2000. Since that pivotal moment, the city has boomed and busted, experiencing unprecedented growth, but with accompanying housing shortages in step with climbing property values.

Yet the convict ethos is set deep within the buttery sandstone of Sin City's buildings. Sydney dazzles with its glamorous beach lifestyle, but the front pages are kept busy with crises, scandals and epidemics. These contradictions are a source of constant tension, making Sydney a triumph of complexity.

THE RENT SQUEEZE

As of September 2015, Sydney had the highest median house price of any city in Australia ($914,056) and asked the most of renters too (a median of $520 a week). Increasingly, this is starting to affect the city's frontline industries. Workers are being squeezed out of the city, and the trend to 'seachanges' and 'treechanges' – moving to the coast or country – is high, with more affordable fringe suburbs and country towns catching the outflow. For the thousands who keep alive the dream of finding a Sydney home, the prospect of cattle-call property inspections with up to 100 others is a constant challenge. What does the State Government plan to do about it? No one is quite sure (least of all, the government itself). The Federal Government's 'first home-buyers grant' of $7,000 has been scrapped and replaced by a $10,000 grant that only applies to brand-new properties, which are likely to be either apartments or houses in the outer suburbs. Investors smile at the squeeze but renters are riled, and the trend for thirtysomethings still living at home with their parents is growing.

GRIDLOCKED

An enduring grievance facing commuters in Sydney is the difficulty in getting to and from work.The creaking train system carries up to a million passengers every day, but services are often late, cancelled or – at best – unpredictable. There are plenty of bus routes operating centrally from Railway Square, at the top of the bustling George Street central precinct, but because 75 per cent of commuters drive their cars to work, the mix makes for a traffic-choked nightmare.

Mayor Clover Moore, now in her third term, vehemently opposes the Federal and State governments' progress through the first stages of 'Australia's biggest urban roads' project – the $12 billion WestConnex link to the west and south-west. This, she says, will introduce yet more traffic into gridlocked areas and will eat up transport funding for decades.

By contrast, Moore's long-running project is to extend the light rail network in the city, to ease traffic congestion. The city invested more than $40 million to undertake feasibility studies and safeguard a light-rail corridor from

Green Square to Central, and another $220 million to extend light rail through the city centre to Moore Park and Randwick.

Moore also introduced a 200-kilometre network of cycleways, spanning the CBD and inner-city areas of Glebe, Camperdown, Erskineville, Pyrmont, Ultimo and Surry Hills. Sure, these green bike paths have stripped some suburbs of parking spaces and car access, but generally they've been embraced as a way for savvy Sydneysiders to beat the traffic, while also cutting emissions and improving public health.

LOCKOUT LAWS

Nothing has reshaped Sydney nightlife as viscerally as the lockout laws introduced to Kings Cross and the CBD in February 2014. Now venues can't let in punters after 1.30am, and alcohol service must cease at 3am. These laws were imposed by the State Government after the death of a man by a 'king hit' punch in 2012 – the latest statistic in a wave of violence. Advocates argue it has worked well – as of August 2015, violent

Light rail.

> *'Nothing has reshaped Sydney nightlife as viscerally as the lockout laws introduced to Kings Cross and the CBD.'*

attacks in Kings Cross are down by 31 per cent – but in reality that troublesome contingent has simply moved the party to the Inner West. There has been an 18 per cent increase of violence in Newtown, which has long been known as an 'alternative' area. Now, weekend partiers flood into Newtown from the suburbs and flit between the late-licence bars, completely changing the demographic. Unsurprisingly, the Newtown sex industry is capitalising on this, with its brothels and sex shops sucking up the custom that has been lost from Kings Cross businesses.

THAT DARLING HARBOUR

While the much-loved Sydney Entertainment Centre is set to be demolished in early 2016, there are bold new developments afoot for Darling Harbour, including a conference, exhibition and entertainment centre – ICC Sydney – opening in December 2016, and a residential village called Darling Square. The 20-hectare transformation will include new light-rail connections – to the CBD, the financial services hub at Barangaroo in the north, and the creative-media and IT hub in the south – and add even more events throughout the year to an already-busy culture calendar and the Saturday-night fireworks displays. These developments are the project of Darling Harbour Live, in partnership with the New South Wales Government, and they're estimated to create 3,700 jobs during construction and a further 4,000 on completion.

CULTURAL CAPITAL

While Melbourne tries to console itself that dismal weather has somehow nurtured a

Vivid Sydney.

helps make the atmosphere at January's Sydney Cricket Test Match utterly loony, even though Mexican waves and 'beer snakes' were banned from the Sydney Cricket Ground as of 2006. In 2013, a $186 million development lifted punters' spirits again with the addition of a new on-site microbrewery. More interested in messing about in boats? Now over 70 years old, the Sydney Hobart Yacht Race is held every Boxing Day and covers 630 nautical miles. The crews tend to joyously imbibe at the Customs House Bar at Circular Quay beforehand. But for a classic Sydney sport experience, it's hard to beat catching a National Rugby League (NRL) game. The grand final has been held in Sydney since 1908, and now attracts a crowd of around 84,000.

TAKING A GAMBLE

All-round leisure complex the Star in Pyrmont has served as an entertainment zone since 1996, with two gaming floors, eight bars, seven restaurants and the Lyric Theatre. It's licensed as the only legal casino in New South Wales. Now its reign has been threatened by the work-in-progress Crown Casino. A sister to the Crown in Melbourne, this will become the city's tallest habitable building, home to a 'six-star' hotel as well as an upmarket entertainment complex and VIP-membership casino. It's the baby of businessman and media mogul James Packer, and will dominate the 22 hectares of prime harbour real estate that is Barangaroo, opening in 2019.

The former shipping site of Barangaroo, known as the 'Hungry Mile', was awarded to Lend Lease in December 2009 to develop a $6 billion project of residential office towers with a new headland park, connecting culture hub Walsh Bay with the food and drinks strip of Cockle Bay and Darling Harbour. But mayhem has ensued, with employment and industry bodies in favour of creating a 'financial gateway' facing off against architects and conservationists appalled at the scale of the designs since the tender was awarded and citing the risk of toxic waste in the harbour. At least, in August 2015, the Barangaroo Reserve was opened to the public; it has been architecturally designed to represent the harbour as it would have looked pre-colonisation, with the installation of 75,000 native trees and plants.

unique cultural ecosystem, it's lazy to dismiss Sydney as being the poor cousin when it comes to the arts and festivals.

Barely has the smoke cleared from the epic New Year's Eve fireworks display then we're in the throes of the Sydney Festival. Every January, world-class local and international acts – from extreme dance to highbrow theatre – flood the city. Winter brings Vivid Sydney, an arts festival centred around the harbour foreshore, with the sails of the Opera House illuminated 24/7 by transformative avant-garde projections, and live music ringing from within. Since the inaugural festival in 2009, attendance has grown to 2.7 million.

Then in October, Good Food Month provides a feast of food festivals, public art displays, island-hopping odysseys and the annual Breakfast on the Bridge, in which the iconic 'Coathanger' is closed to traffic, laid with turf and opened to over 6,000 Sydneysiders to lay down picnic rugs 134 metres above sea level.

SPORTING ENDEAVOURS

Sydney does a sports spectacle very well. Of course, the Barmy Army – aka the Poms – are partly responsible for that. It's this mob that

FUTURE SYDNEY
The mayor's major developments for a greener city.

Sydney's Lord Mayor, Clover Moore, has a dream… of creating 'a city where people are more important than cars'.

ASHMORE PROJECT
One of the City of Sydney's biggest urban development projects is the Ashmore precinct in Erskineville, towards Alexandria. The 17-hectare site will be home to around 6,000 residents, with local shops and cafés, new streets with bicycle lanes, a large central park and systems to manage stormwater.

GREEN SQUARE
Sydney's first eco-village, Green Square is a 278-hectare site between the CBD and Sydney Airport. Moore has committed $440 million to create a commercial and cultural hub that sets new benchmarks in green urban design and will house 33,000 people, with a new library, plaza and aquatic centre.

HAROLD PARK
This urban renewal project in Forest Lodge, near leafy Glebe, aims to provide 1,250 sustainable new homes for low- to moderate-income Sydneysiders. The project, running from 2012 to 2018, will include playgrounds, picnic areas and open grassy spaces.

PADDINGTON RESERVOIR
Already the winner of the nation's highest architectural honours, this once-derelict hangout for graffiti artists on Paddington's Oxford Street is now a sunken wonderland open to the public, with hanging gardens, a lake of contemplation and a *très* cool vibe.

SURRY HILLS LIBRARY
Designed by FJMT architects in collaboration with the City of Sydney, this stunning four-storey creation on Crown Street in Surry Hills set new standards in sustainable design when it opened in 2010, with sun-tracking louvres, a rooftop photovoltaic system and a 'thermal labyrinth' – a series of high-thermal-mass rock baskets, which cools the air within.

SYDNEY PARK
This 44-hectare site formerly used for clay extraction and waste disposal is now central Sydney's biggest park, with a boardwalk weaving through wetlands and a mega children's playground with a bike track. Even the old brickworks have been put to use – as an arts hub and events space.

WALSH BAY
Even actress Cate Blanchett swung into action for the Sydney Theatre Company's $5.2 million Greening the Wharf project to transform its home. It includes rainwater harvesting, smart flush toilets and 1,906 solar panels on the Wharf venue's roof to generate over 70 per cent of the theatre's electricity.

Paddington Reservoir.

Itineraries

*Our morning-to-night
planner for getting the
most out of Sydney.*

1.30PM

4PM

11AM

Day 1

9AM Hop on a ferry to Kirribilli wharf and eat your breakfast as glassy green waves lap up against the wooden wharf at **Anvil Coffee Co** (*p139*).

11AM Naturally, you've pre-booked a **BridgeClimb** (*p48*): a climb to the top of the famous grey icon known as 'the Coathanger' – the **Sydney Harbour Bridge** (*p54*). It's an exhilarating experience, although the climb isn't as arduous or scary as you might

think. It's well worth the effort, and the views from the top are a real thrill.

1.30PM Come back down to earth by strolling around the Walsh Bay wharves, a popular waterside spot for drinks before or after performances at the nearby theatres. After all that bright sunshine and blue water, enjoy lunch at **Café Sopra** (*p163*) or take a short stroll on the Rocks for snacks on the rooftop at the **Glenmore Hotel** (*p56*).

7PM

Clockwise from far left: **Bridge Climb**; **Glenmore Hotel**; **Bennelong**; **Museum of Contemporary Art**.

4PM Do some window-shopping in the colonial-era cobblestoned streets of the Rocks on your way to the **Museum of Contemporary Art** (*p58*). Pick up some arty gifts in the **MCA shop** (*p59*) and take in an exhibition.

5PM Grab a takeaway coffee and head across bustling Circular Quay, past the buskers and the ferry wharves to the iconic **Opera House** (*p58*), from where you can slip into the **Royal Botanic Garden** (*p67*) and have a rest sitting on the grass amid flowers, watching the ferries pass by.

7PM You've booked dinner at **Bennelong** (*p59*): good move. Enjoy your sumptuous meal inside the sails of the Opera House before your concert or opera – also booked ahead.

Top: **Gunther's Dining Room**. Bottom: **LP's Quality Meats**.

11PM It's time for a nightcap. Head to Redfern for a bar crawl that will have you swigging cocktails with the locals. Start at **Arcadia Liquors** (*p86*) and ease into the night with a toasted sandwich and a glass of house wine before checking out the phallic artwork at creative hang-out the **Bearded Tit** (*p86*). Or opt for boogie nights at **Gunther's Dining Room** (*p86*).

Day 2

10AM Head over to Surry Hills for breakfast – try **Reuben Hills** (*p81*) for house-roasted coffee and the 'Dogg's Breakfast', or **Dr Faustus** (*p80*) for a BLT with an experimental French twist.
11.30AM Walk off that breakfast with a window-shop on nearby Crown and Bourke streets, both hip and buzzing thoroughfares.

Check out the independent art galleries and **Cream on Crown** (*p82*) for a vintage outfit or an original little designer piece.

1PM Head for the stylish **Nomad** (*p81*) for house-made charcuterie, pickles and cheeses, or **Longrain** (*p80*) for fun but fancy Thai cuisine.

3.30PM Head over to Chippendale to admire the glory of **White Rabbit** (*p87*), a state-of-the-art, four-storey temple to 21st-century Chinese art.

4PM Pop into **Central Park** mall (*p87*), a glass building covered in vertical gardens, then cross the road and ogle the striking architecture of the University of Technology campus. Time for a drink at **Freda's** (*p87*). Try a 50/50 Sazerac and, if you're in the mood, stick around for '90s R&B anthems or Eurotrash late into the night.

6PM Assuming you've decided not to stay at Freda's for the night, it's time to line your stomach for tonight's revelries: **LP's Quality Meats** (*p87*) is a big venue full of canteen-like timber tables, with a wide open kitchen producing the tastiest Southern smoked meats in Sydney.

8.30PM The night is young. Head into Newtown for a bar crawl. You can't go wrong in this hipster 'burb of indie vibes and small bars. Try **Earl's Juke Joint** (*p134*) and **Mary's** (*p134*). Finish your night with a playlist of rock 'n' roll classics at the **Midnight Special** (*p135*). The small neighbourhood bar keeps the party going until midnight most evenings of the week.

FREE SYDNEY

Enjoy the city but hang on to your cash.

Art Gallery of NSW.

It's easy to spend money in Sydney, but exploring will cost you nothing and the city also has a good crop of free attractions. Begin your free day at the **Rocks** (*p54*). It's Sydney's oldest area, with twisty laneways, sandstone stairs and cobblestoned streets – well worth a couple of hours' exploration.

Nearby, on the Domain, the **Art Gallery of NSW** (*p63*) is Sydney's leading art museum, with a large permanent collection; it's free to enter. And at the tip of the Domain, jutting out into the harbour, is one of the most photographed performing arts venues in the world. The pearly shells of the **Sydney Opera House** (*p58*) are an intrinsic part of Australia's image – and an iconic part of Sydney's skyline. It costs nothing to have a look inside.

Take time out to lounge around in **Customs House** (*p57*) and make the most of the free Wi-Fi as you thumb the extensive collection of free newspapers from around the world. While you're there, tread across a scale model of Sydney set under the glass floor of the lobby.

Next, head for some luxury window-shopping: first, head to the **Queen Victoria Building** (*p69*). You don't have to spend anything to admire the 19th-century architecture. If you are tempted, though, you'll find typical Aussie merchandise here, ranging from the cheap (a Haigh's chocolate frog) to the very expensive (an opal from one of the many jewellery boutiques).

For a break from the city, beautiful **Barangaroo** (Hickson Road, Millers Point) – the newly opened nature reserve along the western Harbour foreshore – has walking tracks, picnic areas and a giant cavern called the Cutaway. You'll have to fight for space as the locals love it, but there are deck chairs for the taking if you're there early enough or on weekdays. Alternatively, the **Royal Botanic Gardens** (*p67*) provides a lush green escape, and a relaxing way to walk between the Art Gallery of New South Wales and the Opera House.

Our top tip for free stuff in Sydney, though, is to skip across the **Sydney Harbour Bridge** (*p54*). Look up and you can spot the bridge climbers, but the best view is at eye level; from here you can take in the whole Emerald City in one glorious panorama.

Diary

*Our year-round guide
to Sydney's best
festivals and events.*

Sydney Festival. *See p33.*

Everything is upside-down on this side of the globe. Australians celebrate Christmas in summer and winter festivals kick off in June. Sydneysiders make the most of their clement weather all year round – from the spectacular fireworks that colour the harbour for New Year's Eve to the glittering floats that glide through Oxford Street in Mardi Gras. Crowds flock to the streets for annual sporting events such as the gruelling City2Surf fun run and everyone stops work to join in the festivities surrounding the nation's most famous horse race, the Melbourne Cup. Come spring, locals and visitors flood the coastal paths for cultural celebrations like Sculpture by the Sea and kite-flying extravaganza the Festival of the Winds. For vibrant, boundary-pushing arts and culture, there are major annual festivals: Vivid in winter and the Sydney Festival in summer. And they still manage to squeeze in citywide festivals for craft beer, plus Fashion Week, ferry races and noodle-eating competitions.

Spring

Primavera

Museum of Contemporary Art, 140 George Street, the Rocks (9245 2400, www.mca.com.au). **Date** Sept.

Every year, the Museum of Contemporary Art invites an artist to curate its Primavera exhibition, a showcase for artists under 35. Beyond this, the format is flexible – the artists and events to be programmed, and whether it is existing or new work, or a combination. That flexibility is the show's greatest asset, allowing each artist-curator to put their stamp on the show; you might say that Primavera is as much an artwork as an exhibition of artworks.

Blackmores Running Festival

www.sydneyrunningfestival.com.au. **Date** Sept.

This festival for the fit takes scenic routes around Sydney, over the Harbour Bridge, past the iconic sails of the Sydney Opera House and along the harbour foreshore through the Botanic Gardens. There are four separate races, from a three-kilometre family run to a marathon.

Festival of the Winds

Bondi Beach (www.waverley.nsw.gov.au). **Date** Sept.

Head to Bondi Beach for a sky-high festival of kite flying. Local and international kite-flyers gather to take advantage of ocean breezes to show off their skills and colourful handmade kites. Giant animals, flowers and traditional kites of all kinds fill the skies. You can fly your own kite or join a kite-making workshop and test out your new creation. The family-friendly day has food stalls, puppet shows, wandering performers and an art exhibition at the beachside Bondi Pavilion. *Photo p30.*

Cabramatta Moon Festival

Cabramatta (www.moonfestival.com.au). **Date** Sept.

Less than an hour from Sydney is a bright and beautiful night-time street festival and convivial Asian cultural celebration. There's a lantern parade led by the Moon Goddess and multitudes of food stalls – packed with delicious flavours from all across Asia – plus music and dancing. Visitors can compete in mooncake-eating, noodle-eating and prawn-peeling contests and are also treated to temple blessings and fishing displays.

Football Grand Finals

Various venues (www.afl.com.au). **Date** Sept-Oct.

Australian rules football is elegant and brutal. It's a hard-running, hard-kicking game with balletic leaps and jaw-dropping tackles. Australians go nuts around grand final season, with three varieties of the game of football – NRL (rugby league) and rugby, as well as Aussie rules – all hotting up to

Diary

Clockwise from left: **Festival of the Winds**
(see p29); **Sydney Hobart Yacht Race**;
Sculpture by the Sea.

decide on the ultimate winners for the season. Grand
final game tickets are hard to come by, but you can
immerse yourself in the fanatical atmosphere by
watching games at the pub with the locals.

Sculpture by the Sea
Around Bondi (www.sculpturebythesea.com).
Date Oct.
Over 100 artists transform the cliff tops and beaches
along the Bondi to Tamarama coastal walk into
an amazing sculpture park. Sculpture by the Sea
is a key annual arts event drawing huge numbers
to enjoy site-specific sculptures by top artists and
emerging talents from Australia and abroad. There
are two walking routes to choose from: the longer
walk from Bondi to Tamarama and a shorter loop on
flatter ground with no steps.

Craft Beer Week
Various venues (www.sydneycraftbeerweek.com).
Date mid Oct.
Ten massive days across 70 of Sydney's best pubs
and venues, this is craft beer heaven. Events range
from the indoor 'sports' night Beerlympics to the Hair
of the Dog Breakfast, with eight beers served over
six courses of breakfast. There are more traditional

tasting sessions too, plus special events for beer geeks, casual beer drinkers and foodies.

Good Food Month

Various venues (sydney.goodfoodmonth.com). **Date** Oct.
This month-long celebration of food is held all across Sydney, from expensive restaurants to hip cafés, pubs, small bars and even the green room at the Sydney Opera House (an area usually off-limits to the public). But it's the night noodle markets in Hyde Park – with all the sounds and smells of an Asian market – that draw the biggest crowds.

Parramasala

Parramatta (www.parramasala.com). **Date** Oct.
Parramatta is the geographical centre of the Greater Sydney region. An hour inland from the big smoke, this satellite city turns up the heat for an annual festival celebrating food, film, music and dance from India and South Asia. The opening night street parade is a feast of colour and sound, and the festival days are packed with performances, screenings and exhibitions. Food stalls complete the picture.

Graphic Festival

Sydney Opera House, Bennelong Point, Circular Quay (graphic.sydneyoperahouse.com). **Date** Oct.
This cutting-edge festival celebrates storytelling in comic books, music and animation. Featuring world première performances and specially commissioned works, the festival allows a first look at ambitious new works. The programme of ticketed and free events runs from graphic films and documentaries to talks with Q&As.

Melbourne Cup

Celebrated around Sydney. **Date** Nov.
The Melbourne Cup takes place in Melbourne, but that doesn't slow down the party here in Sydney. It's a race that stops the nation; Australians all over the country finish work and find a way to join in the festivities. Most bars, pubs and restaurants host a special Cup Day event where you can watch the race on telly, join in a sweepstake and drink champagne for as long as you can stand.

Newtown Festival

Camperdown Memorial Rest Park, Newtown (www.newtownfestival.org). **Date** Nov.
Newtown is home to the alternative, bohemian and unclassifiable, and Newtown Festival is a celebration of neighbourhood pride and inclusivity. Once a year, as many as 90,000 people flock to Camperdown Memorial Rest Park for five stages of live music, hundreds of market stalls, and family-friendly activities such as a dog show. The 'Newtown locals' element sees pop-ups from neighbourhood bars, cafés and restaurants – plus locally brewed beers on tap. Look out for details on featured authors for the Writers' Tent and hands-on activities in the Vocal Local Village.

Corroboree

Around Sydney (www.corroboreesydney.com.au). **Date** Nov.
Corroboree Sydney is a vibrant celebration of Australia's rich Indigenous heritage, featuring leading Aboriginal and Torres Strait Islander artists, writers, dancers and musicians showcasing their creativity and sharing their stories in over 100 events across the city and harbour foreshore. Part of the festival is the Black Art Market, a rare chance to meet the Aboriginal and Torres Strait Islander makers behind rare artworks and original designs at the one-day market. There'll also be homewares and design, bush foods and body products, music and literature for sale.

Summer

Sydney Hobart Yacht Race

Sydney Harbour (www.rolexsydneyhobart.com). **Date** 26 Dec.
At 1pm on Boxing Day, a fleet of racing yachts leaves Sydney and races across the open ocean to Hobart, Tasmania. The twin start lines are just north of Shark Island. To see the jostling fleet leave the harbour, head to parklands on North or South Head. You can even watch from the water if you're lucky enough to score a place on a boat.

New Year's Eve

Around Sydney (www.sydneynewyearseve.com). **Date** 31 Dec.
The biggest party of the year, absolutely everywhere in Sydney, is filled to bursting with revellers. Wander the crowded streets of the Rocks and soak up the atmosphere or book yourself into one of hundreds of party events all across town. To watch the legendary

PUBLIC HOLIDAYS

New Year's Day
1 Jan

Australia Day
26 Jan

Good Friday
25 Mar 2016, 14 April 2017

Easter Sunday
27 Mar 2016, 16 April 2017

Easter Monday
28 Mar 2016, 17 April 2017

Anzac Day
25 Apr

Queen's Birthday
13 June 2016, 12 June 2017

Labour Day
3 Oct 2016, 2 Oct 2017

Christmas Day
25 December

Boxing Day
26 December

Above: **Ferrython**.
Top right: **Chinese New Year**.

fireworks, bag your spot early as more than one million people crowd the city and surrounds to watch the 9pm and midnight fireworks displays. Some public parks are alcohol-free zones, so check the official website before you bring your booze.

Flickerfest
Bondi (flickerfest.com.au). **Date** Jan.
See the world's best short films under the stars at Bondi Beach. Sydney's original outdoor film festival attracts the best short films from around the world – not least because a win in one of the competition categories qualifies films for consideration for an Oscar nomination. The best 100 films are selected from more than 2,000 submissions from around the world. There are pop-up food stalls to enjoy too.

Water Polo by the Sea
Bondi Icebergs Club, 1 Notts Avenue, Bondi (waterpolobythesea.com). **Date** Jan.
Sunshine, cocktails, DJs and stunning ocean views are the backdrop for world-class athletes wandering around in their swimwear. Water Polo by the Sea sees the Australian men's water polo team (Aussie Sharks) take on a super-team made up of the world's

best water polo players in the Bondi Icebergs pool. This hip event in the sun sells out fast, so organise your tickets early.

Sydney Festival

Various venues (www.sydneyfestival.org.au). **Date** Jan.

The huge New Year's celebrations are followed by a massive festival. The hot days and balmy nights are filled with delightful, challenging or mind-blowing events, taking place in venues from the Opera House all the way out to Parramatta. It's a good idea to study the programme as there really is a crazy amount going on around town, from free open-air concerts in the Domain to street-wide discos and smaller events hidden in the nooks and crannies of the city. Hyde Park in the CBD is festival HQ, hosting the festival village and wonderful artworks, performances, pop-up bars, eateries and two Spiegeltents. It's a great space to relax between events, soak up the festival vibe and plan what to do next. The festival is well known for its high standard of art, big ideas and kaleidoscopic programming. More than 350 performances and 100 events take place, with over 700 artists, and many of the events are free. Big names are a regular feature; artists appearing have included Björk, Brian Wilson, Grace Jones, Manu Chao, Elvis Costello, AR Rahman, Cate Blanchett, Ralph Fiennes, Sir Ian McKellen, David Byrne and St Vincent. *Photo p28.*

Ferrython

Sydney Harbour (www.sydneyfestival.org.au). **Date** 26 Jan.

Sydney's iconic ferries are usually steady passenger boats carrying commuters to work and sightseers to the other side of the harbour, except for one day a year when they rev up their engines and race for glory. It's an Australia Day tradition to make for a grassy spot near the harbour to watch the ferries go head-to-head in a race from Circular Quay to Shark Island, finishing at the Sydney Harbour Bridge.

Twilight at Taronga

Taronga Zoo, Bradleys Head Road, Mosman (twilightattaronga.org.au). **Date** Jan-Mar.

Taronga Zoo is just a quick ferry ride across the harbour to the North Shore from Sydney CBD. For the past 20 years, it has played host to a series of musical events at dusk. Sydneysiders flock to the attractive venue for the Twilight at Taronga music series, with concerts and picnics under the stars, against a gobsmacking backdrop that includes the city skyline, the Opera House and that beloved bridge.

Chinese New Year

Chinatown & around Sydney (www.sydney chinesenewyear.com). **Date** from 8 Feb 2016; from 28 Jan 2017.

The city hosts one of the biggest Chinese New Year festivals outside China, with vibrant celebrations in

Chinatown and around the city. It kicks off with a launch party at Dawes Point, followed by a month-long programme of free and ticketed events. Catch the thrilling Dragon Boat Races, sate your hunger with Lunar Feast set menus and enjoy the colourful procession of the Twilight Parade.

Laneway Festival
Rozelle (sydney.lanewayfestival.com). **Date** Feb.
In a city full of music festivals, Laneway stands out for its good vibes, cool stalls (food, vinyl, vintage) and distinct lack of beefed-up bros in the crowd. The sheer talent in the line-up (local up-and-comers and seriously major acts) each year usually ensures you get good value for money. You'll get to see a heap of the most critically acclaimed musicians of the year in a single day for less than you'd splash out for a new pair of jeans.

Autumn

Biennale of Sydney
Cockatoo Island & various venues (www. biennaleofsydney.com.au). **Date** 18 Mar-5 June 2016.
Every two years, the Biennale of Sydney takes over the city's major art institutions and Cockatoo Island to create a wonderland of contemporary visual art. The Biennale attracts huge numbers of international guests as well as local visitors; it runs for three months and presents a jaw-dropping range of innova-tive work from Australian and international artists.

Opera on the Harbour
Sydney Royal Botanic Gardens, Mrs Macquaries Road, CBD (opera.org.au). **Date** Mar.
Take Sydney Harbour, add over-the-top set design, raz-zle-dazzle costumes, dance rou-tines and acrobatics and drop in one high-drama opera classic. Finish with a dash of fireworks, and serve the best balmy sum-mer Sydney has to offer. The result is the perfect mix of the glitzy, hyperactive energy of a Broadway musical mixed with world-class opera on the water.

Clockwise from left: **Laneway Festival**; **Mardi Gras**; **Art Month**; **Opera on the Harbour.**

Mardi Gras
Around Sydney (www.mardigras.org.au).
Date Mar.
Gay, lesbian, transgender, queer – everyone is welcome to join the hectic and colourful celebration that draws thousands upon thousands of interstate and international visitors to Sydney. Mardi Gras is three weeks of dazzling events, out-and-proud behaviour and some of the most smashing parties on the planet. The fabulous parade down Oxford Street features 10,000 people marching in an unbridled celebration of pride and diversity, and the after party is one of the biggest LGBT celebrations in the world. For more, *see p193* **Hurrah for Mardi Gras!**

Australian Tattoo & Body Art Expo
Various venues (www.tattooexpo.com.au).
Date Mar.
Join thousands of ink aficionados at the biggest tattoo expo in the southern hemisphere. Check out more than 200 local and international tattoo artists, daily tattoo competitions, live entertainment and market stalls from industry vendors. Get some fresh ink or begin the crucial research and inspiration phase for working out just what you'll get for your first-ever tattoo.

Taste of Sydney
Centennial Park (www.taste ofsydney.com.au). **Date** Mar.
A four-day food and wine festival in Centennial Park that showcases the talents of the city's hot chefs, top restaurants and best producers. Each participating restaurant prepares three or four signature dishes in small taster-sized portions, so you can create your own dream menu. In addition to all the eating and drinking, the festival hosts tasting masterclasses, cooking lessons and chef demonstrations.

Art Month
Varies venues (www.artmonthsydney.com.au).
Date Mar.
An annual festival that aims to engage people with contemporary art and artists. It's an explosion of exhibitions, talks and discussions, tours and pop-up art bars. More than 100 galleries open their doors for parties – an open invitation to take a look inside the galleries in Sydney's hottest art precincts.

Sydney Royal Easter Show
Sydney Olympic Park (www.eastershow.com.au).
Date Mar-Apr.
An agricultural show, gymkhana and funfair all in one, this huge show sees as many as 14,000 animals on site for breed competitions, rodeos, equestrian events and displays. Sydneysiders line up to ride rollercoasters, watch wood-chopping races, sample regional produce and marvel at the giant district displays made of 50,000 pieces of fruit and vegetables.

Mercedes-Benz Fashion Week
Carriageworks, 245 Wilson Street, Eveleigh (mbfashionweek.com/australia). **Date** Apr.

Sydney's top fashion festival is a week-long celebration of style. Catwalk shows from established and up-and-coming designers from Australia and the world are held in Carriageworks, a cool warehouse site with an industrial vibe. The festival is packed with industry events and runway shows and also includes Fashion Saturday, a city-wide shopping event with special deals from retailers, interactive street events, workshops and exhibitions.

Sydney Comedy Festival
Various venues (www.sydneycomedyfest.com.au). **Date** Apr-May.
Split your sides with Sydney's massive month-long laugh fest. Kicking off with two gala events – the Sydney Comedy Festival Gala at the Sydney Opera House and Cracker Night at the Enmore Theatre – Sydney Comedy Festival sees comedians taking to stages all over the city for a month. If you're canny, you can see a show a day, from international and Australian comedians across all genres and including fresh new talent.

Sydney Writers' Festival
Various venues (www.swf.org.au). **Date** May.
Held at Hickson Bay Wharf and venues such as the Sydney Town Hall, the Sydney Writers' Festival has a mammoth line-up that includes in-conversation events with big-name authors and indie favourites, talks, workshops and storytelling events, all featuring local and international writers. There's a different theme each year, and the festival hosts pop-up stalls for food, drinks and books, as well as a huge 'zine fair.

World Press Photo Exhibition
State Library, Macquarie Street, CBD (www. worldpressphoto.org). **Date** May.
The State Library of New South Wales hosts one of Sydney's most popular annual exhibitions, featuring award-winning photographs from the

Left: **Mercedes-Benz Fashion Week**. See *p35*.
Below: **Sydney Writers' Festival**.

HAPPY NEW YEAR

Where to see Sydney's famous fireworks.

There's one annual event that draws all eyes to Sydney – its famous New Year fireworks. Here are some great vantage points to see the pyrotechnics.

If it's your first Sydney New Year, you may want to join the milling throngs hugging the sails of the **Opera House**. There's no doubt you'll be in the thick of it, but be prepared for a tight squeeze. Thousands also pack the grand dame of vantage points – **Mrs Macquarie's Point** on the tip of the Domain. There's no BYO here (and strictly no glass); food and alcohol can be bought on site, though, and there's a large police presence.

If you're in the Kings Cross area, the place to go is **Embarkation Park** in Potts Point (access via Victoria Street or Cowper Wharf Road). It's heavily policed and you can't bring in alcohol nor buy it here, but there are food stalls. Glebe's **Bicentennial Park** (Federal Road, access via Chapman Road) is another good spot with waterside seats along the industrial side of the harbour. Food is on sale, but load up on alcohol before you go as there's none on sale.

Over at Milsons Point on the North Shore, **Bradfield Park** (access via Broughton Street or Alfred Street South) is another popular viewing spot and the slope of the hill makes for a decent view. Again, you can't bring alcohol but food and booze are for sale on site. At the eastern tip of Balmain, the **Illoura Reserve** at Peacock Point (Weston Street) is another great vantage point. You'll need to stake your spot mid afternoon in this pretty park. Don't come by car as public transport is great here. Food is for sale and you can bring your own alcohol too.

For a spectacular viewing point in a leafy setting, there's **Cremorne Point Reserve** (access via Milson Road). This is a great spot for families. Food is on sale but booze is banned.

To really make a night of it, there's **Cockatoo Island**. The former shipyard, reformatory and jail is open to campers for the big night. Bring along a tent and perch in prime position for both the western and city fireworks. You can't bring in alcohol but it's available to buy on the island.

World Press Photo Contest. It is an astonishing, thought-provoking and often beautiful exhibition of images ranging from sports and nature photography to snapshots from the frontlines of war, staged portraits and remarkable candid shots.

Head On Photo Festival

Various venues (www.headon.com.au). **Date** May.
Head On Photo Festival covers every permutation of photography, from documentary and photojournalism to commercial and fine art, and moving images, with exhibitions, talks, workshops and international guests. The flagship event of the festival is the Head On Portrait Prize, showcasing the best in Australian photographic portraiture. The 40 finalists are exhibited at the Museum of Sydney.

Vivid

Sydney foreshore (www.vividsydney.com).
Date May-June.
Vivid Sydney transforms the city into a dazzling playground of light installations and projections. One of the highlights each year is the Lighting of the Sail – an artwork projected on to the Sydney Opera House. Once the 'house' is all lit up, the city follows with light installations and projections from Circular Quay to Martin Place, Darling Harbour to Pyrmont, the University of Sydney and Central Park. Take time to check out the large-scale animation projected on to Customs House and the Museum of Contemporary Art. All in all, this is a festival of three parts: a packed programme of live music, light and ideas. Venues around town host ground-breaking collaborations between musicians, with big international acts and local talent in an eclectic line-up. The Ideas programme is designed to spark discussion and debate around creativity, with talks and masterclasses at the MCA, Sydney Convention & Exhibition Centre, Powerhouse Museum and the Seymour Centre. Around Circular Quay, the crowds are thick. Leave plenty of time to arrive for shows, as you'll find yourself wading through thousands of awestruck visitors and you'll want to stop for a selfie, trust us.

Winter

Sydney Film Festival

Various venues (www.sff.org.au). **Date** June.
A long time ago in a galaxy far, far away, people went to the movies to be challenged, thrilled and to see things they'd never seen before. You still can at the Sydney Film Festival, an event that champions 'courageous, audacious and cutting-edge' films. Screened across the city in beautiful independent cinemas, stately old theatres, art galleries and even retail shops and out-of-town drive-ins, the festival is a city-wide event. Pick up a flexi-pass and catch as many films as you can.

The Rocks Aroma Festival

The Rocks (www.therocks.com). **Date** July.
Wind your way through the cobblestone streets of
Sydney's oldest area and decide for yourself who
makes the best coffee in town. The Rocks Aroma
Festival sees crowds lining up for anything from flat
whites to speciality brews (with many tasting cups
of coffee costing just $2), plus chocolates and creamy
gelato. In the lead-up to the festival, there are activities and workshops tailored to coffee enthusiasts.

Sydney Manga & Anime Show (SMASH!)

Rosehill Gardens, Rosehill (www.smash.org.au).
Date July.
This annual festival celebrates well-loved aspects of
Japanese popular culture, including manga, anime,
cosplay, Gundam and gaming. It routinely draws
celebrity guests from Japan and thousands of fans to
participate in cosplay competitions, panels, discussions, screenings, demonstrations and more.

Fifties Fair

*Rose Seidler House, 71 Clissold Road, Wahroonga
(sydneylivingmuseums.com.au).* **Date** Aug.
Held in the time capsule of Rose Seidler House –
the fair is an annual magnet for hipsters, rocka-
billy-heads and '50s enthusiasts. The fair is a neat
intersection of many of Sydney's favourite things:
dapper dressing, Danish design, retro decor and
records. The annual best-dressed competition and
the display of vintage cars guarantees some serious
eye-candy. Expect stalls selling vintage and reproduc-
tion fashion, accessories, vinyl, furniture and objects,
plus live music, swing dancing and food stalls.

Underbelly Arts Festival

Cockatoo Island (underbellyarts.com.au).
Date Aug.
A festival for emerging and experimental art,
Underbelly Arts takes over the island in the middle of Sydney Harbour for one weekend a year. It
includes over 100 artists producing works to tickle
your fancy, mind, ears and eyes. What started as
an ambitious juggernaut of dreams has become a
key player in Sydney's arts scene; more than 7,000
punters attended the last festival.

City2Surf

Sydney to Bondi (www.city2surf.com.au). **Date** Aug.
Sydney's favourite fun run is a big one – 14km (nine
miles) can feel a lot longer than it sounds. Get your
training schedule sorted before you sign up for this
race, as Heartbreak Hill's a bitch. The run starts in
the CBD and winds its way to stunning Bondi Beach.
There's music and entertainment along the course.

Left: **Vivid.**
Right: **Fifties Fair.**

Sydney's Best

Check off the essentials with our hand-picked highlights.

Hyde Park Barracks.

Sightseeing

VIEWS
Bondi to Coogee coastal walk p106
Take a leisurely seaside stroll, looking out for whales, dolphins and surfers.
South Head p115
To the left: the beautiful city. To the right: views far out to sea.
Shark Island p83
Admire the Harbour Bridge from the best spot in the harbour.
Blu Bar on 36 p56
This lofty hotel bar is the place for panoramic views with a cocktail in hand.
Harbour Bridge p54
The city's splendour laid before you as you cross the bridge.

MUSEUMS
Art Gallery of New South Wales p63
The most important public gallery in Sydney.
Museum of Contemporary Art p58
World-class exhibitions in an impressive new building by the Quay.
White Rabbit Gallery p87
Eye-catching Chinese contemporary art – and it's free.

HISTORY
North Head Quarantine Station p149
Built in 1828, the station was the prison – and burial place – of scores of unfortunate souls.

Quay.

Cockatoo Island p83
Imagine the prison, the school, the dockyard and the gum trees of days gone by.
Lord Nelson Brewery Hotel p56
Drink like a convict in Sydney's oldest continually licensed pub.
Hyde Park Barracks p63
Find out how the convicts lived, slept, toiled and built this very building.

OUTDOORS & WILDLIFE

Royal Botanic Gardens p67
Get lost in the shaded pathways and herbariums.
Sydney Opera House p58
The forecourt is one of the world's most spectacular outdoor performance spaces.
Taronga Zoo p180
Lions, tigers, bears – and koalas and kangaroos.
Sea Life Sydney Aquarium p75
Get a real feel for life under the sea.

Eating & drinking

BLOWOUT

Bennelong p59
World-class food in a world-class building.
Momofuku Seiobo p76
Creative Korean-inspired dining – part of David Chang's global food empire.
Quay p59
Beautiful cooking with views over the Opera House.
Rockpool p68
The restaurant that defined modern Australian dining.

LOCAL

ACME p111
Time Out's Restaurant of the Year 2015 features some highly creative cooking.

Watsons Bay Boutique Hotel.

LP's Quality Meats p87
American barbecue,
Sydneyfied, plus merchandise
for sale, and rock 'n' roll tunes.
Ester p87
Chippendale's hidden
gem has a top-notch $65
banquet menu.
Billy Kwong p89
It's Australia on a plate.
Chinese style, with but
with native ingredients.
Papi Chulo p150
Manly's shining star: harbour
views and epic food.

BARS
Shady Pines Saloon p79
Casual, foot-stomping fun
and impressive cocktails
for midnight cowboys.
Freda's p87
This casual, friendly party bar
keeps the good times rolling
in Chippendale.
Eau de Vie p78
Plush and moody decor
and dynamite cocktails draw
those in the know to this bar
at the back of the Kirketon
hotel in Darlinghurst.

Earl's Juke Joint p134
Cocktails are king at this
Newtown bar hidden behind
a butcher's shop façade.
Manly Wine p151
Watch the breakers roll in with
a bottle of the good stuff.
Baxter Inn p69
Walls of whisky in an
underground bunker.

CAFES
Single Origin CBD p68
Pick up one of Sydney's best
coffees (and this city knows
good coffee) in the CBD.
Smalltown p152
Escape to Avalon for the
beach – and the doughnuts.
Showbox Coffee Brewers
p150
For beachside eats at Manly
– without the queues.
Edition Coffee Roasters p77
A prime example of Japanese
and Nordic influences taking
over the Sydney food scene.
Black Star Pastry p163
It's all about the compressed
watermelon cake at this
Rosebery warehouse café.

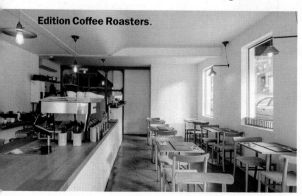

Edition Coffee Roasters.

latest in shopping centre architecture. Now, it's a great place to pick up a Sydney keepsake.

BOOKS & MUSIC
Press Books p88
An offshoot of a photography publication that also dabbles in independent publishing. Three-quarters of the books are independent stock.
Kinokuniya p69
More manga and anime than you can shake a comic book at, in the Galeries mall.
TITLE p145
This Surry Hills store has an impressive collection of cult DVDs, paperbacks and vinyl.

FASHION & DESIGN
Incu p95
Local labels and global brands come together in one inviting boutique.
Collector Store p82
Split over two levels of Surry Hills terrace, Collector Store stocks fashion, jewellery and homewares.

OUTDOOR DRINKING
Watsons Bay Boutique Hotel p116
It doesn't get better than a sunset spritz and a sashimi boat at this beer garden with million-dollar harbour views.
Bondi Icebergs p104
Panoramic views of Bondi from the second-floor bar.
Courthouse Hotel p134
One of the best-loved beer gardens in the Inner West.
Glenmore Hotel p56
Pub with a rooftop bar overlooking Circular Quay and the Sydney Opera House.
Coogee Pavilion p109
A great place to spend an afternoon, with salty sea air and a carafe of wine.

Aquabumps p110
Take a look at photographer Eugene Tan's stunning shots of Bondi Beach and its inhabitants.
Strand Arcade p70
When it opened in 1862, it was considered the very

Shopping

GIFTS AND SOUVENIRS
MCA Gift Shop p59
Pick up a child's toy version of one of Sydney's iconic ferries or a colourful silk scarf from Australiana queen Jenny Kee.

Kinokuniya.

Carriageworks Market.

Newtown Social Club.

Koskela p163
This industrial warehouse is a homeowner's dream, packed with vintage and new furniture, toys and lighting fixtures.

MARKETS

Carriageworks Market p87
Sydney's biggest farmers' market attracts throngs of hip Inner West shoppers. Set the alarm and have breakfast as you shop.

Bondi Market p104
Sundays by the beach can hardly be improved upon, which is partly why these weekly markets are so popular. Head here for bric-a-brac, up-and-coming brands and fresh juice.

Rozelle Markets p120
This is the closest Sydney comes to having its own European flea market – there's trash 'n' treasure galore, and it's only a bus ride from the city centre.

Nightlife

CLUBS

Goodgod Small Club p202
Like a bunker of underground good times in the middle of Chinatown – whether it's Wednesday trivia night or 1990s dance parties.

Cliff Dive p200
Look for the pineapple painted on the doors of this hidden Oxford Street gem.

Ivy p202
The rooftop pool alone is worth the flight of stairs. Take a cocktail with your dip, and stay for mainstream dance music on a Saturday night.

Standard Bowl p203
Free bowling, free gigs, free arcade games and a great view of Taylor Square.

downstairs for a boozy night on the tiles.

Metro p206
From big-name DJs to touring indie-rock bands, hit up the Metro any time of the year.

Civic Underground p200
Boogie the night away to electro-dance music in the heart of the city.

Oxford Art Factory p208
This is where you'll catch a local act before it tours Europe and the US.

Arts

THEATRE

Sydney Theatre Company p213
Head to the wharf for a show – and nab a table for pre- or post-show dining at the Bar at the End of the Wharf, under the shadow of the Harbour Bridge.

Belvoir p213
This once shabby tomato sauce factory now hosts a respected theatre company.

Griffin Theatre Company p213
The city's only theatre company solely dedicated to new Australian work.

FILM

Hayden Orpheum p184
Catch a retro flick in a retro cinema with all the trimmings.

Golden Age Cinema p184
A tiny underground cinema in an art deco building.

Sydney Film Festival p38
Winter's saviour: a packed programme of award-winning movies showing in unusual locations.

OPERA & BALLET

Sydney Opera House p221
The iconic Opera House stages work ranging from the puppet-peppered *Magic Flute* to rarer fare such as *The Love For Three Oranges*.

Bangarra Dance Theatre p218
A unique mix of contemporary style with ancient Aboriginal traditions of storytelling through movement.

Marquee p202
Nightclubs don't come any bigger in this city. Take your casino winnings and blow it all on a table and some bubbly.

MUSIC

Newtown Social Club p208
Go upstairs for up close and personal gigs. Stay

Oxford Art Factory.

Explore

Sydney Tours

Sydney's a beautiful city – sprawling, diverse and teeming with water views. But she can be daunting to navigate for all of those reasons too. Newbies may be best served by a guide, whether that be in the form of a classic harbour ferry, a bike-riding architecture enthusiast or your own smartphone. Whether you want to scale the mighty Coathanger, as the Harbour Bridge is known, or be chauffeured to picturesque secret Sydney beaches in a classic EH Holden car, there are plenty of options for touring the Emerald City.

EXPLORE

ON FOOT

Bridgeclimb
Meet at 3 Cumberland Street, the Rocks (8274 7777, www.bridgeclimb.com). Circular Quay rail or ferry. **Tours** Daily by appt. **Tickets** $158-$358.
For a look at the Harbour from a very different angle, make a booking at Bridgeclimb. You'll take in the most beautiful harbour in the world from atop its most famous structure, Sydney Harbour Bridge. You'll be climbing for three hours or so, but that view from the top is worth every second spent getting there.

FREE I'm Free Walking Tour of Sydney
Meet at Town Hall Square, 483 George Street, Chinatown (0405 515 564, imfree.com.au). Town Hall rail. **Tours** 10.30am daily.
Tickets free (donations welcome).
There are several free walking tour operators in Sydney but this one is a cut above. The fun tour takes you through a smörgåsbord of famous sights, bouncing between the city's culture and lifestyle belts while delving into Sydney's history, stories and secrets. It's a three-hour, easy walk and there's no need to book.

Razorhurst
Meet at Darlo Village Hotel, 234 Palmer Street, Darlinghurst (www.razorhurst.com.au). Bus 389 or Oxford Street buses. **Tours** 1hr (self-guided).
Downloads $2.49 from iTunes.
Razorhurst is both an interactive game set in 1920s Darlinghurst – Sydney's notorious crime capital back then – and a historical walking tour. Palmer Street's Darlo Village Hotel, one of the infamous Kate Leigh's

favoured haunts, is the starting point for the adventure. Leigh was the sly, brothel-keeping grog queen of the Sydney underworld and in the game her stash is seized during a police raid. Players must help her replenish stocks as they tour the bygone underworld.

Sydney Connection
0435 050 367, www.thesydneyconnection.com.au. **Tours** 10am-6pm Tue, Wed, Fri; by appt Sat.
Tickets from $150.
Walkers can choose between the Surry Hills Hipster, the Darlinghurst Cowboy, Potts Point Princess or the Sydney CBD Suit. Each provides an intimate (tours are kept to a maximum of four people) insider's guide to top Sydney food, fashion and design store picks.

FREE Sydney Culture Walk
Free download for iPhone & Android from the App Store, Google Play & at sydneyculturewalksapp.com.
This free walking tour app from the City of Sydney guides you as you explore the city's best public art gems, hidden laneways and historical nooks and crannies. There are ten virtual routes to choose from, and 400-plus historical and cultural points of interest.

Taste Cultural Food Tours
www.tastetours.com.au. **Tickets** $52-$76.
Love food? Love culture? Roll them into one with these delicious tours of Sydney's west. Over the course of these four-hour guided food-tasting tours – there are over 20 to choose from – you'll sample local specialties spanning Lebanese, Vietnamese, Balkan and Bangladeshi cuisines, in western Sydney neighbourhoods including Liverpool, Lakemba, Granville and Fairfield.

ON WHEELS

Bonza Bike Tours

9247 8800, www.bonzabiketours.com. **Tours** 2.15pm Mon, Fri, Sat. **Tickets** $109-$129.

Bonza do some great bike tours – have a look at the website for all the options – but our favourite is Manly. The Manly Beach Cycle Tour & Sunset Cruise begins aboard the ferry to Manly. From there, it rolls you past Manly beach and out to stunning North Head. You'll skirt coastal cliffs, catch glimpses of fairy penguins or humpback whales and then head back to Circular Quay with the fireball sun setting behind the Opera House, Harbour Bridge and city skyline.

My Sydney Detour

0404 256 256, mysydneydetour.com. **Tours** daily by appt. **Tickets** $399-$999.

In-the-know Sydneysider Richard Graham takes visitors on unique and luxurious private tours in his beautiful sky-blue EH Holden. Choose from a selection of signature tours – including My Gadigal Detour, which focuses on Indigenous history, and My Hawkesbury Detour, which concentrates on Sydney's untouched natural beauty – and let Graham show you the sites and the city's best eats in a classic Australian car.

SAW Bike Tours

Meet at Town Bike Pitstop, 156 Abercrombie Street, Redfern (0403 888 390, www.sydney architecture.org). Redfern rail. **Tours** see website for dates. **Tickets** $80-$90. Bike & helmet hire $30.

These three-and-a-half-hour architectural tours are a workout for your mind, bum and thighs. On the two-wheeled architectural safari with the scruffy Eoghan Lewis as your dude of a tour guide, you'll be engaging with the natural topography of the land and Sydney's urban design at the same time – while maintaining a cyclist's heightened awareness of what's around you.

BY WATER

Cockatoo Island Ferry

Departs Circular Quay (131 500, www.transport nsw.info). Circular Quay rail or ferry. **Ferries** every half hour, around 6.30am-11.30 daily. **Tours** by appt; $16. **Tickets** *Ferry* $6.20-$15.20 return.

Eighteen hectares in size and set at the intersection of the Parramatta and Lane Cove rivers, Cockatoo Island was an Aboriginal fishing spot before settlement saw it become a prison built to house convicts from Norfolk Island. Since then, Nick Cave has curated a

My Sydney Detour.

EXPLORE

music festival here, the Sydney Biennale has made it its home, and the island has allowed overnight camping stays and audio- and tour-guided historical walking tours. See www.cockatooisland.gov.au to book a tour. Pack a picnic (and your imagination).

Darling Harbour Ferry

Departs Circular Quay (131 500, www.transport nsw.info). Circular Quay rail or ferry. **Ferries** every half hour, around 6am-11.30pm daily. **Tickets** $6.20-$15.20 return.

If you're after a bite-size taste of the Sydney ferries experience, the trip to Darling Harbour from Circular Quay lasts about 20 minutes. The ferry scoots you under the Harbour Bridge and around the Opera House, often via the gourmet village of Balmain, with its bars, cafés and restaurants. The final destination, Darling Harbour, is full of cool family attractions, including the IMAX Theatre, Sydney Aquarium, Wildlife World, Chinese Gardens and Powerhouse Museum.

Manly Ferry

Departs Circular Quay (131 500, www.transport nsw.info). Circular Quay rail or ferry. **Ferries** every half hour, around 6am-midnight daily. **Tickets** $6.20-$15.20 return.

For 155 years, the Manly Ferry has been the classic Sydney adventure. Today, stepping aboard one of these noble craft bound for lunching, walking, shopping or beaching experiences is to know why Manly is 'seven miles from Sydney, a thousand miles from care'. For less than $20, you can enjoy the soothing chug of the motors, the tranquil churn of the big blue beneath, the thrill of the vistas passing by and the smug serenity in knowing that only in Sydney can such a trip be made.

Mosman Ferry

Departs Circular Quay (131 500, www.transport nsw.info). Circular Quay rail or ferry. **Ferries** every half hour, around 6am-midnight daily. **Tickets** $6.20-$15.20 return.

Balloon Aloft.

EXPLORE

Gliding past Cremorne Point, Taronga Zoo, south Mosman, Old Cremorne and finally Mosman Bay, you'll see how the other half live as you gawp open-mouthed at some of the city's most expensive, sought-after and architecturally impressive harbourside homes (including the prime minister's residence, Kirribilli House).

Parramatta Ferry

Departs Circular Quay (131 500, www.transport nsw.info). Circular Quay rail or ferry. **Ferries** every half hour, around 6.30am-midnight daily. **Tickets** $6.20-$15.20 return.

Sydney's greater west is the fastest-growing area in Australia. And little wonder – Parramatta is a thriving maelstrom of restaurants, art galleries, theatres and band venues, old and new bars and, increasingly, major festivals. But when you consider the 23km (14 miles) of noisy, often-congested highway between Parramatta and the CBD, there's really no smarter or sexier a way to get there than via ferry.

Watsons Bay Ferry

Departs Circular Quay (131 500, www.transport nsw.info). Circular Quay rail or ferry. **Ferries** 7.15am, 8am, 4.05pm, 5.20pm, 6pm, 6.20pm, 7.10pm daily. **Tickets** $6.20-$15.20 return.

Long lunchers rejoice! The ferry to Watsons Bay is one of the most nourishing Sydney offers, both for its views, and culinary feast awaiting at the end of your journey. Leaving Circular Quay, your ferry goes to Garden Island, Darling Point, Double Bay and Rose Bay before arriving at Watsons Bay, where a cluster of cafés and restaurants, a thriving and chic beer garden in the Watsons Bay Boutique Hotel (*see p116*), and a series of charming coastal walks await. Puritans beware: nearby Lady Bay is a legal nude beach.

BY AIR

Balloon Aloft

4990 9242, www.balloonaloft.com. **Tours** daily by appt. **Tickets** from $299.

Ballooning offers a serenity of air travel no plane or helicopter can match. Balloon Aloft provides the chance to chase the sunrise 1,000 metres above Sydney on a variety of different flight routes, most of which finish with a champagne breakfast. Weekday trips meet at Old Government House, Parramatta Park; while at weekends, you'll meet at Camden Valley Inn, Camden. All flights last an hour and include flight certificates.

Blue Sky Helicopters

9700 7888, www.blueskyhelicopters.com.au. **Tours** daily by appt. **Tickets** from $150.

Blue Sky Helicopters offers a deluxe private charter service for up to four passengers on one of its elite R44 or Jet Ranger choppers. A Harbour & Beach Discovery flight spans just 15 minutes but buzzes you over the panorama that is Sydney Harbour, taking in the Opera House, Harbour Bridge, Fort Denison, Watsons Bay and Bondi Beach. Other flights will take you as far as the Blue Mountains in the west or on specialised whale-watching or horse-racing jaunts.

Sydney Seaplanes

1300 732 752, www.seaplanes.com.au. **Tours** daily by appt. **Tickets** from $200.

One of the most classic Sydney experiences is to fly to a seafood feast by the beach. Perhaps the most scenic of these airborne adventures is the seaplane to Jonah's acclaimed restaurant at Whale Beach (*see p152*). Taking flight at picturesque Rose Bay, you'll watch Sydney Harbour and the golden sandy strips of the northern beaches slide beneath you as you pass over places such as Freshwater, Curl Curl, Newport and Palm Beach. Landing at Barrenjoey Headland, you'll then be collected by a small boat and whisked to where a car awaits for the final glide to Jonah's.

EXPLORE

Circular Quay & the Rocks

Circular Quay – which wraps around Sydney Cove, is bookended by the Harbour Bridge and Opera House and opens out on to the Royal Botanic Gardens – is your starting point in this city. It's a bustling nexus for travellers and Sydneysiders, and offers art, theatre, drinking and dining experiences with zillion-dollar views and all kinds of transport.

Adjacent, the historic Rocks is no longer the preserve of tourists thanks to the arrival of some cool pubs, bars and galleries. And its evolution from inner-city slum to cultural precinct (after protracted battles between developers and greenies) has set the blueprint for other parts of central Sydney to smarten up their acts.

Sydney Ferry

Don't Miss

1 **Sydney Harbour Bridge** The mighty Coathanger is a Sydney icon (p54).

2 **Sydney Opera House** One of the planet's most identifiable buildings, home to world-class arts (p58).

3 **Sydney Ferry** The city's favourite form of transport (p57).

4 **MCA (Museum of Contemporary Art)** Be amazed and inspired (p58).

5 **Quay** Beautiful food, world-class views (p59).

EXPLORE

THE ROCKS

Tourist-friendly it remains, but the big news out of the Rocks is that it's no longer off-limits to locals. A higher concentration of fine-grain creativity has enriched this historic part of Sydney and today its famous cobblestones regularly come alive for visitors and locals of all ages and tastes. There are still high-class restaurants, historic pubs, curio shops selling Australiana and rustic cafés galore, but now local artisans also sell their independent wares from pop-up shops, troubadours busk from corners and burlesque performers set up their red-light delights in the many alleyways and coves.

Community gatherings are also plentiful hereabouts – the Rocks' Friday night markets are thriving and street festivals devoted to music, coffee, beer, light installations and more run throughout the year. It's now common for culture vultures hitting the nearby Opera House and Walsh Bay theatres to wet their whistles, fill their bellies and fuel their conversations in the Rocks before and after shows. And why not? With views across the Harbour and of the **Sydney Harbour Bridge**, a wealth of nearby transport connections close by and surprises around every corner, the Rocks is rocking once more.

Sights & Museums

S H Ervin Gallery

National Trust Centre, Watson Road, next to the Observatory (9258 0173, www.shervingallery.com. au). Circular Quay rail or ferry, or Wynyard rail. **Open** 11am-5pm Tue-Sun. **Admission** $10. **Map** p55 D2 ❶

A spectacular setting on Observatory Hill and an impressive line-up of annual exhibitions and themed shows are the draws at the National Trust S H Ervin Gallery. It specialises in Australian art (painting, sculpture and works on paper), both historical and contemporary in nature.

Susannah Place Museum

58-64 Gloucester Street, at Cumberland Place Steps (9241 1893, sydneylivingmuseums.com.au). Circular Quay rail or ferry. **Tours** 2pm, 3pm, 4pm daily. **Admission** $4-$8. **Map** p55 D3 ❷

Built in 1844, this terrace of four houses – including a corner shop, original brick privies and open laundries – gives an idea of what 19th-century living was really like. Entry to the museum is by guided tour only; book ahead if possible. Note that steep, narrow stairs are involved.

Sydney Harbour Bridge & Pylon Lookout

Bridge & Pylon Lookout accessible via stairs on Cumberland Street (9240 1100, www.pylon lookout.com.au). Circular Quay rail or ferry.

Open 10am-5pm daily. **Admission** *Pylon Lookout* $6.50-$13. **Map** p55 A4 ❸

The bridge has been declared one of the seven new wonders of the world, and its refurbished Pylon Lookout, in the south-east pylon, is well worth a visit. Climb 200 steps, past three levels of exhibits celebrating the history of the bridge and its builders, and find magnificent open-air views from the top. To look at the bridge from another angle, book Bridgeclimb (*see p48*).

Sydney Observatory

Watson Road, off Argyle Street, Observatory Hill (9921 3485, www.sydneyobservatory.com.au). Circular Quay rail or ferry. **Open** *Museum* 10am-5pm daily. **Admission** *Museum & gardens* free. *Day tours* $10; $8 reductions. *Night tours* $18; $12-$14 reductions. **Map** p55 C2 ❹

Built in 1858, Sydney Observatory gained international recognition under Henry Chamberlain Russell, government astronomer from 1870 to 1905, who involved Sydney in the International Astrographic Catalogue, the first complete atlas of the sky. Interactive displays include a virtual-reality tour over the surfaces of Venus and Mars, and night tours include a talk and tour, 3-D Space Theatre session and viewing through a 40cm reflecting telescope.

Restaurants & Cafés

Ananas

18 Argyle Street (9259 5668, www.ananas.com.au). Circular Quay rail or ferry. **Open** noon-3pm, 6-10pm Mon-Thur; noon-3pm, 6-11pm Fri; 6-11pm Sat. **Main courses** $33-$45. **Map** p55 C3 ❺ **French**

In a beautifully designed room with pineapples as far as the eye can see, you'll find classic French dishes. Don't leave without sampling the salt-caramel eclair – soft, light choux pastry holds a core of whipped caramel cream and a slick of salt caramel on the top.

Fine Foods Store

Corner of Mill & Kendall Lanes (9252 1196). Circular Quay rail or ferry. **Open** 7am-5pm Mon-Fri; 7.30am-4.30pm Sat, Sun. **Main courses** $12-$18. **Map** p55 C3 ❻ **Café**

As well as its well-stocked grocery shelves and sweets by famous Sydney bakers, Fine Foods has a café that is one of your best options for breakfast and lunch in the Rocks. Do not ignore the sausage and egg panini – we never do.

Pancakes on the Rocks

4 Hickson Road (9280 3791, www.pancakeson therocks.com.au). Circular Quay rail or ferry. **Open** 24hrs daily. **Main courses** $12-$34. **Map** p55 B3 ❼ **Café**

You can eat breakfast 24 hours a day at this tourist favourite. Yes, that's right, folks – eat a pancake breakfast complete with bacon, eggs and bananas at three in the morning, with a beer chaser. We dare you.

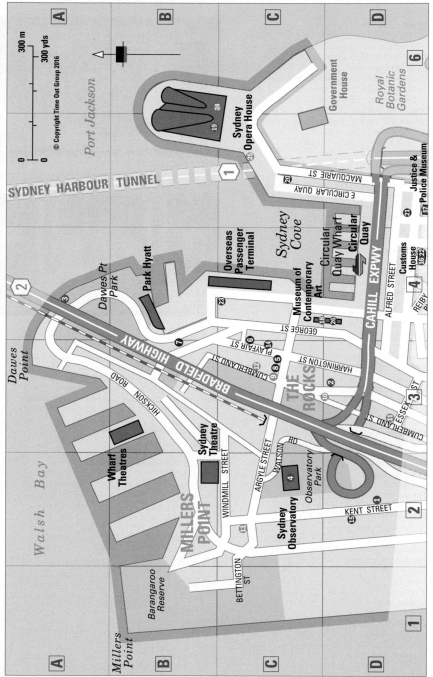

EXPLORE

EXPLORE

Saké
12 Argyle Street (9259 5656, www.sakerestaurant. com.au). Circular Quay rail or ferry. **Open** noon-10.30pm daily. **Main courses** $29-$45. **Map** p55 C3 **8 Japanese**
In an area more known for its beer swilling than cocktail drinking, Saké stands out. And it should – there's some excitement to be found in this Japanese restaurant and bar. The drinks menu is extensive; bar snacks are bite-sized and pack a tasty punch; and the sashimi is top-notch.

Bars

Argyle
18 Argyle Street (9247 5500, www.theargyle rocks.com). Circular Quay rail or ferry. **Open** 11am-midnight Mon-Wed, Sun; 11am-1am Thur; 11am-3am Fri, Sat. **Map** p55 C3 **9**
This suits 'n' tourists watering hole boasts a pizza canteen with mismatched couches and comfy armchairs, dishing out $15 wood-fired pizzas at top speed. You'll also find five bars over two levels, including a huge beer garden and a more dance-friendly space with gloriously tacky disco lights, a big-beat soundtrack and velvet couches.

Australian Heritage Hotel
100 Cumberland Street (9247 2229, www. australianheritagehotel.com). Circular Quay rail or ferry. **Open** 10.30am-midnight daily. **Map** p55 D3 **10**
The Australian Heritage Hotel strikes a comfortable balance between historic tourist stop and a pub that hard-bitten Sydneysiders still want to frequent. Keep hand and jaw busy with a packet of spiced, local jerky while you peruse the impressive craft beer collection. Then sample the bizarre pizzas: Peking duck, tandoori chicken, and the famous Coat of Arms pizza with emu and pepper kangaroo meat.

Blu Bar on 36
Level 36, Shangri-La Hotel, 176 Cumberland Street (9250 6000, www.shangri-la.com). Circular Quay rail or ferry. **Open** 5pm-late Mon-Thur; 5pm-1am Fri, Sat; 5-11pm Sun. **Map** p55 D3 **11**
Forget touristy pretenders: Blu Bar is the best place in Sydney to down a cocktail while floating up in the clouds. Embedded high in the Shangri-La tower, it has floor-to-ceiling windows overlooking the best bits of Sydney's great expanse. The drinks here are carefully concocted by a team of crack mixologists. They also serve a list of cocktails spanning the ages, so you can drink yourself through time.

Glenmore Hotel
96 Cumberland Street (9247 4794, www.glenmore hotel.com.au). Circular Quay rail or ferry. **Open** 11am-midnight Mon-Thur, Sun; 11am-1am Fri, Sat. **Map** p55 C3 **12**

The rooftop bar has unbelievable harbour views, taking in the majesty of the Harbour Bridge and hooking around past the Opera House sails to the glittering CBD – and Pimm's and mule cocktails are available by the jug. Downstairs, you'll find smaller rooms with pool tables and couches; out on the street, a picnic table is a great spot for people-watching over a classic pub meal such as fish and chips or chicken schnitzel.

Lord Nelson Brewery Hotel
19 Kent Street (9251 4044, www.lordnelson brewery.com). Circular Quay rail or ferry. **Open** 11am-11pm Mon-Sat; noon-10pm Sun. **Map** p55 C2 **13**
Being the oldest continuously licensed pub in the city, the Lord Nelson has had a lot of practice at being awesome. It brews its own beer here, and a fresher pint in Sydney is hard to find. Not a beer drinker? These guys aren't the type to judge. Instead, they'll simply whip you up a Nelson Nudie cocktail using fresh bottled juices. Prep your stomach with the Nelson's primer of choice: the beef pie.

Shops & Services

Candle Factory
29 Playfair Street (9241 3365, www.thecandle factory.com.au). Circular Quay rail or ferry. **Open** 10am-5pm daily. **Map** p55 C3 **14 Gifts & souvenirs**
This waxy wonder has been charming visitors for over 30 years. Drop in for quality candles including

Customs House.

EXPLORE

melts, lanterns and votives handcrafted on site, as well as favourite brands Ecoya, Circa Home, Palm Beach and Glasshouse.

Day Spa at the Langham Hotel

Langham Hotel, 89-113 Kent Street (8248 5250, www.langhamhotels.com). Wynyard rail. **Open** 6am-9pm Mon-Fri; 7am-9pm Sat, Sun. **Map** p55 D2 ⓯ **Health & beauty**
This is the place to go if you want to play king or queen for a day. Not just for hotel guests, the spa and fitness facilities can be used by anyone who fancies indulging in a casual afternoon swim, steam, sauna or Babor facial – the spa's signature treatment.

CIRCULAR QUAY

As you arrive in Circular Quay, preferably on one of the city's much-loved green-and-cream ferries, mull over how things have changed since the First Fleet planted flags in 1788. That said, the societal split that arose in those early days of the colony – the bigwigs in their grand sandstone buildings to the east, the convicts and carousing sailors in their tumbledown cottages and seedy drinking dens in the Rocks to the west – is still evident today.

There's nothing quite like Circular Quay, the heart of central Sydney. From here, you get the view of the solid iron struts of the Sydney Harbour Bridge over the gentle undulating sails of the **Opera House**. It will take your breath away time and time again. **Opera Bar** on the eastern side pulls in alfresco drinkers and diners nightly, and the **Overseas Passenger Terminal** on the west side, with its wealth of swish eating and drinking spots, is a welcome addition for the 'it crowd'. The gastronomic heart of the city might just be at the Quay nowadays, where world-class chefs Neil Perry, Guillaume Brahimi, Matt Moran and Peter Gilmore face off nightly.

Sights & Museums

FREE Customs House

31 Alfred Street (9242 8551, www.cityofsydney. nsw.gov.au/customshouse). Circular Quay rail or ferry. **Open** 8am-midnight Mon-Fri; 10am-midnight Sat; 11am-5pm Sun. **Admission** free. **Map** p55 D4 ⓰
Built in 1885, Customs House was one of government architect James Barnet's finest works. Its double-pillared colonnade, wrought-iron panels and long clean lines give it a feeling of space and majesty, underlined by the open area in front. The building houses a highly stylish public library – with decor slick enough to make boutique hotel junkies drool – and some local businesses. Don't miss the fantastic scale model of the city under glass on the ground floor.

Justice & Police Museum

Corner of Albert & Phillip Streets (9252 1144, www.hht.net.au). Circular Quay rail or ferry. **Open** 10am-5pm Sat, Sun. **Admission** $5-$10. **Map** p55 D5 ⓱

EXPLORE

THE CITY'S ORIGINAL ICON
Sydney Harbour Bridge has been wowing visitors since the 1930s.

Long before the Opera House was built, Sydney had 'the coat hanger' as its icon. Locals had dreamed for decades of a bridge to link the north and south shores before construction of the 'All Australian Bridge' began in 1924, by which time Sydney's ferries were struggling to carry 40 million passengers a year.

The winning design came from English firm Dorman, Long & Co, but used Australian steel, stone, sand and labour. Families within the path of the new bridge and its highways were displaced without compensation, and 800 houses were demolished. A total of 1,400 workers toiled on the structure, which is 134m (440ft) high and 1,149m (3,770ft) long, and was the world's largest single-span bridge when it was constructed. It took eight years to build, and workers grafting without safety rails took great risks: 16 died. The opening ceremony was held in 1932, and broadcast around the world.

The refurbished Pylon Lookout, in the south-east pylon, is well worth a visit. Climb 200 steps, past three levels of exhibits celebrating the history of the bridge and its builders. Stained-glass windows feature a painter, riveter, stonemason, rigger, concreter and surveyor. Original bridge memorabilia from the 1930s is also on display; more up-to-date souvenirs are available in the shop on level two. And the open-air views from the top are magnificent. The bridge has been declared 'one of the seven wonders of the modern world' – though not everyone

admires it. Writer James Michener commented in the 1950s that it was 'big, utilitarian and the symbol of Australia... But it is very ugly. No Australian will admit this.'

For listings, *see p54*.

Fittingly, the Justice & Police Museum has been a Water Police Court (1856), Water Police Station (1858) and plain old Police Court (1886). Death masks of some of Australia's more infamous crims are on display, as well as mugshots, assorted deadly weapons and newspaper reports of sensational wrongdoings. Also on view is a recreated 1890s police charge room, a dark and damp remand cell, and a restored Court of Petty Sessions with its notorious communal dock, which could hold up to 15 prisoners at a time.

FREE MCA (Museum of Contemporary Art)
140 George Street (9245 2400, www.mca.com.au). Circular Quay rail or ferry. **Open** 10am-5pm Mon-Wed, Fri-Sun; 10am-9pm Thur. **Admission** free. **Map** p55 D3 ⑱

Once the administration offices of the Maritime Services Board, this waterside museum was overhauled head to toe (well, almost) in 2011 and re-opened in March 2012 with light, airy, uncluttered interiors, more floor space and a boxy new façade. The gallery hosts a mix of blockbuster local and international retrospectives and innovative group shows, and there's a rooftop café and sculpture terrace boasting ripper views too.

FREE Sydney Opera House
Bennelong Point (tours 9250 7250, www. sydneyoperahouse.com). Circular Quay rail or ferry. **Open** 9am-after last performance daily. **Tours** 9am-5pm daily. **Admission** free. *Tours* Sydney Opera House Tour $37; $20 reductions. See website for other tours. **Map** p55 B5 ⑲

As one of the most photographed and famous (if controversial) performing arts venues in the world, the pearly shells of the Sydney Opera House are synonymous with Australia's image – an iconic and irreplaceable part of the Sydney skyline. The Opera House is all about performance, invitation and suspense. From its intricate corridors to its aesthetially pleasing and sound-enhancing performance halls, to its slanted windows (so you can look out on to the Harbour without a reflection), there's plenty to marvel at. Various tours allow you to get intimate with the building, including full 'experience' packages. But if you don't feel like shelling out, it's still free to sit on the steps for a quick lunch and walk by the water and gaze in marvel at those 1,056,000 pearly, self-cleaning Swedish tiles.

Restaurants & Cafés

The restaurant at **Bennelong** (*see right*) serves superb contemporary Australian cuisine.

Aria
1 Macquarie Street (9252 2555, www.aria restaurant.com.au). Circular Quay rail or ferry. **Open** noon-2.30pm, 5.30-11.30pm Mon-Fri; 5-11.30pm Sat; 6-10.30pm Sun. **Set meal** $105 2 courses; $130 3 courses. **Map** p55 C5 ⑳
Contemporary Australian
TV's Matt Moran is much more than just another celebrity chef. He really can cook. Few places can compare on service, the wine list is multi-award winning and the stylish room makes for a special evening. Roast chicken on creamy mash and covered with an aromatic avalanche of sliced truffle is a festival of richness, and calamari fronds gently poached in shiitake broth are similarly successful.

Cafe Nice
2 Phillip Street (8248 9600, fratellifresh.com.au). Circular Quay rail or ferry. **Open** noon-3pm, 6-11pm Mon-Fri; 6-11pm Sat. **Main courses** $24-$39. **Map** p55 D5 ㉑ **French**
At this Niçoise restaurant, you'll find an accomplished menu served by some of the friendliest (and Frenchiest) staff in town. Try the *pissaladière*. It's the South of France's version of pizza – flaky pastry with anchovies, caramelised onions, black olive bits and garlic. Or, opt for the salade niçoise – mixed right at the table.

Cafe Sydney
31 Alfred Street (9251 8683, www.cafesydney. com). Circular Quay rail or ferry. **Open** noon-11pm Mon-Fri; 5-11pm Sat; noon-4pm Sun. **Main courses** $36-$39. **Map** p55 D4 ㉒ **Contemporary Australian**
Cafe Sydney has some of the best views in the city. The huge balcony juts straight over Circular Quay with a bird's-eye view of the Harbour Bridge, Opera House and Sydney ferries choofing their way across the sparkling blue water. Main course combinations

might include grilled swordfish with pea purée, carrots, broad beans, nasturtium and tarragon cream. Or, if you're in full impress-your-mates mode, order a seafood platter with a selection of yabbies, bugs, crab, marron and prawns.

Quay
Overseas Passenger Terminal (9251 5600, www. quay.com.au). Circular Quay rail or ferry. **Open** 6-10pm Mon; noon-2.30pm Tue-Fri; noon-2:30pm, 6-10pm Sat, Sun. **Set meal** $185 tasting menu. **Map** p55 C4 ㉓ **Contemporary Australian**
Even the bread and butter is beautiful at Quay. The food is sophisticated, forward-thinking and made with ultra-seasonal and rare local produce. The smallest flowers. The weirdest peanuts. Berries that grow in the dung of camels in outback Australia. Peter Gilmore's palate and palette know no bounds as he creates food that's almost too beautiful to ruin with cutlery. Almost.

Bars

Bennelong Bar
Sydney Opera House, Bennelong Point (9241 1999, www.bennelong.com.au). Circular Quay rail or ferry. **Open** 5.30pm-late Mon-Sat. **Map** p55 B6 ㉔
Being situated in the smallest sail of the Sydney Opera House does give Bennelong Bar something of an unfair advantage. The soaring ceiling is stunning, the harbour views rock, the superb wine list and service make you feel grown-up and sexy, and the Saarinen chairs are the gods' gift to lounging.

Opera Bar
Lower Concourse, Bennelong Point (9247 1666, www.operabar.com.au). Circular Quay rail or ferry. **Open** 11.30am-late daily. **Map** p55 C5 ㉕
On the day you snag a seat facing the Harbour Bridge up on the raised promenade, you should go buy a lottery ticket, because lady luck has smiled on you. If you want to complete the perfect Sydney Instagram pic with a cocktail, there are about a dozen concoctions that favour sweet, fruity, brightly coloured ingredients designed to pop with the right filter. We recommend ordering a classic instead – a negroni is never a bad idea.

Shops & Services

MCA Store
140 George Street (9245 2400, www.mca.com.au). Circular Quay rail or ferry. **Open** 10am-5pm Mon-Wed, Fri-Sun; 10am-9pm Thur. **Map** p55 C4 ㉖ **Books & music**
The MCA Store is replete with art books of every stripe: scholarly works, collections of prints, catalogues, coffee-table art pieces and more, for everyone from the interested fan to the trained expert. They've also got loads of gift ideas.

EXPLORE

Central Sydney

What makes Sydney great are its fabulous little burgs – and that is certainly true of central Sydney. The one-time theatre and dance hub of Walsh Bay is now a fully fledged entertainment district that's not only home to the Sydney Theatre Company and Sydney Dance Company, but great eating and drinking options too. Chinatown pumps out Australia's most awesome Cantonese food. Darling Harbour has enough family activity venues to keep even the most hyperactive of kids amused for days on end. Meanwhile, Kings Cross, Darlinghurst and Surry Hills retain their urban bohemian edge, with the coolest drinking, dining, clubbing and shopping spots in the city. Gentrification is spreading all over central Sydney – even city-fringe ruffians Redfern and Waterloo are getting in on the act, thanks to an urban renewal programme and a wealth of slick new apartment blocks.

Eau de Vie.

Don't Miss

1 **Royal Botanic Gardens** An oasis of calm amid the urban jungle (p67).

2 **Eau de Vie** Arguably the best damn cocktails in the city (p78).

3 **White Rabbit** Backstreet temple to 21st-century Chinese art (p87).

4 **Momofuku Seibo** Just plain excellent (p76).

5 **Art Gallery of NSW** The permanent collection is a thing of wonder (p63).

Art Gallery of NSW.

EXPLORE

THE CBD

It's an exciting time to be in the centre of town. Fuelled by a small-bar renaissance and some creative reawakenings in the local laneways, the CBD (Central Business District) has enjoyed a revival in recent years. The roads between skyscrapers now have some of the coolest small bars, pubs, cafés and craft beer bars in the country. Tucked away on tiny Bridge Lane, two-level Canto-extravaganza **Mr Wong** is bringing a sense of sleek and chic to central Sydney Chinese food. Nearby **Bistrode CBD** works a similar angle for classic Brit-fare. In need of a stiff drink? Whiskey haven the **Baxter Inn** has got your back. Or, if you prefer rum, hot-foot it straight to **Lobo Plantation**.

Drinking and dining options aside, the CBD boasts elegant Macquarie Street and Martin Place, reaching out to the **Royal Botanic Gardens**, giving a sense of the history of the city and how the land of the First Australians has been re-shaped by the settlers who have arrived since 1788. The huge **St Andrew's Cathedral** in Sydney Square, built in Gothic revival style and now restored to its original glory, is Australia's oldest cathedral. And beautiful green **Hyde Park** is a fine sight at night, with fairy lights in the trees and possums scampering up trunks and

foraging among the plants. In summer, office workers flop down on the grass, while ibis pick their long-legged way around the supine bodies. The parks and gardens of the **Domain** lead from the CBD to Woolloomooloo Wharf, Mrs Maquaries Point and the Royal Botanic Gardens. It's full in the morning with keep-fit classes, at lunchtime with joggers and soccer players, and is an evening venue for numerous events.

The CBD is a solid shopping destination too. The **Queen Victoria Building**, the **Galeries** and **Strand Arcade** house high-end chain stores and boutiques selling great fashion, while **Westfield Sydney**, off buzzing Pitt Street Mall, is the most luxe and lavish mall in Sydney.

Sights & Museums

Andrew (Boy) Charlton Pool

Mrs Macquaries Road, the Domain (9358 6686, www.abcpool.org). Bus 411. **Open** *Apr-Sept* 6am-7pm daily. *Oct-Mar* 6am-8pm daily. **Admission** $3.80-$5.50. **Map** p65 G3 ❶
A $10-million refurbishment has made this harbourside pool the place for inner-city summer swimming. The baths have an eight-lane, heated 50m pool; learners' and toddlers' pools; a sun deck; and a great café. The pool's harbourside edges are glazed, allowing swimmers unparalleled views across the bay.

EXPLORE

IN THE KNOW GETTING AROUND

The CBD is easily walkable – virtually all of its major thoroughfares are built on ancient Gadigal walking tracks. But if you want to save your feet, there are also trains that go underground around the City Circle loop, covering Central, Town Hall, Wynyard, Circular Quay, St James and Museum stations.

Australian Museum

6 College Street, at William Street (9320 6000, www.austmus.gov.au). Museum or St James rail. **Open** 9.30am-5pm daily. **Admission** $5-$10. **Map** p65 E6 ❹
The Australian Museum (established 1827) houses the nation's most important animal, mineral, fossil and anthropological collections, and prides itself on its innovative research into Australia's environment and indigenous cultures. Any serious museum-tripper should see a few of the local stuffed animals, and the displays should answer all your questions about Australian mammals.

Great Synagogue

166 Castlereagh Street, between Park & Market Streets. Entry for services: 187A Elizabeth Street (9267 2477, www.greatsynagogue.org.au). St James or Town Hall rail. **Open** *Services* summer 6.15pm Fri; 8.45am Sat. Winter 5.30pm Fri; 8.45am Sat. *Tours* noon Tue, Thur. **Admission** $10; $5-$7 reductions. **Map** p65 E6 ❺
Sydney's Jewish history dates back to convict times – there were around 16 Jews in the First Fleet – and the Great Synagogue, consecrated in 1878, is deemed the mother congregation of Australian Jewry.

Hyde Park Barracks Museum

Queens Square, corner of Macquarie Street & Prince Albert Road (8239 2311, www.hht.net.au). Martin Place or St James rail. **Open** 9.30am-5pm daily. **Admission** $10; $5 reductions. **Map** p65 E5 ❻
Designed by convict architect Francis Greenway, the barracks were completed in 1819 to house 600 male convicts, who were in government employ until 1848. Subsequently used as an immigration depot and an asylum for women, they eventually metamorphosed into a museum. The courtyard houses a pleasant café for moments of quiet contemplation.

Museum of Sydney

Corner of Bridge & Phillip Streets (9251 5988, www.hht.net.au). Circular Quay rail or ferry. **Open** 10am-5pm daily. **Admission** $10; $5 reductions. **Map** p65 E3 ❼
This modern building stands on one of the most historic spots in Sydney, site of the first Government

FREE Anzac Memorial

Hyde Park, between Park & Liverpool Streets (9267 7668). Museum rail. **Open** 9am-5pm daily. **Admission** free. **Map** p65 E6 ❷
Sydney architect Bruce Dellit was only 31 when he won the 1930 competition to design this beautiful grey-pink granite memorial to the Australian and New Zealand troops who fell in World War I, particularly those involved in the bloody battle for the Gallipoli peninsula. His art deco vision caused a sensation when it opened in 1934. Now, an act of remembrance is held here at 11am daily. Guided tours can be arranged at the reception desk in the monument's base, where you'll also find a small museum dedicated to Australia's military.

★ FREE Art Gallery of NSW

Art Gallery Road, the Domain (9225 1700, www.artgallery.nsw.gov.au). Bus 441. **Open** 10am-5pm Mon, Tue, Thur-Sun; 10am-10pm Wed. **Admission** free. **Map** p65 F4 ❸
Established in 1871, this gallery is one of Australia's foremost cultural institutions. It holds significant collections of Australian, European and Asian art, and presents nearly 40 exhibitions annually. Every Wednesday night, the Art After Hours programme features workshops, celebrity talks and film screenings. Matt Moran's new contemporary restaurant Chiswick is also here, plus a café.

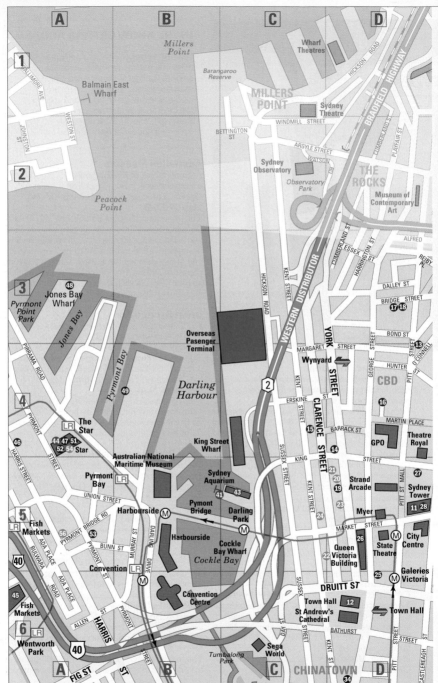

EXPLORE

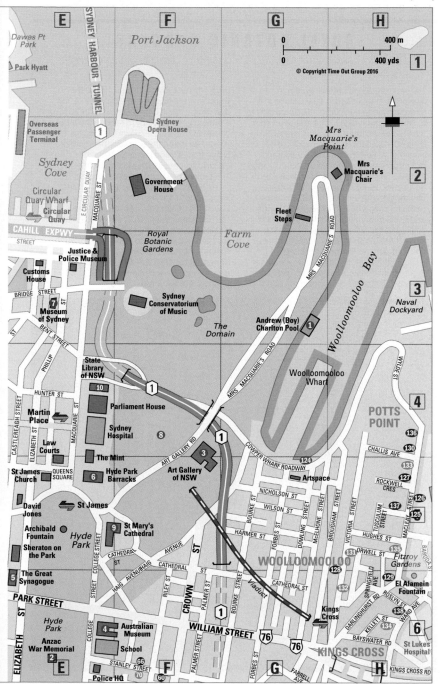

ROYAL BOTANIC GARDENS

With its possums and rare cacti, this is more than just a place to rest.

The beautiful Royal Botanic Gardens (*see p63*), established in 1816, make a sweeping green curve from the Opera House to Woolloomooloo Bay. It's a gorgeous spot, full of majestic trees, spacious lawns, bird-filled ponds, statues, native wildlife and ornamental flowerbeds – all in the heart of a major city. The Domain surrounds the gardens: in colonial times, this land acted as a buffer between the governor's home and the penal colony, but by 1831 roads and paths had been built to allow public access, and it has remained a people's place ever since. The Palm Grove is a good place to start: there's a shop and visitor information counter, café, restaurant and toilets.

Highlights from the 30 hectares include the Tropical Centre, spectacular rose gardens, cacti collection, possums and the living fossil Wollemi pine, one of the world's rarest species, discovered in 1994 by a ranger in the Blue Mountains. In 2012, a project got under way to remove the large cohort of fruit bats – known as flying foxes – that had made the Gardens their home. Noise at dawn and sunset was used to disturb the bats as they were roosting. The project has been largely successful.

The Fleet Steps provide a classic Opera House photo-op. There are free guided walks (10.30am daily), or you can take the 'trackless train' ($10, $5 reductions), which stops at areas of interest around the gardens, ending up at the Opera House. To learn more about the Aboriginal life in the area, visit the Cadi Jam Ora gardens or book a walk with an Aboriginal guide (9231 8134, $38, $18 reductions).

House, built in 1788 by Governor Arthur Phillip. Now, it offers a mix of state-of-the-art installations, nostalgic memorabilia and changing exhibitions. This area was the first point of contact for the indigenous Gadigal people and the First Fleet, so the museum also explores issues of colonisation, invasion and contact.

★ FREE Royal Botanic Gardens

Mrs Macquaries Road (9231 8111, www. rbgsyd.nsw.gov.au). Bus 441. **Admission** free. **Map** p65 F4 ❽

Over the years, this 30-hectare site has withstood fires, cattle grazing, invasions of flying foxes, a windmill, an aviary and even a zoo. Today, save a few sulphur-crested cockies, it's an oasis of calm in an urban jungle. There are free guided walks on offer and decent coffee going at the Botanic Gardens Restaurant. *See also p66.*

FREE St Mary's Cathedral

Corner of College Street & Cathedral Square (9220 0400, www.stmaryscathedral.org.au). St James rail. **Open** 6.45am-6pm Mon-Fri; 9am-6.30pm Sat; 7am-6.30pm Sun. *Tours* 10.30am Sun; also by appt. **Admission** free. **Map** p65 F4 ❾

St Mary's Cathedral is the seat of the Roman Catholic archbishop of Sydney and stands on the site of Australia's first Catholic chapel. William Wilkinson Wardell's design replaced the original cathedral, ruined by fire in 1865. In the winter months, the forecourt is iced for a skating rink.

FREE State Library of New South Wales

Corner of Macquarie Street & Cahill Expressway (9273 1414, www.sl.nsw.gov.au). Martin Place rail. **Open** 9am-8pm Mon-Thur; 9am-5pm Fri; 10am-5pm Sat, Sun. *Tours* 11am Tue; 2pm Thur. **Admission** free. **Map** p65 E4 ❿

The State Library is essentially two libraries in one: the modern General Reference Library provides access to five million books and other media (stored across five floors below ground), while the 1910 Mitchell Wing (closed Sundays) holds the world's greatest collection of Australiana, including James Cook's original journals and the logbook of Captain Bligh of the *Bounty*. The library also has one of the most significant collections of maps in Australia.

Sydney Tower Eye

100 Market Street, between Castlereagh & Pitt Streets (9333 9222, www.sydneytowereye.com.au). St James or Town Hall rail. **Open** 9.30am-8.45pm daily; Skywalks run every 30-60mins. **Tickets** *Skywalk & Observation Deck* $70; $49 reductions. **Map** p64 D5 ⓫

First opened to the public in 1981, Sydney Tower provides a panoramic 360° view, with the Pacific Ocean in the east and the Blue Mountains in the west. If you manage to get past the five levels of the Westfield Sydney Shopping Centre, then the most dangerous

part is over. Pass through the metal detector and into one of the three double-decker lifts that ascend above the city skyline. Arrive at the Observation Deck and gaze out on every rooftop in Sydney. If you're feeling more adventurous, take a heart-pulsing stroll along the Skywalk – an external walkway of Sydney Tower – where you'll get far-reaching views from 268m (880ft) above the ground. You'll want to watch your step, though. Not that there's any danger of tumbling off the edge – a guide is on hand to soothe nerves and share points of interest – but the glass-floored viewing platform offers breathtaking views of the CBD below.

FREE Sydney Town Hall

Corner of George & Druitt Streets (9265 9189, www.cityofsydney.nsw.gov.au). Town Hall rail. **Open** 8.30am-6pm Mon-Fri. **Admission** free. **Map** p64 D6 ⓬

Built on a graveyard, completed in 1889 and given a sustainability-driven overhaul in 2010, Sydney Town Hall is an impressive High Victorian building, topped by a clock tower with a two-ton bell. It has retained its original function and interiors, including the council chamber and lord mayor's office. Centennial Hall is dominated by a magnificent 8,000-pipe organ: with a capacity of 2,048, it was once the largest concert hall in the world and is still used for organ recitals and other musical events.

Restaurants & Cafés

★ Bentley

Radisson Blu Hotel, 27 O'Connell Street (8214 0505, www.thebentley.com.au). Wynyard rail. **Open** noon-3pm, 6pm-late Mon-Fri; 6pm-late Sat. **Main courses** $36-$49. **Map** p64 D4 ⓭

Contemporary Australian

What started out back in 2006 as a little venue in Surry Hills offering kooky wines and some pretty crazy modern Australian snackage has morphed into one of the city's more exciting restaurants inside enormous new CBD digs. Treat yourself to a full meal, or pop in for a bowl of chips, a sandwich and a glass of Chablis.

Bistrode CBD

Level 1, 52 King Street (9240 3000, merivale.com. au/bistrodecbd). Wynyard rail. **Open** noon-3pm, 6-10pm Mon-Fri. **Main courses** $26.50-$41.50. **Map** p64 D4 ⓮ **British**

Classic British stylings in a stunning city dining room meet outstanding Brit-fare by Jeremy Strode, whose artfully simple cooking has encouraged a whole generation of young chefs to embrace a less-is-more attitude.

Cross Eatery

155 Clarence Street (9279 4280). Wynyard rail. **Open** 6.30am-4pm Mon-Fri. **Main courses** $12-$18. **Map** p64 C4 ⓯ **Café**

EXPLORE

This CBD café delivers brunch vibes to your mid-day meal. The queues build quickly after noon as people clamour for a slice of salad bar action. Dig into roasted root vegetables with almonds and a feta dressing. Or go tart and fresh with pink grapefruit on a jumble of brussels sprouts, chicory and walnuts.

Felix

Ivy, 2 Ash Street (9240 3000, merivale.com.au/felix). Wynyard rail. **Open** noon-3pm, 5.30-10.30pm Mon-Fri; 5.30-10.30pm Sat. **Main courses** $34-$49. **Map** p64 D4 ⑯ **French**

Felix takes its cues from New York brasserie to the stars Balthazar, itself a homage to the classic Parisian bistro. The menu of bistro classics is deceptively simple but beautifully executed. And at the back of the mammoth French-style brasserie, there is a small bit of bar-hugging real estate that makes for excellent CBD tippling too.

Mr Wong

3 Bridge Lane (9240 3000, merivale.com.au/mr wong). Circular Quay rail or ferry. **Open** noon-late daily. **Main courses** $30-$38. **Map** p64 D3 ⑰ **Chinese**

This two-level Canto-extravaganza offers everything from fancy dim sum to green beans stir-fried with pork mince and house-made XO sauce. Upstairs features a big, beautiful bar run by Doron Whaite – and

he sure makes a fine cocktail. Mr Wong is a popular choice, so at lunchtime go early – say, noon, when it opens – for a guaranteed seat, if you haven't booked.

★ Rockpool

11 Bridge Street (9252 1888, www.rockpool. com/rockpoolsydney). Circular Quay rail or ferry. **Open** noon-3pm, 6pm-late Mon-Fri; noon-3pm Sat. **Main courses** (lunch only) $29-$140. **Set meal** $185 tasting menu. **Map** p64 D3 ⑱ **Contemporary Australian**

The restaurant that defined modern Australian fine dining in Sydney moved house recently. And you know what? We're glad. The new digs are flash and grand, but still accessible. And the dinner? A long and luxurious tasting menu, with little plates of deliciousness such as white spruce urchin with bernaise custard, scallops with squid ink and chilli and wagyu grilled with wasabi and pickled chrysanthemum.

★ Single Origin CBD

89 York Street (0425 223 952, singleorigin roasters.com.au). Wynyard rail. **Open** 6.30am-4pm Mon-Fri. **Main courses** $10-$14. **Map** p64 D5 ⑲ **Café**

There are seemingly thousands of places in the CBD serving coffee. But for great quality, look no further than this spinoff from beloved Surry Hills institution Single Origin Roasters. Pair its excellent

Barber Shop.

coffee with banana bread slathered with espresso butter for the best kind of morning.

Bars

Barber Shop

89 York Street (9299 9699, thisisthebarbershop. com). Wynyard rail. **Open** 4pm-midnight Mon, Tue; 2pm-midnight Wed-Fri; 5pm-midnight Sat. **Map** p64 D5 ⓴

It's a barber out front and a party out the back at this inner city bar, where the gin flows freely. There are 47 types of the spirit listed on the menu, and that doesn't take into account owner Mikey Enright's vintage gin collection or the Genever – the pride of the Netherlands.

Baxter Inn

156 Clarence Street (no phone, thebaxterinn. com). Wynyard rail. **Open** 4pm-1am Mon-Sat. **Map** p64 D5 ㉑

This basement-level hooch sanctuary can be found (after some serious searching) on a nondescript laneway off Clarence Street. The sister venue to Shady Pines is a legendary candlelit basement bar with a thick carpet, offering jazz and blues – and toilets with some of the best acoustics in town. It's kind of modelled on an old-school Irish American sports bar, only with no sport and much better whisky.

Grandma's Bar

Basement Level, 275 Clarence Street (9264 3004, www.grandmasbarsydney.com.au). Town Hall rail or bus 500, 504, 506, 507, 510, 515, 518, 520, M50, M52. **Open** 3pm-late Mon-Fri; 5pm-late Sat. **Map** p64 D5 ㉒

Down the quiet end of Clarence Street is good ol' Grandma's. The below-street-level bar's walls are lined with bright yellow lorikeet-printed wallpaper, and vintage kitchen canisters, crochet blankets and Grandma's rum selection fill out the space. The sugarcane spirit is the star of the tiki-skewed menu, which features Sydney's only peanut butter colada.

Lobo Plantation

209 Clarence Street (no phone, thelobo.com.au). Wynyard rail. **Open** 4pm-midnight Mon-Thur, Sat; 2pm-midnight Fri.* **Map** p64 D5 ㉓

Like rum? Then this exotic stop is a must. With its emerald walls, rattan lamps and bentwood bar stools, Lobo captures the faded grandeur of a Caribbean summer house. Lobo's signature creation is the Old Grogrum, with spiced rum, fresh lemon, sugar and Lobo's own vermouth – and flames. Be warned, though: you'll want to make this an early-in-the-week visit if you're a non-queuer.

Papa Gede's

Rear of 348 Kent Street, via laneway (www.papa gedes.com). Wynyard rail. **Open** 5pm-midnight Mon-Sat. **Map** p64 C5 ㉔

A block away from the Baxter Inn (*see p68*) is a charming little voodoo bar lit by candles and decorated with skulls, beads and half-finished incantations scrawled on the polished concrete floor. The drinks are all pretty much on the bitter, brown spirits and boozy end of the spectrum, and very often combine all the above in one glass. There are free Burger Rings too.

Shops & Services

Galeries

500 George Street (9265 6888, www.thegaleries. com). Town Hall rail. **Open** 10am-6pm Mon-Wed, Fri, Sat; 10am-9pm Thur; 11am-5pm Sun. **Map** p64 D6 ㉕ **Mall**

This shopping precinct houses Time Out favourites such as women's clothing store Gorman, two spacious men's and women's Incu stores, beauty brand Mecca Cosmetica and Melbourne-based streetwear label Alphaville. The mammoth Kinokuniya bookstore has classic, contemporary and pulp fiction, a huge range of Japanese-language books and manga.

★ Queen Victoria Building

455 George Street, between Market & Druitt Streets (9264 9209, www.qvb.com.au). Town Hall rail. **Open** 9am-6pm Mon-Wed, Fri, Sat; 9am-9pm Thur; 11am-5pm Sun. **Map** p64 D5 ㉖ **Mall**

EXPLORE

Mamak

Designed by George McRae to resemble a Byzantine palace, the QVB occupies an entire block on George Street, and once dominated the Sydney skyline with its dramatic domed roof – an inner glass dome encased by a copper-sheathed outer one. On the hour, shoppers gather on the second floor to watch the Royal Automata Clock display a moving royal pageant. Home to over 100 shops – from Camper to Victoria's Secret – the QVB is a stalwart of high-end high-street shopping in Sydney.

Strand Arcade

412-414 George Street (9232 4199, www.strand arcade.com.au). Town Hall or Wynyard rail. **Open** 9am-5.30pm Mon-Wed, Fri; 9am-8pm Thur; 9am-4pm Sat; 11am-4pm Sun. **Map** p64 D5 **27** **Mall**
When it opened in 1892, the Strand Arcade was regarded as the very latest in shopping-centre architecture. Wedged between George and Pitt Streets, the narrow, multi-level thoroughfare houses premium Australian fashion designers, including Jac + Jack, Lover, Sass & Bide and Sydney darling Dion Lee.

Westfield Sydney

Corner of Pitt Street Mall & Market Street (9231 9300, www.westfield.com). Martin Place rail. **Open** 9.30am-6.30pm Mon-Wed, Fri, Sat; 9.30am-9pm Thur; 10am-6pm Sun. **Map** p64 D5 **28** **Mall**
A seven-storey shopping centre featuring more than 170 stores, a number of local and international high-end fashion brands, and an impressive food and dining precinct.

CHINATOWN & HAYMARKET

Ah, delicious Haymarket – home to the walk-through supermarket and food court that is Chinatown, and destination for many a mega-musical at the beautiful and historic **Capitol Theatre** (*see p214*). The area, which stretches from Railway Square to Darling Harbour, also counts among its sites the **4A Centre for Contemporary Asian Art** and the **Golden Water Mouth**, a sculpture based on a dead tree trunk, partly covered with gold leaf, installed in 1999. But you're probably here because you followed your nose to the district around Sussex and Dixon Streets: so hit up late-night legend **Golden Century**, the great and always packed **BBQ King**, queue-worthy Malaysian hotspot **Mamak** and the cheap and cheerful **Chinese Noodle Restaurant**. **Marigold** has yum cha (like dim sum). If it's street food, exotic meats and Asian bric-a-brac you're after, then head for the **Chinatown Night Market**. And if you're looking for a bright and cheap phone cover, **Paddy's Markets** is your go-to. Feel like a beverage? Hit the **Civic Hotel** – and go late so you can join the party at the **Civic Underground** (*see p200*).

Sights & Museums

FREE 4A Centre for Contemporary Asian Art
181-187 Hay Street (9212 0380, www.4a. com.au). Capitol Square light rail. **Open** 11am-6pm Tue-Sat. **Admission** free. **Map** p72 D2 ②
This non-profit arts organisation and gallery aims to present different cultures through a regular schedule of exhibitions, performances and public programmes with local and international Asian and Australian artists.

Restaurants & Cafés

Chinese Noodle Restaurant
Shop 7, 8 Quay Street (9281 9051). Central rail. **Open** 11am-late daily. **Main courses** $9-$19. **Map** p72 C2 ③ **Chinese**
This place is so popular, the lines snake out the doors every lunchtime, which means you either need to get there super-early or be prepared to queue. Once inside, you'll be eating hand-pulled noodles with pork mince and light-as-a-feather dumplings.

Golden Century
393-399 Sussex Street (9212 3901, www.golden century.com.au). Capitol Square light rail. **Open** noon-4pm daily. **Main courses** $19-$71.50. **Map** p72 C1 ③ **Chinese**
The Golden C may be most famous among pub-going Sydney residents for its awesome late night dishes, such as pork and preserved egg congee, salt and pepper squid and roast pork, but this impressive Canto-palace is one of the most lavish places for a night on the town with a menu including pipis in XO sauce, crisp-skinned chicken and steamed parrot fish.

Mamak
15 Goulburn Street (9211 1668, www.mamak. com.au). Capitol Square light rail. **Open** 11.30am-2.30pm, 5.30-10pm Mon-Thur, Sun; 11.30am-2.30pm, 5.30pm-2am Fri, Sat. **Main courses** $14-$19. **Map** p72 C1 ② **Malaysian**
The queues are long but worth it at this famous Malaysian eatery. Order the roti to start – paper-thin pieces of dough, fried on a hotplate and served with curry (or ice-cream!) – and round the meal out with one of the tastiest *nasi lemaks* in town. The room is pretty much a concrete block with tables and chairs, but the food more than makes up for anything lacking in the style department.

Marigold
Levels 4 & 5, 683-689 George Street (9281 3388, www.marigold.com.au). Capitol Square light rail. **Open** 10am-3pm, 5.30-11pm daily. **Main courses** $22-$68. **Map** p72 C2 ③ **Chinese**
Make this your go-to joint when yum cha cravings hit. Best bets at Marigold are the pork knuckles, beef tendon, fried radish cakes and prawn dumplings.

Banquetting it up? Expect stuffed crab claw, scallops in bird's nest and all your seafood favourites.

Menya Mappen
Shop TG8, 8 Quay Street (9267 4649, menya. com.au). Central rail or Capitol Square light rail. **Open** noon-3pm, 6-10pm Mon-Sat. **Main courses** $10-$13. **Map** p64 D6 ② **Japanese**
This city noodle bar wows soup fans with crisp tempura and brilliant udon noodles. Don't fancy soup? One of the tastiest things here is the dragon – hot noodles covered in a spicy, chilli-studded pork mince and boiled egg garnish.

N2 Extreme Gelato
43/1 Dixon Street (no phone, n2extremegelato.com. au). Town Hall rail or bus 500, 504, 506, 507, 510, 515, 518, 520, M50, M52. **Open** 1-11pm daily. **Ice-cream** $7-$9. **Map** p72 C1 ③ **Ice-cream**
This lab-like gelato bar attracts huge queues on a Friday night and has outlandish flavours such as Chinese Cough Medicine, Rosemary's Baby and gorgonzola. It also churns through 1,000 litres of liquid nitrogen a week. Watch on as your sweet treat freezes before your eyes.

Seoul Orizin
203-209 Thomas Street (8541 7531). Central rail or Capitol Square light rail. **Open** 11am-11pm daily. **Main courses** $13-$37. **Map** p72 C2 ③ **Korean**
A must-visit for fried chicken fans. No soggy bottoms here: the coating is crisp and ultra-crunchy, and makes a satisfying shattering sound when you bite into it. One cannot live on fried chicken alone, so give your arteries a break with the *japchae*: glass noodles tossed with courgettes, carrots and mushrooms.

Bars

Bear
Thomas Lane (0451 029 226, www.thebearbar. com.au). Central rail or Capitol Square light rail. **Open** 5pm-midnight daily. **Map** p72 D1 ③
Take a walk down dark and dodgy Thomas Lane and look for the flashing Christmas tree in lieu of a security guard manning the door. Occupying the old storeroom of a pâtisserie, this small bar with a Scandi/Alpine twist can barely fit 30 people. Order a classic cocktail and a house-made fondue pot and imagine you're holidaying in a ski cabin.

Civic Hotel
388 Pitt Street (8080 7000). Museum rail. **Open** 10am-3am daily. **Map** p72 D1 ③
Some people love the Civic for its art deco finishes, craft beer specials and location convenient to most city offices. Another – very separate – group of people love the Civic for its underground nightclub Civic Underground (*see p200*), with matching loose and lively club nights and one of the best sound systems around these parts.

EXPLORE

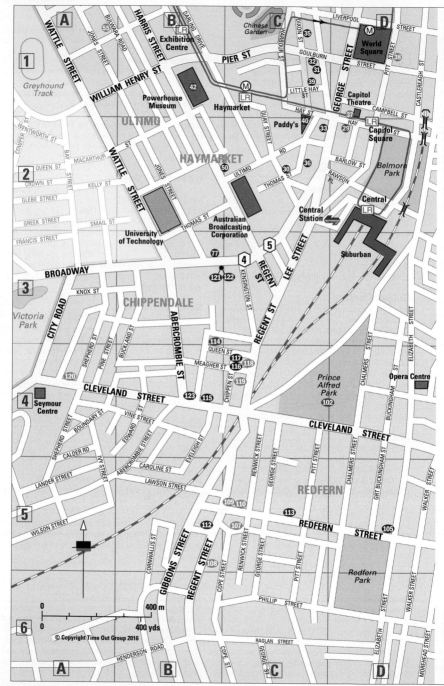

EXPLORE

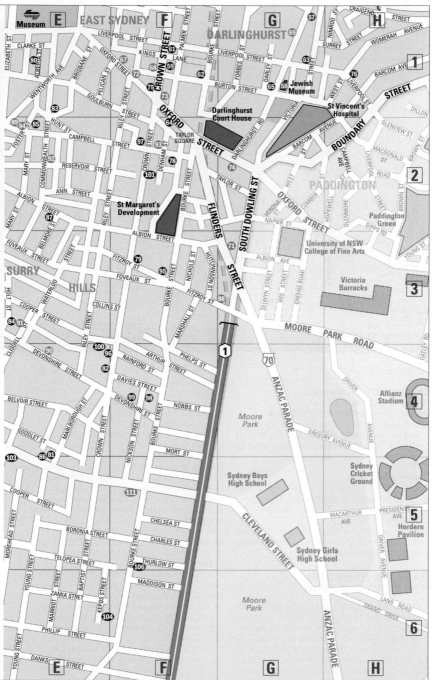

EXPLORE

EXPLORE

Paddy's Markets.

Shops & Services

Chinatown Night Market

Dixon Street. Paddys Market's light rail.
Open 4-11pm Fri. **Map** p72 C1 **㊴ Market**
You can get your street food and exotic meats here
– octopus balls, yum! – and ten different types of
Asian-style liquorice, but we love this place for the
plush toys and only-in-Asia bric-a-brac.

Paddy's Markets

*Corner of Hay & Thomas Streets (9325 6200,
www.paddysmarkets.com.au). Paddy's Markets
light rail.* **Open** 9am-5pm Wed-Sun. **Map** p72 C2
㊵ Market
The stallholders at this 150-year-old institution hawk
food, fashion, bric-a-brac, not very convincing knock-
offs, tourist tat and mobile phone covers.

DARLING HARBOUR, PYRMONT & ULTIMO

We're **Pyrmont** defenders here at Time Out, and
here's why: long dismissed as a bit dull, we reckon
Pyrmont has a lot going for it. First of all, there
is the obvious stuff: the **Fish Market** – now
complete with one of Sydney's best yum cha dens;
the casino, recently refurbished and revived as the
Star and jam-packed with awesome things to eat,

such as Messina ice-cream and Adriano Zumbo
pâtisserie treats, plus **Momofuku Seiobo**,
David Chang's only restaurant outside New
York. And if you're after something fancier
in the area, **Flying Fish** at Jones Bay Wharf
is still going great guns.

The inner-city area of **Ultimo** is a hive of
academic activity and home to thousands of
TAFE, UTS and Sydney University scholars
rushing between classes and back home to study.
Ultimo is primarily a residential neighbourhood
but there are still plenty of gems hidden away
on its leafy side streets. Your Ultimo visit should
include a pop-in at the **Powerhouse Museum**,
which often has free exhibitions that appeal to
kids and adults in equal measure; a pint or two at
the **Lord Wolseley**; and a coffee at any of the
many storefront cafés that dot its streets.

Darling Harbour is Sydney tourism
central, featuring numerous restaurants, bars,
the **IMAX** (*see p187*) cinema and the starting
point for boat tours and water taxis. Since its
recent refurbishment, Darling Harbour is more
family-friendly than ever before: the classic
carousel is still in place, as are the train tours
up and down the wharves, but it now also has
a fantastic mega-playground that'll keep kids
(and probably most adults) entertained for
literally hours.

Sea Life Sydney Aquarium

1-5 Wheat Road, Darling Harbour (9333 9245, www.sydneyaquarium.com.au). Town Hall rail or Darling Harbour ferry. **Open** 9.30am-7pm (last entry 6pm) daily. **Admission** $28-$40; $19.60-$31.50 reductions. **Map** p64 C5 ➍➌

The world's largest indoor system of Australian marine life features 60 tanks and three oceanaria filled with more than 12,000 animals from 650 different species. Highlights include Shark Valley, the Great Barrier Reef exhibit, Japanese Spider Crabs and the Bay of Rays. The cheaper entry prices are available by booking online.

Star

80 Pyrmont Street, Pyrmont (1800 700 700, www.star.com.au). The Star light rail. **Open** 24hrs daily. **Map** p64 A4 ➍➍

Opened in 1997, the casino formerly known as Star City had a massive revamp in 2011, to become a restaurant, nightlife and hotel hub. The $870-million facelift saw the building given a new glass façade facing harbourside, and five new signature restaurants – BLACK by ezard (*see below*), Balla, Sokyo (*see p76*), Momofuku Seibo (*see p76*) and the Century.

Sydney Fish Market

Bank Street, Pyrmont (9004 1100, www.sydney fishmarket.com.au). Wentworth Park light rail or bus 443, 501. **Open** 7am-4pm daily. **Map** p64 A6 ➍➎

This working fishing port – with many types of fishing vessels in Blackwattle Bay, wholesale and retail fish markets, shops, a variety of indoor and outdoor eateries, and picnic tables on an outdoor deck – is well worth the journey to Pyrmont.

Restaurants & Cafés

Bar Zini

78 Harris Street, Pyrmont (9660 5718). The Star light rail or bus 443. **Open** 7am-4pm Mon, Tue; 7am-4pm, 5pm-late Wed-Fri; 8am-4pm, 5pm-late Sat. **Main courses** $13-$25. **Map** p64 A4 ➍➏
Italian

This sweet little Pyrmont café-cum-restaurant has an Italian bent. There are breakfast dishes, panini and salads at lunchtime, and a changing dinner menu. Head here for the roast and vino Wednesday special.

BLACK by ezard

Ground Level, The Star, 80 Pyrmont Street, Pyrmont (9657 9109, www.star.com.au). The Star light rail. **Open** 5.30-9.30pm Tue-Thur; noon-3pm, 5.30-10pm Fri; noon-2.30pm, 5.30-10pm Sat; noon-2.30pm, 5.30-9.30pm Sun. **Main courses** $29-$48. **Map** p64 A4 ➍➐
Contemporary Australian

This is big casino dining for high rollers. Start out with a drink in the bar – they push the boat out with their cocktails and you'll be sipping them in a deluxe, blinged-up room with views over the bay. The menu

Sights & Museums

Madame Tussauds

1-5 Wheat Road, Darling Harbour (1800 205 851, www.madametussauds.com/sydney). Town Hall rail or Darling Harbour ferry. **Open** 9.30am-8pm daily (last entry 7pm). **Admission** $28-$40; $19.60-$31.50 reductions. **Map** p64 B5 ➍➊

Expect to encounter historical figures (Captain Cook, Sir Charles Kingsford Smith), political leaders (Julia Gillard, Barack Obama), sports stars (Lleyton Hewitt, Layne Beachley), Hollywood A-listers (Brad Pitt, Leonardo DiCaprio) and movie stars (Marilyn Monroe, Audrey Hepburn) at Sydney's branch of the famous wax museum.

Powerhouse Museum

500 Harris Street, Ultimo (9217 0111, maas. museum/powerhouse-museum). Exhibition Centre light rail or bus 501. **Open** 10am-5pm daily. **Admission** $15; free under-16s. **Map** p72 B1 ➍➋

This science, technology, creativity and pop culture museum sits on the site of the old Ultimo Power Station. It's the largest in Australia, with a collection of 385,000 objects, 22 permanent and five temporary display spaces, and more than 250 interactive exhibits. We love the reconstructed art deco cinema showing films and newsreels from the 1920s and '30s and the steam-powered locomotive from the 1850s.

EXPLORE

is broken into four sections: starters and mains up the top; the grilled gear and sides down the bottom. Focus on the top half – beef tartare with heirloom beets, herb mayonnaise and mustard ice-cream, say, followed by poached hapuka with calamari 'risotto', seasonal vegetables and escabeche dressing – and you won't go wrong.

Flying Fish

Lower Deck, Jones Bay Wharf, 19-21 Pirrama Road, Pyrmont (9518 6677, flyingfish.com.au). Bus 443. **Open** 6-10.30pm Mon; noon-2.30pm, 6-10.30pm Tue-Sat; noon-2.30pm Sun. **Main courses** $38-$48. **Map** p64 A3 (48) **Seafood**

This beautifully designed waterside seafood restaurant resides on an original wharf site, with many of its industrial-maritime beginnings preserved. Go for the views, stay for the blue eye trevalla.

LuMi

56 Pirrama Road, Pyrmont (9571 1999, www.lumidining.com). The Star light rail or bus 443. **Open** 6.30pm-late Wed, Thur; noon-2.30pm, 6pm-late Fri, Sat; noon-2.30pm, 6.30pm-late Sun. **Set meal** $55 4 courses (lunch); $95 tasting menu. **Map** p64 B4 (49) **Italian/Japanese**

Expect new wave Italian right on the water at LuMi, with a side order of Japanese. Federico Zanellato's eight-course degustation menu features the likes of plump spelt ravioli holding a thin layer of melted brown butter and pumpkin purée, and stinging nettle spaghetti with porky pangrattato. There are wine pairings for an extra $80.

Mecca Espresso

646 Harris Street, Ultimo (9280 4204, www.meccaespresso.com). Bus 501. **Open** 7am-4pm Mon-Fri; 7am-3pm Sat. **Map** p72 C2 (50) **Café**

This coffee shop is all about the pour-over method. Like a fancier form of filter coffee, it offers very different notes, flavours and textures from espresso-style coffee.

★ Momofuku Seiobo

Ground Level, The Star, 80 Pyrmont Street, Pyrmont (momofuku.com/sydney/seiobo). The Star light rail. **Open** 6.30-10pm Mon-Thur; noon-2pm Fri; 6-10pm Sat. **Set meal** $185 tasting menu. **Map** p64 A4 (51) **Korean**

What started as a noodle joint on 13th Street in Manhattan's East Village over a decade ago is now a global food force, headed by chef David Chang. The team have planted the flag on the other side of the world – inside a casino. Naturally. The tasting menu? Delicious, crazy and probably for our buck, top of its game on the fancy stakes in Sydney.

Sokyo Sushi Bar

Ground Level, The Star, 80 Pyrmont Street, Pyrmont (9657 9161, www.star.com.au). The Star light rail. **Open** 7-10am, 5.30-9.30pm Mon-Wed, Sun; 7-10am, 5.30-10.30pm Thur-Sat. **Main courses** $30-$46. **Map** p64 A4 (52) **Japanese**

Chefs Chase Kojima and his new offsider Takashi Sano command the most impressive sushi counter in Sydney. The only challenge is landing a seat. They experiment quite a lot here, whether that's ageing fish for weeks on end, or perfecting that crisp, almost crackling-like nori.

Tappo Osteria

Corner of Pyrmont & Bunn Streets, Pyrmont (9552 1509, tappo.com.au). Bus 443, 501. **Open** 5-10.30pm Tue, Sat; noon-2.30pm, 5-10.30pm Wed-Fri. **Main courses** $26-$31. **Map** p64 A5 (53) **Italian**

Tappo offers damn fine pizza and an impressive collection of Italian craft beers. Order the Calabrese: it's a rich and mouth-searing mix of n'duja (the spicy Calabrian pork paste Sydney's come to know and love), *cimi de rapa*, and plenty of garlic and chilli oil, all on a thin yet soft and puffy base. There are pasta dishes and mains too.

Bars

Black Bar

The Star, 80 Pyrmont Street, Pyrmont (1800 700 700, www.star.com.au). The Star light rail. **Open** 5.30-9.30pm Tue-Thur; noon-3pm, 5.30-10pm Fri; 5.30-10pm Sat. **Map** p64 A4 (54)

This classic cocktail bar is heavy on the class and light on the frou frou. Try a Royal Cocktail – a riff on the 1930s classic of gin, dry vermouth and cherry brandy that's unctuous and musky. Or a Domo Arigato – a full-bodied and nicely balanced shake-up of yuzu, Japanese whisky, spiced sugar syrup and two types of bitters.

Lord Wolseley

265 Bulwara Road, Ultimo (9660 1736, www.lordwolseleyhotel.com.au). Exhibition Centre light rail. **Open** 11am-midnight Mon-Fri; noon-midnight Sat; noon-10pm Sun. **Map** p72 A1 (55)

In a leafy pocket of Ultimo, you'll find this old timer which strikes a comfortable balance between the old ways and the new. Traditional pub fixings still have pride of place in the public bar; but in the back bistro, Pub Life Kitchen is pumping out experimental and exceptional burgers.

Quarrymans

214-216 Harris Street, Pyrmont (9660 0560, www.quarrymanshotel.com.au). Bus 443, 501. **Open** 11am-midnight Mon-Sat; 11am-10pm Sun. **Map** p64 A5 (56)

At this excellent Pyrmont pub, you'll find 24 craft beer taps and one hand pump for real-ale enthusiasts. The coppery pipes supply everything from super-refreshing After Battle pale ale through to a strawberry wheat beer, a blueberry Hefeweizen and an alcoholic ginger beer.

EAST SYDNEY & DARLINGHURST

The razors have been blunted in Sydney's former centre of sex, drugs and crime. Now, lanes where you once dared not walk are home to bars you'd kill to get into – shady little places at the forefront of the city's small-bar movement such as **Hazy Rose** and the hidden-if-not-very-small **Shady Pines Saloon** and **Cliff Dive**. Food in the blocks between Oxford Street and the Cross has also picked up – Victoria Street is chock-a-block with great eats, and home to Sydney's most popular ice-cream shop in **Messina** – and you'll find one of Sydney's thinnest, most perfectly crisp (and ruthlessly authentic) pizzas at **Lucio**.

Oxford Street has lifted its game big time in the last decade, from thumping new-age gay bars to hipster gig venue of choice the **Oxford Art Factory**. Darlo is still the place to get royally trashed in this city – and it can still be as shady as it ever was. The difference now is that you can do it with a bit of style… and get the best pork roll going at **Mr Crackles** when you need that 4am stomach-filler. It's also a shopping hotspot, with vintage and new fashion boutiques aplenty.

Sights & Museums

Govindas
12 Darlinghurst Road, Darlinghurst (9380 5155, www.govindas.com.au). Kings Cross rail or bus 311, 378. **Open** see website for session times and prices. **Map** p73 G1 ⑰
This Hare Krishna-run centre is a haven from the evening antics of nearby Kings Cross. Attend a meditation class in the lotus room, then have a vegetarian dinner in time for a late session in the boutique cinema.

Sydney Jewish Museum
148 Darlinghurst Road, Darlinghurst (9360 7999, www.sydneyjewishmuseum.com.au). Kings Cross rail or bus 311, 378. **Open** 10am-4pm Mon-Thur, Sun; 10am-2pm Fri. **Admission** $10; $7 reductions. **Map** p73 G1 ⑱
Take a 45-minute guided tour at noon on Monday, Wednesday, Friday or Sunday for the best look at this wonderful little museum's exhibits, which focus on Sydney and Australian Jewish history.

Restaurants & Cafés

Chaco Bar
238 Crown Street, Darlinghurst (9007 8352). Oxford Street buses. **Main courses** $24. **Map** p73 F1 ⑲ **Japanese**
It's all sticks, all the time, at this tiny yakitori restaurant. You want liver? Gizzards? Gristle? They've got 'em, along with plenty more pieces of protein that aren't quite as gutsy. Move through the skewer menu with your choice of saké in this loud and buzzy venue.

Downstairs
83 Stanley Street, Darlinghurst (0420 645 373, www.downstairsrestaurant.com). Bus 389. **Open** 5-10.30pm Tue-Fri; 10am-3pm, 5-10.30pm Sat; noon-late Sun. **Main courses** $15-$29. **Map** p65 F6 ⑳ **British**
Beneath the excellent Hazy Rose cocktail bar (*see p79*), you'll find pared-back, solid Brit fare perfect for the colder months. Order the smoked ham hock to better understand what British cuisine is actually all about: produce-driven food that heats you from the inside.

Edition Coffee Roasters
265 Liverpool Street, Darlinghurst (www.editioncoffeeroasters.com). Bus 389. **Open** 7am-3.30pm Mon-Fri; 8am-3.30pm Sat, Sun. **Main courses** $12-$19. **Map** p73 F1 ㉑ **Café**
At this sleek Japanese-Nordic fusion café, you'll find a cool, calm design oasis in which to eat the likes of black rice pudding, hot cakes with pepper roasted pineapple, and smoked king salmon on firm, sweet pumpernickel triangles with crème fraîche, fish roe, black and white sesame seeds and fronds of dill.

Lucio Pizzeria
248 Palmer Street, Darlinghurst (9332 3766, www.luciopizzeria.com.au). Bus 389. **Open** 6-10pm Mon, Wed-Sun. **Main courses** $14-$24. **Map** p73 F1 ㉒ **Pizza**
The Lucio is this pizzeria's crowning glory, and its answer to the much-loathed (by pizza chefs) 'half 'n' half'. You really need to see it to believe it, but it's half a margherita (tomato, mozzarella, baby basil) and half a calzone (just like a pizza only folded), filled with fluffy ricotta and strips of ham. Oh, mamma!

Messina
241 Victoria Street, Darlinghurst (8354 1223, www.gelatomessina.com). Kings Cross rail. **Open** noon-11pm daily. **Ice-cream** $4. **Map** p73 G1 ㉓ **Ice-cream**
Thumping house plays inside and a 50-person queue snakes down the street outside as you try and choose between flavours such as milk chocolate with choc-peanut fudge, dolce de leche and pannacotta with fig jam and amaretti biscuits. It doesn't really matter: they're all delicious.
Other locations The Star, 80 Pyrmont Street (9571 1918); 389 Crown Street, Surry Hills (9332 1191); G6/61 Hall Street, Bondi (9130 2877); 283 Church Street, Parramatta (9635 3064).

Mr Crackles Carryout
155 Oxford Street, Darlinghurst (8068 2832, www.mrcrackles.com.au). Oxford Street buses. **Open** 11am-8pm Mon-Wed; 11am-9pm Thur; 11am-3am Fri; noon-3am Sat; noon-9pm Sun. **Main courses** $12-$17. **Map** p73 F2 ㉔ **Sandwiches**
After throwing in the fine-dining towel a few years back, chefs Carlos Justo and Sam Horowitz started

EXPLORE

Eau de Vie.

hawking their delicious roast sandwiches at Rozelle Market. Now, they've settled in a little shopfront in Darlinghurst, and they're serving the best roast pork sandwich in Sydney – until well into the morning.

Playa Takeria
132 Darlinghurst Road, Darlinghurst (9332 4206, www.playa.net.au). Kings Cross rail. **Open** 6-10pm Mon; 11am-3pm, 6-10pm Tue-Thur; 11am-3pm, 6-11.30pm Fri; 11am-11.30pm Sat; 5-9pm Sun. **Main courses** $14-$21. **Map** p73 G1 ⑥⑤ **Mexican**
The chefs at Playa Takeria have their burrito game on lock (not to mention tacos and quesadillas). Your night will be incomplete without an agave-based beverage to go with your choice. This place will fill your mind with Mexican sunshine whether you go the brisk Tommy's Margarita route, or opt for the longer and surprisingly sweeter Paloma.

Sagra
62 Stanley Street, Darlinghurst (8307 0430, sagrasydney.com.au). Bus 389. **Open** noon-3pm, 6-10.30pm Mon-Fri; 6-10.30pm Sat. **Main courses** $30-$31. **Map** p65 F6 ⑥⑥ **Italian**
Sagra offers deceptively simple Italian food in a sweet corner setting. And you can book ahead – a rarity on the Sydney dining scene. There'll be complimentary Sicilian green olives and house-made bread to start; then you'd best move on to the light, crisp courgette flowers before your main of choice. There's a weekday lunch special of a main course and glass of wine for just $20 too.

Bars

Cliff Dive
16-18 Oxford Square, Darlinghurst (www.the diffdive.com.au). Oxford Street buses. **Open** 6pm-late Wed-Sat. **Map** p73 F1 ⑥⑦
Head to Sydney's only under-the-sea-themed Papua New Guinean dancehall for a sweet and fruity tiki cocktail and a late-night slow grind beneath a school of light-up paper fish on the sunken dancefloor. *See also p200.*

Commons
32 Burton Street, Darlinghurst (9358 1487, www.thecommons.com.au). Oxford Street buses. **Open** 6pm-midnight Tue, Wed; noon-late Thur, Fri; 8.30am-late Sat, Sun. **Map** p73 F1 ⑥⑧
Scattered plants and cosy wooden tables in the courtyard make the Commons a summer hotspot, but the bar's sandstone rooms are where it's at all year round. There's table service, so old faithfuls such as whisky sours and vodka espressos keep coming all night.

★ Eau de Vie
The Kirketon, 229 Darlinghurst Road, Darlinghurst (0422 263 226, eaudevie.com.au). Kings Cross rail. **Open** 6pm-1am Mon-Sat; 6pm-midnight Sun. **Map** p73 G1 ⑥⑨
Hidden in the back of the Kirketon hotel is a terrific bar with a plush and moody fit-out and dynamite cocktails. There are few greater drinking treats than nabbing a seat at EDV on a quiet night and commanding the full attention of the guys behind the bar.

Hazy Rose

1/83 Stanley Street, Darlinghurst (9357 5036, www.thehazyrose.com.au). Bus 389. **Open** 5-11pm Tue; 5pm-midnight Wed, Thur; 3pm-midnight Fri, Sat. **Map** p65 F6 ⑩
A dark little bar, upstairs in an old terrace (underneath is Downstairs, *see p77*). A well-tended back bar, friendly service, comfy seating and some of the most forgiving lighting in town makes an attractive combo.

Local Taphouse

122 Flinders Street, Darlinghurst (9360 0088, www.thelocal.com.au). Bus 373, 377, 392, 394, 396, 397, 399, M10. **Open** noon-midnight Mon-Wed; noon-1am Thur-Sat; noon-11pm Sun. **Map** p73 G3 ⑪
This Inner East beer barn has led the beer charge for half a decade, and its love of craft shows no signs of flagging. A beer-tasting paddle is both an education and a damn good way to spend $17 and an hour or two of your time.

Oxford Art Factory

38-46 Oxford Street, Darlinghurst (9332 3711, www.oxfordartfactory.com). Oxford Street buses. **Open** 6pm-late daily. **Map** p73 F1 ⑫
Oxford Art Factory hasn't quite made its mind up. Is it a bar, a club, a live music venue or an art space? But that's exactly why we love it. The small gallery bar is designed so you can drink in there, oblivious to the gig next door. The main room hosts up-and-coming local bands as well as international stars. *See also p208.*

★ Shady Pines Saloon

Shop 4, 256 Crown Street, Darlinghurst (www. shadypinessaloon.com). Oxford Street buses. **Open** 4pm-midnight daily. **Map** p73 F1 ⑬
Sydney's rootinist, tootinist, most taxidermy-filled bar keeps on attracting midnight cowboys and Surry Hillbillies. Just look for the shittiest door on Crown Lane, near the hot yoga place. The genius of this much loved saloon is its ability to provide casual, foot-stomping fun and impressive cocktails.

This Must Be The Place

239 Oxford Street, Darlinghurst (9331 8063, www.tmbtp.com.au). Oxford Street buses. **Open** 3pm-midnight daily. **Map** p73 G2 ⑭
Spritzers, salty snacks and stationery-themed art are the orders of the evening at this excellent establishment from two bar-scene veterans. Our spritzer pick is the Gloss, a blushing pink mix of citron vodka, watermelon infused riesling, rose-water and a strawberry shrub (a syrup that results after vinegar is left to infuse over fruit) for a balanced sweetness.

Shops & Services

American Apparel

82 Oxford Street, Darlinghurst (9358 2666, www.americanapparel.net). Oxford Street buses. **Open** 10am-7pm Mon-Wed, Fri, Sat; 10am-8pm Thur; 11am-5pm Sun. **Map** p73 F1 ⑮ **Fashion**
Sydney hipsters can't get enough of the LA brand's bright body-con wares. Make a beeline for this two-level store if a leotard or legging urge strikes.

Blue Spinach

348 Liverpool Street, Darlinghurst (9331 3904, www.bluespinach.com.au). Bus 311, 389. **Open** 10am-6pm Mon-Wed, Fri, Sat; 10am-7pm Thur; 11am-4pm Sun. **Map** p73 H1 **76 Fashion**
Whether it's a Comme des Garçons diamond-embossed wallet or a Stella McCartney silk dress that catches your eye, you can get it at this legendary vintage boutique for a snippet of the original price.

Platform72

72 Oxford Street, Darlinghurst (www.platform 72.com.au). Oxford Street buses. **Open** 11am-7pm Tue-Sat; 11am-5pm Sun. **Map** p72 B3 **77 Gallery**
Platform72 is a collaborative venture between Kaleidoscope Gallery, Metta Media and the City of Sydney. Expect to see paintings, sculptures, drawings, photography and more by emerging artists, designers, makers and craftspeople.

Zoo Emporium

180 Campbell Street, Darlinghurst (9380 5990). Oxford Street buses. **Open** 11am-6pm Mon-Wed, Fri, Sat; 11am-8pm Thur; noon-5pm Sun. **Map** p73 F2 **78 Fashion**
No one does vintage quite like Zoo. The store – over two floors – specialises in 1970s and '80s funk and retro tees. The ground floor is devoted to sale items.

SURRY HILLS

Once the scruffy home to Sydney's rag trade and a former local haunt for such nefarious folk as legendary underworld figure Kate Leigh, Surry Hills is now Sydney's buzziest and most happening neighbourhood. Want clothes? Hop along to Crown and Bourke streets or hit the monthly markets at Shannon Reserve on Crown Street (first Saturday of the month) for some seriously cool vintage threads.

In addition, 'Surry', as locals call it, is a virtual urban food court brimming with Sydney's most innovative chefs – including those rockabilly **Porteño** boys…

Thirsty? From classic cocktails to big bold reds, Surry Hills has got you covered. In fact, so transformed has this steep little slice of Sydney been that some are wondering whether it's lost its rougher charms. Maybe. But when you're six-in at the **Cricketers** on a Friday afternoon, mixing it with the gentrifiers and the gentrified, it's hard to think of a place in Sydney you'd rather be.

Restaurants & Cafés

Bang

3/410 Crown Street (8354 1096, www.bangstreet food.com.au). Bus 301, 302, 303, 352. **Open** 6pm-late Tue-Thur; noon-late Fri, Sat. **Main courses** $20-$32. **Map** p73 F3 **79 Bangladeshi**

The food at this new and oh-so-cool Bangladeshi restaurant doesn't weigh you down, and is treated with a sophisticated understanding of the cuisine. As for drinks, feel free to spike your lassi with a shot of dark rum, and don't ignore the Porto Grande cocktail either.

Berta

17-19 Alberta Street (9264 6133, www.berta. com.au). Bus 311, 378. **Open** 6pm-late Tue-Thur, Sat; noon-late Fri. **Main courses** $32-$46. **Map** p73 E1 **80 Italian**
The seasonally focused menu of Italian small plates changes virtually every day and the wine list and moody industrial setting are excellent. On Tuesday nights, Berta hosts Sagra dinners – a four-course meal ($65) in which a different ingredient is highlighted each week.

Dr Faustus

80 Cleveland Street (0416 914 170, drfaustus. com.au). Bus 352, 372, 393, 395, M50. **Open** 5-10pm Tue-Thur; 11.30am-10pm Fri; 9am-10pm Sat; 9am-4pm Sun. **Main courses** $13-$16. **Map** p73 E4 **81 Café**
There's no clear breakfast and lunch divide at this antique-y café. Yes, there's a BLT on the menu, but here your bacon gets dolled up with onion, gruyère and a swipe of foie gras on a French bread roll. Or you can get a German sausage on a milk bun with mustard and pickled cabbage.

Four Ate Five

485 Crown Street (9698 6485, fouratefive.com). Bus 301, 302, 303, 352. **Open** 7am-4pm Mon-Fri; 7.30am-4pm Sat; 9.30am-2.30pm Sun. **Main courses** $14-$18. **Map** p73 E4 **82 Café**
Four Ate Five is the type of café we'd love to eat in every day. It's got brilliant food, friendly service and a pulled pork sandwich that visits us in our dreams. Order it with a huge juice (watermelon, lemon and mint, say, or apple, pineapple and mint) and a Single Origin coffee and you'll know why.

Longrain

85 Commonwealth Street (9280 2888, longrain. com). Bus 301, 302, 303. **Open** 6pm-late Mon-Fri; 5.30pm-late Sat, Sun. **Main courses** $22-$40. **Map** p73 E1 **83 Thai**
A decade and a half since its arrival transformed Sydney's understanding of high-end Thai cuisine, Longrain remains a buzzing destination on the local dining scene. The interior is fun but fancy enough, the service warm and accommodating. And the food kicks ass.

Movida

50 Holt Street (8964 7642, movida.com.au). Central rail. **Open** noon-late Mon-Sat. **Main courses** $24.50-$32. **Map** p73 E3 **84 Tapas**
Nab a seat at the bar if possible, for maximum fun and credit card carnage. The tapas here is perfectly

suited to grazing – try the creamy, crunchy salt cod croquette – but there are bigger plates too. Don't miss the churros with hot chocolate.

Nomad

16 Foster Street (9280 3395, nomadwine.com.au). Central rail. **Open** 6pm-late Mon; noon-2.30pm, 6pm-late Tue-Fri; noon-2pm, 6pm-late Sat. **Main courses** $18-$39. **Map** p73 E2 **⑮ Middle Eastern**
Nomad is good fun. Its wine list is a smart combination of approachable and challenging; the beautifully designed room is open plan and sunlit, and filled with Danish-style furniture; and the crunchy spanner crab-spiked falafel and house-made halloumi are excellent.

★ Porteño

358 Cleveland Street (8399 1440, www.porteno. com.au). Bus 352, 372, 393, 395, M50. **Open** 6pm-late Tue-Sat. **Main courses** $22-$50. **Map** p73 E4 **⑯ Argentinian**
This rockabilly Argentinian restaurant is a legend on the Sydney dining scene. The South American-centric wine list is one of the finest in town, and the meats – roasted for eight hours over an ironwood bar fire – are perfection. Top tip: order a side of brussels sprouts. Trust us.

Reuben Hills

61 Albion Street (9211 5556, www.reubenhills. com.au). Central rail. **Open** 7am-4pm daily. **Main courses** $8-$18. **Map** p73 E2 **⑰ Café**
At Reuben Hills, they roast the beans themselves, which are sourced from the owners' trips to El Salvador, Honduras, Panama, Colombia and Costa Rica. It makes for damn fine espresso to pair with – you guessed it – a Reuben sandwich and the best salt caramel milkshake in the city.

Bars

121BC

Shop 4, 50 Holt Street (9699 1582, 121bc.com.au). Central rail. **Open** 5pm-midnight Tue-Sat. **Map** p73 G3 **⑱**
It's one of the busiest little bars in Surry Hills, offering wines by the glass from most areas of the boot (that's Italy, you guys). Trying to get a seat past 7pm is a fool's errand, though we can tell you that turning up either early or late in the evening will result in some good vinous fun.

Bar H

80 Campbell Street (9280 1980, www.barhsurry hills.com). Central rail. **Open** 6pm-late Mon-Sat. **Map** p73 E2 **⑲**
Asian-inspired cocktails and a ripper saké list make this moody corner bar/restaurant. Hungry? The menu is Japan's version of Chinese food – made with lots of native Australian ingredients. Tokyo via Sichuan with a detour through rural Victoria…

Bang.

EXPLORE

EXPLORE

Cricketers Arms

106 Fitzroy Street (9331 3301, www.cricketers armshotel.com.au). Bus 339, 374, 376, 391. **Open** 3pm-midnight Mon-Fri; 1pm-midnight Sat; 1-10pm Sun. **Map** p73 E4 ㏿

As more and more great old Sydney pubs go under the knife, the Cricketers Arms remains resolutely as it ever was, wearing its sticky floor and chipped original tiles with the grizzled pride of an old-timer who's refused to move with the times. And with good reason – everybody loves the Crix.

Dove & Olive

156 Devonshire Street (9699 6001, doveandolive. com.au). Central rail. **Open** 10am-midnight Mon-Fri; 11am-midnight Sat, Sun. **Map** p73 E3 ㏿

With delicious beers, damn fine steak and a winning attitude, the Dove & Olive is getting the pub vibes right. Staff keep things traditional with trivia Tuesdays, and get experimental and weird with the odd opera performance. Yes, really.

Royal Albert Hotel

140 Commonwealth Street (9281 2522, www. royalalberthotel.com.au). Central rail. **Open** noon-midnight Mon-Sat; noon-10pm Sun. **Map** p73 E2 ㏿

When a hot dog and a craft brew is all your heart desires, then it's time to cannonball down the slopes of Surry Hills to the Royal Albert Hotel. Here, they play old-school soul and rock 'n' roll tunes – and there's a dumpling house for Asian-style bar snacks out the back.

Surly's

182 Campbell Street (9331 3705, surlys.com.au). Bus 301, 302, 303, 352. **Open** noon-midnight Tue-Sun. **Map** p73 F2 ㏿

At this American-themed bar, there are Coors and PBR to accompany your barbecue platter and chilli cheese fries, and Clamato juice in the fridge. Bloody Caesars for all!

Wild Rover

75 Campbell Street (9280 2235, www.thewildrover. com.au). Central rail. **Open** 4pm-midnight Mon-Sat. **Map** p73 E2 ㏿

There's no sign, but you'll see this bar from the slip of golden light coming from under the heavy doors. Inside is a two-level haven of exposed brick, deco-style wall-mounted lamps and fine cocktails. Try the refreshing Virginia Venette, with gin, red grapefruit juice, thyme syrup, rhubarb bitters and a splash of Aperol and lemon, topped with sparkling wine; or the Irish Penicillin, with two kinds of whiskey, lemon, honey and ginger. The long whiskey list features bottles from Ireland, Scotland and the New World.

Shops & Services

A.P.C.

2/406-410 Crown Street (9380 2010, usonline. apc.fr). Bus 301, 302, 303, 352. **Open** 10am-6pm Mon-Wed, Fri, Sat; 10am-7pm Thur; 11am-5pm Sun. **Map** p73 F3 ㏿ **Fashion**

The Surry Hills boutique by A.P.C. (Atelier de Production et de Création) is styled as minimally and as elegantly as one might expect from the French brand. If you're keen to improve your weekend wardrobe, one of its classic Demi Lune leather bags in beige or dark navy is a great place to start.

Collector Store

473 Crown Street (9699 7740, www.collectorstore. com.au). Bus 301, 302, 303, 352. **Open** 10am-6pm Mon-Wed; 10am-7pm Thur; 10am-5.30pm Fri, Sat; 10am-5pm Sun. **Map** p73 E4 ㏿ **Fashion/ homewares**

Split over two levels of a traditional Surry Hills terrace, Collector Store has a desirable selection of ladies' and gents' fashion, jewellery and a substantial range of homewares. Top brands include Herschel backpacks, cushions and throws from Harvest Textiles, fabrics from Utopia Goods and Rittenhouse clothing.

Cream on Crown

32/277-285 Crown Street (9331 5228, www. creamonline.com.au). Oxford Street buses. **Open** 10am-6pm Mon-Wed, Fri-Sun; 10am-8pm Thur. **Map** p73 F2 ㏿ **Fashion**

Cream is known for its reconstructed denim and an abundance of cowboy boots. It's the ultimate Americana vintage-shopping spot in Sydney.

Ici et La

7 Nickson Street (8339 1173, www.icietla.com.au). Bus 355. **Open** 10am-5pm Mon-Sat. **Map** p73 F4 ㏿ **Homewares**

This rustic French design store peddles goods as various as espadrilles, antique French deckchairs, zinc letters, industrial light shades and vibrant striped fabrics. Marcel, the resident French bulldog, alone makes the joint worth a visit.

Kit & Ace

276 Devonshire Street (www.kitandace.com). Bus 355. **Open** 10am-5pm daily. **Map** p73 F4 ㏿ **Fashion**

The clothes here mesh technical elements with luxury fibres and carry the wearer from day to night – think machine-washable cashmere, for starters.

ISLAND HOPPING
Explore the Sydney Harbour Peninsula.

Sydney Harbour is sprinkled with islands. Some are off-limits. On others, however, you can cast yourself away or take a tour.

The largest island is **Cockatoo Island** (8969 2100, www.cockatooisland.gov.au), managed by the Sydney Harbour Federation Trust. The trust runs informative 90-minute walking tours ($16), which depart from Circular Quay and must be pre-booked. There are also self-guided routes. Cockatoo Island was once a convict prison and later an enormous shipbuildng and repair operation; structures associated with both these eras still stand like ghostly sentinels to an alternately dark and industrious past. There's a camping ground with 135 sites for tents, plus showers and other facilities. Full camping packages, including tent hire, are available. The site has amazing views across the Parramatta River to Hunters Hill, plus there's a café and bar.

The other islands that can be visited are under the auspices of the National Parks & Wildlife Service (9247 5033, www.national parks.nsw.gov.au). **Fort Denison**, just off Mrs Macquaries Point, served as an open-air prison and was once known as Pinchgut

Island thanks to the starvation rations served to its inmates. In 1862, a fort with a distinctive Martello tower was added and the island was renamed Fort Denison after then-governor William Denison. There is a restaurant and tea house on the island, and it's easy to access by water taxi or ferry; tours with ferry trip included are available from Matilda Cruises (www.matilda.com.au). Information on visiting can be found on www.fortdenison.com.au.

Shark Island, off Point Piper, is great for picnics, as there are large grassy areas, lots of trees, picnic shelters, toilets, a gazebo and a wading beach. (There's no café.) Get there by Matilda Cruises ferry or water taxi.

Popular with wedding parties who like to hire their own island exclusively, **Clark Island**, near Darling Point, and **Rodd Island**, west of the Harbour Bridge in Iron Cove, are open to day-trippers. Visitor numbers are limited; you must book in advance with the NPWS and arrange your own transport by private boat, chartered ferry or water taxi from the NPWS list of licensed operators. There's a landing fee of $7 per person. Boats are allowed to drop off and pick up at the island's wharfs, but not to tie up.

EXPLORE

Cockatoo Island.

Kepos Street Kitchen.

EXPLORE

Paper2

*477 Crown Street (9318 1121, www.paper2.com.
au). Bus 301, 302, 303, 352.* **Open** 10am-5.30pm
Mon-Sat; noon-4.30pm Sun. **Map** p73 E4 ⑩
Stationery

Paper, ribbons and notebooks line the walls of this
cheerful shop. We challenge you to leave without
making a purchase from a selection that comes from
Tokyo, London, Frankfurt and New York, as well as
Paper2's own range, designed and printed in-house.

Wheels & Doll Baby

*259 Crown Street (9361 3286, www.wheels
anddollbaby.com). Oxford Street buses.* **Open**
10am-6pm daily. **Map** p73 F2 ⑩ **Fashion**

If it's tight, low-cut or leopard-printed, Wheels &
Doll Baby has it in spades. In its 20-odd years of trad-
ing, the label has been worn by stars such as Debbie
Harry, Gwen Stefani, Katy Perry and Kate Moss.

REDFERN, EVELEIGH
& WATERLOO

The artfully ragged seams of Surry Hills extend
west to Central Station (just beyond the rag-trade
centre on and around Foveaux Street) and south
to Cleveland Street, the border with Redfern.
Aboriginal people from rural areas started
moving into **Redfern** in the 1920s because of
its proximity to Central Station, cheap rents and
local workshops offering regular work. More
arrived during the Depression of the 1930s, and
by the '40s the area had become synonymous

with its indigenous population. Following
the 1967 national referendum, which gave
indigenous people citizenship rights, Redfern's
Aboriginal population increased to 35,000,
causing mass overcrowding.

In the decades that followed, government
programmes (some helpful, some not) have
disseminated the area's indigenous people,
and today the area is undergoing intensive
reinvention, with some pockets hurtling
upmarket. But the central patch of run-down
terraces in a one-hectare area bounded by
Eveleigh, Vine, Louis and Caroline Streets –
which made up the Block, the beleaguered heart
of a black-run Aboriginal housing co-operative
– remains an indigenous enclave. Forty years
after its inception, the last 75 residents of the
Block were evicted in 2010 to allow for demolition
and commencement of the Pemulwuy Project –
designed to redevelop the area with commercial
space and housing for local residents.

But the suburb long famous as a centre for
Sydney's indigenous community is at something
of a crossroads of late – gentrifying bar and café
owners seep in from the Surry Hills side while
longtime locals defend their turf. It's the suburb
where you'll find Redfern Oval – the spiritual, if
no longer actual, home of the Rabbitohs rugby
league team. And no matter where you stand on
gentrification in these parts, it's brought some
pretty great venues: for café fare, **St Jude** is a
gem. And for a drink, **Arcadia Liquors** might
just be the friendliest little hipster bar in town.

EXPLORE

In neighbouring **Waterloo**, development is also running rife. **Danks Street**, at the heart of a previously industrial area, now has a fine range of eateries and design shops. And in **Eveleigh**, multidisciplinary arts centre **Carriageworks** (*see p217*), on Wilson Street, the new incarnation of the Eveleigh Rail Yards, hosts edgy music, theatre and art shows, plus the city's most respected **farmers' market** every Saturday.

Sights & Museums

Prince Alfred Park Playground
Cnr Chalmers and Cleveland Streets, Redfern (www.cityofsydney.nsw.gov.au). Redfern rail. **Map** p72 D4 ⓲
Prince Alfred Park has recently undergone a $9 million facelift. The seven-hectare park now has two new basketball courts, barbecue and picnic areas and a heated pool, plus fitness stations. Kids love the two playgrounds with custom play equipment.

Restaurants & Cafés

House of Crabs
305 Cleveland Street, Redfern (9699 3177, houseofcrabs.com.au). Bus 352, 372, 393, 395, M50. **Open** 6pm-midnight Tue-Sat; noon-4pm Fri. **Main courses** $32-$45. **Map** p73 E4 ⓲
American seafood
You'll find this homage to the American seafood shack above the Norfolk pub. The nautical paraphernalia is laid on with a trowel, with glass fishing floats,

plastic crabs and old ropes adorning the bar. Be prepared to leave poise at the door – there's nothing dainty about smashing a bag full of crabs.

John Smith Cafe
1 John Street, Waterloo (0422 855 811, www. facebook.com/johnsmithcafe). Bus 355, 370. **Open** 6.30am-4pm Mon-Fri; 7am-5pm Sat, Sun.
Café
Inside a warehouse-style structure just off a not particularly enticing stretch of Botany Road are exceptional coffee beans from Rebel Roasters, ground and pressed into exceptional coffees. Pair your cup with a classic cronut for a perfect afternoon snack.

Kepos Street Kitchen
96 Kepos Street, Redfern (9319 3919, keposstreet kitchen.com.au). Redfern rail. **Open** 7.30am-3pm Tue; 7.30am-3pm, 6-10pm Wed-Fri; 8am-3pm, 6-10pm Sat; 8am-3pm Sun. **Main courses** $17-$29. **Map** p73 E6 ⓲ **Café**
Pop your name on a list, order a takeaway coffee and bask on the sunny benches outside until you're called. Once seated, you'll be eating soft-baked eggs and tomato shakshuka, or a tower of tender steak, wilted spinach, juicy roast tomato, sweet and sticky onion jam and aïoli layered between toasted sourdough.

Moon Park
34 Redfern Street, Redfern (9690 0111, www. moon-park.com.au). Redfern rail. **Open** 5.30pm-late Tue-Sat; noon-3pm Sun. **Main courses** $15-$34. **Map** p72 D5 ⓲ **Korean**

It's Korean food, but not as you know it – probably. The menu is broken into little and larger dishes meant for sharing, but there's also a four-course tasting menu for $50. On that menu there's *bibimbap* and *bulgogi*, fried chicken and *tteokbokki*. To finish, moon pie has peaks of soft meringue strewn with pieces of torn ginger jelly and little confit pear rounds.

St Jude
728 Bourke Street, Redfern (9310 3523). Bus 301, 302, 303, 355. **Open** 7am-3pm daily. **Main courses** $14-$19. **Map** p73 F5 **106** Café
The Peruvian, organic and fair-trade blend of coffee is expertly offset by a beautifully original dish. An almost-toffeed date paste is spread over toasted rye, which is then topped with warm and salty blue cheese. Grilled, fat asparagus and whole-roasted truss tomatoes sit on top of balsamic onion. Yum.

Bars

Arcadia Liquors
7 Cope Street, Redfern (8068 4470, www.arcadia liquors.com). Redfern rail. **Open** 4pm-midnight Mon-Fri; noon-midnight Sat; noon-10pm Sun. **Map** p72 C5 **107**

White Rabbit.

This popular neighbourhood bar is easy on the pocket – in Sydney terms, that is. Cocktail prices have stayed deliciously low – you can get a $14 negroni – and while the majority of the wines by the glass will cost a tenner, the house option is always six bucks. Decor is understated but nice and homey.

Bearded Tit
183 Regent Street, Redfern (8283 4082, www. thebeardedtit.com). Redfern rail. **Open** 4pm-midnight Mon-Thur; noon-midnight Fri, Sat; noon-10pm Sun. **Map** p72 B5 **108**
This densely populated creative space on Regent Street celebrates art and beer in no particular order. Lost? Look for the fluffy plush penises. They're hand-knitted and on display in the front window where they float, hang, drape and furiously jizz strands of alpaca wool against a backdrop of ferns and waterfalls. Inside, you'll find cocktails and a long list of spirits as well as beers and wines.

Dock
182 Redfern Street, Redfern (0405 757 458). Redfern rail. **Open** noon-midnight Mon-Sat; noon-10pm Sun. **Map** p72 C5 **109**
The Dock feels like a house party where everyone is invited and you don't need to carve out fridge space behind some Thai leftovers and half an elderly watermelon for your drinks. It's a cosy, low-lit, ramshackle place where the playlist is a freewheeling mix of cheesy but secretly awesome school-disco bangers.

Gunther's Dining Room
180 Redfern Street, Redfern (www.facebook.com/ redferncontinental). Redfern rail. **Open** 5pm-late Tue-Sat. **Map** p72 C5 **110**
Redfern's newest small bar gives off serious *Boogie Nights* vibes. There are green velour booths, and German rod chandeliers are mounted on the walls and hang from chains on the ceiling, while a nearby mirrorball spins at a swift clip. You'll feel like Dirk Diggler surrounded by the heady fragrance of a grapefruit and maraschino liqueur in your Hemingway daiquiri.

Lord Raglan
12 Henderson Road, Alexandria (9699 4767, www.lordraglan.com.au). Bus 355. **Open** noon-midnight Mon-Sat; noon-10pm Sun.
Go to the Lord Raglan for the love of beer. It has 12 taps and supplementary fridges for the fancy bottled stuff (a Sierra Nevada Northern Hemisphere Harvest wet hop ale longneck is a cool $22). Drink your brew with a side of salty crab cakes with corn salsa and tartare sauce for optimum results.

Vasco
421 Cleveland Street, Redfern (0406 775 436, www.vascobar.com). Bus 355. **Open** 5pm-midnight Tue-Sat. **Map** p73 F5 **111**

Even the bar stools are Fender at Sydney's only Italian rock bar. The drink names are all plays on classic tunes – a Lucy in the Sky, an Eagle Rock, the Hendrix Experience – and many of them lean on herbaceous Italian bitters and liqueurs. Knock 'em back and fist pump. Or, sip slowly, you animal.

Shops & Services

★ Carriageworks Farmers Market
245 Wilson Street, Eveleigh (http://carriageworks. com.au). Redfern rail. **Open** 8am-1pm Sat. **Market**
In just a few short years, the Carriageworks Farmers Market, formerly the Eveleigh Farmers Market, has become Sydney's premier fresh food market. Stalls by Billy Kwong or Bird Cow Fish are the stars, but don't forget the Blini Bar up back: its ham, cheese and mushroom crêpe is wonderfully gooey and spongy.

Retro on Regent
88 Regent Street, Redfern (0408 839 493, www.retroonregent.com.au). Redfern rail. **Open** 11am-5pm Fri-Sat. **Map** p72 B5 **⓬ Homewares**
This store is full of tons of authentic midcentury modern furniture, glassware and ceramics for all you *Mad Men* obsessives.

Seasonal Concepts
122 Redfern Street, Redfern (0430 044 383, www.seasonalconcepts.com.au). Redfern rail. **Open** 10am-5pm Tue-Sat. **Map** p72 C5 **⓭ Florist/homewares/taxidermy**
The name of this Redfern shop and its entrance are unassuming, but what's inside may astound you. Taxidermy – ducks, peacocks, kookaburras, stags, a wolf rug and, most startlingly, the towering neck and head of a giraffe named Roger. And that's just the start. This emporium also stocks pre-1950s furniture, ceramics and kitchenware, plus contemporary linens and jewellery – and operates as a florist.

CHIPPENDALE

Sandwiched between Cleveland Street and Broadway, and a longtime favourite of the Sydney Uni set, Chippo packs a lot of punch for a little fella. The area has just welcomed the mammoth **Central Park** development of the old Carlton & United brewery site, and there's an increasing amount of eating, drinking and art-watching to be done: hit up the always excellent **White Rabbit**, **Brickfields** and **Ester**, and party late after a deep-fried Golden Gaytime at the **Gladstone**.

Sights & Museums

★ FREE White Rabbit
30 Balfour Street (8399 2867, www.white rabbitcollection.org). Parramatta Road buses.

Open 10am-5pm Wed-Sun. **Admission** free. **Map** p72 B3 **⓬**
White Rabbit is a state-of-the-art, four-floor temple to 21st-century Chinese art hidden on a Chippendale backstreet in a former Rolls-Royce service depot, funded solely by owner Judith Neilson's philanthropic foundation. The gallery also houses a gift shop, and a tea house that also serves dumplings.

Restaurants & Cafés

Brickfields
206 Cleveland Street (9698 7880, brickfields. com.au). Bus 352. **Open** 7am-3pm Mon-Fri; 8am-4pm Sat-Sun. **Main courses** $10-$14. **Map** p72 B4 **⓯ Café**
This beautiful bakery serves the best bread in the city. Try it sandwiching rich, juicy anchovy-mayo-soaked-brisket with chilli and gherkins. And add a house-made soda, Persian love cake, croissant or very attractive-looking crostata on the side.

★ Ester
46-52 Meagher Street (8068 8279, ester-r16 chiestaurant.com.au). Bus 352. **Open** 6pm-late Mon-Thur, Sat; noon-3pm, 6pm-late Fri; noon-5pm Sun. **Main courses** $28-$36. **Map** p72 C4 **⓰ Contemporary Australian**
This modest Chippendale establishment was named Time Out Sydney's Restaurant of the Year in 2014. Chef Mat Lindsay has turned up the strange on an untamed menu of wood-fired smoke and funk. Mains might be cobia (a fish), with grilled peas and lardo, and sea blight. Or flank steak with fermented rice and leeks. The wine list – as eccentric and smart as the menu – features obscure and rare treats and crowd-pleasing tipples.

LP's Quality Meats
Unit 1, 16 Chippen Street (8399 0929, www.lps qualitymeats.com). Bus 352. **Open** 5-11pm Wed, Thur, Sat; noon-3pm, 5-11pm Fri. **Main courses** $32-$42. **Map** p72 C4 **⓱ Smokehouse**
This meat-centric restaurant has a bouncer out the front, merchandise for sale, and rock 'n' roll tunes turned up to 11. There's a deep, all-pervading smoke through everything you eat here, but it's all salty and absolutely delicious. *Photo p88.*

Bars

Freda's
109 Regent Street (8971 7336, www.fredas.com. au). Redfern rail or bus 352. **Open** 5pm-midnight Tue-Sat; 4-10pm Sun. **Map** p72 C4 **⓲**
The 100-year-old warehouse that houses this bar has been given a simple and sympathetic refit, and there's an attractive list of cocktails including a 50/50 sazerac. Freda's also hosts eclectic mini dance parties – Eurotrash tunes or a vogueing extravaganza – on most Friday and Saturday nights.

EXPLORE

LP's Quality Meats. *See p87.*

Lord Gladstone

115 Regent Street (9690 2350). Redfern rail or bus 352. **Open** 10am-late Mon-Wed; 10am-3am Thur-Sat; noon-10pm Sun. **Map** p72 C4 ⑲
There are many reasons to love the recently revamped Gladstone, and at the top of that list is its deep-fried Golden Gaytime – the Aussie ice-cream of champions. There's also a crumbly and cool corner beer garden and a solid roster of promoters pushing great late-night party action.

Rose Hotel

54 Cleveland Street (9318 1133, www.the rosehotel.com.au). Bus 352, 370, 422, 423, 426, 428, M30. **Open** 11am-late daily. **Map** p72 A4 ⑳
Looking for a place to spend a relaxing drinking afternoon? Set up camp in the beer garden at this much-loved Chippendale institution and make jugs of beer and pizzas vanish without a trace. These guys also do weekend breakfasts that include a big, English-style fry-up.

Shops & Services

Capsule

Level 1, Central at Central Park Shopping Centre, 80 Broadway (8097 9207, www.capsulestore.com.au). Paramatta Road buses. **Open** 10am-8pm daily. **Map** p72 B3 ㉑ **Fashion/accessories**
Men's apparel, footwear and accessories from over 35 cool-as-hell brands, including Herschel, London Undercover, Mr Simple and Vanishing Elephant.

Daiso

Level 1, Central at Central Park Shopping Centre, 80 Broadway (www.mydaiso.com.au). Paramatta Road buses. **Open** 9am-8pm Mon-Wed, Fri, Sat; 9am-9pm Thur; 10am-9pm Sun. **Map** p72 B3 ㉒ **Discount store**
Affordable apparel? Cheap chopsticks? Bargain beauty products? They've got shelves of the stuff at Daiso – Japan's famous discount store – with more than 200,000 products all priced at $2.80 each.

Press Books

116 Abercrombie Street (www.press-books.co). Redfern rail. **Open** 10.30am-6pm daily. **Map** p72 B4 ㉓ **Books & music**
Press Books is an offshoot of the Heavy Collective, a photography outfit that also dabbles in independent publishing. Three-quarters of the items in store are independent stock, such as photographic titles *Aint-Bad Magazine* and *LIT*.

KINGS CROSS, POTTS POINT & WOOLLOOMOOLOO

Kings Cross, formed by the intersection of Darlinghurst Road and Victoria Street as they cross William Street, has long been the city's red-light district, although today it's dominated as much by amazing bars and restaurants as drugs and prostitution. It remains Australia's most populated district per square mile and it fairly bursts at the seams. The on-show seedy action is pretty much confined to 'the Strip', stretching along **Darlinghurst Road** from William Street to the picturesque El Alamein fountain. Visitors should stick to the main streets here, especially at night when the winding roads leading back towards Potts Point and the Cross tend to become drug alleys. Along Darlinghurst Road you'll find Australia's first legal 'shooting gallery', a monitored, fully staffed injecting room opened in 2001. Despite much controversy, the centre has remained open, and many in the know say it has reduced the number of heroin deaths in the area while providing desperately needed support for the growing number of users. Alas, as heroin's grip loosened, so arrived the new scourge of ice (crystal meth). Nonetheless, the Cross's neon lights still pull in hordes of backpackers, sustained by a network of hostels, internet cafés and cheap and cheerful restaurants. The good news for tourists is that there are plenty of police on the beat, and when the night turns ugly, as it inevitably does for some, you needn't get caught in the trouble.

Yep, it's still sleazy, and it's a helluva rowdy ride on a Saturday night, but there's plenty of hipster eating, drinking and shopping to be had here too. The **Roosevelt** shows there's more to the Cross's drinking culture than stumbly blokes in tight tees, and late-night restrictions have led to a blossoming restaurant culture. If you want theatre, the Griffin, which is based at the **Stables Theatre** (*see p217*), is probably the most exciting play-making company in Sydney.

Some clichés exist for a reason: the 'Potts Point is like Paris' line is one such. Just around the bend from the seediest strip in Sydney – which we kind of love – **Potts Point**, anchored by Macleay Street, really is like a little slice of the French capital. Tree-lined streets, gorgeous old art deco buildings, painted-up old beauties smoking at cafés with lapdogs… seriously, save yourself the Air France fare. Bordered by the Cross and Woolloomooloo, just like Paris, Potts is a place for foodies: **Billy Kwong**, **Yellow** and **Monopole** are all excellent.

Waterside **Woolloomooloo**, down the hill from Kings Cross, is an area that gives everyone pause (when they're trying to spell it). Home to the Matthew Talbot Hostel, the largest hostel for homeless men in the southern hemisphere, Woolloomooloo is Sydney's most dramatically gentrified suburb – at least around the **Finger Wharf** (home to what is probably the coolest apartment block in the whole of Australia).

Sights & Museums

FREE **ArtSpace**
43-51 Cowper Wharf Road, Woolloomooloo (9356 0555, www.artspace.org.au). Kings Cross rail. **Open** 11am-5pm Tue-Fri; noon-4pm Sat, Sun. **Admission** free. **Map** p65 G5 ⓬⓸
Many have called Woolloomooloo's historic Gunnery Building 'home' over the years, including squatting artists in the 1980s. Now, it's a contemporary art gallery with an annual programme including exhibitions, artist residencies, talks and symposiums.

Restaurants & Cafés

Apollo
44 Macleay Street, Potts Point (8354 0888, www.theapollo.com.au). Kings Cross rail. **Open** 6pm-late Mon-Thur; noon-11pm Fri, Sat; noon-9.30pm Sun. **Main courses** $26-$34. **Map** p65 H5 ⓬⓹ **Greek**
Elegant family-style Greek dining is what the Apollo is all about. Do the Full Greek for just $55 a person – it's all the stuff you'll want to order off the menu (taramasalata, Greek salad, a big bowl of sticky roast lamb ribs with lemony roast potatoes, and filo pastry cigars filled with chopped walnuts, honey and olive oil).

Billy Kwong
1/28 Macleay Street, Potts Point (9332 3300, www.billykwong.com.au). Bus 311. **Open** 5.30pm-late daily. **Main courses** $21-$45. **Map** p65 H5 ⓬⓺ **Contemporary Chinese**
This is the place to go for creative modern Chinese cooking that's mixing things up with native Australian ingredients and bugs. That's right, Billy Kwong features a select few menu items that include mealworms and crickets. There's nothing run-of-the-mill about a meal here.

Cho Cho San
73 Macleay Street, Potts Point (9331 6601, chochosan.com.au). Bus 311. **Open** 6-11pm daily. **Main courses** $16-$42. **Map** p65 H5 ⓬⓻ **Japanese**
The food at this popular spot is not your average Japanese cuisine. The best menu picks are the small things, raw things and the sides. Fried chicken is ultra-light with a glutinous yet crisp batter, and utterly wonderful with a whisky, apple and ginger slushy. And if you crush on saké, you've come to the right place.

Ms G's
155 Victoria Street, Potts Point (9240 3000, www.merivale.com). Kings Cross rail. **Open** 5-11pm Mon-Thur; noon-midnight Fri; 5pm-1am Sat; 1-10pm Sun. **Main courses** $25-$38. **Map** p65 H5 ⓬⓼ **Pan-Asian**
Start with a drink in the upstairs bar, where staff shake up what looks on paper to be a bunch of very loopy, bubble-tea-inspired drinks, and then dig into the restaurant's mod-Asian menu of snappy flavours and big spicy ideas.

EXPLORE

Wilbur's Place

36 Llankelly Place, Kings Cross (9332 2999, www.wilbursplace.com). Kings Cross rail. **Open** 8am-10pm Tue-Sat. **Main courses** $25-$28. **Map** p65 H6 ⓑ **Contemporary Australian**

Share a bench outside in the evening and order from the old-school felt pin board. It boasts bargains such as fall-off-the-bone roast duck leg with crisp, golden polenta chips and roast plums, creamy duck liver parfait with toast, and a side of lightly pickled cauliflower and a sharp-yet-rich salad of pork belly, walnuts, apple and witlof.

Yellow

57-59 Madeay Street, Potts Point (9332 2344, www.yellowsydney.com.au). Bus 311. **Open** 6pm-late Mon-Fri; 8am-3pm, 6pm-late Sat, Sun. **Main courses** $17-$18. **Map** p65 H4 ⓑ **Bistro**

The famous Yellow House has been a pâtisserie, an Italian restaurant, a pop-up and, now, a mod bistro. Start with a big bowl of beef tendon crisps that arrive snapping and crackling, and move on to the sirloin – it comes out rosy pink with mustard leaves and a very fancy jacket potato (topped with whipped sour cream and chopped chives).

Bars

Chester White

3 Orwell Street, Potts Point (www.chesterwhite diner.com.au). Kings Cross rail. **Open** 5-11pm Wed, Thur; noon-11pm Fri, Sat. **Map** p65 H5 ⓑ

Chester White is about quick-fire negronis and big plates of meat, all on the balcony of an old cottage in Potts Point. Or, give that pairing a miss and go straight for a bowl of kale chips and a glass of Trumer Pils.

Jimmy Liks

186-188 Victoria Street, Potts Point (8354 1400, www.jimmyliks.com.au). Kings Cross rail. **Open** 5pm-late Mon-Thur; noon-late Fri-Sun. **Map** p65 H6 ⓑ

Ten years on and this dark mod-Asian restaurant-bar still hits the spot. Expect spicy cocktails (such as a refreshing chilli-infused cucumber martini) and even spicier food, together with chilled house beats and great service.

Monopole

71A Madeay Street, Potts Point (9360 4410, monopolesydney.com.au). Bus 311. **Open** 5pm-late Mon-Fri; noon-late Sat, Sun. **Map** p65 H5 ⓑ

A wine bar that also has delicious eats. Or a restaurant with delicious wine, if you prefer. The wine list is really, truly excellent. And behind the bar is a glass case where chef-owner Brent Savage cures a bunch of meats – duck ham, brisket, venison sausage and bresaola are served in wispy slices with a side of pickles.

Powder Keg

7 Kellett Street, Potts Point (8354 0980, www.thepowderkeg.com.au). Kings Cross rail. **Open** 5pm-late Wed, Thur; 4pm-2.30am Fri, Sat; 2-11.30pm Sun. **Map** p65 H6 ⓬
You can book, but genial staff are just as happy if you pop in on a whim for a cocktail (gin is the main squeeze) and a snack. The tunes are just a few volume hikes from becoming full-blown dancefloor fillers.

Roosevelt

32 Orwell Street, Potts Point (0423 203 119, www.theroosevelt.com.au). Kings Cross rail. **Open** 5pm-midnight Tue-Fri; noon-4pm, 5pm-midnight Sat; 3-10pm Sun. **Map** p65 H5 ⓭
Bringing back a touch of old-world class to the Cross, the Roosevelt harks back to the days when dinner and drinks meant something more than a taco and a shot, a time when nightclubs were places where you sat down for cocktails after dinner.

Shops & Services

Arida

61 Madeay Street, Potts Point (9357 4788, www.arida.com.au). Bus 311. **Open** 10am-6pm Mon-Sat; 11am-5pm Sun. **Map** p65 H4 ⓰ **Fashion**
Arida stocks men's and women's collections from Lanvin, Givenchy, Rick Owens, Celine, Superfine, L'Agence and James Perse. It also carries unique furniture, homewares and decorative objects.

Becker Minty

7/81 Madeay Street, Potts Point (8356 9999, www.beckerminty.com). Bus 311. **Open** 10.30am-6pm daily. **Map** p65 H5 ⓱ **Homewares**
The owners pride themselves on hand-picking original and unexpected furnishings, and the lighting, ornaments and fashion items here have been chosen for their unusual style and worldly elegance.

Skarfe

4C Roslyn Street, Potts Point (8021 4961, www.skarfe.com). Bus 311. **Open** 10am-6pm Mon-Sat; noon-4pm Sun. **Map** p65 H6 ⓲ **Accessories**
Luxurious wraps, scarves and accessories from Italy, France, Belgium, Africa, Mongolia and Australia. It's like walking into a rainbow of silk and cashmere.

Roosevelt.

Eastern Suburbs

Over the past 20 years, the Eastern Suburbs have been completely transformed by a young, go-getting moneyed set who want to live the high life close to the city. The east has always had a certain cachet – the back streets of Woollahra, Double Bay, Vaucluse, Darling Point, Rose Bay and Centennial Park are lined with grand colonial mansions. But Paddington, Bondi, Tamarama, Watsons Bay and Coogee are where the upwardly mobile are staking their claim. Old-timers recall the beachside suburbs as largely working-class enclaves and Paddington as a slum, but all that is ancient history. Today, the young and hip have taken over, transforming Paddington's tiny terraced houses into TARDIS-like structures. And in Bondi – at the Junction and around the famous beach – ritzy apartment blocks are increasingly dominating the skyline, with rents and house prices at a record high.

EXPLORE

Bondi Icebergs.

Don't Miss

1 Bondi to Coogee walk Clifftop track with world-class views (p106).

2 Buon Ricordo Splash your cash at one of the city's best eateries (p111).

3 Bondi Icebergs Watch the Sunday swimming or enjoy a cocktail (p104).

4 William Street Home to leading local fashion designers (p94).

5 Centennial Park Inner east park with fields, swamps and bushland (p98).

IN THE KNOW BAREFOOT BOWLS

Paddo Bowls (2 Quarry Street, Paddington, 9363 1150, www.paddobowls.com.au) claims to have spearheaded the barefoot bowls trend in Sydney – its games focus on the social aspect over the competition – and it's certainly a popular joint with the younger crowd. Barefoot bowls sessions run three times daily, every day of the week, and start at $12. After a quick tutorial, settle in for a relaxing afternoon of bowls, served with a hearty meal and jugs of beer from the newly refurbished bar.

EASTERN PROMISE

The magnetism of the east lies with its easy proximity to the city and its natural beauty. The water – be it ocean or harbour – is never far away, and in many suburbs it's the main view. There is a host of pretty beaches with something for everyone, from family-centric Nielsen Park to sunbathers' haven Tamarama, surf paradise Bondi or peaceful Parsley Bay. Add to this great shops – Paddington is the appointed home of the city's fashion designers, many trading from terraced homes – plus enough restaurants, cafés and bars to keep locals busy. Even if you're just spending a few hours here, it's pretty clear why the east has become the place to settle.

PADDINGTON

A luxe, boutique-strewn suburb, Paddo (as the locals call it) is famous for fine threads, good-looking residents and a very Eastern Suburbs private-school vibe. And let's face it: that's why we love it. Come here to be transported. Narrow **William Street** and curvy **Glenmore Road** have got you sorted for high-end duds, while all the big shops have a home on **Oxford Street**. The Saturday **Paddington Markets** are well worth a rummage if you're looking to save a few pennies – perhaps to have a drink at **Wine Library**, or the **Four in Hand**. If you want to get in with the well-heeled young pros who love a game of rugby as much as they do a well-tailored suit, the **London** is your bet.

But Paddington's about more than boozing and clothing. Want a book? **Ariel** has you sorted. Fancy a flick? The **Palace Verona** (*see p185*) shows the latest arthouse and foreign films.

Sights & Museums

ᴿᴿᴱᴱ Paddington Reservoir Gardens
Corner of Oatley & Oxford Streets. Bus 333, 352, 378, 380, M40. **Admission** free. **Map** p96 B5 ❶

One of Sydney's top-secret art grottoes and unique abandoned spaces has been reborn. The Paddington Reservoir, built 142 years ago, was decommissioned in 1914 and became a garage. Now, with almost $10 million worth of restoration work complete, the new Paddington Reservoir Gardens has a stunning Romanesque sunken garden with a lake of contemplation at its centre, a hanging garden canopy around the perimeter and an eastern chamber left empty but for the wall art. This blank canvas 'cultural precinct' hosts markets, art and film festivals.

Victoria Barracks
Oxford Street, between Greens & Oatley Roads (9339 3170). Bus 333, 352, 378, 380, M40. **Open** *Museum* 10am-3pm Sun. *Tour* 10am Thur. **Admission** *Museum* $2 donation. *Tour* free. **Map** p96 B5 ❷

Built with local sandstone between 1841 and 1849, the Regency-style Victoria Barracks were designed by Lieutenant-Colonel George Barney, who also built Fort Denison and reconstructed Circular Quay. Nowadays, the old barracks are used as a military planning and administration centre. The museum is housed in the former 25-cell jail, also home to a ghost, Charlie the Redcoat, who hanged himself while incarcerated for shooting his sergeant.

Restaurants & Cafés

10 William St
10 William Street (9360 3310, 10williamst. com.au). Bus 333, 352, 378, 380, M40. **Open** 5pm-midnight Mon-Thur; noon-midnight Fri, Sat. **Main courses** $24-$30. **Map** p96 C5 ❸ **Wine bar**

The menu is small-plates-o-rama at this two-level wine bar and restaurant just off Oxford Street. The beautifully hand-cut beef tartare is a favourite. As are the juicy green peppers pan-fried with salt, or pickled radish and celery. On the wine side, 10 William has a penchant for crazy, raw, wild and feral Italians. And they're excellent.

Guillaume
92 Hargrave Street (9302 5222, www.guillaumes. com.au). Bus 389. **Open** 5.45pm-late Tue-Thur; noon-3pm, 5.45pm-late Fri, Sat. **Set meal** $145 4 courses. **Map** p96 D4 ❹ **French**

Guillaume is our top pick for French cuisine. You'll get all the thrills with plenty of frills at this restaurant from top chef Guillaume Brahimi. Exquisite dishes feature local produce: moreton bay bug with pork cheek, radish, cauliflower and sea spray, say, or squid from South Australia, with mussels, fennel and ham. You'll need to book weeks – sometimes months – in advance. It's that good.

Lucio's
47 Windsor Street (9380 5996, www.lucios. com.au). Bus 389. **Open** 12.30-2.45pm,

6.30-10.15pm Tue-Sat. **Main courses** $44-$46.
Map p96 D4 **❺ Italian**
Gaze at a dizzying art collection (Olsens, Smarts and Storriers) as you eat some of the city's best contemporary Italian food – the likes of crudo of kingfish with pickled green tomato, avocado, fennel, radishes and chives; or wagyu rump carpaccio with jerusalem artichoke, cress and bagna cauda. It's a big, expensive night out but well worth it.

Bars

Four in Hand

105 Sutherland Street (9362 1999, www.fourin hand.com.au). Bus 389. **Open** noon-10pm Mon, Sun; noon-11pm Tue-Sat. **Map** p96 D4 **❻**
This watering hole in the backstreets is not as fancy as you'd think a pub adjoining a fine-dining restaurant would be, but that's a large part of its appeal. Food by chef Colin Fassnidge is the best pub grub going.

Grand National

161 Underwood Street (9363 3096, thegrand nationalhotel.com.au). Bus 333, 352, 378, 380, M40. **Open** noon-midnight Mon-Sat; noon-10pm Sun. **Map** p96 D5 **❼**
Forget steak: this pub puts béarnaise sauce on its burgers. A proper medium-rare beef patty with cheddar melted on top comes secured in a well-toasted sesame-seed bun. And on Mondays, it's just a tenner.

London

85 Underwood Street (9331 3200, hotellondon. com.au). Bus 333, 352, 378, 380, M40. **Open** noon-midnight Mon-Sat; noon-10pm Sun. **Map** p96 C5 **❽**
The London may be one of many in the Paddington pub cluster but this prettied-up old terrace keeps sport-loving locals on side with friendly staff, cold beers and a tasty burger joint upstairs. Wednesdays are cheap pizza nights, and they do a juicy pub steak for $10 on Thursdays. You beauty!

Print Room

11 Glenmore Road (0424 034 020, www.print room.net.au). Bus 333, 352, 378, 380, M40. **Open** 3pm-late Wed-Fri; noon-11pm Sat; noon-10pm Sun. **Map** p96 A4 **❾**
The oldest pub in Paddington is surrounded by high-end fashion boutiques, stylish shoppers and latte-sipping ladies of leisure by day. So perhaps it's no surprise that upstairs in this historic building, there's an elegant wine and cocktail lounge without a pint in sight – just look for the separate entrance on the left, painted dusty pink.

Wine Library

18 Oxford Street (9360 5686, www.wine-library. com.au). Bus 333, 352, 378, 380, M40. **Open** 11.30am-11.30pm Mon-Sat; 11.30am-10pm Sun. **Map** p96 D6 **❿**
You want a sure bet when it comes to drinking good wine? This is it. The wine list offers plenty of delicious bottles and glasses, for very few dollars, and the meatballs are damn fine too.

Shops & Services

Aesop

72A Oxford Street (9358 3382, www.aesop.com). Bus 333, 352, 378, 380, M40. **Open** 10am-6pm Mon-Sat; 11am-5pm Sun. **Map** p96 A4 **⓫ Health & beauty**
Go natural with Aesop's bath and body products. The Paddington store gives facial treatments using Aesop's divine beauty products, and the shop design alone makes a visit worthwhile.
Other locations throughout the city.

Alpha60

15 Glenmore Road (8084 2592, www.alpha 60.com.au). Bus 333, 352, 378, 380, M40. **Open** 10am-6pm Mon-Wed, Fri, Sat; 10am-7pm Thur; 11am-5pm Sun. **Map** p96 A4 **⓬ Fashion**
Monochromatic men's and women's garments are synonymous with boutique streetwear label Alpha60, which was founded in 2005 by brother-sister duo Georgie and Alex Cleary. The Melbourne label transforms classic shapes into edgy pieces.

Ariel

42 Oxford Street (9332 4581, www.arielbooks.com. au). Bus 333, 352, 378, 380, M40. **Open** 9am-midnight daily. **Map** p96 A4 **⓭ Books & music**
It always makes a difference when a bookstore chooses its stock with care. Ariel has been a Paddington landmark since 1985, thanks to its knowledgeable staff and superb selection of quality titles. And it stays open late too.

Corner Shop

43 William Street (9380 9828, www.thecorner shop.com.au). Bus 333, 352, 378, 380, M40. **Open** 10am-6pm Mon-Sat; noon-5pm Sun. **Map** p96 C5 **⓮ Fashion**
This beautifully merchandised boutique stocks international and standout local labels, and is the perfect introduction to Aussie greats Christopher Esber, Magdalena Velevska and swimwear label Anna & Boy.

Incu

256 Oxford Street (9331 6070, www.incu.com/ store-locations/paddington). Bus 333, 352, 378, 380, M40. **Open** 10am-6pm Mon-Wed, Fri, Sat; 10am-7pm Thur; 11am-5pm Sun. **Map** p96 C5 **⓯ Accessories**
You can't go past Incu if you're serious about fashion accessories. Brands such as Brilliant (for its leather chain cuffs) and Marc by Marc Jacobs make appearances, as do staff favourites Tatty Devine and Princess Tina.

EXPLORE

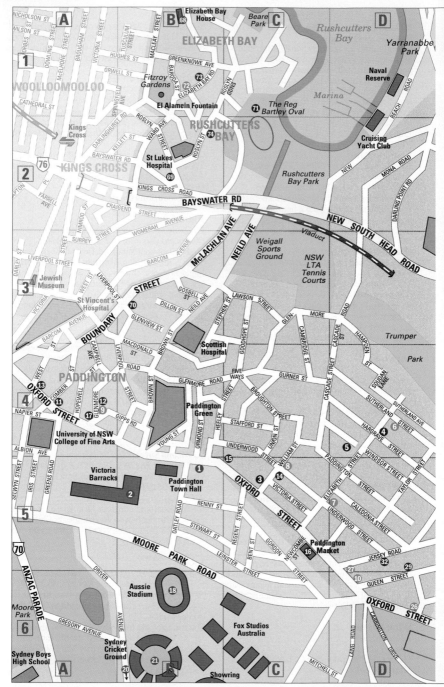

EXPLORE

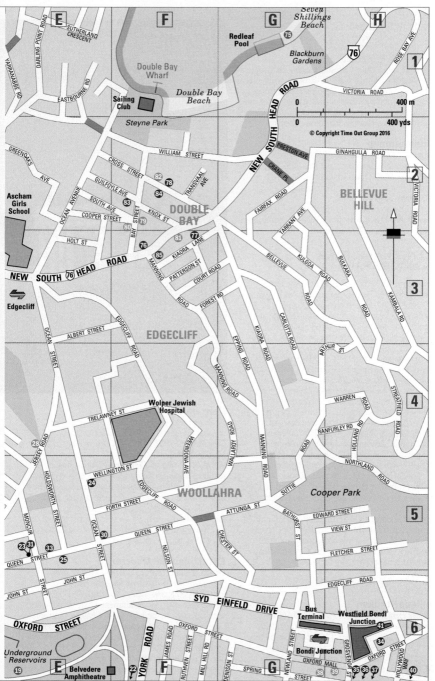

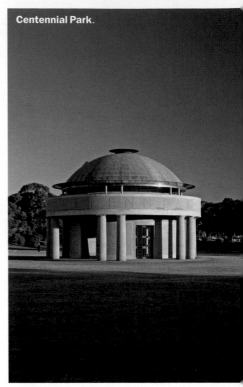
Centennial Park.

Paddington Markets
395 Oxford Street (9331 2923). Bus 333, 352, 378, 380, M40. **Open** 10am-4pm Sat. **Map** p96 C5 ⑯ **Market**
Shop at more than 150 stalls every Saturday at Paddington Uniting Church. This is where local labels such as Dinosaur Designs and Sambag got their start, and it's a must if you're looking for interesting Aussie-designed fashions and accessories, as well as candles, flowers, records and the like.

Zimmermann
Shop 2, 2-16 Glenmore Road (9357 4700, www.zimmermannwear.com). Bus 333, 352, 378, 380, M40. **Open** 10am-6pm Mon-Wed, Fri, Sat; 10am-7pm Thur; 10am-5pm Sun. **Map** p96 A4 ⑰ **Fashion**
If there's a souvenir outfit to take home, it has to be glamorous beachwear from Australian designers Nicky and Simone Zimmermann.

CENTENNIAL PARK & MOORE PARK

If it's greenery you're after, head to the top of Oxford Street, where **Centennial Park** awaits. It's hard to believe that such a huge and lush expanse of breathing space and picnic spots lies so close to the inner city. Filled with artificial lakes, fields, bridle paths and cycle tracks, the park attracts a mix of families looking for the perfect spot for a toddler's birthday party, outdoor fitness fanatics and casual strollers. Rolling all the way down to Randwick Racecourse and across to Queens Park and Moore Park (home to Sydney's first zoo), Centennial Park was created in the 1880s on the site of the Lachlan Swamps as part of the state celebrations to mark the centenary of the landing of the First Fleet. The three parks (Centennial, Moore and Queens) encompass 3.8 square kilometres (1.5 square miles) and are collectively known as Centennial Parklands.

The former Royal Agricultural Society Showground on the west side of Centennial Park has been redeveloped by Fox Studios Australia into a film studio and entertainment complex, the **Entertainment Quarter**. Next to the complex (approached from Moore Park Road or Driver Avenue), the huge white doughnuts that form **Sydney Cricket Ground (SCG)** and **Allianz Stadium** light up the sky for miles around at night.

Sights & Museums

Allianz Stadium
Moore Park Road, Moore Park (9360 6601, www.allianz.com.au/stadium). Bus 355, 391, 392, 394, 396, 397, 399. **Tickets** see website for fixture times and prices. **Map** p96 B6 ⑱
If you are visiting the taller of the twin stadiums at Moore Park, rugby is probably on the agenda.

Centennial Park
Between Oxford Street & York, Darley, Alison & Lang Roads (9339 6699, www.cp.nsw.gov.au). Bus 333, 352, 355, 378, 380. **Open** 24hrs daily. **Map** p97 E6 ⑲
A weekend trip to Centennial Park, especially in summer, reveals Aussies at their leisurely best. There's an outdoor fitness station, and you can hire in-line skates and bikes or even go horse-riding. Statues, ponds and indigenous Australian flowers make it one of Sydney's prettiest places to spend a day. Keep your eyes peeled for the Moonlight Cinema (*see p187*) from December to March.

Entertainment Quarter
Driver Avenue, Moore Park (8117 6700, www. entertainmentquarter.com.au). Bus 355, 373, 374, 376, 377, 391, 392, 396. **Map** p96 B6 ⑳
The super-slick Entertainment Quarter complex, with cinemas, shops, a barrage of eateries and some huge entertainment spaces, also hosts a weekend crafts market and a farmers' market on Wednesdays and Saturdays (both open 10am-4pm). Kids will have a ball at the two state-of-the-art playgrounds, seasonal ice-rink, ten-pin bowling centre, crazy golf

EXPLORE

course and the popular Bungy Trampoline. Max Watt's music venue (*see p206*) is also here, as is the popular Comedy Store (*see p211*).

Sydney Cricket Ground

Driver Avenue, Moore Park (9360 6601, www. sydneycricketground.com.au). Bus 355, 391, 392, 394, 396, 397, 399. **Tickets** see website for fixture times and ticket prices. **Map** p96 B6 ㉑
Sydney's pre-eminent and most-loved sporting colosseum, the Sydney Cricket Ground (SCG) has come a long way in its 134-year history. Today, it is the active home ground of the NSW Blues cricket team in summer and the Sydney Swans AFL squad in winter and – all year round – the spiritual home of Sydney rugby league and rugby union... and all Sydney sports lovers.

Restaurants & Cafés

Centennial Parklands Dining

Grand Drive, Centennial Park (9380 9350, www. cpdining.com.au). Bus 333, 352, 355, 378, 380. **Open** noon-3pm daily. **Main courses** $20-$26. **Map** p97 F6 ㉒ **Contemporary Australian**

There are a few dining options at the heart of Sydney's most famous park: there's a kiosk so you can grab something on-the-go, plus a private dining room and a café full of locally sourced produce – beer-battered fish with chips and tartare sauce, say, or pork belly kimchi sliders with coleslaw, pork crackling and chilli mayo.

WOOLLAHRA

If you love the smell of trees and money in the morning, you'll love Woollahra. From the Aboriginal word for 'camp' or 'meeting spot', Woollahra's one of Sydney's ritziest postcodes and boasts the kind of shopping, restaurants and bars to match.

Queen Street is the closest thing in eastern Sydney to an old-fashioned English high street, and the villagey feel will make you think the city is hours rather than minutes away. Pricey antique shops, galleries, delis, homewares stores and boutiques line the first stretch (from Centennial Park), leading down to the upmarket village of Woollahra. The antique shops are not for the bargain hunter, but are surprisingly rich in wares.

Bistro Moncur.

Our shopping highlight has to be **Victor Churchill**, a butcher shop so luxe, refined (and expensive) that Sydney's chefs call it 'Tiffany'.

Walking east along Queen Street, turn left at the traffic lights on to Moncur Street at French restaurant **Bistro Moncur**, then round to the right into Jersey Road, and you'll come to the **Lord Dudley Hotel**. The Dudley is an oasis for nostalgic Poms looking for a touch of home; it positively screams English pubdom, from its ivy-clad exterior down to its cosy bar with British beers on tap. It's also popular with mature moneyed locals and revellers from the nearby **Paddington Bowling Club** (*see p94* **In the Know**), who meet at the pub for a post-match tipple.

A walk from the east end of Queen Street, via Greycairn Place and Attunga Street, to **Cooper Park** – which runs east into the suburb of Bellevue Hill – is a pleasure in jacaranda season (late November to December), when the streets are flooded with vivid purple blossoms. At the east end of Cooper Park, across Victoria Road, you'll find small **Bellevue Park**, which has some amazing views of the harbour.

The suburbs from Woollahra to Double Bay, Bellevue Hill, Bondi Junction and Bondi, are home to Sydney's Jewish community. On Friday evenings and Saturday mornings, the streets are busy with the devout walking to and from the various synagogues dotted throughout the area.

Restaurants & Cafés

Bistro Moncur
Woollahra Hotel, 116 Queen Street (9327 9713, woollahrahotel.com.au). Bus 389. **Open** noon-3pm, 6pm-late Mon-Thur; noon-3pm, 5.30pm-late Fri; noon-3pm, 3.30-10.30pm Sat; noon-3pm, 3.30-9pm Sun. **Main courses** $32-$46. **Map** p97 E5 ❷ **French**
French bistro classics under the guidance of head chef Sam Kane are some of this postcode's favourite eats – the likes of fillet steak with béarnaise sauce, and Bistor Moncur pork sausages with potato purée and lyonnaise onions. The high-end restaurant has a loyal local following – and we can see why.

Chiswick
65 Ocean Street (8388 8688, www.chiswick restaurant.com.au). Bus 200, 400. **Open** noon-2.30pm, 6-10pm Mon-Thur; noon-3pm, 5.30-10pm Fri, Sat; noon-3pm, 6-9pm Sun. **Main courses** $31-$38. **Map** p97 E5 ❷ **Contemporary Australian**
This Sydney institution by chef Matt Moran and restaurateur Pete Sullivan is set in lush garden sur-rounds. The roasted lamb shoulder, raised on the Moran family property just outside of Bathurst, is a hit, served with a side salad picked from the kitchen

garden. Consume with a tipple from the exciting wine list and finish with one of the ace bourbons, such as a slug of Pappy Van Winkle.

Ladurée
111 Queen Street (9221 9538, www.laduree.com). Bus 389. **Open** 10am-6pm Mon-Fri; 9am-6pm Sat; 10am-5pm Sun. **Map** p97 E5 ㉕ **Café**
The fanciest French macarons, chocolates from Les Marquis de Ladurée confectionary, teas and perfumed candles fill the shelves at this darling café.

Bars

Hotel Centennial
88 Oxford Street (9362 3838, www.centennial hotel.com.au). Bus 333, 352, 378, 380, M40. **Open** noon-midnight Mon-Sat; noon-10pm Sun. **Map** p96 D6 ㉖
At this elegant design hotel, everything looks expensive – and everything is. Wander past the giant orchid display in the formal entrance and you'll find yourself in a tricked-out public bar that looks like it should be hosting Russian oligarchs and old-school Wall Street tycoons. A nice, high-class pub for a high-end suburb.

Light Brigade Hotel
2A Oxford Street (9357 0888, www.lightbrigade. com.au). Bus 333, 352, 378, 380, M40. **Open** 11am-midnight Mon-Thur; 11am-1am Fri, Sat; 11am-10pm Sun. **Map** p96 D5 ㉗
Straddling the Woollahra–Paddington divide, this place is low on upmarket posturing; but it's by no means a divey pub either. It has gently masculine decor, and a great range of beers on tap. La Scala, the restaurant upstairs, does rustic Italian fare such as slow-cooked lamb, grilled pizzas and fresh pasta.

Lord Dudley
236 Jersey Road (9327 5399, www.lorddudley. com.au). Bus 200, 389. **Open** 11am-11pm Mon-Wed; 11am-midnight Thur-Sat; noon-10pm Sun. **Map** p97 E4 ㉘
This family-run pub likes the old ways as much as we do. The vast, red-brick premises looks more like a British country manor than an Inner East establishment, and staff serve great pies that take 25 minutes to bake to golden brown. Grab a Guinness and settle in for a spot of Scrabble.

Shops & Services

Ginkgo Leaf
43A Queen Street (9328 0585, ginkgoleaf.com.au). Bus 389. **Open** 10am-5.30pm Wed-Fri; 11am-5pm Sat, Sun. **Map** p96 D5 ㉙ **Homewares**
Ginkgo Leaf stocks contemporary design products from Japan. The Woollahra store has a curated collection of homewares, from Kyoto's Hosoo textiles to Kaico kitchen products.

.M Contemporary
37 Ocean Street (0415 692 294, mcontemp.com). Bus 200, 389. **Open** 10am-5pm Tue-Sat; 10am-4pm Sun. **Map** p97 E5 ㉚ **Gallery**
South African-born art collector Michelle Paterson opened this commercial gallery in August 2013. The gallery is aimed at cross-cultural discussion, programming emerging and established artists from Australia and overseas.

Moncur Cellars
Woollahra Hotel, 116 Queen Street (9327 9715, www.woollahrahotel.com.au). Bus 389. **Open** 10am-9pm Mon, Sun; 10am-10pm Tue-Sat. **Map** p97 E5 ㉛ **Food & drink**
The Woollahra Hotel's cellar boasts an impressive selection of French and Italian regional wines as well as Australian bottles. Stop off at the shopfront on your way out to grab cheese, duck terrine (made next door at Bistro Moncur) and sausages to pair with your newly acquired bottles.

Olsen Irwin Gallery
63 Jersey Road (9327 3922, www.olsenirwin.com). Bus 333, 352, 378, 380, 389, M40. **Open** noon-5pm Mon, Sun; 10am-6pm Tue-Fri; 10am-5pm Sat. **Map** p96 D5 ㉜ **Gallery**
Formerly the site of Tim Olsen Gallery, this new incarnation of the space represents a partnership between the well-known gallerist (and son of John Olsen) and powerhouse dealer Rex Irwin. The gallery presents a broad spectrum of Australian and international art.

Victor Churchill
132 Queen Street (9328 0402, www.victor churchill.com.au). Bus 389. **Open** 9am-6pm Mon-Fri; 8am-6pm Sat; 9am-5pm Sun. **Map** p97 E5 ㉝ **Food & drink**
Victor Churchill is a shrine to meat, and if Salvador Dali and Elton John got together to open the world's fanciest butcher, it'd look very much like this. It's not cheap, but you're paying as much for the friendly staff who will answer your every protein-related question as you are for quality and the unforgettable experience of shopping here.

BONDI JUNCTION & WAVERLEY

While it's the beach that is the focus for most, the Junction, with its monster mall – the **Westfield Bondi Junction** – has become the place to shop in eastern Sydney, if you don't mind crowds. It boasts every brand-name shop from Oxford Street and the city, plus supermarkets, restaurants, a multi-screen cinema and even a state-of-the-art gym with great views over Sydney. The proximity of the city by train or bus has turned Bondi Junction into a booming residential and commercial hub, and although the older parts look relatively shabby in the

EXPLORE

shadow of the Westfield, on the whole the place has finally come into its own – particularly in terms of drinking and dining thanks to new additions including **El Topo**, **Nelson Road Tuck Shop** and the **Traditional Chip Shop**.

From the Junction, there are two roads that lead to Bondi Beach (we are as confused as you are about why the train stops at Bondi Junction rather than venturing closer to the actual beach). Old South Head Road turns away from the ocean and winds north to Watsons Bay (take the turn-off at O'Brien Street or Curlewis Street). It tends to be quieter than the other route, Bondi Road, which can be thick with buses; in summer, when the crowded vehicles trundle at a snail's pace, it's often quicker to walk (about 30 minutes). Snaking through Waverley into Bondi (increasingly called 'Bondi Heights' by estate agents keen to exploit its trendiness), Bondi Road is a mixed bag of alternative shops and international restaurants.

Restaurants & Cafés

El Topo
Level 3, The Eastern Hotel, 500 Oxford Street, Bondi Junction (8383 5959, theeastern.com.au/ eltopomexican). Bondi Junction rail. **Open** 4-10pm Mon; noon-late Tue-Sat; noon-midnight Sun. **Main courses** $18-$32. **Map** p97 H6 ❹ **Mexican**

Welcome to the first Mexican restaurant in Sydney where you can order fried crickets. This is some benchmark Mexican food, right here, and the design is awesome to boot, with hand-painted Oaxaca tiles on the tables and walls, candlelit skulls and tiny dioramas. Oh, and they spike the *horchata* with rum!

Nelson Road Tuck Shop
60 Bronte Road, Bondi Junction (9387 6505, www.nelsonroad.com.au). Bondi Junction rail. **Open** 7am-3pm daily. **Main courses** $16-$20. **Map** p97 H6 ❸ **Café**

This grown-up tuck shop serves flavoured milks and rotating Your Own Adventure lunches from 11.30am. On our last visit, staff were pushing roast pork and stuffed chicken, destined to be mixed and matched with peach, radicchio, lentil and prosciutto salad or a jumble of corn, quinoa and green beans held together by a super garlicky aïoli.

Ruby's Diner
Shop 1, 173-179 Bronte Road, Waverley (0404 379 585, www.rubysdiner.com.au). Bus 314, 316, 317, 348, 353, 378. **Open** 6.30am-3.30pm Mon-Fri; 7am-3.30pm Sat; 8am-3.30pm Sun. **Main courses** $11-$20. **Map** p97 H6 ❸ **Café**

The coffee at Ruby's Diner really is something, and they've got you covered whether you want an

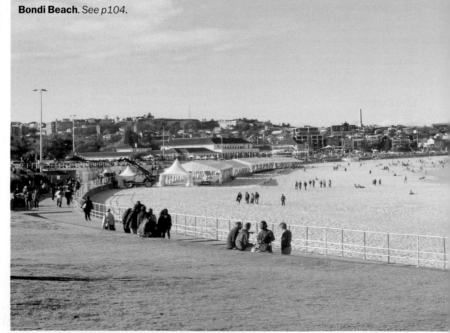

Bondi Beach. *See p104.*

espresso, floral cold drip, pour-over or filter coffee. If you don't get your kicks from caffeine, order the Monkey Magic – a sweet and sticky vegan smoothie of banana, dates, chia seeds and almond milk gently spiced with cinnamon.

Traditional Chip Shop

78 Bronte Road, Bondi Junction (1300 244 774, www.thechipshop.com.au). Bondi Junction rail. **Open** 11.30am-10pm Mon-Wed; 11.30am-11pm Thur, Fri; 11am-11pm Sat; 11am-9.45pm Sun. **Main courses** $8-$13. **Map** p97 H6 **❸**
Fish & chips
This is a good chippy. It's distinctly British, and it's worth the trip if you're not staying nearby. This is dinner that's designed to be eaten with your hands down the shipyards – no fancy embellishments or fanfare, just excellent, British-style fish and chips.

Bars

Jam Gallery

Underground, 195 Oxford Street, Bondi Junction (9389 2485, www.jamgallery.com.au). Bondi Junction rail. **Open** 7pm-3am daily. **Map** p97 G6 **❸**
Like a delicious condiment for retail-dominated Bondi Junction, Jam Gallery is spicing things up with an underground, multipurpose music venue, gallery space, bar and eaterie.

Spring Street Social

Underground, 110 Spring Street, Bondi Junction (9389 2485, www.facebook.com/SpringStreet Social). Bondi Junction rail. **Open** 4pm-3am Tue-Sat. **Map** p97 H6 **❸**
Bondi Junction was never known for small bars or live music but Spring Street Social and the Jam Gallery (*see left*) are changing that. At this underground club, all are welcome, for great cocktails (Chase the Dragon has apple-pie-infused rye whisky, cognac, bitters, cinnamon and applewood smoke) and tasty bar snacks.

Shops & Services

East Side Ink

Suite 1, 2A Waverley Street, Bondi Junction (9389 8370, www.eastsideinkbondi.com). Bondi Junction rail. **Open** 10am-6pm daily. **Map** p97 H6 **❹ Tattooist**
This parlour's no-gimmick approach makes it our favourite – no tatt is too intricate or too minimal, too hardcore or too pretty. Look out for the work of artist Wilson Arbis, who has quite a following.

Westfield Bondi Junction

500 Oxford Street, Bondi Junction (westfield.com. au/bondijunction). Bondi Junction rail. **Open** 9.30am-6pm Mon-Wed, Sat; 9.30am-7pm Thur; 10am-6pm Sun. **Map** p97 H6 **❹ Mall**

EXPLORE

There's a wealth of high-street fashion, electronics, furniture and fancy boutiques inside this huge shopping complex, including an Apple store, emerging designer market 100 Squared, Aesop, Chanel, Louis Vuitton, natural skincare brand Kiehl's, Sydney labels Dion Lee and Vanishing Elephant, Melbourne label Gorman, European high-street giant Zara and several supermarkets.

BONDI BEACH TO COOGEE BEACH

Bondi Beach is anything but a romantic, stroll-in-the-moonlight sandy spot. It's the closest ocean beach to the city and at first glance could easily be dismissed as a tacky tourist trap. But don't be fooled: there's a reason that some die-hard Sydneysiders wouldn't live anywhere else, to the extent that they venture out of the area only when they absolutely have to.

Before you do anything else, make a beeline for the south end of the beach itself, and embark on the most popular walking route in Sydney – the Bondi to Coogee coastal track. The views are fabulous from Bondi's southern headland, which turns inwards to show off Bondi Beach in all its glory. Past Waverley Cemetery, the coastal walk continues south to lovely Clovelly Beach and then on to dramatic Coogee Beach, with its historic Wylie's Baths and the deservedly popular women's pool.

The main thoroughfare of Bondi is noisy, four-lane **Campbell Parade**, which runs parallel to the beach and is lined with restaurants, cafés and souvenir shops, all of them usually packed at weekends. Below that is dinky **Bondi Park** – housing the 1928 Bondi Pavilion and the Bondi Surf Bathers' Life Saving Club (claiming to be the first of its kind in the world, although that boast is hotly contested by rival clubs) – and after that the sand itself. Bondi is a good surfing beach, and there are plenty of places to hire wetsuits and surfboards along Campbell Parade; check out **Let's Go Surfing**, which provides info on surf lessons too.

Campbell Parade thumps and pumps for interlopers and blow-ins at weekends and offers more languorous delights for locals during the week, but to get a feel for why some people live and die in Bondi, you need to look around the corners and backstreets. **Hall Street** is the villagey heart of Bondi Beach, with such everyday necessities as banks, a post office and travel agents, as well as a gaggle of cafés and restaurants – including awesome café **Bills** – that make it a great daytime strolling location. Nearby **Gould Street** has a small but significant collection of designer shops, many of whose keepers started selling their wares at the famous **Bondi Market** (Bondi Beach Public School, Campbell Parade,

www.bondimarkets.com.au), which takes place in a school playground every Sunday.

Bondi is popular with backpackers for good reason: it's loud, crowded and anything goes. Backpackers and locals both love the **Beach Road Hotel**, and there's plenty of solid smaller drinking spots such as **Anchor** and **Neighbourhood**.

The north end of the beach has blossomed with its share of cafés and eating establishments, including **Sean's Panorama** and **North Bondi Fish**. The outdoor gym, which is really just a collection of bars set up for pull-ups, is now generally acknowledged as the number one spot for tanning, posing and mutual admiration among Sydney's gay men.

Bondi is also home to the famous **Bondi Icebergs Club**, housed in a strikingly modern, four-storey building at the southern end of the cove. Throughout the winter, members of the club (formed in 1929) gather every Sunday morning for their ritual plunge into the icy waters of the outdoor pool. The club also houses the upmarket **Icebergs Dining Room & Bar** – both the bar and restaurant are ideal for panoramic views over the beach.

Generally acknowledged to be Bondi's poorer cousin in terms of fashion, restaurants, bars and even its beach, **Coogee** has raised its game in the past few years. Although still littered with backpackers – who find the rates cheaper here than at overpriced Bondi – it's answered a need for more palatable eating and drinking spots. The **Coogee Bay Hotel** has traditionally dominated seafront socialising but has been joined by Justin Hemmes' lavish **Coogee Pavilion** in place of the Coogee Palace Hotel. The **Little Kitchen** is a casual-looking gem, and there are also Indian, Thai and Japanese restaurants, plus breakfast spots aplenty.

Sights & Museums

Bondi Icebergs Club

1 Notts Avenue, Bondi (9130 3120). Bus 333, 380, 381, 382. **Open** *Gym* 6am-8.30pm Mon-Fri; 8am-5pm Sat, Sun. *Pool* 6am-6.30pm Mon-Fri; 6.30am-6.30pm Sat, Sun. **Admission** *Gym* $15. *Pool* $5; $3 reductions. **Map** p105 ❷
Although most famous for its all-weather swimming club, Icebergs houses a number of other attractions. There's a pool, gym, sauna and deck on the ground floor, all open to the public, plus the national headquarters of Surf Life Saving Australia and a small museum on the first floor.

Bondi Pavilion

Queen Elizabeth Drive, Bondi (8362 3400, www.waverley.nsw.gov.au/recreation). Bus 333, 380, 381, X84. **Open** varies. **Admission** varies. **Map** p105 ❸

EXPLORE

Bondi Icebergs Club.

The Bondi Pavilion started life as the Bondi Municipal Surf Sheds, a series of 1,000 dressing sheds dedicated to the 'clean and healthful pastime of surf bathing'. The building is now safe on the NSW heritage register and is currently an arts and cultural centre, home to the Tamarama Rock Surfers theatre group, a rehearsal and recording studio, and the Bondi Pavilion Gallery.

Restaurants & Cafés

A Tavola
75-79 Hall Street, Bondi (9130 1246, atavola.com. au/bondi). Bus 389, X89. **Open** noon-3pm Mon, Tue; noon-3pm, 5.30pm-late Wed-Sun. **Main courses** $31-$38. **Map** p105 ❹ **Italian**
The Bondi outpost follows the same cues that made the original A Tavola in Darlinghurst such a hit, especially the marble communal tables that double as a workbench for the chefs rolling out fresh pasta. The wine list is 100% Italian, there's a team of stupendously friendly Italian waiters and the quality of the pasta is excellent.

Bills
79 Hall Street, Bondi (8412 0700, www.bills.com. au). Bus 389, X89. **Open** 7am-10pm Mon-Fri; 7.30am-10pm Sat, Sun. **Main courses** $14.50-$33. **Map** p105 ❺ **Brasserie**
Every man, woman and their French bulldog is lining up for a seat at the brand new Bills in Bondi. Seats outdoors spill on to Hall Street, where most people

are eating classics à la Bills – corn fritters, creamy scrambled eggs, hotcakes. Inside, squashy leather banquettes and big-ass wood-and-rattan chairs work against a backdrop of caramel wooden ceilings. Come the evening, creative dinner dishes have global twists. **Other locations** throughout the city.

Da Orazio Pizza & Porchetta
3/75-79 Hall Street, Bondi (8090 6969, daorazio. com). Bus 389, X89. **Open** 5pm-midnight Mon-Fri; noon-midnight Sat; noon-10pm Sun. **Main courses** $18-$27. **Map** p105 ❻ **Italian**
Restaurateur Maurice Terzini and chef Orazio D'Elia have teamed up to offer outstanding pizza and roast meats, minutes from the sea. Tasty, gutsy stuff.

Drake Eatery
Corner of Curlewis & Gould Streets, Bondi (9130 3218, drakeeatery.com.au). Bus 380, 381, 382. **Open** 7am-late daily. **Main courses** $29-$32. **Map** p105 ❼ **Contemporary Australian/café**
Drake is open daily for breakfast, lunch, dinner, snacks and drinks, and seasonal, fresh, locally sourced produce is at its heart. We love the pan-seared thyme gnocchi with golden raisins, hazelnuts and Pecora blue cheese.

Icebergs Dining Room & Bar
1 Notts Avenue, Bondi (9365 9000, idrb.com). Bus 333, 380, 381, 382. **Open** noon-midnight Tue-Sat; noon-10pm Sun. **Main courses** $40-$70. **Map** p105 ❽ **Italian**

WALK BONDI TO COOGEE
Surfing, swimming, sculpture – and superb views.

Character Dramatic ocean views.
Length 6km (3.5 miles) one way.
Difficulty Easy; some uphill climbs and steps.
Transport Bondi Junction rail then bus 333, 380, 381, 382.

This coastal walk through some of the prettiest beaches in suburban Sydney takes about two-hours. You don't have to go all the way to Coogee – you can stop at any of the beaches en route – and you can, of course, do the walk in reverse.

Start at the southern end of Bondi Beach, where steps take you up to Notts Avenue and past the stylish Icebergs clubhouse and outdoor pool (see p104). The path starts to the left of Notts Avenue, dropping down then going up some steep steps to Marks Park on the spectacular cliff-top Mackenzies Point, with its 180° views along miles of coastline. This first stretch – as far as Tamarama Beach – is the site of the annual Sculpture by the Sea festival in November (see p30). It's a fantastic sight but attracts occasionally overwhelming crowds. After another headland, the path drops down to Tamarama, which has a park, a little café next to the beach and plenty of surfers.

At the southern end of Tamarama, steps lead up to the road, which after a few hundred coast-skirting metres takes you to Bronte Beach. Bronte is popular with surfers and families (especially the southern end, around the outdoor pool), and good for picnics and barbecues. There are also shower and toilet blocks and a kiosk, plus a cluster of cafés and restaurants on the road just behind the beach.

Walk through the car park and take the road uphill via steps through Calga Reserve to Waverley Cemetery. Spreading over the cliffs, the cemetery is a tranquil, well-kept area, and the view out to sea makes this a fitting resting place. Take the oceanside path through the adjoining Burrows Park to the warm welcome of Clovelly Beach. Equipped with a café and a pub just up the hill, this is one of the prettiest of the walk's beaches and a great place to stop for a bite to eat or a swim. It's at the end of a long, narrow inlet, meaning that the waves are small and manageable, making it popular with families.

As you continue around the next headland, the last patch of sand before Coogee is Gordon's Bay; there's not much of a beach, but the view over the water is stunning. Then comes Dunningham Reserve, where a sculpture commemorates those who died in the 2002 Bali bombings. Two plaques nearby list the victims from Sydney: six from the local Dolphins rugby league club and 20 from the Eastern Suburbs. Then it's down to Coogee Beach. At the far end is South Coogee, where you'll find Wylie's Baths, a pretty nature walk and dog park. To get back to the city, take the 372, 373, 374 or X73 bus from Arden Street.

A word to the wise: avoid the walk if it's a windy day, as the cliffs are exposed. If you insist on going in the midday sun, take plenty of water and a hat. Oh, and watch out for the joggers – they brake for no one!

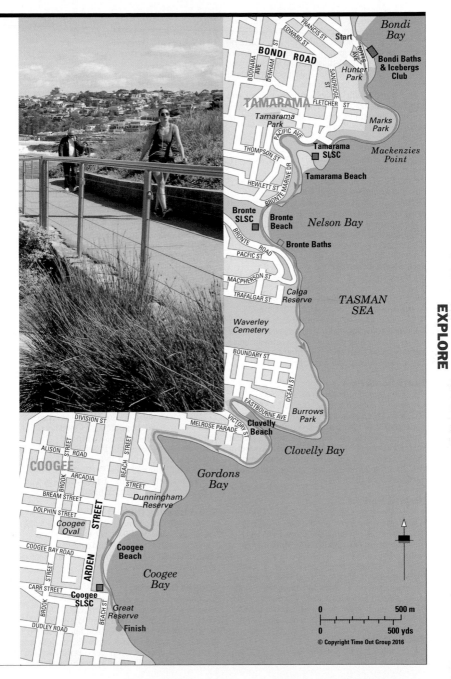

There's no denying the completely beautiful setting of Icebergs: jutting over the ocean pool below and looking straight out to Bondi Beach. Diners do have a tendency to give off a 'comfortable on any size yacht' vibe. But letting that get in the way of what could potentially be an epic lunch would be a mistake. Antipasti could include a *crudo di pesce* or a local burrata with bresaola, capers, croûtons and lemon. Mains focus on top quality, sustainable fish and meat, beautifully prepared. This is a restaurant at the height of excellence.

Little Kitchen

275 Arden Street, Coogee (0450 118 744, www.thelittlekitchen.com.au). Bus 313, 314, 372, 373, M50. **Open** 7am-4pm Mon-Thur; 7am-10pm Fri, Sat. **Main courses** $15-$30. **Café**

Kedgeree, bacon and egg butties, and a full English breakfast are nods to Brit-chef Neil Thompson's heritage at this pretty little room just up from the beach. They appear on the menu beside Aussie café favourites such as iced chocolates and burgers.

Lox Stock & Barrel

140 Glenayr Avenue, Bondi (9300 0368, loxstockandbarrel.com.au). Bus 389. **Open** 7am-3.30pm Mon, Tue, Sun; 7am-3.30pm, 6pm-late Wed-Sat. **Main courses** $15-$18. **Map** p105 (49) **Café**

This shiny new Bondi café is the little brother of popular brekkie spot Brown Sugar, just around the corner on Curlewis Street. But unlike Brown Sugar's fairly straight, surf-style café fare, Lox Stock & Barrel offers bagels, brioche and brisket.

North Bondi Fish

120 Ramsgate Avenue, Bondi (9130 2155, www.northbondifish.com.au). Bus 380, 381, 382, X84. **Open** noon-late Wed-Sun. **Main courses** $27-$36. **Map** p105 (50) **Seafood**

Seafood, sand, sun and sangria make for a perfect summer lunch at North Bondi Fish. Make your own fun here, in one of the most beautiful locations in the world, with some mates, great seafood dishes and a fistful of nice wine.

Porch & Parlour

17/110 Ramsgate Avenue, Bondi (9300 0111, www.porchandparlour.com). Bus 380, 381, 382, X84. **Open** 6.30am-4pm Mon, Tue; 6.30am-10pm Wed-Sun. **Main courses** $14-$22. **Map** p105 (51) **Café**

This Bondi café isn't rewriting the rules – it just has the good sense to serve tasty food made with excellent produce. Service is tight and comes with a smile, making Porch & Parlour a lovely place to start your day with snazzy versions of breakfast classics such as french toast, porridge and poached eggs.

Sean's Panaroma

270 Campbell Parade, Bondi (9365 4924, seanspanaroma.co). Bus 380, 381, 382, X84. **Open** 6pm-late Wed, Thur; noon-late Fri-Sun. **Main courses** $32-$48. **Map** p105 (52) **Contemporary Australian**

Sean's Panaroma is pure Sydney – if you can handle forking out top dollar for three (sometimes two) elements on a plate (perhaps you're paying for what they have the good sense to leave off). Chef Sean Moran has a tendency to wax herbal at times, but his baseline is good-quality, local ingredients treated with integrity.

Sefa Kitchen

292 Bondi Road, Bondi (8068 6461, sefakitchen.com). Bus 333, 380, 381, 382. **Open** 6pm-late Tue-Sat; 9am-3pm Sun. **Main courses** $18-$36. **Map** p105 (53) **Middle Eastern**

In ex-Rockpool chef Simon Zalloua's hands, warm halloumi with a drizzle of honey and sprinkle of za'atar spice is delicate, simple and extremely tasty, and tender beef short ribs with Moroccan aubergine salad are short in length but not in flavour. The room is handsome, with the decor, artwork, dinnerware and tiling all working the Middle Eastern theme well.

Bars

Anchor

8 Campbell Parade, Bondi (8084 3145, anchorbarbondi.com). Bus 380, 381, 382, X84. **Open** 4.30pm-late Tue-Fri; 12.30pm-late Sat, Sun. **Map** p105 (54)

From the outside, it looks innocent enough – dark timber, a small bar, kitchen and a few tables – but this local has a tendency to incite unexpected good times.

Beach Road Hotel

71 Beach Road, Bondi (9130 7247, www.beachroadbondi.com.au). Bus 389, X89. **Open** noon-1am Mon-Sat; 11am-10pm Sun. **Map** p105 (55)

When you're the size of the Beach Road Hotel, you can be a little something to everyone: sports bar, gastropub, live music venue. On Wednesday nights Sosume presents a line-up of buzzy indie pop and EDM acts, and there are local hip-hop nights too.

Bondi Bowling Club

1 Warners Avenue, Bondi (9130 2383, www.bondibowlingclub.com). Bus 386, 387. **Open** 3-11pm Tue-Fri; noon-late Sat, Sun. **Map** p105 (56)

Outdoor drinking, great bistro food and barefoot bowling if you fancy it.

Coogee Bay Hotel

253 Coogee Bay Road, Coogee (9665 0000, www.coogeebayhotel.com.au). Bus 313, 314, 372, 373, M50, X73. **Open** 10am-late daily.

Being by the beach is all well and good, but once the sun goes down the surfboards, goggles and togs (that's Aussie for swimsuits) get put away and those sun-kissed bodies need a place to let off steam.

And that place is the Coogee Bay Hotel. Early in the week it's a quiet spot for an outdoor drink, but it turns into a bit of a zoo at the pointy end of the week, especially when Selina's nightclub opens on Saturday nights.

Coogee Pavilion

169 Dolphin Street, Coogee (9240 3000, merivale. com.au/coogeepavilion). Bus 313, 314, 372, 373, M50, X73. **Open** *7.30am-late daily. Rooftop bar* noon-midnight Wed-Sun.

Despite its multi-million dollar location right on the northern headland, the old Coogee Palace never even came close to living up to its potential as a destination pub – it got a C-minus at best. But with the opening of the Coogee Pavilion (and its Rooftop bar) we now have an A-grade beachside pub just a short bus ride from the city.

Neighbourhood

143 Curlewis Street, Bondi (9365 2872, neighbourhoodbondi.com.au). Bus 380, 381, 382, X84. **Open** *5.30-11pm Mon-Thur; 11am-11pm Fri; 9am-11pm Sat; 9am-10pm Sun.* **Map** p105 ⑤⑦

Think of Neighbourhood, the Bondi bar offering excellent cocktails in fairly modest surrounds, as a great bar in board shorts. It's all about spicy margaritas and cheeseburger toasties here.

Stuffed Beaver

271 Bondi Road, Bondi (9130 3002, stuffed beaver.com.au). Bus 333, 380, 381, 382. **Open** noon-late daily. **Map** p105 ⑤⑧

The innuendos are ubiquitous and never-ending at this sports-lovin' bar. Throw in boozy booze, sporty sports and loud music and you've got a recipe for a night of cheeky double entendres.

Shops & Services

Annex

Shop 8, 178 Campbell Parade, Bondi (9300 8888, www.theannex.com.au). Bus 380, 381, 382. **Open** 10am-6pm Mon-Wed, Fri-Sun; 10am-7pm Thur. **Map** p105 ⑤⑨ **Fashion**

Sandwiched between Aesop and Sonoma, this small menswear boutique is a dark and moody store that mirrors the loose-fitting, androgynous and industrial aesthetic of its own-brand clothing. It also stocks Chronicles of Never, Sunday Somewhere and the exclusive Mere Footwear collection developed by Manly designer James Noakes.

Aquabumps

151 Curlewis Street, Bondi (9130 7788, www.aquabumps.com). Bus 380, 381, 382, X84. **Open** 10am-6pm daily. **Map** p105 ⑥⓪ **Gallery**

It's hard not to get drawn into this long, narrow gallery shop just to take a look at photographer

Eugene Tan's latest stunning shots of Bondi Beach and its inhabitants. Prices start from $35 for a small, unframed print.

Camilla Frank's Beach House Store

132A Warners Avenue, Bondi (9130 1430). Bus 380, 381, 382, X84. **Open** 9.30am-5.30pm Mon-Fri; 10am-5pm Sat, Sun. **Map** p105 ⑥① **Fashion**

Camilla Frank's flagship store is a stone's throw from the sand and surf. Her flamboyant silky kaftans, displaying a bohemian collection of tribal patterns and bird-of-paradise colour palettes, line the beach-house boutique. It's like being in Camilla's closet.

Carousel

4/95 Gould Street, Bondi (0424 325 432, www. carouselbondi.com.au). Bus 380, 381, 382. **Open** 9.30am-6pm Mon-Wed, Fri, Sat; 9.30am-8pm Thur; 10am-8pm Sun. **Map** p105 ⑥② **Fashion**

This corner store on Gould Street has a striking collection of neon dresses. Bypass those and seek out the store's We Are Handsome swimwear at the back, or the brand's own hot label, Oscar the Third.

Earth Food Store

81A Gould Street, Bondi (9365 5098, www.earth foodstore.com.au). Bus 380, 381, 382. **Open** 7am-7pm daily. **Map** p105 ⑥③ **Food & drink**

Organic, gluten-free, kosher – they know their food at Earth Food Store. And for the past 20-odd years, this café-cum-grocer has been nourishing the health-conscious community with fresh, organic fruit and veg, a huge variety of almond milk, tribal energy bars and seeds you didn't know existed.

Gertrude & Alice

46 Hall Street, Bondi (9130 5155, www.gertrude andalice.com.au). Bus 389, X89. **Open** 7am-9.30pm daily. **Map** p105 ⑥④ **Books & music**

Some come for the 25,000 paperbacks stacked from floor to ceiling, some for the coffee. We come for both. Tilt your head to the ground for the $5 crates of children's lit and a dog-eared copy of *Don Quixote*.

Let's Go Surfing

128 Ramsgate Avenue, Bondi (9365 1800, www. letsgosurfing.com.au). Bus 380, 381, 382, X84. **Open** 9am-5pm daily. **Map** p105 ⑥⑤ **Surfing**

Let's Go Surfing offers hands-on lessons in small groups (usually a maximum of five people) to make sure you are getting a more personal approach to surfing; plus private lessons are available for individuals and families. Bonus for the gals: the school offers two-hour lessons designed specifically for females.

Tuchuzy

Shop 11, The Beach House, 90 Gould Street, Bondi (9365 7775, www.tuchuzy.com). Bus 380, 381, 382. **Open** 9am-6pm Mon-Wed; 9am-7pm Thur-Sat; 10am-6pm Sun. **Map** p105 ⑥⑥ **Fashion**

EXPLORE

Locals know they don't need to leave the hood to get their hands on the latest Bassike, Dion Lee, Jac+ Jack, Josh Goot, Rag & Bone and Willow collections – they've got them all here.

Yellow Bungalow

221 Bondi Road, Bondi (9365 3850, yellow bungalow.com.au). Bus 333, 380, 381, 382. **Open** 10am-5pm Mon-Fri; 10am-4pm Sat, Sun. **Map** p105 ⑰ **Homewares**

This year-old store has a bizarre and beautiful collection of modern Nordic designs and vintage oddities. Looking for a vintage grey TV chair? A concrete coffee table? A folding children's globe? You've come to the right place.

ELIZABETH BAY & RUSHCUTTERS BAY

On Sydney Harbour, **Elizabeth Bay** begins beyond Fitzroy Gardens at the southern end of Macleay Street. Gone are the backpackers and crowded streets: here, the calm, quiet roads are lined with residences that date from the 1930s. Worth a peek are **Elizabeth Bay House** and **Boomerang** (corner of Ithaca Road and Billyard Avenue), a 1930s Alhambra-esque fantasy that has been home to some of Sydney's highest flyers – and fastest fallers. On the edge of Elizabeth Bay is **Beare Park**, one of many little green edens that dot the harbourside.

The next inlet east is the romantically named Rushcutters Bay, so called because of the convicts who really did cut rushes here: two of them were the first Europeans to be killed by the local Aboriginal inhabitants, in May 1778. There's now a large and peaceful park lined by huge Moreton Bay figs. The bay is also home to the **Cruising Yacht Club of Australia (CYCA)** on New Beach Road: its marinas are a frenzy of activity every December when the club is the starting point for the Sydney Hobart Yacht Race. If you fancy trying your hand at some sailing yourself, or simply want to sit back, glass of wine in hand, while someone else steers you around the harbour, **Eastsail** (d'Albora Marinas, New Beach Road, 9327 1166, www. eastsail.com.au) will make life easy for you, with boats, yachts and crew for hire.

Sights & Museums

Elizabeth Bay House

7 Onslow Avenue, Elizabeth Bay (9356 3022, www.hht.net.au). Kings Cross rail or bus 311, 312. **Open** 9.30am-4pm Fri-Sun. **Admission** $4-$8. **Map** p96 B1 ⑱

No expense was spared on this handsome Greek Revival villa, designed by John Verge for NSW colonial secretary Alexander Macleay in 1839. Elizabeth Bay House boasted the first two flushing toilets in the country, the finest staircase in Australian colonial architecture, and breathtaking views of Elizabeth Bay and the harbour. The beautiful house (now run by the Historic Houses Trust) still breathes noblesse, wealth and good taste. Rooms are furnished as they would have been in its 1839-45 heyday.

Restaurants & Cafés

ACME

60 Bayswater Road, Rushcutters Bay (8068 0932, www.weareacme.com.au). Bus 324, 325, 326, 327. **Open** 5-10pm Tue-Fri; noon-4pm, 5-10pm Sat. **Main courses** $18-$24. **Map** p96 B2 ⑲ **Global**

We wouldn't call chef Mitch Orr's food straight-up Italian. He's been known to say he takes more influence from Chinatown than he does the Cinque Terre. So what the hell do you call a restaurant serving a menu of seven pastas, a baloney sandwich and cucumber spears pickled in gin? Italianese? Chitalian? It probably doesn't matter. The more important message here is that it's fun and good.

Michael Reid Gallery. See p112.

EXPLORE

Buon Ricordo

*108 Boundary Street, Rushcutters Bay
(9360 6729, www.buonricordo.com.au).
Bus 389.* **Open** noon-4pm, 6-11pm Tue-Sat.
Main courses $31.50-$62. **Map** p96 B3 **70**
Italian
Over the past 21 years, the walls of Buon Ricordo
– one of Sydney's most established Italian restaurants – have held some of Sydney's biggest hitters.
Everyone from Cate Blanchett to Packer family captain John Alexander has been spotted here, and it's
easy to see why: if you've got the moolah, you're in
for something exceptional.

Rushcutters Bay Kiosk

*New Beach Road, Rushcutters Bay (9331 3119,
rushcuttersbaytennis.com.au/kiosk). Bus 328.*
Open 7am-7.30pm daily. **Main courses** $8.50-
$16.50. **Map** p96 C1 **71** **Café**
Rushcutters Bay Kiosk is smack-bang in the middle
of Rushcutters Park, with tables and chairs set outside. The coffee is good and the menu is fresh and
simple. The kids can play and eat at the same time,
and you can just relax and enjoy the sun and the view
over the bay.

Bars

Gazebo

*2 Elizabeth Bay Road, Elizabeth Bay (9357 5333,
www.gazebowinegarden.com.au). Kings Cross rail.*
Open 3pm-midnight Mon-Thur; noon-midnight
Fri-Sun. **Map** p96 B1 **72**
The late twenty- and thirtysomething crowd at this
greenhouse-like bar lacks pretentiousness, the wine
list is well priced, and the 1980s classics over the ivy-
clad speakers are, well, music to our ears. Chicken
liver pâté and crisp squid are good options too.

Shops & Services

Bloodorange

*35 Elizabeth Bay Road, Elizabeth Bay (9357 2424,
www.bloodorange.com.au). Bus 311.* **Open** 11am-
4pm Mon, Sun; 11am-6pm Tue, Wed, Fri; 11am-7pm
Thur; 10am-5.30pm Sat. **Map** p96 B1 **73** **Fashion**
This small store bursts at the seams with stylishly pared-back offerings from A.P.C, Alexander
Wang and Filippa K. Well-priced goodies such as
K Jacques sandals and Lover swimsuits are the
answer to the blues.

EXPLORE

Murray Rose Pool.

Michael Reid Gallery

44 Roslyn Gardens, Elizabeth Bay (8353 3500,
www.michaelreid.com.au). Bus 324, 325, 326, 327.
Open 11am-5pm Wed-Sat. **Map** p96 B2 ❼ **Gallery**
This small commercial gallery specialises in art education and works by highly collectable Australian
artists. *Photo p110.*

DARLING POINT & DOUBLE BAY

Bordered by Rushcutters Bay Park to the west
and Edgecliff to the south, **Darling Point** is
another of Sydney's most salubrious areas,
with spectacular views as standard – the best
of these can be sampled free from **McKell
Park** at the northern tip of Darling Point Road.

Fancy a really remote picnic? **Clark Island**, a
small, 0.9-hectare nugget just off of Darling Point,
is a popular picnic spot and wedding destination,
but it was once a simple veggie patch. Lieutenant
Ralph Clark, who came over with the First Fleet,
had tried to set up a little vegetable garden on the
island in the 18th century, but other produce-
loving settlers kept pinching the fruits – and
veg – of his labour. There are no ferries to Clark
Island, but you can visit for a picnic ($7 landing
fee) – there are tables and toilets – or hire the
island exclusively for a function. You'll have to

take your own boat, or a water taxi, and book
ahead of time with the Sydney Harbour
National Park Information Centre (9253 0880).

The next suburb to the east is Double Bay
– or 'Double Pay', as it was unceremoniously
known. Not so long ago, this area was considered
something of a ghost town by most Sydneysiders.
Its verdant streets were peppered by high-priced
eateries, ladies who lunch and their cute dogs,
hoity-toity day spas and… well, that was about
it. No more. The more recent openings of bars
such as **Pelicano** and **Mrs Sippy** have come
on the heels of a welcome revival that's drawing
younger, hipper crowds to the area. And the faded
Ritz-Carlton hotel, once a favourite haunt of
celebrities, has reopened as the Intercontinental
Sydney Double Bay, drawing a whole new raft of
cool venues, including the **Stillery**, to the area.

New South Head Road is the main thoroughfare
through the Bay. The **Sheaf** hotel is a popular
watering hole with four bars catering to drinkers
of all ages and tastes. The bistro is exceptional,
and the busy beer garden is especially fun on
Sunday afternoons. The gorgeously curated
boutiques that put Double Bay on the map are
still here, peddling wares you won't find
anywhere else in the city. But it's the food and
drink options that are really expanding in this

sophisticated European-style village, and they're reason enough to head out to this pretty little area – along with the stunning purple blooms of the jacaranda trees that set Double Bay ablaze in springtime.

There are also two beaches at Double Bay, but only one of them is suitable for swimming. The beach next to Steyne Park sadly isn't, but it's a nice place to wander and is always bustling with yachties. On summer weekends, you can see the famous 18-foot sailing boats that compete in the annual Sydney Hobart Yacht Race rigging up and practising their moves, ready for battle.

If you do want to swim in Double Bay, continue east for ten minutes on New South Head Road to **Murray Rose Pool** (a shark-netted swimming area) and **Seven Shillings Beach**. This adorable little harbour beach is well hidden from the road, has a lovely garden setting and welcomes everyone. Behind the beach, next to Blackburn Gardens, is the attractive Woollahra municipal council building.

Sights & Museums

FREE Murray Rose Pool
New South Head Road, Double Bay (www. woollahra.nsw.gov.au). Bus 324, 325. **Open** 24hrs daily. **Admission** free. **Map** p97 G1 🄐
Murray Rose Pool can be found in Double Bay's Blackburn Cove and provides swimmers with a safe harbourside tidal enclosure. There's a wrap-around deck, which makes for a lovely walk and begs for a dive into the cool water, where you can swim to a floating pontoon that's perfect for sunbathing. Feeling peckish? Head to the kiosk on the hill, grab a snack and take in the views of Sydney's wondrous harbour while you eat.

Restaurants & Cafés

Chinta Kechil
342 New South Head Road, Double Bay (9327 8888). Edgecliff rail or bus 324, 325. **Open** 11.30am-9.45pm Mon-Sat. **Main courses** $17-$26. **Map** p97 F3 🄐 **Malaysian**
At this temple of Malay deliciousness, *char kway teow, nasi lemak* and *laksa* are all on the menu.

Little Jean
1 Kiaora Road, Double Bay (9328 0201, www.littlejean.com.au). Edgecliff rail or bus 324, 325. **Open** 6.30am-4pm Mon, Tue, Sun; 6.30am-late Wed-Sat. **Main courses** $16-$33. **Map** p97 F3 🄐 **Café**
Offerings at this light-filled café are fresh, seasonal and modern, with a focus on house-baked pastries and breads, local market produce and eggs sourced from Archerfield Farm in Richmond. Breakfast and lunch are served seven days a week. Dinner,

from Wednesday to Saturday, features the likes of seared herb-crusted tuna with cherry tomato, black garlic and yuzu; or confit duck leg with tamarind glaze, with herb mash and green beans.

Saké
Beneath the InterContinental Hotel, 33 Cross Street, Double Bay (8017 3104, www.sake restaurant.com.au/double-bay). Edgecliff rail or bus 324, 325. **Open** 11am-midnight daily. **Main courses** $31-$42. **Map** p97 F2 🄐 **Japanese**
Take a seat at the sushi counter and watch the masters do their thing on the white-hot charcoal at the custom-made robata grill. And whatever you do, don't leave without catching a glimpse of the highly dramatic dragon egg dessert – an ovum-shaped chocolate creation that arrives in a dramatic flourish, with white smoke billowing over the sides of the plate.

Bars

Mrs Sippy
37 Bay Street, Double Bay (9362 3321, mrs sippy.com.au). Edgecliff rail or bus 324, 325. **Open** noon-11pm Tue-Sat; 11am-6pm Sun. **Map** p97 F2 🄐
Since opening in late 2014, Mrs Sippy has become a buzzing little inn, serving brunch, lunch, dinner and cocktails to the well-dressed bar-hoppers of the Eastern Suburbs. The ten-page wine list is dominated by Australian varieties, and for those skinny Eastern Suburbs gals, there is a special selection of low-calorie, low-alcohol (and, frankly, skip-able) 'healthy' wines.

Pelicano
24 Bay Street, Double Bay (8021 4050, www. pelicanobar.com.au). Edgecliff rail or bus 324, 325. **Open** 6pm-midnight Wed, Thur; noon-2am Fri, Sat; noon-10pm Sun. **Map** p97 F2 🄐
You'll find Mediterranean fare in the company of the original Lichtensteins and Basquiats that decorate this 1960s, Harry Seidler-designed building. Drinks include cocktails such as the Duke – earl grey-infused gin, Fernet-Branca, mint, lemon juice and a sugar rim – plus a good selection of champagnes.

Sheaf
429 New South Head Road, Double Bay (9327 5877, thesheaf.com.au). Edgecliff rail or bus 324, 325. **Open** 10am-1am Mon-Wed; 10am-2am Thur-Sat; 11am-midnight Sun. **Map** p97 F3 🄐
From Wednesday to Saturday, the enormous beer garden gets packed with high heels, pressed collars, tanned limbs and white teeth, with DJs to keep energy levels high and fruity cocktails for sustenance. But come here on a Sunday afternoon and it's a different story. The dress code still leans towards preppy but it's a more relaxed vibe, with people catching up over fish and chips and sashimi salads, with their designer dogs at their feet.

EXPLORE

Stillery

InterContinental Hotel, 33 Cross Street, Double Bay (8388 8372, www.stillerydoublebay.com.au). Edgecliff rail or bus 324, 325. **Open** 7am-late daily. **Map** p97 F2 ⏱
At Stillery, the bar off the hotel lobby, you'll find more than 60 local and international gins and a list of house cocktails (make ours a Four Pillars gin martini with olives) alongside ciders, wines and more spirits.

Shops & Services

Christensen Copenhagen

2 Guilfoyle Avenue, Double Bay (9328 9755, www.christensencopenhagen.com.au). Edgecliff rail or bus 324, 325. **Open** 10am-6pm Mon-Fri; 10am-5pm Sat; noon-5pm Sun. **Map** p97 F2 ⏱
Fashion
This beautiful boutique stocks pieces from DVF by Diane Von Furstenberg, McQ Alexander McQueen, M Missoni, Herve Leger, Marcus Lupfer, By Malene Birger and Jonathan Saunders.

Harlequin Market

Shop 8, 20-26 Cross Street, Double Bay (9328 5430, www.harlequinmarket.com). Edgecliff rail or bus 324, 325. **Open** 10am-5pm Mon-Sat. **Map** p97 F2 ⏱ Fashion/accessories
You'll find it all here, from snakeskin gloves to cat-shaped bangles. A huge range of vintage gear and costume jewellery is available, along with a large range of designer clothes.

White Ivy

Shop 2, 365 New South Head Road, Double Bay (9326 1830, www.whiteivy.com.au). Edgecliff rail or bus 324, 325. **Open** 10am-5.40pm Mon-Fri; 10am-4pm Sat. **Map** p97 F3 ⏱ Accessories
One of Sydney's most exclusive lingerie stores, with a clientele list that has boasted Vivien Leigh and even Queen Elizabeth II, this Double Bay diamond is still a fairly well-kept secret and has been since it first opened its doors in the late 1940s.

POINT PIPER, ROSE BAY, VAUCLUSE & WATSONS BAY

These stunning, wealthy harbourside suburbs can easily be experienced on the cheap. By ferry from Circular Quay, you can take in Darling Point (*see p112*), Rose Bay and Watsons Bay – though not every ferry stops at every destination, and there's no service to Darling Point at weekends.

From Double Bay, small harbour beaches dot the shore up to **Point Piper**, which is full of stunning high-walled mansions. You can enjoy the multi-million-dollar views for free from the tiny **Duff Reserve** on the edge of the harbour – a good picnic spot if you can beat the crowds.

Stillery.

Lyne Park in **Rose Bay** is where the city's seaplanes land. You can watch them in more comfortable surroundings at the bayside restaurant **Catalina**. On the other side of New South Head Road is Woollahra Golf Course, which is very charitably open to the general public, unlike the snooty Royal Sydney Golf Course next door.

The streets from Rose Bay to **Vaucluse** feature yet more millionaire mansions: for the jealously inclined, the hidden jewels of the **Hermitage Foreshore Reserve** and an arm of **Sydney Harbour National Park**, which run around the peninsula, come as compensation. They are reached by a walking track that starts at Bayview Hill Road, below the imposing stone edifice of Rose Bay Convent, and offer fine views of the Harbour Bridge, as well as picnic spots aplenty and glimpses of the lifestyles of the rich and comfortable. The walk emerges at **Nielsen Park**, off Vaucluse Road, where there is an enclosed bay, Shark Beach – particularly beautiful on a summer evening.

Further along, on Wentworth Road, the estate that became **Vaucluse House** was bought by newspaperman and politician William Charles Wentworth in 1827. It's open to the public, along with its fine tearooms. Next to Vaucluse Bay, **Parsley Bay** is a lesser-known, verdant picnic spot popular with families.

EXPLORE

It is claimed that **Watsons Bay** was the country's first fishing village. Now, it's largely the province of the lovely and rather large **Watsons Bay Boutique Hotel**, which has stunning views back across the harbour to the city. Other epic harbour views can be taken in while walking north to the First Fleet landing spot at **Green Point Reserve** and on to **Camp Cove** and **Lady Bay** beaches, and the Hornby lighthouse on the tip of **South Head**.

On the other (ocean) side of the peninsula from Watsons Bay beach is the bite in the sheer cliffs that gives the **Gap** its name – and from which many have jumped to their doom. **Gap Park** is the start of a spectacular cliff walk that runs south back into Vaucluse.

Sights & Museums

FREE **Nielsen Park**

Greydiffe Avenue, Vaucluse (9337 5511, www.nationalparks.nsw.gov.au). Bus 325. **Open** 5am-10pm daily.
Generations of Sydneysiders have been flocking to Nielsen Park for family get-togethers since the early 1900s. They sit on Shark Beach or the grassy slopes behind, or climb the headlands either side for a great view across the harbour. With its abundance of shady trees, gentle waters, panoramic views and the

excellent Nielsen Park Café & Restaurant (9337 7333, www.nielsenpark.com.au), it's the perfect picnic spot.

FREE **Strickland House**

52 Vaucluse Road, Vaucluse (9337 5999, www.woollahra.nsw.gov.au). Bus 325. **Open** *Grounds* daylight hours. **Admission** free.
At the bottom of a tiny, steep laneway is a narrow park that runs around the coast from Rose Bay. Descend the stairs and, at the forked path, veer right to the discreet Hermit Bay and, further along, Tingara Beach. Keep on until you reach the 1850s harbourside villa grounds of Strickland House and a dazzling view of the harbour. Swim at Milk Beach or walk to Nielsen Park.

Vaucluse House

Vaucluse Park, Wentworth Road, Vaucluse (9388 7922, www.hht.net.au). Bus 325. **Open** *House* 9.30am-4pm Fri-Sun. *Grounds* 10am-5pm Tue-Sun. **Admission** $8; $4 reductions.
The oldest 'house museum' in Australia nestles prettily in a moated 19th-century estate, surrounded by ten hectares (28 acres) of prime land, with its own sheltered beach on Vaucluse Bay. From 1827 to 1853, and 1861 to 1862, this was the opulent home of William Charles Wentworth. The Historic Homes Trust has endeavoured to keep the place as it was when the Wentworths were in residence. *Photos pp116-117.*

FREE Watsons Bay Baths

Marine Parade, Watsons Bay. Bus 325.
Open 24 hrs daily. **Admission** free.
Near to other well-known swimming holes Parsley Bay and Nielson Park, Watsons Bay Baths offers a convenient spot to take a dip with a great view of the city.

Restaurants & Cafés

Catalina

Lyne Park, 1 Sunderland Avenue, Rose Bay (9371 0555, www.catalinarosebay.com.au). Bus 323, 324, 325. **Open** noon-10pm daily. **Main courses** $36-$49. **French/seafood**
With an amazing view over Rose Bay and an exceptional wine list, Catalina specialises in seafood but also does gutsy French classics such as pig's head with *sauce gribiche*. It also has its own sushi chef, who'll slice you a piece of fish faster than you can say *mushi mushi*.

Vaucluse House Tearooms Cafe

Wentworth Road, Vaucluse (9388 8188, www. vauclusehousetearooms.com.au). Bus 325. **Open** 10am-4.30pm Wed-Fri; 8am-4.30pm Sat, Sun. **Main courses** $24-$32. **Café**
Nestled in the 19th-century surrounds of historic Vaucluse House, the Tearooms present the perfect opportunity to enjoy lunch (say linguine with king prawns, cherry tomatoes, garlic, chilli and parsley) or an indulgent afternoon tea with a view of the estate's impeccable gardens and extensive lawns.

Bars

Watsons Bay Boutique Hotel

1 Military Road, Watsons Bay (9337 5444, watsonsbayhotel.com.au). Bus 325. **Open** 10am-midnight Mon-Sat; 10am-10pm Sun.
Get in early for prime seats by the bannister, which is all that separates you and the shoreline. Seafood plays a key role on the menu – and prices reflect this – but it means you can order spiced mulloway, miso-glazed salmon, lobster rolls, soft-shell crab sliders and smoked trout with your wine.

RANDWICK & KENSINGTON

There's lots to love in **Randwick**, home to a good number of historic buildings (be sure to check out the stunning, Gothic-style Nugal Hall), the University of New South Wales, the National Institute of Dramatic Art (alma mater of Nicole Kidman and Mel Gibson) and the **Royal Randwick Racecourse**, which buzzes in summer as the races and popular music festivals take root on its expansive grounds. And then there's the **Ritz** (*see p181*), a beloved art deco landmark cinema with an upstairs bar and an old-school vibe. There's a bevy of before- or after-screening meal options at one of the many restaurants along Belmore Road.

Anzac Parade is one long highway, but it will lead you to **Chairman Mao** in **Kensington** – a Chinese joint popular with locals, but also Sydney's chefs, including Neil Perry, Dan Hong

Vaucluse House. *See p115.*

and Morgan McGlone. Just up the road is the pinkest department store you'd ever hope to see, **Peter's of Kensington**. Also on Anzac Parade is the **Parade Theatre**, popular for musicals and dance.

Sights & Museums

Royal Randwick Racecourse
Alison Road, Randwick (9663 8400, www. australianturfclub.com.au). Bus 348, 370, 890, 891, M50. **Open** varies. **Admission** $20-$165.
The historic Royal Randwick Racecourse is the scene of exciting race meets throughout the year.

Restaurants & Cafés

Chairman Mao
189 Anzac Parade, Kensington (9697 9189). Anzac Parade buses. **Open** 5-10pm Mon, Wed, Thur; 5-11pm Fri, Sat. **Main courses** $17-$32. **Chinese**
This suburban Chinese restaurant is serving some of the most interesting food in town. It's the combination of textures that really gets us going: broad beans with pork mince has the chalky, squishy, chubby little beans coated in spicy, sweet, fried pork mince – the combination is pretty life-changing.

Four Frogs Creperie
30 St Pauls Street, Randwick (9398 3818, www.fourfrogs.com.au). Bus 314, 316, 317, 372, 373, 376, 377, 394, M50. **Open** 11am-9pm Mon-Wed; 7am-10.30pm Thur-Sat; 7am-9pm Sun. **Main courses** $11.50-$18. **Crêperie**
After great success in Mosman, the Four Frogs team opened up a second venue in Randwick so that the east could get in on their delicious crêpe action – in all its sweet and savoury goodness.
Other location 175 Avenue Road, Mosman (9960 1555).

Bars

Charing Cross Hotel
1 Carrington Road, Waverley (9389 3093, charing crosshotel.com.au). Bus 313, 314, 316, 317, 348, 353, 378. **Open** 10am-midnight Mon-Thur; 10am-2am Fri, Sat; 10am-10pm Sun.
In Waverley, to the north of Randwick, the newly renovated Charo has gone all out on the fancy gastropub front with an eco beach-house vibe: woven lampshades, cane and bentwood chairs, gleaming copper beer taps and a sandstone fireplace. Grab comfy chairs near the fireplace, and settle in.

Shops & Services

Peter's of Kensington
57 Anzac Parade, Kensington (9662 1099, www. petersofkensington.com.au). Anzac Parade buses. **Open** 9.30am-5.30pm Mon-Fri; 9.30am-5pm Sat. **Department store**
The famous can't-miss pink building stocks kitchen staples, stationery, travel items and even perfumes among other home-based knick knacks.

Inner West

Despite the usual attempts to gentrify the more fashionable suburbs in this underrated area, the Inner West remains a mix of grunge and glamour. At one extreme is the alternative hub of Newtown – home to goths, punks, musos, artists, writers, gays and lesbians – and the university student hangout of Glebe; at the other end, the cafés and restaurants of harbourside Balmain and trendy Leichhardt attract yuppie out-of-towners. Foodies also flock to Rozelle, Haberfield and Petersham to pick up delicacies from multicultural delis and bakeries.

Property prices are almost as high as in the Eastern Suburbs, and there's plenty of modernisation, but much of the Inner West likes to pretend it's still down-to-earth and 'real' by comparison. Overall, it holds on to its status as an intriguing bohemian village, but you have to look a bit harder than you once did to find the cheap, quirky gems that make it so special.

EXPLORE

Oscillate Wildly.

Don't Miss

1 Dawn Fraser Baths Take a dip at this harbourside pool (p120).

2 Adriano Zumbo Pastry perfection (p122).

3 Italian Forum Italian culture in downtown Leichhardt (p126).

4 Oscillate Wildly Go on a food safari at this tiny Newtown joint (p134).

5 Earl's Juke Joint Cool cocktails flow freely at this classically styled bar (p134).

EXPLORE

BALMAIN, BIRCHGROVE & ROZELLE

Snuggled in the Inner West's harbour, a six-minute ferry ride from Circular Quay or a 20-minute bus trip from the city centre, **Balmain** was settled in the 1830s by boat builders; today, it's increasingly home to on-the-make moneyed types. **Darling Street** – the spine of the area – starts at Balmain East Wharf and curves uphill past the sandstone Watch House (built in 1854, it was once the police lock-up and is now the headquarters of the Balmain Historical Society).

Further up in central Balmain, Darling Street is lined with countless food options interspersed with homewares and clothing shops, all winding along in a pleasingly low-key, two-storey way. A cluster of impressive Victorian buildings – the Post Office, Court House, Town Hall and Fire Station – are testament to Balmain's prosperity in the 1880s. **Balmain Market**, held on Saturdays in the grounds of St Andrew's Church, opposite Gladstone Park, is always worth a browse.

Pockets of urban cool include tiny pizza joint **Rosso Pomadoro** on Buchanan Street, while newcomer **Efendy**, just off the main drag, serves modern Turkish food in a contemporary setting. Cafés abound, too, including legendary brunch spot **Kazbah** dishing up Middle Eastern fare. Sydney's rock-star pastry chef is Adriano Zumbo – whose goal in life is to 'caramelise the nation' – and his original pâtisserie can be found in Balmain. After an appearance on the all-time ratings hit *MasterChef*, Zumbo sold 6,000 macaroons in a single day.

On the northern side of Darling Street is **Birchgrove**, flanked on three sides by water. Pubs are still the lifeblood of Birchgrove and Balmain, and the area has its fair share of old-man establishments. In fact, as you wander through the streets, it feels like there's one on just about every corner. But as the demographic becomes less blue collar and more blue Mercedes, a lot of the old watering holes have pulled up their socks and started catering to an upmarket crowd. And leading the pack is the **Riverview Hotel**, for years owned by legendary Olympic gold medal-winning swimmer Dawn Fraser, and now one of the suburbs' most-loved gentrified bloodhouses.

Fraser's name lives on at the carefully restored harbourside pool at the edge of charming **Elkington Park**. The park overlooks **Cockatoo Island**, the largest of the harbour's islands and a former prison and shipyard. Another park can be found at the end of Ballast Point Road. With its decorative petrol station pieces and stark flora, the new **Ballast Point Park** has divided opinion between eyesore and urban planning genius.

To reach **Rozelle**, simply continue west along Darling Street. Wander around its windy lanes and you'll quickly forget that you're in the big

smoke. Charmingly old-school pubs and welcoming cafés line the streets, with lovely old terraced houses overlooking the harbour.

Treasure-hunters can get lost among the stalls at the **Rozelle Markets** (Rozelle Public School, 9am-4pm Sat, Sun) or peruse one of the many vintage stores lining Victoria Street. Sydney's prettiest educational institution, **Sydney College of the Arts**, can also be found on Balmain Road, housed in what was once a psychiatric hospital. In February, a sea of hipsters floods on to the campus for the annual Laneway Festival, one of the country's leading music events.

Sights & Museums

FREE Constellation Playground
Manning Street, Rozelle (www.leichhardt.nsw. gov.au). Bus 440, 444, 445.
Stop off on your cycle, walk or jog around the Bay Run for a play break at this intergalactic-themed playground. There are tall hillside slides to climb up and slide down, large tripod swings big enough for the whole family to jump on and a super-fast flying fox. The playground is suitable for all ages and there are superb waterside views.

Dawn Fraser Baths
Elkington Park, Fitzroy Avenue, Balmain (9555 1903). Bus 434, 444, 445. **Open** *Mar, Oct, Nov* 7.15am-6.30pm daily. *Dec-Feb* 6.45am-7pm daily. Closed Apr-Sept. **Admission** $5; $1.60-$3.30 reductions; free under-5s.
Australia's oldest swimming club features a handsome tidal-flow saltwater pool. The adjacent kiosk serves snacks, ice-cream and coffee, and there are hot-water showers.

Restaurants & Cafés

Efendy
79 Elliott Street, Balmain (9810 5466, www.efendy. com.au). Bus 434, 444, 445. **Open** 5-10pm daily. **Main courses** $18-$45. **Turkish**
You can eat upstairs in elegant, white-cloth surroundings, but the real fun at Efendy is to be found in the downstairs diner. The walls are covered in Turkish comic-book posters, there's an open fire, and the Turkish-style grills are top-notch.

Kazbah
379 Darling Street, Balmain (9555 7067, www.kazbah.com.au). Bus 434, 444, 445. **Open** 8pm-late daily. **Main courses** $18-$22.50. **Middle Eastern**
Kazbah's hearty Middle Eastern fare will keep you firing on all cylinders. Highlights include a lamb tagine with Turkish toast, pitta bread and a squeeze of lemon, or *foul medammas* (a peasant dish of beans mashed with olive oil and spices).

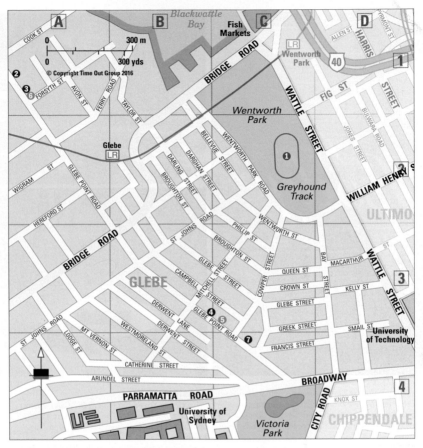

Rosso Pomadoro
*Shop 90-91, 24 Buchanan Street, Balmain
(9555 5924, www.rossopomodoro.com.au).
Bus 441, 442.* **Open** 6-10pm Tue-Sun.
Main courses $19-$25. **Pizza**
This tiny little shop is a loud and local slice, serving
traditional pizza from (gasp!) an electric oven. Be
warned: they've got some pretty strict topping rules
here. Try ordering a ham-and-pineapple or a half-
and-half and you'll be laughed out of Balmain.

Bars

Lodge Bar
*3/415 Darling Street, Balmain (8084 2502, www.
thelodgebar.com.au). Bus 434, 444, 445.* **Open**
4-10pm Tue, Wed; 4-11pm Thur-Sat; noon-5pm Sun.
In a suburb dedicated to the pub in all its guises, this
tiny, subterranean wine bar is going for a different
crowd. Blood-red velvet drapes are drawn aside

to let the light filter in through the hanging plants
that decorate the raised outdoor terrace. An evening
at the Lodge is all about enjoying wine and cheese in
elegant surroundings. *Photos p122.*

Riverview Hotel
*29 Birchgrove Road, Balmain (9810 1151, www.
theriverviewhotel.com.au). Bus 434, 444, 445.*
Open noon-midnight Mon-Sat; noon-10pm Sun.
At this spruced-up pub, the charcoal paint job and
glossy red doors are straight out of picture-book
England, and the warm glow from the fire draws
people in from the in-no-way-mean streets of the
Inner West. It's worth a visit for the winning Sunday
roast alone – $15 with all the trimmings.

Welcome Hotel
*91 Evans Street, Rozelle (9810 1323, www.the
welcomehotel.com). Bus 434, 441, 442, 444, 445.*
Open 11.30am-11.30pm Mon-Sat; noon-10pm Sun.

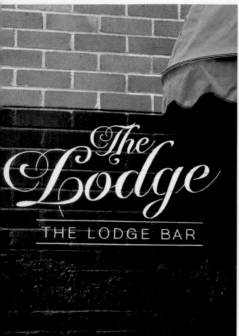

Lodge Bar. See p121.

A degree of extra care has been given to the food and drink menus here – the Italian-accented mains take pub food to new heights, and the craft beers on tap reflect the evolving boutique brewing scene in Sydney.

Wilhelmina's
332 Darling Street, Balmain (8068 8762, www.wilhelminas.com.au). Bus 434, 444, 445. **Open** 4pm-late Mon-Wed; noon-late Thur-Sun.
This little bar-restaurant is about snappy cocktails such as the Darling Street Derby – a riff on the classic cocktail involving a slug of bourbon, sweet vermouth and fresh mandarin juice. Bar snacks include the likes of pork croquettes – crunchy pucks of shredded, breaded and then deep-fried pork cheek.

Shops & Services

Adriano Zumbo
296 Darling Street, Balmain (9810 7318, www.adrianozumbo.com). Bus 433, 442, 444, 445. **Open** 8am-6pm Mon-Sat; 8am-4pm Sun.
Food & drink
The Zumbo legend was born in this sliver of a store on Darling Street. Buy a selection of macaroons and a coffee, then head to the nearby park to scoff them.

Bassike
361 Darling Street, Balmain (8457 6884, www. bassike.com). Bus 434, 444, 445. **Open** 10am-5pm Mon-Fri; 9.30am-5pm Sat; 11am-4pm Sun.
Fashion
Australian-made organic cotton label Bassike has racks of loose-fitting pants and luxurious tops. And as young hipsters and yummy mummies fill the cafés along the Balmain stretch of Darling Street, it now carries Birkenstocks and baby outfits too.

Belle Fleur
658 Darling Street, Rozelle (9810 2690, www.bellefleur.com.au). Bus 434, 444, 445. **Open** 9am-6pm Mon-Fri; 9am-5pm Sat; 10am-4pm Sun.* **Food & drink**
At this little corner of Bruges in Rozelle, the chocolatiers wield some serious skill in the window-display department, constructing elaborate sculptures of anything from a woodwork bench complete with chocolate mallets and chocolate wood shavings through to 6ft chocolate Christmas trees.

Mint Condition
134 Victoria Road, Rozelle (www.mintcondition vintagefashionboutique.com.au). Bus 500, 501,

502, 504, 505, 506, 507, 508, 510, 515, 518.
Open 11am-5pm Wed-Fri; 10am-5pm Sat;
10am-4pm Sun. **Fashion/accessories**
Stepping into this vintage store is like walking on to
the set of *Mad Men*. There are Jackie Onassis pill-
box hats, Audrey Hepburn full-skirt frocks and silk
scarves that deserve a spin around the room.

GLEBE

There was a time when **Glebe** felt like little more
than the backyard of some shared student digs:
all ramshackle and filled with cheap takeaway
joints. But lately, the suburb once owned by the
Anglican church has been staking its claim as a
place to be reckoned with. There are cute new bars
and cafés, such as the **Little Guy** and **Madame
Frou Frou**, both on and off the main drag of
Glebe Point Road.

Of course, not everything's changing: you can
still visit one of the city's best bookshops in long-
surviving **Gleebooks** or watch dogs chase
things at **Wentworth Park**. And a walk through
Sydney University, just beyond Victoria Park
on City Road, is as pretty a stroll as you'll find this
end of town. For a feel of what Sydney used to be

like before the money took over, visit
Wentworth Park Greyhound Track,
Sydney's premier dog-racing venue, which
has meets every Monday and Saturday night.
It's a great night out – there are bars and a
bistro, and the betting ring is about the only
place where you'll still see pork-pie hats worn
without a trace of irony.

At the Rozelle Bay end of Glebe Point Road
is the large twin expanse of **Jubilee Park**
and **Bicentennial Park**. The area has
undergone a major facelift to become a
pleasantly marshy play zone. **Pirrama Park**
is the latest sustainable green space built along
this waterfront, with $20 million spent in 2010
on reworking an old Water Police site into
playgrounds, native plantings, walking trails
and community squares, much of it themed
in tribute to the peninsula's original Gadigal
inhabitants and the stevedores who toiled here
in the 19th century.

Well-served by the light rail, and with a buzzy,
up-and-coming vibe, Glebe should definitely
be on your Sydney hit list. If you're in town in
November, look out for the one-day Glebe Street
Fair, the city's longest-running street party.

Sights & Museums

Wentworth Park Greyhound Track
Wentworth Park Road (8587 1203, www. wentworthpark.com.au). Wentworth Park light rail. **Open** varies. **Admission** $6; free under-18s. **Map** p121 C2 **1**
Wentworth Park has been inner Sydney's home of racing since way back in 1938. Place your bets, buy your drinks and get yourself ready for a barking good time at a true inner-city institution.

Restaurants & Cafés

Glebe Point Diner
407 Glebe Point Road (9660 2646, www.glebe pointdiner.com.au). Bus 431. **Open** 6pm-late Mon-Thur; noon-2.30pm, 6pm-late Fri, Sat; noon-2.30pm Sun. **Main courses** $28-$38. **Map** p121 A1 **2**
Contemporary Australian
GPD's success is based around locally sourced ingredients cooked with great skill. Tuck into the likes of Ulladulla yellowfin tuna with ratatouille or Rangers Valley beef with aubergine, mushrooms, celeriac purée and pecorino. The menu changes daily and the wine list is local with an eye to the biodynamic.

Madame Frou Frou
381 Glebe Point Road (no phone). Bus 431. **Open** 7am-5pm daily. **Main courses** $14-$20. **Map** p121 A1 **3** **Café**
It's the simple things that make this place: pastries from Black Star, Victoire bread for the toast and sandwiches, and coffee from Melbourne star roasters St Ali. The layout is simple too: old cinema seats line the walls, which are decorated with block-mounted posters of magicians from the 1920s and '30s. Service is super-friendly.

Thievery
91 Glebe Point Road (8283 1329, thethievery. com.au). Bus 431. **Open** 6-11pm Tue-Thur; 6pm-midnight Fri; 11am-3pm, 6pm-midnight Sat. **Small plates** $9-$18. **Map** p121 B3 **4** **Lebanese**
They're mixing things up just right at this new Lebanese eaterie. A tall dome of creamy houmous is doused with nutty, paprika-tinted melted butter, and smoky baba ganoush is served with a generous folding of crunchy pine nuts and big dollops of tart sheep's yoghurt. The kebabs are superb too: try the wagyu beef shawarma with harissa, pickled chilli and smoked garlic sauce. The Lebanese-themed cocktails are as good as the food.

EXPLORE

Bars

Little Guy

87 Glebe Point Road (thelittleguy.com.au). Bus 431.
Open 4pm-midnight Mon-Fri; 1pm-midnight Sat;
3-10pm Sun. **Map** p121 C3 ❺

Duck in for a barrel-aged negroni and a bowl of
popcorn at this quaint neighbourhood bar. There's
free live music every Sunday afternoon, and a raft of
craft beers on tap and by the bottle.

Timbah

375 Glebe Point Road (9571 7005). Bus 431.
Open 4-9pm Tue-Thur; 4pm-midnight Fri;
2pm-midnight Sat; 2-8pm Sun. **Map** p121 A1 ❻

Early in the week, it's pretty easy to nab a table and
fill it with great wine and snacks (deep-fried pork
gyoza or Turkish-style pizza with aubergine and
lots of cheese). Weekends see the 'Bah spilling over,
while Johnny Cash and Blondie fill the air.

Shops & Services

Gleebooks

49 Glebe Point Road (9660 2333, www.gleebooks.
com.au). Bus 431. **Open** 9am-7pm Mon-Wed,
Sun; 9am-9pm Thur-Sat. **Map** p121 C4 ❼

Books & music
Frequently named the best independent bookshop
in Sydney, Gleebooks stocks a wonderfully diverse
range of fiction and non-fiction, and hosts talks from
local and international writers.

ANNANDALE & LEICHHARDT

Annandale was once earmarked as a model
township, hence the look of its main thoroughfare:
broad, tree-lined Johnston Street (named after
Lieutenant George Johnston, the first man to step
ashore from the First Fleet in 1788 – albeit on the
back of a convict). Located between Glebe and
Leichhardt, it soon became a predominantly
working-class district. These days, it's gradually
upping its foodie quotient on Booth Street to cope
with the growing influx of residents decamping
from the east. There's a strong café culture – try
Revolver in north Annandale – and plenty of
local colour. For instance, did you know that Mark
Twain spent a stretch here? He was hosted by
Sir Henry Parkes.

Further west still lies **Leichhardt**. Formerly
known as the 'Little Italy' of the west, it's long

Thievery.

outgrown that title. The main thoroughfare, Norton Street, now pumps with a whole new nightlife vibe, although young, slick Italians still have a firm grip on the territory. A cluster of Australian heritage buildings on Norton Street includes the two-storey **Leichhardt Town Hall**, built in 1888, which often hosts visiting art exhibitions. But it's the **Palace Norton Street Cinema** (*see p184*), a four-screen arthouse specialist, that pulls in the crowds. Check out the **Italian Forum** for a right-there-in-Italy feel (of a semi-genuine nature), and get down with old Med boys at **Bar Italia** to snap up cheap focaccia, great ice-cream and hearty pasta dishes.

Sights & Museums

FREE Italian Forum

23 Norton Street, Leichhardt (9518 3396, www. italianforum.com.au). Parramatta Road buses. **Open** 10am-6pm Mon-Wed; 10am-9pm Thur; 10am-8pm Fri; 10am-6pm Sat, Sun. **Admission** free.
The Forum is a cultural centre with a bona fide Italian piazza in downtown Leichhardt, including restaurants, cafés and gift shops.

Restaurants & Cafés

Bar Italia

169 Norton Street, Leichhardt (9560 9981). Parramatta Road buses. **Open** 7am-11pm daily. **Main courses** $6.50-$12. **Italian**
Bar Italia is one of the busiest places to eat in Leichhardt, with queues out the door and a room full of hungry punters squished together on benches. You can eat here for less than $15 (baked cannelloni and other Italian classics), there's excellent *gelati* for dessert, and if your date isn't up to much conversation, it's loud enough to hide any awkward silences.

Braza

13 Norton Street, Leichhardt (9572 7921). Parramatta Road buses. **Open** 6pm-midnight Mon-Wed; noon-3.30pm, 6pm-midnight Thur-Sun. **Churrasco** $38-$49. **Brazilian**
This Brazilian *churrascaria* is good-value if you're hungry enough: $38 gets you all the meat you can eat plus all sorts of sides, such as cassava and sticky banana fritters. Drinks-wise, there are plenty of cocktails and bottled beers, including 750ml long-necks – something you very rarely see in restaurants.

Jasmin1

116 Marion Street, Leichhardt (8084 2692, www.jasmin1leichhardt.com.au). Bus 370, 436, 438, 439, 445. **Open** noon-10.30pm daily. **Main courses** $16-$18. **Lebanese**
There was a time when you'd have to schlep out to Lakemba for a plate of Jasmin's falafels, but now they've opened a branch in Leichhardt. As well as

the crisp pucks of spiced chickpea and coriander, there's outstanding baba ganoush – an incredibly smoky aubergine dip that's perfect with slices of spiced grilled lamb.

Revolver

291 Annandale Street, Annandale (9555 4727). Bus 433. **Open** 8am-4pm daily. **Main courses** $9.50-$18. **Café**
Formerly an old corner store, this hidden gem deep in the heart of North Annandale is now full of street-art-inspired screens mixed with Italian-style frescoes and antique shelving (complete with trundling library ladder). The big breakfast is a thing of wonder: house-made baked beans, mushrooms, bacon and pork sausage topped with two baked eggs, served in a cast-iron pan. Lunch options include cheeseburgers and old-fashioned milkshakes, and Revolver brews an excellent cup of coffee too. Just don't count on getting a seat at the weekend.

Bars

Empire

103A Parramatta Road, Annandale (9557 1701, www.empirehotelannandale.com.au). Parramatta Road buses. **Open** 11am-midnight Mon-Fri; 10am-midnight Sat; noon-10pm Sun.
With a working fireplace, frosted glass, art deco light fixtures, velvet chaises longues and high-backed leather armchairs, Empire feels like it was made for the consumption of craft beer. The taps change weekly, and if the beers aren't calling your name, the bistro does two-for-one specials on Sunday and Monday nights. Bargain.

Royal

156 Norton Street, Leichhardt (9569 2638, www. royalhotelleichhardt.com.au). Parramatta Road buses. **Open** 10am-1am Mon-Thur; 10am-3am Fri, Sat; 10am-midnight Sun.
Upstairs at the Royal, there's a 1950s botanical theme, with bright fern-print carpet, hanging plants and big arched windows that let the afternoon sun pour in. The bartenders will whip you up a civilised cocktail such as the Hendrick's Tea Cup with rose-and-apple tea and cucumber. Downstairs, you'll find more traditional pub vibes, with crooner tunes and a good selection of tap beers.

Shops & Services

Vintage Record

31A Parramatta Road, Annandale (9550 4667, www.thevintagerecord.com). Parramatta Road buses. **Open** 11am-6pm Mon-Fri; 11am-5pm Sat, Sun. **Books & music**
The warm tones of vinyl are making a comeback, and this is a great place to start or refresh your collection. The Vintage Record covers all genres, including rock, classical, soul and even comedy.

HABERFIELD, ASHFIELD & SUMMER HILL

Situated to the west of Leichhardt, **Haberfield** is the more recently discovered Little Italy of the west – 'little' being the operative word. Yet despite its diminutive size, it remains the true heartland of homeland authenticity – just check out the queue at **A & P Pasticceria**.

Nearby **Summer Hill** is a suburb with a lot of love to give. It's home to one of the world's most awesome old-school milk bars (the Rio on Smith Street has been delighting the Inner West since 1952), as well as foodie fave the **Drugstore**. In need of a drink? Head for the **Temperance Society**. You'll find it in an ancient row of Smith Street shopfronts with original leadlight windows and auburn tiles, and even on a Monday night you can hardly find an indoor perch – there are plenty of night owls in this leafy suburb keen for after-hours cavorting close to home.

Slightly further afield, **Ashfield** is known for its shallot pancakes, soup-filled dumplings and cheap butchers, but first of all, sample a coffee at beautiful, bleached-wood café **Excelsior Jones**.

Restaurants & Cafés

A & P Pasticceria

119 Ramsay Street, Haberfield (9797 0001). Bus 436, 438, 439, L38. **Open** from 9am daily. **Café** The queue snakes around the tables and customers ogle the glass cabinets full of pastries, *biscotti* and other baked goods. Indulge in a fat *cannoli* stuffed with chocolate, vanilla or custard, or chocolate-dipped, jam-filled biscuits. The *pasticceria* also does a great line in *gelati*, and the tiramisu cake is stunning.

EXPLORE

Royal.

Cremeria De Luca
84 Ramsay Road, Five Dock (0498 656 088,
www.cremeria-deluca.com). Bus 415, 438, 439,
460, 492, L38, L39. **Open** 9am-10pm Tue-
Thur; 9am-11pm Fri, Sat; 9am-6pm Sun.
Ice-cream
Cremeria De Luca serves Sydney's best gelato and it's
got the pedigree to prove it – the De Luca family has
been making ice-cream since 1937. For the ultimate
indulgence, order the gelato burger: two scoops of
ice-cream and whipped cream sandwiched in a brioche bun spread with Nutella. Definitely one to eat
sitting down.

Drugstore
140 Smith Street, Summer Hill (no phone).
Summer Hill rail. **Open** 5am-noon daily.
Main courses $12-$20. **Café**
Drugstore has stripped back your morning ritual to
bare bones. They do coffee and they do it very well,
pumping out punchy Campos Dark City shots from
a shining La Marzocco machine – it's worth queuing
for. Got time for a sit-down? You can nestle into the
squashy, well-worn vinyl sofa, pull up an old-school
chair to one of the Formica tables or perch at the
counter and study the swathe of tour posters lining
the walls.

Excelsior Jones
139A Queen Street, Ashfield (9799 3240,
www.excelsiorjones.com). Bus 418. **Open**
7.30am-4pm Mon-Fri; 8am-4pm Sat, Sun.
Main courses $10-$16. **Café**

Head to this Ashfield café for the superb all-day
breakfast menu. Highlights include pork-hock hash
– shreds of smoky meat mixed with fried buckwheat
and slivers of shallot, topped off with a perfectly
poached egg.

Bars

Temperance Society
122 Smith Street, Summer Hill (8068 5680,
www.facebook.com/thetemperancesocietybar).
Summer Hill rail. **Open** 4-11pm Mon-Thur;
noon-midnight Fri, Sat; noon-10pm Sun.
The Temperance Society is a welcoming small bar
in Summer Hill. It's a simple operation – you can get
Young Henrys cider, Rocks lager or Ironbridge ale
in a $5 pot, a $10 pint or a $17 jug. There are plenty
of Sydney wine bars where ten bucks will barely
buy you a scoop of olives, so hurry up and order a
bowl of Sicilians for $3.50 before they go and adjust
their pricing.

Shops & Services

Rino Saffioti's Chocolate Shop
129 Ramsay Street, Haberfield (9716 7671).
Bus 415, 438, 439, 460, 492, L38, L39.
Open 8am-5pm Mon-Sat. **Food & drink**
This divine chocolate shop stocks all manner of
treats: dark chocolate baubles filled with red wine
liqueur, white chocolate topped with pink pepper-
corns with a spicy tahini filling, and glossy chocolate
fingers stuffed with gianduja.

St Nicholas, Marrickville.

MARRICKVILLE & PETERSHAM

Once upon a time, all the cool kids lived in
Newtown. Then came Surry Hills. Now, well,
the coolest kids all live in Marrickville – a suburb
once best known for its mall. No more: today, this
spread-out 'burb seven kilometres south of the
CBD is packed with a multicultural mix of
residents, students and arty types chasing the
affordable rents. Make your first port of call
Cornersmith for a locally sourced breakfast.
The **Marrickville Markets** are a Sunday
essential for fruit and veg, tzatziki-covered corn
fritters and vintage kimonos. There's excellent,
cheap Vietnamese food to be found here too. Due
to licensing restrictions in the CBD, many of
Sydney's best club promoters are heading west
to put on all-night parties at unexpected venues
such as the **Marrickville Bowling Club** and
more mainstream options such as the **Factory
Theatre**. Keep you ears peeled in the suburb's
backstreets and you might even be lucky enough
to come across an underground warehouse party.

Petersham lies north-west of Enmore; if
you're driving, turn right off Enmore Road into
Stanmore Road, which becomes New Canterbury
Road, the main thoroughfare. Until very recently,
the neighbourhood was home to the **Oxford
Tavern** that hulks at its gateway, flashing
'24-hour lingerie waitresses' in screaming neon.
Now, the tavern pulls in crowds with its shirt on
– but it's still a loose-collar kind of joint where
good times are the whole point. A fleet of

excellent traditional Portuguese restaurants and
pâtisseries line the few blocks of New Canterbury
Road from Audley Street to West Street, and
crowds flock from all over Sydney to sample
the butterflied, grilled and spiced chicken on
offer at **Petersham Charcoal Chicken**.

Restaurants & Cafés

Bourke Street Bakery

2 Mitchell Street, Marrickville (9569 3225).
Bus 423, 426, M30. **Open** 7am-4pm Mon-Fri;
8am-4pm Sat, Sun. **Café**
Get your hands on the famous pork-and-fennel
sausage rolls and crusty sourdough loaves without
having to brave the hungry crowds at the original
outpost in Surry Hills.
Other locations throughout the city.

Cornersmith

314 Illawarra Road, Marrickville (8065 0844,
www.cornersmith.com.au). Marrickville rail.
Open 6.30am-3.30pm Mon-Wed; 6.30am-3.30pm,
5.30pm-late Thur, Fri; 7.30am-3.30pm, 5.30pm-
late Sat, Sun. **Main courses** $9-$18. **Café**
The menu changes according to what's available that
week at this buzzy ethical café, but operates within a
loose framework of morning toasts, muesli, eggs and
lunchtime plates. You may not be able to predict the
dishes on any given day, but rest assured that it'll be
top-notch. Cornersmith has also started serving dinner a few nights a week, with a focus on locality, sea-
sonality and preserved fruit and veg. The food from

EXPLORE

Stead House, Marrickville.

chef Maxim Roberts is unpretentious but thoughtful, and the whole place has a welcoming vibe.

Daisy's Milkbar
340 Stanmore Road, Petersham (8065 3466, daisysmilkbar.com). Petersham rail. **Open** 7am-3pm Mon-Fri; 8am-3pm Sat, Sun. **Main courses** $8-$16. **Café**
This is a contender for the cutest little café and milk bar ever. Booth seating out the back, milkshakes out the front, and sweets as far as the eye can see – what's not to love? The coffee, by Double Roasters, pride of Marrickville, is definitely worth a nudge. And savouries-wise, the meatball sandwich is a rustic two-handed number on herbed bread, covered in melted parmesan and roasted capsicum.

Marrickville Pork Roll
236A Illawarra Road, Marrickville (0411 167 169). Marrickville rail. **Open** 7am-6pm daily. **Rolls** from $4. **Vietnamese**
Banh mi are almost a Sydney religion, and here they make them cheap and crunchy. This might just be the best bargain lunch in town.

Petersham Charcoal Chicken
98 New Canterbury Road, Petersham (9560 2369). Petersham rail. **Open** 9am-9pm daily. **Main courses** $17-$20. **Grill**
Giant hot pits of coal, huge braziers, iron cages filled with meat and queues out the door for the *frango de churrasco* (barbecued chicken) are what you'll find here. It doesn't look like much outside or in, but head out the back to the seated area and you'll find beers in the fridge and house-made hot sauce in squeezy bottles – perfect on the fried pork sandwich. The chicken is the main event here, though: butterflied, grilled and spiced with plenty of hot sauce.

Bars

Batch Brewing Co
44 Sydenham Road, Marrickville (batchbrewingco. com.au). Bus 418, 425. **Open** 2-8pm Thur; noon-8pm Fri-Sun.
This bare-bones company in Marrickville has a brewery operation out the back and a tasting bar at the front. Depending on when you visit, they might have a milk stout made with Campos coffee for an extra kick, or perhaps a few bottles of Christmas in July porter brewed with star anise, allspice, vanilla and ginger.

Camelot Lounge
103 Railway Parade (entrance at 19 Marrickville Road), Marrickville (9550 3777, www.camelot lounge.com). Sydenham rail. **Open** varies.
This artist-curated space houses a main music stage marked by a 1930s German grand piano that hosts big band, gypsy jazz, funk, gospel, reggae and world music. There's also a 'sideshow' stage for smaller acts and performances.

Henson.

Henson

91 Illawarra Road, Marrickville (9569 5858, www.thehenson.com.au). Bus 423, 426, M30. **Open** 11am-midnight Mon-Sat; 11am-10pm Sun.

For many years, the Henson Park Hotel was an abandoned, rotting shell of a pub hidden in the backstreets of Marrickville. But a massive revamp means it's now one of the most family-friendly watering holes in the Inner West. Craft beers, great tunes and good pub food – if we could live in the Henson, we would.

Oxford Tavern

1 New Canterbury Road, Petersham (8019 9351, theoxfordtavern.com.au). Petersham rail. **Open** noon-midnight Mon-Thur; noon-3am Fri, Sat; noon-10pm Sun.

There may be a lot less jelly and nudity all round at the Oxford Tavern, but the spirit of the former topless bar lingers in the poles built into the bar and the Jelly Wrestle shared dessert of jelly, ice-cream, waffles and sundae trimmings that you eat with gloved hands.

Shops & Services

Addison Road Centre

142 Addison Road, Marrickville (9569 7633, www.arcco.org.au). Bus 428. **Market**

This laid-back community hub is home to the weekly Marrickville Market on Sundays, as well as the Addison Galleries, Reverse Garbage, Aerialize, Sidetrack Theatre and many, many more creative and inventive types.

NEWTOWN, ERSKINEVILLE & ENMORE

You can choke it with renovators and young families, you can tart up the rough edges with smart shops, but **Newtown** somehow manages to remain stubbornly and comfortably down-at-heel, like an old drag queen in her glitter rags. Lying to the south of Annandale and Glebe, Newtown has it all: few other areas accommodate so many subcultures – grungy students from the nearby University of Sydney, young professional couples, goths, spiky punks, gays and lesbians – and all in apparent harmony. See the community in all its glory during the Newtown Festival in November.

In Newtown, some things change while others stay very much the same. The backstreets and courtyards are still perfumed by the rich, ripe smell of reefers; fluoro dreads and stacked boots still pass down streets lined with fair-to-average Thai food. But there's been a tectonic shift on the Newtown plate. Besides being Sydney's premier alt-suburb, it's become a town of small bars, craft

EXPLORE

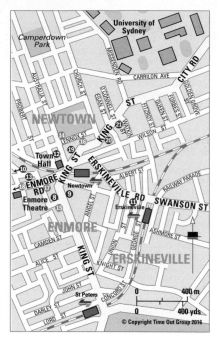

beers, cocktails and excellent coffee. It's also great for music – notably the **Enmore Theatre** (*see p206*) and jazz stronghold the **Vanguard** (*see p210*). The soundtrack on offer at the **Courthouse** is worth a listen too.

You'll have no trouble finding somewhere to linger over a cappuccino – every second shopfront houses a café, and new places seem to open every week. Head to **Black Star Pastry** for a macaroon or individual tarte tatin with your coffee. Next door, tiny, wacky **Oscillate Wildly** will take you through a progressive dinner degustation that'll rock your world. **Bloodwood** burns brightest on a warm night when you can bag a seat on the open balcony and gorge on fried chicken wings, garlic prawns and polenta chips.

While in Newtown, it's also worth ducking off King Street to the two 'E' suburbs, **Erskineville** and **Enmore**. To reach the former – which is rapidly expanding into a crowd-puller in its own right – turn off King Street at Erskineville Road and keep walking. You may recognise the landmark art deco **Imperial Hotel** from *Priscilla, Queen of the Desert*. After lunch at **Fleetwood Macchiato**, walk it off along the backstreets as you marvel at the adorable terraced homes and miners' cottages that lend the suburb its inimitable charm.

To get to Enmore, return to Newtown and turn off King Street onto Enmore Road. Tucked away

between Newtown, Stanmore and Marrickville, Enmore has long been overshadowed by vibrant King Street up the road: but no more. Bustling Enmore Road and the surrounding streets are home to many hidden gems; try Lebanese treats at **Emma's Snack Bar** or the new **Stinking Bishops** for a plate of deliciously smelly cheese. Perhaps one of the oddest yet coolest additions to the Sydney nightlife scene is **Slyfox**; the music varies nightly, alternating between house, electro, techno, drum 'n' bass, rock and goth, while Wednesday brings Sydney's lesbians out in force for the weekly Birdcage night.

Restaurants & Cafés

Bach Eatery

399 King Street, Newtown (8084 4093, bach eatery.com.au). Newtown rail. **Open** 5pm-late Wed-Fri; noon-late Sat, Sun. **Main courses** $18-$24. **Map** p132 ❽ **New Zealand**
Despite being located on one of the Inner West's most hectic main drags, Bach's vibe transports you to a world far removed from the noise outside. The name refers to 'baches', which is what New Zealanders call holiday homes and beach houses. As such, there's a surfboard propped up against the wall and low-key tunes on the stereo. Food-wise, former Bistro Moncur executive chef Darrien Potaka (a Kiwi himself), dishes up classy cooking: grain-fed steak with crispy fried onions, smoky braised lettuce and a smooth caramelised onion purée is a triumph of textures.

Bloodwood

416 King Street, Newtown (9557 7699, www. bloodwoodnewtown.com). Newtown rail. **Open** 5pm-late Mon-Fri; noon-3pm, 5pm-late Sat, Sun. **Main courses** $15-$32. **Map** p132 ❾ **Contemporary Australian**
Bridging the gap between cheap Thai food and Oscillate Wildly's multi-course molecular journey, Bloodwood is a very welcome addition to the area. It's a neighbourhood restaurant bashing out tapas-style plates such as chickpea pancakes with feta, quinoa and toasted pumpkin seeds.

Emma's Snack Bar

59 Liberty Street, Enmore (9550 3458, www. facebook.com/emmassnackbar). Bus 355, 423, 426, 428, M30. **Open** 6pm-late Tue-Sat. **Main courses** $10-$18. **Map** p132 ❿ **Lebanese**
At this smart-casual Lebanese diner, don't miss the smoky, feather-light baba ganoush. Or the Moorish chicken – marinated morsels of meat in Lebanese bread with tangy spices and shaved red onion. To drink, a frosty bottle of 961 pale ale or an Almaza pils – or take advantage of the BYO wine option.

Fleetwood Macchiato

43 Erskineville Road, Erskineville (9557 9291, fleetwoodmacchiato.tumblr.com). Erskineville rail.

SMALL IS BEAUTIFUL

Drink like an Inner Westie at one of these 'small bars'.

Known locally as 'small bars', pint-sized independent bars are the beating heart of Sydney's bar scene… and nowhere mixes indie and booze quite like the Inner West.

Glebe's very first small bar is still going strong, serving locals all through the week and into the night. **Timbah's** (*see p125*) isn't exactly cheap (around $12 a glass for the non-house gear), but if you dig through the list you'll find a few $25 quaffers by the bottle.

Also in Glebe is the **Little Guy** (*see p125*), a pretty, light space filled with ferns and big comfortable bar stools. As well as craft beers, there's a short cocktail list including a take on a tommy's margarita (they're calling it Don's Agave Margarita) and a Jamaican Me Crazy – with rum, vanilla and apple juice. Nice.

The walls of the **Hive Bar** (93 Erskineville Road, 9519 9911, www.thehivebar.net) in Erskineville are covered in event posters, stencils and murals by local artists, and record-sleeve menus boast a long list of local ales and lagers, including the St Peters Cinnamon Girl Spiced Ale, Doss Blockos Pale Lager, White Rabbit and Mountian Goat, as well as Boston's Mill Pale Ale and the citrusy 4 Pines Kolsch.

Balmain is shrugging off the Bugaboo image as more small bars open around the blue-chip Inner West suburb. The **Lodge Bar** (*see p121*) is a pocket-sized watering hole where the decor is part bordello and part terrarium, while the

Cottage (342 Darling Street, 8084 8185, thecottagebalmain.com.au) is a restaurant and bar offering a casual place to drink and dine in the heart of Darling Street.

Over in Newtown is the **Midnight Special** (*see p135*). We don't really want to make too much of this place, mainly because it's only got a 50-person capacity and, frankly, we don't want any more competition to get in. So let's emphasise that it's only open until midnight. Awesome drinks, delicious snacks, comfy booths in the back, friendly staff and excellent music provide absolutely no reason for you to go. Seriously.

Staying in Newtown, the cocktail list is short, sweet and simple (boody marys, manhattans, martinis) at **Bloodwood** (*see p132*), though the wine list needs depth. Still, it's reasonably priced and it's not that much of a mission digging up something you'll be happy drinking. We have a soft spot for another King Street bar, **Corridor** (no.153, 0405 671 002, www.corridorbar.com.au). What we like about the folks at Corridor is that they're friendly and down to earth. They're just doing what they do – and they're doing it well: long necks for $12, simple mixers (get them to do you a ginger beer with rum and limes), local wines by the glass (in red and white)… you get the picture. That's what this new crop of small bars are about: neighbourhood joints offering a community atmosphere.

EXPLORE

Little Guy.

Oscillate Wildly.

Open 7am-3pm Mon-Fri; 8am-3pm Sat, Sun.
Main courses $12-$22. Map p132 ⓫ **Café**
The Fleetwood team bring their A-game on the food front. Sure, it all fits easily into categories such as baguettes, soup, salads, eggs and toast – but like Darryl Kerrigan (from seminal Aussie flick *The Castle*) famously said: 'It's what you do with it.'

Oscillate Wildly

275 Australia Street, Newtown (9517 4700, www.oscillatewildly.com.au). Newtown rail. **Open** 6.30pm-late Tue-Sat. **Set meal** $120 tasting menu. Map p132 ⓬ **Contemporary Australian**
The tasting menu at this progressive restaurant changes regularly, but it's consistently impressive. Chef Karl Firla dishes up plates such as blood plum and cassis-flavoured edible paper or wagyu beef on egg yolk with white radishes. You can BYO on Tuesday, but the wine selection is excellent.

Stinking Bishops

Shop 5, 63/71 Enmore Road, Newtown (9007 7754, www.thestinkingbishops.com). Newtown rail. **Open** 5-10pm Tue, Wed; 11am-10pm Thur, Fri; 11.30am-4.30pm, 5.30-10pm Sat; 11am-6pm Sun. Map p132 ⓭ **Cheese bar**
It's time to confess your fondness for *fromage* to the Stinking Bishops – a well-stocked Enmore cheese bar. It's $20 for two, $29 for three or $36 for four cheeses, and you get to choose each and every one. Only serious cheese fiends should attempt the pungent mac and cheese, though.

Bars

Courthouse Hotel

202 Australia Street, Newtown (9519 8273). Newtown rail. **Open** 10am-midnight Mon-Sat; 10am-10pm Sun. Map p132 ⓮
There's nothing to dislike about this old boozer, and we suspect if anyone ever tried to refurbish the Courthouse there'd be rioting in the streets. The outdoor space is at least twice the size of the indoor area, and the beer garden is where you want to be when the sun is shining and jugs of cider, or beer and a burger, are the order of the day.

Earl's Juke Joint

407 King Street, Newtown (no phone). Newtown rail. **Open** 4pm-midnight Mon-Sat; 4-10pm Sun. Map p132 ⓯
The drinks flow freely and the music jumps from the speakers at this classically styled Newtown bar, with a dark room lined with pictures of jazz greats and a deep wooden bar that's built to last. Order a Jelly Roll Morton's Zombie – a tiki-licious mix of rums, cognac, lime, spiced grapefruit, absinthe and bitters.

Mary's

6 Mary Street, Newtown (no phone). Newtown rail. **Open** 4pm-midnight Mon-Sat; noon-10pm Sun. Map p132 ⓰
Formerly home to an STI clinic (called the Sanctuary – how creepy is that?), a masonic hall, a Greek club and a pool hall, this unassuming little building next

Stinking Bishops.

to Kelly's on King is now a small bar called Mary's serving fine renditions of two of Sydney's current obsessions – cocktails and burgers.

Midnight Special
44 Enmore Road, Newtown (9516 2345, www.themidnightspecial.com.au). Newtown rail. **Open** 5pm-midnight Tue-Sat; 5-10pm Sun. **Map** p132 ⑰
Space is a premium at this small Enmore bar, so the owners devote what they have to the important elements of a good night out. The playlist provides punters with a solid rock 'n' roll education and there's a short, solid six-cocktail list. Order an Eastside, which uses lime juice, mint, cucumber, sugar and a generous glug of gin to great effect.

Slyfox
199 Enmore Road, Enmore (9557 1016). Bus 355, 423, 426, 428, L23, M30. **Open** 10am-4am Mon-Thur; 10am-6am Fri, Sat; 10am-midnight Sun. **Map** p132 ⑱
This all-night party haven pushes a huge range of musical genres through its speakers. Hit the dance floor to techno, house, two-step or hip hop, or relax with a beer in its 1970s-themed front room.

Shops & Services

Cream on King
371 King Street, Newtown (9565 2955, www. facebook.com/creamonline). Newtown rail.
Open 10am-6pm Mon-Wed, Fri, Sat; 10am-8pm Thur; 11am-6pm Sun. **Map** p132 ⑲ **Fashion**
Rock the vintage bohemian look at moderately priced, well-stocked Cream on King. It's a one-stop shop for all things retro, from flannel and floral to a big, old pair of Docs (very old-school Newtown). The store specialises in 1970s-'90s styles.

Maple Store
244 King Street, Newtown (9555 2352, www.maplestore.com.au). Newtown rail.
Open 10am-6pm Mon-Wed, Fri, Sat; 10am-9pm Thur; 11am-5pm Sun. **Map** p132 ⑳ **Fashion**
Maple is a surefire sign that the once-bohemian suburb of Newtown is now in gentrification phase 2.0. Alongside high-waisted Marilyns and James Dean roll-ups from labels such as Dr Denim, Neuw and Nudie, this is also the place to pick up forest-scented Triumph & Disaster grooming kits, sleek Sunday Somewhere shades, Funkis clogs, Saltwater sandals and a big choice of of striped tees.

Pretty Dog
5A Brown Street, Newtown (9519 7839, www.prettydog.com.au). Newtown rail.
Open 11am-5.30pm Tue-Sat; noon-5pm Sun. **Map** p132 ㉑ **Fashion**
Seek out beautiful terrace boutique Pretty Dog and you won't be disappointed. Those Karen Walker, Romance Was Born, House of Holland and Jenny Kee designs need to be taken for a whirl around the room, even if you can't afford to take them all home.

North Shore

Crossing the bridge to the north side of Sydney has always meant joining the comfortable set. Since 1932, anyway. Until the construction of the Harbour Bridge that year, the north shore was largely undeveloped and the rugged coastline was thick with bushland and fauna. Much remains in the north side's waterside parks and reserves, but the area is now also home to North Sydney, the city's northern business district; the luxurious and moneyed Mosman, home to the must-see Taronga Zoo; serene waterside spots such as McMahons Point and Balmoral; and quaint food and drink hubs including Neutral Bay and Kirribilli. Note that the 'north shore' is not an officially designated area: rather, it's a term to lump together the suburbs on the north side of the harbour that are south and/or west of the northern beaches. And getting around the north shore isn't easy. Its size and sprawl mean that you're best off in a car, and many of its hidden beaches can only be reached on foot (if you're prepared for the hills) or by charter boat (if you're not).

EXPLORE

Hayden Orpheum Picture Palace.

Don't Miss

1 Luna Park Walk through the clown's mouth for all the fun of the fair (p139).

2 Tim Ho Wan Some of the best dumplings in town (p143).

3 Hayden Orpheum Picture Palace A beautiful art deco cinema (p140).

4 Ormeggio Exquisite Italian food with a waterfront view (p141).

5 North Sydney Olympic Pool Practise your crawl under Harbour Bridge (p139).

Luna Park.

KIRRIBILLI, MILSONS POINT, MCMAHONS POINT & NORTH SYDNEY

The north shore starts at Kirribilli and Milsons Point, tiny suburbs nestled on either side of the Harbour Bridge and boasting sweeping vistas of the city and the Opera House. Despite the apartment blocks that have sprung up in between the old houses, both suburbs are Victorian in feel, with many original buildings still standing.

The southern tip of **Kirribilli** is home to the official Sydney residences of the prime minister (Kirribilli House, a Gothic Revival-style building dating from 1855, flanked by rolling, manicured lawns) and the governor-general (Admiralty House, a classic colonial mansion built in 1844-45). There's a distinctly villagey feel to Kirribilli, and its residents continue to fill the cafés and restaurants around the hub of Fitzroy, Burton and Broughton streets. A particularly good time to visit Kirribilli is on the fourth Saturday of the month, when one of Sydney's oldest bric-a-brac, fashion and antiques markets is held in **Bradfield Park**, on the corner of Burton and Alfred streets.

On a sunny day, treat yourself to a ferry trip from Circular Quay, gliding past the Opera House to **Milsons Point wharf** (Alfred Street South). From here, you can take the harbourside walk in either direction. The ferry pulls up right in front of the grinning face and huge staring eyes of

Luna Park. To the right (with your back to the water), is the historic **North Sydney Olympic Pool**, which must be the top contender for the 'most stunningly located swimming pool in the world' award: it's on the water's edge, beneath the northern pylon of the Harbour Bridge. The foreshore walk ends at **Mary Booth Lookout**, a patch of green with a great view that's perfect for picnics.

In the other direction from Luna Park, the foreshore walk winds around **Lavender Bay**: it's especially dazzling at sunset, when the city lights shimmer in the golden glow. Make a stop at **Clark Park** (Lavender Street) to take in **Wendy's Secret Garden**. It's the 'optical erotica' that inspired Australian artist Brett Whiteley at the foot of his Lavender Bay home, and it is still beautifully maintained by Whiteley's widow, Wendy.

Just beyond Lavender Street is Blues Point Road, which slices down from North Sydney through the heart of McMahons Point. It's one of Sydney's great people-watching strips, and there are numerous cafés, pubs, delis and restaurants from which you can take in the view. Allow time to walk down to **Blues Point Reserve**, a swathe of open parkland at the southern tip of **Blues Point** that provides a great photo op for that obligatory Sydney Harbour holiday snap.

The northern end of Blues Point Road merges into Miller Street, dominated by the office blocks

of North Sydney and constituting Sydney's main business district after the CBD. It's buzzing during the week, and mostly a ghost-town on the weekend. Its ripper burger joint, **Five Points Burgers**, makes it a good dining stop before heading further north.

Sights & Museums

★ FREE Luna Park
1 Olympic Drive, Milsons Point (9033 7676, www.lunaparksydney.com). Milsons Point rail or ferry. **Open** 11am-6pm Mon-Thur; 11am-11pm Fri; 10am-11pm Sat; 10am-6pm Sun (later in school holidays). **Admission** free. Unlimited ride pass $20-$43.
The huge laughing clown's mouth that marks the entrance to Luna Park is visible from Circular Quay. Walk through that mouth and you'll find a 1930s-style fun park and performance venue. You can ride a rollercoaster and visit a sideshow, and there's no shortage of fixes for addicts of high speeds and heights.

★ North Sydney Olympic Pool
4 Alfred Street South, Milsons Point (9955 2309, www.northsydney.nsw.gov.au). Milsons Point rail or ferry. **Open** 5.30am-9pm Mon-Fri; 7am-7pm Sat, Sun. **Admission** $3.20-$6.50.
This outdoor swimming pool, situated between the Harbour Bridge and Luna Park, holds a special place in the hearts of many a Sydneysider. Opened in 1936,

the building has wonderful art deco stylings and decorative plasterwork, most of it still intact. A total of 86 world records have been set here. *Photo p140.*

Restaurants & Cafés

Anvil Coffee Co
Kirribilli Commuter Wharf, Kirribilli (www.anvil cc.com.au). Kirribilli rail or ferry. **Open** 6.30am-3pm Mon-Fri; 7am-3pm Sat; 8am-3pm Sun. **Main courses** $8.50-$16. **Café**
The set-up here is like a boat driver's quarters turned café. Anvil serves excellent coffee alongside the likes of house-toasted muesli with flaky nuts and topped with soft, braised rhubarb, and buttered 'Arabian eggs' – poached, served with sweet onion relish, chilli and lemon, licks of yoghurt and creamy butter, and sourdough bread.

Coco Chocolate
Shop 12, 3A-9B Broughton Street, Kirribilli (9922 4998, cocochocolate.com.au). Kirribilli rail. **Open** 10am-6pm Mon-Sat. **Café**
Coco Chocolate hand-tempers all of its chocolate on marble – if that's not lavish, we don't know what is – and staff are trained how to explain the chocolate process from bean to bar. Enjoy the product in-house with one of 12 varieties of drinking chocolate or a cup of Sacred Grounds coffee.

Five Points Burgers
Entry via Berry Street, 124 Walker Street, North Sydney (no phone). North Sydney rail. **Open** 11.30am-5pm Mon-Fri. **Main courses** $9.50-$12.50. **Burgers**
Ever since Five Points Burgers opened in 2015, people have been going crazy for the patties and buns. Not only is chef Tomislav Martinovic a Fat Duck alumnus, but the New York-themed interior and ripper burgers are a dream match. Try the Bronx: a charred but tender patty cooked medium-rare is sandwiched between two melted slices of American cheese, with sweet onion jam, a heap of sour pickles and a big, crunchy leaf of iceberg lettuce. There's also bacon, tomato sauce and mustard. It looks like it's going to topple over, it's so deeply filled, but the sturdy, soft bun keeps things in check.

Bars

Botanist
17 Willoughby Street, Kirribilli (9954 4057, thebotanist.com.au). Kirribilli rail. **Open** 4pm-late Mon, Tue; 11.30am-midnight Wed-Fri; 11am-midnight Sat, Sun.
The room is – unsurprisingly – botanical. There are hanging plants and floral lampshades, and vines crawl from stacks of old suitcases. To drink, we recommend the fruity cocktails, which look innocent but pack plenty of punch. Shared plates such as sliders, pizza and tacos will keep hunger at bay.

EXPLORE

Kirribilli Hotel

37 Broughton Street, Milsons Point (9955 1415,
www.kirribillihotel.com.au). Kirribilli rail. **Open**
10am-midnight Mon-Sat; 10am-10pm Sun.
This is not an ostentatious pub. Its rounded, art deco,
red-brick façade tucks neatly into the row of shopfronts lining Broughton Street and an impressive
craft beer selection is reason enough to swing by.

CREMORNE, NEUTRAL BAY, MOSMAN, BALMORAL & THE SPIT BRIDGE

The main commercial centre of the lower north
shore is Military Road, a low-slung, seemingly
endless strip of shops, cafés and innovative
restaurants that heads east through **Neutral
Bay**, the lower north shore's food, drink and
entertainment centre. If you continue east
along Military Road, you will arrive at some
of Sydney's richest suburbs: Cremorne,
Mosman and Balmoral, where the heavily
moneyed live in conspicuous splendour.

Cremorne Point, a sliver of a peninsula,
offers one of the finest panoramas of Sydney
Harbour. It's the perfect setting for a harbourside
stroll. Inland, **Cremorne** is home to a beautiful
art deco cinema, the **Hayden Orpheum Picture
Palace** (*see p184*). From Cremorne Point, you can
hop on the ferry to **Mosman Bay** wharf, where
an uphill walk or bus will take you into **Mosman**
village. Further east lies **Taronga Zoo** (*see
p180*), which occupies a splendid vantage point
overlooking Bradleys Head. North of the zoo,
Mosman's commercial centre runs along Military
Road – a good place to people-watch and shop.

Over on the 'Middle Harbour' side of Mosman
is **Balmoral**, one of Sydney's prettiest harbour
suburbs. With two beaches, lots of green space
and a curiously Romanesque bandstand, it's a
great spot for a sunset meal of fish and chips. But
watch out for the seagulls – they are a particularly
robust flock here and will steal the chips straight
from your hands. For **Balmoral Beach**, *see p169*.

Head further north and you'll hit the **Spit
Bridge**, the beautiful bottleneck faced by
those wanting to head towards Manly and the
northern beaches (*see pp146-153*). The view
driving down Spit Road from Military Road
is one of Sydney's most amazing, with boats

North Sydney Olympic Pool. See p139.

bobbing in the marina either side of the narrow causeway and swanky mansions clinging to the rocky cliffs. Traffic comes to a halt when the bridge lifts to let boats pass beneath.

Restaurants & Cafés

Barrel Bar & Dining
3/362 Military Road, Cremorne (9904 5687, barrelbar.com.au). Bus 227, 228, 230, 236, 244, 245, 247, 257. **Open** 5pm-late Mon-Fri; 3pm-late Sat; 3-10pm Sun. **Main courses** $31-$37. **Contemporary Australian**
Barrel Bar & Dining is on a consistently busy stretch of Military Road in Cremorne, next to the lovely Hayden Orpheum Picture Palace (*see p184*). It features great wine chosen by three of Sydney's most seasoned sommeliers (Stephen Thompson, Tony Binning and Alex Searle), and awesome food to match. The contemporary Australian cooking, with the finest ingredients and Mediterranean influences, produces small plates such as scallop ceviche with blood orange, candied orange zest, fried capers, lemon oil and black salt, or mains such as slow-cooked beef cheeks with confit leek, turnip and puréed parsnips.

Chiosco
The Jetty, d'Albora Marinas, the Spit, Mosman (9046 7333, www.chiosco.com.au). Bus 143, 144, 151, 169, 178, 179, 180, 183, 184, 185, 190, 248. **Open** 8am-4pm Mon; 8am-late Tue-Sun. **Main courses** $30-$36. **Seafood/Italian**
An affordable seafood restaurant that does BYO and has water views? No, it's not a myth: it's right by the Spit. It's a casual, trattoria-style Italian restaurant with smiling young wait staff in white tees and striped aprons, serving the likes of mussels with garlic, chilli and tomato sauce, and baby snapper with tomatoes and olives. *Photos pp142-143.*

★ Ormeggio
The Jetty, d'Albora Marinas, the Spit, Mosman (9046 7333, www.ormeggio.com.au). Bus 143, 144, 151, 169, 178, 179, 180, 183, 184, 185, 190, 248. **Open** noon-3pm, 6-11pm Tue-Sat; noon-3pm Sun. **Set meal** tasting menu $119; $199 (including wine). **Italian**
One of Sydney's best long-lunch spots. Brescian-born-and-raised chef Alessandro Pavoni serves a regional menu from his part of Italy. It's paired with very drinkable, very Italian wine. The location doesn't hurt either – behind a boat shop, right on the water.

Salt Meats Cheese
3/803 Military Road, Mosman (www.saltmeats cheese.com.au). Bus 227, 228, 230, 236, 244, 245, 247, 257. **Open** 8am-10pm daily. **Main courses** $6-$14. **Italian**
Aside from featuring walls stacked with beautiful handmade pastas and carefully curated cheeses and salumi, this Italian *providore* is open all day and into the evening as a café and restaurant. Slices of wood-fired pizzas, calzone, pastas and salads, as well as house speciality meat platters, are on the menu.

Bars

Minskys Hotel
287 Military Road, Cremorne (9909 8888, www.minskyshotel.com.au). Bus 227, 228, 230, 236, 244, 245, 247, 257. **Open** 10am-4am Mon-Thur; 10am-5am Fri, Sat; 10am-midnight Sun.

IN THE KNOW VIEWPOINTS

From this side of the city, you get postcard views of the Harbour Bridge and the Opera House – the best, of course, is from **Kirribilli House** (see p138). Other dreamy spots include **Cremorne** foreshore (see p140), where laughing kookaburras and sweetly screeching rainbow lorikeets nestle in weeping figs, and **Balmoral Beach** (see p169), Sydney's most sophisticated oceanside suburb.

EXPLORE

A decade ago, had you suggested a drink at the Megahole (as Minskys Hotel used to be called in certain circles) people might have worried that you'd taken leave of your senses. These days, however, it's a stylish, welcoming pub with a blue-tiled kitchen pumping out typical European tavern fare (salt and pepper squid, burgers), and is an excellent spot for a craft beer or glass of wine.

Side Car
394 Military Road, Cremorne (9909 2496).
Bus 227, 228, 230, 236, 244, 245, 247, 257.
Open 4pm-midnight Tue-Sat; 4-10pm Sun.
Side Car's modest shopfront is marked by lanterns out on the footpath; the flickering candlelight acts like a will-o'-the-wisp, drawing you into a skinny bar packed with battered leather couches and cow hides. It's a low-lit, comfortable nook for low-key drinks. There's a tasty cheese board too.

Shops & Services

Fourth Village Providore
5A Vista Street, Mosman (9960 7162, www.fourthvillage.com.au). Bus 227, 228, 230, 236, 244, 245, 247, 257. **Open** 7am-6.30pm Mon-Fri; 7am-6pm Sat, Sun. **Food & drink**

Head here for the kind of fresh fruit and veggies that belong on a Sicilian postcard. There are floor-to-ceiling shelves fit to bursting with preserves, condiments, spices and dry goods, and in the centre of the store is a veritable cornucopia of fresh produce, laid out in baskets, boxes, trays and barrels. There's also an Italian restaurant (where the pizzas are available to take away).

Spoilt Rotten
Shop 10, 601-611 Military Road, Mosman (9960 6095). Bus 227, 228, 230, 236, 244, 245, 247, 257. **Open** 10am-5pm Mon-Fri; 10am-4pm Sat. **Children**
It's worth crossing the bridge for the beautiful kids' bedding, paintings, clothing, backpacks and toys at this lovingly curated Mosman boutique.

CHATSWOOD

This popular business district in northern Sydney is home to a large number of corporate headquarters. But while it's definitely a business hub – and has the grey-glass high-rise buildings that come with that – Chatswood is also one of Sydney's great cultural hubs, and a focus for the Asian community. The latter explains the great

Chiosco. See p141.

dumpling outlets found dotted throughout the suburb: it's here that you'll find **Din Tai Fung** and **Tim Ho Wan**. In addition, Chatswood is home to both the high-end **Chatswood Chase** shopping centre, and cultural venue the **Concourse**, an arts centre where you can hear music, see plays and watch movies under the stars in summer.

Sights & Museums

FREE The Concourse
409 Victoria Avenue (9020 6968, www.the concourse.com.au). Chatswood rail. **Open** varies. **Admission** free.
This elegant grey steel-and-glass concert hall could be mistaken for the Guggenheim Museum Bilbao's straight-laced younger brother. Inside, you'll find a captivating programme of orchestral concerts, contemporary music gigs and theatre shows. (An outdoor screen shows live performances of sold out shows.) It is also home to several pieces of art in its public spaces, as well as changing exhibitions in the Art Space. Venue tours run every Tuesday at 11am and there are plenty of places to eat and drink. The precinct also includes Chatswood Library and two green spaces. *See also p221.*

Restaurants & Cafés

Din Tai Fung
Shop 332-336, Westfield Shopping Centre, 1 Anderson Street (9415 3155, www.dintai fungaustralia.com.au). Chatswood rail. **Open** 11am-2.30pm, 5-8.30pm Mon-Wed; 11am-2.30pm, 5-9pm Thur, Fri; 11am-3.30pm, 5pm-9pm Sat; 11am-3.30pm, 5-8.30pm Sun. **Main courses** $10-$17. **Chinese**
The demand for Din Tai Fung's dumplings and soups has become so great that the eaterie now has dumpling houses in Chatswood, Chippendale, North Sydney, Pyrmont, Chinatown and the CBD. Experience the silky morsels at this north shore branch.
Other locations throughout the city.

Tim Ho Wan
Corner of Victoria Avenue & Railway Street (9898 9888, www.timhowan.com.au). Chatswood rail. **Open** 10am-9pm daily. **Dumplings/small dishes** $6-$9. **Chinese**
Love dumplings? Who doesn't? Well, Tim Ho Wan is home of the world's most highly lauded dumplings. Each of its Hong Kong outlets boasts a Michelin star and – unsurprisingly – the queue at this Chatswood branch stretches down the street.

EXPLORE

SYDNEY FERRIES

Sydney's water transport provides one of its most emblematic icons.

No trip to Sydney would be complete without clambering aboard one of the picture-postcard green-and-yellow ferries that ply the harbour (all depart from Circular Quay ferry terminal) and are used daily by hundreds of commuters. These stately vessels – a key feature of Sydney's tourism industry – are a great way to explore the harbour and further afield: there's plenty of room to take pictures from the decks or just to sit in the sun and enjoy the ride.

Although the first ferry service offered on Sydney Harbour was the Rose Hill Packet (aka 'The Lump'), which putt-puttered to Parramatta from 1789, the first official (albeit privatised) Sydney Ferries route was that of the North Shore Ferry Company, in operation since 1878 (the company changed its name in 1899). Today, 21st-century Sydneysiders can recreate that historic trip and get up close to Sydney's inner northern suburbs while they do it. Gliding past Cremorne Point (see p140), Taronga Zoo (see p180), south Mosman, Old

Cremorne and finally Mosman Bay (see p140), you'll see how the other half live as you gawp at some of the city's most expensive, sought-after and architecturally impressive harbour-side homes (including the prime minister's official residence, Kirribilli House).

If you're after a bite-size taste of the beauty of the Sydney Ferries experience, the trip to Darling Harbour from Circular Quay lasts about 20 minutes and scoots you under the Harbour Bridge (see p54) and around the Opera House (see p58), often via the gourmet village of Balmain (see p120), with its nexus of bars, cafés and restaurants. Your end point of Darling Harbour (see p74) is full of cool family attractions – the IMAX Theatre, Sydney Aquarium, Wildlife World, Chinese Gardens and Powerhouse Museum, not to mention an assortment of shops in the Harbourside complex, and restaurants, bars and cafés at Cockle Bay and King Street Wharf.

For more information, visit www. sydneyferries.info.

EXPLORE

Bars

465 the Avenue
465 Victoria Avenue (9423 2888, www.465the avenue.com.au). Chatswood rail. **Open** 7am-11pm Mon; 7am-midnight Tue-Fri; 11am-midnight Sat.
A lively neighbourhood bar where you can start the day with pancakes or end it with a glass of the ballsy Arido malbec and – if you need a time out from shopping – a Prickly Moses red ale in between.

Shops & Services

Chatswood Chase
345 Victoria Avenue (9422 5316, www.chatswood chaseshopping.com.au). Chatswood rail. **Open** 9.30am-5.30pm Mon-Wed, Fri; 9.30am-9pm Thur; 9am-5pm Sat; 10am-5pm Sun. **Mall**
This luxury shopping centre is home to Aussie design faves including Alannah Hill, Gorman, David Lawrence and Carla Zampatti.

CROWS NEST & GREENWICH

Getting its name thanks to its elevated position – it's one of the highest points of all of the northern suburbs – **Crows Nest** is home to a strip of family-owned mid-range restaurants, with a bunch of Vietnamese, Thai and Japanese joints dotted all the way along Willoughby Road. It's also home to some of the lower north shore's first small bars, plenty of friendly little cafés and loads of furniture shops and cute, browse-worthy boutiques.

If you travel out of Crows Nest, down River Road and towards the harbour, you'll find the green waterside suburb of **Greenwich**. It's worth a visit for the beautiful harbour views from Greenwich Point and a dip at the enclosed **Greenwich Baths** (Albert Street, 9438 5922).

Restaurants & Cafés

Johnny Lobster
48 Willoughby Road, Crows Nest (9436 4672, www.johnnylobster.com.au). Bus 263, 267. **Open** 11am-9.30pm daily. **Main courses** $18-$32. **Seafood**
The king of crustaceans still costs $30 at Johnny Lobster, located on buzzy Willoughby Road, so don't throw your dollar bills in the air with glee just yet. But it will cost upwards of double that amount most anywhere else in Sydney, so this is a great deal – especially considering it's sustainably caught.

Bars

Foxtrot
28 Falcon Street, Crows Nest (no phone). Bus 143, 144. **Open** 5pm-midnight Tue-Wed; 5pm-1am Thur; 5pm-2am Fri, Sat; 4-10pm Sun.

IN THE KNOW EARLY SETTLERS

The north shore settlers of the early 1800s were land dealers, and its development into a place of white estates and family homes stems from that time. The Cammeraygal, Gorualgal and Wallumedegal tribes who inhabited the area when the First Fleet arrived at Sydney Cove in 1788 had largely been driven out of the region by the 1860s. The Cammeraygal, recorded as being a powerful and numerous tribe, 'most robust and muscular', lived along the foreshore, in the bushland and cliffs, and in rock shelters. Places such as Berry Island, Balls Head, Kirribilli, Cremorne and Cammeray are dotted with cultural remnants of the tribe's heyday.

The Foxtrot opened back in 2011 and has steadily climbed its way to the top of the list of bars worth hitting north of the Bridge. The wine list is skewed towards lighter Australian drops, and the bartenders are more than happy to recommend a good whisky. There's an AstroTurfed indoor garden mezzanine, but make a beeline to the back room. There you'll find couches so comfy you'll want to nick them.

Hayberry
97 Willoughby Road, Crows Nest (8084 0816, www.thehayberry.com.au). Bus 257, 273. **Open** 4pm-midnight Tue-Thur; noon-midnight Fri, Sat; noon-10pm Sun.
Here, the lights are low, there's a rustic timber bar, pictures of Ned Kelly line the wall and the music is loud. And cocktails are boozy, juicy numbers such as the Apple Pip – with vodka, caramel liqueur and just-squeezed green apple juice – which tastes like someone juiced a caramel apple.

Shops & Services

TITLE
92 Willoughby Road, Crows Nest (9437 4997, titlestore.com.au). Bus 257, 273. **Open** 10am-6pm daily. **Books & music**
If your taste in entertainment is left of centre and refined, you'll spend hours browsing this hand-picked selection of cult DVDs, books and music.

Top 3 by Design
168 Willoughby Road, Crows Nest (www. top3.com.au). Bus 257, 273. **Open** 10am-6pm Mon-Fri; 10am-5pm Sat; 10am-4pm Sun. **Homewares/accessories**
As the name indicates, this shop stocks three products for each category, chosen according to design values – everything form a handy bottle-opener ring to the perfect Alessi fruit bowl.

EXPLORE

Northern Beaches

Beyond the city lies a secret – the seemingly endless stretch of surf beaches that line the north coast like a string of pearls. This is a wonderful place, and the locals know it – which is why they have fiercely protected the northern beaches from tourist overload. It's not for nothing that this area is dubbed the 'insular peninsula'. The northern beaches start over the Spit Bridge, which crosses Middle Harbour and connects Mosman to Seaforth and Manly. Busy, touristy Manly, where there's a plethora of hotels, kicks off the run of beaches; but it's the more distant suburbs such as Collaroy, Narrabeen, Newport, Avalon, Whale Beach and Palm Beach that set the tone for the area, which is lush, laid-back and totally devoted to living well in the great outdoors. The beaches themselves remain largely untouched, with deep pink sand and crashing waves. For more about them, *see pp164-175* **Sydney's Best Beaches**.

Papi Chulo.

Don't Miss

1 **Manly Surf School** Learn to tame the waves (p151).

2 **Jonah's** This B&B takes beachy R&R to the next level (p152).

3 **Papi Chulo** Be prepared to queue at Manly's must-try restaurant (p150).

4 **North Head Quarantine Station** Spook yourself silly on a ghost tour (p149).

5 **Cranky Finns Holidae Inn** 1950s surf shack vibes and cocktails (p153).

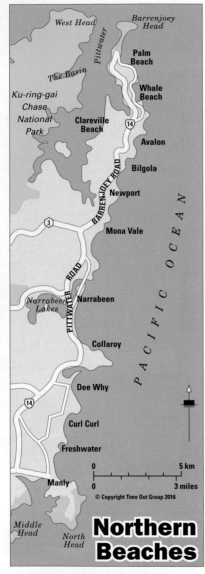

West Head

Barrenjoey Head

Pittwater

The Basin

Palm Beach

Whale Beach

Ku-ring-gai Chase National Park

Clareville Beach

14

Avalon

Bilgola

BARRENJOEY ROAD

Newport

3

Mona Vale

PITTWATER ROAD

Narrabeen Lakes

Narrabeen

Collaroy

P A C I F I C   O C E A N

Dee Why

14

Curl Curl

Freshwater

0   5 km
0   3 miles
© Copyright Time Out Group 2016

Manly

Middle Head

North Head

Northern Beaches

EXPLORE

was slipping into decline and had the feel of a faded British seaside resort, but it has since rejuvenated itself and is now a vibrant, dynamic suburb with a bevy of amenities and some good festivals that attract major crowds. While some Sydneysiders have mixed feelings about Manly, its perennial holiday atmosphere and 1.5 kilometres (one mile) of tree-lined ocean beach are irresistible to visitors. The tourists heading to Manly are a curious mix of the well-heeled (who stay at the area's expensive hotels), a burgeoning backpacker brigade holing up in cheap hostels and pubs, and day-trippers delivered by ferry from the Sydney suburbs.

To get to Manly, take one of the Manly ferries (30 minutes) from Circular Quay to the slickly refurbished Manly Wharf, with its cafés, pubs and restaurants, on Manly Cove. Here, you'll also find a peaceful patch of harbourside sand (though no surf, and the water is a tad murky for swimming). Nearby, at the western end of the cove, is popular **Oceanworld Manly**, and further west is the start of a fine ten-kilometre (six-mile) walk through bushland and along clifftops to Spit Bridge.

The main pedestrian precinct, the Corso, links Manly Wharf with Manly Beach, and is lined with restaurants, surf shops, fast-food joints and tourist shops. You'll also find a clutch of high-street chains, plus cool clothing and footwear stores, amid the myriad cafés and restaurants. The **Manly Arts & Crafts Market**, worth a browse for handmade jewellery and souvenirs, is held every weekend on the lower end of Sydney Road, just off the Corso. The **Manly Farmers Markets** (9315 7011, Short Street Plaza) are a magnet for green gourmets on Saturdays.

The suburb's main attraction, though, is **Manly Beach** itself, a long crescent of sand and ocean surf, fringed by a promenade lined with giant Norfolk pines that's a draw for surfers, sunbathers, cyclists, in-line skaters and beach volleyball enthusiasts. Surfboards, wetsuits and beach umbrellas are all available for hire on the beach, and novice surfers can hone their skills with the **Manly Surf School**. For more on the beach, *see p173*.

A must is the 15-minute walk to **Shelly Beach** (*see p173*). Also unmissable is the spectacular view from North Head, the northern of the two Heads that form the gateway to Sydney Harbour. North Head is also home to the historic **North Head Quarantine Station**. You might even spot some of Sydney's famous fairy penguins, tiny versions of their Antarctic cousins, living in the heart – and the heat – of the city.

MANLY & NORTH HEAD

A summery explosion of shops, restaurants, cafés, surfboards, people and colour, this famous beachside suburb nestles on its own peninsula, boasting both ocean and harbour beaches, plus views from every corner. A decade ago, **Manly**

Sights & Museums

FREE Manly Art Gallery & Museum
West Esplanade, Manly (9976 1420, www.manly australia.com.au/manlyartgallery). Manly ferry. **Open** 10am-5pm Tue-Sun. **Admission** free. **Map** p151 ❶

Manly Art Gallery.

Although Manly isn't exactly synonymous with high culture, you can pop into this small gallery/museum if all the surfer lingo starts to curdle your brain. Opened in 1930, it has an 845-strong collection of paintings by Australian artists, more than 2,000 historic photographs of the northern beaches area, some impressive ceramics, and exhibitions by local students and photographers.

Manly SEA LIFE Sanctuary

Western Esplanade, Manly (1800 199 742, www.manlysealifesanctuary.com.au). Manly ferry. **Open** 9.30am-5pm daily (last entry 4.30pm). **Admission** $17.50-$25; $11.90-$20 reductions. **Map** p151 ❷

The Manly SEA LIFE Sanctuary is about as good as aquariums get. The three-level attraction has a floor devoted to dangerous Australian creatures (poisonous snakes, funnel-web spiders, giant monitor lizards, crocodiles) and another to tropical fish, corals and venomous sea creatures. The main attraction, on the lower level, is the oceanarium, which holds the largest sharks in captivity in Australia, plus giant rays and turtles.

North Fort

North Fort Road, off North Head Scenic Drive, North Head (9976 6102, www.north fort.org.au). Manly ferry, then bus 135. **Open** 9am-4pm Wed-Sun. **Admission** $5-$11. **Map** p151 ❸

The remote location of North Fort means its landscape has changed little since early colonial paintings of the spot. Today, it's home to the Royal Australian Artillery National Museum, once part of the School of Artillery, built between 1935 and 1938 in the shadow of impending war and the need to defend Sydney Harbour from naval attack. You can still tour the fortifications and tunnels, and there's also a memorial walkway.

★ North Head Quarantine Station

North Head Scenic Drive, North Head (9976 6220, www.quarantinestation.com.au). Manly ferry, then bus 135. **Open** Pre-booked tours only. **Admission** $19-$25. **Map** p151 ❹

The ghost tours here are very creepy. Built in 1828, the station was the prison – and burial place – of scores of unfortunate souls, who were quarantined here for a minimum of 30 days if their ship was suspected of carrying an infectious disease. You'll be led through its black streets, old fumigation rooms, shower blocks and cemetery by a guide with a kerosene lamp.

Restaurants & Cafés

Chica Bonita

9 The Corso, Manly (9976 5255, chicabonita manly.tumblr.com). Manly ferry. **Open** 11.30am-3pm, 6pm-late Tue-Sun. **Main courses** $12-$15. **Map** p151 ❺ Taqueria

Chica Bonita (Spanish for 'beautiful girl') is a tiny taqueria hidden in a dingy walkway just off the Corso in Manly. It's a magical wonderland of margaritas, chimichangas, and the likes of Little Richard, Elvis, Chuck Berry and Chubby Checker on the speakers.

Pantry
Ocean Promenade, North Steyne, Manly (9977 0566, thepantrymanly.com). Manly ferry. **Open** 7.30-11.30am, noon-10pm daily. **Main courses** $23-$38. **Map** p151 **6** **Brasserie**
Directly overlooking the beach, this deli-style beach house boasts a stunning location, consistently good service and awesome eats – breakfasts, sharing plates, salads, tapas and modern brasserie fare.

Papi Chulo
22-23 Manly Wharf, Manly (9240 3000, merivale. com.au/papichulo). Manly ferry. **Open** noon-10.30pm Mon-Sat; 11.30am-9pm Sun. **Main courses** $29-$36. **Map** p151 **7** **Smokehouse**
North America meets South America in a tidal wave of sour, hot, spicy and fun at this new beachside smokehouse that's got everyone talking. *Photos pp152-153.*

Showbox Coffee Brewers
19 Whistler Street, Manly (9976 5000, www.showboxcoffee.com.au). Manly ferry.

Open 7am-4pm Mon-Sat; 8am-4pm Sun. **Main courses** $11.50-$19. **Map** p151 **8** **Café**
This café provides fuzzed-out rock and full-throttle coffee first thing in the morning. Try a 'pegg roll' – a sesame-seed bun stuffed with cheesy scrambled egg, crisp fried pancetta, rocket, onion relish and mayo.

Bars

Daniel San
55 North Steyne Road, Manly (9977 6963, www.danielsan.com.au). Manly ferry. **Open** 3pm-midnight Mon-Thur; noon-2am Fri, Sat; noon-11pm Sun. **Map** p151 **9**
At this pan-Asian/surftown fusion bar, you'll find martial arts trophies, Japanese beers, rock pumping through the speakers, and sashimi and skewers.

Hemingway's
48 North Steyne, Manly (9976 3030, www. hemingwaysmanly.com.au). Manly ferry.
Open 8am-midnight Mon-Sat; 8am-10pm Sun. **Map** p151 **10**
The sort of place you wouldn't feel weird drinking in during the day. In fact, the tiny, kooky beachside bar also offers breakfast. Grab some toasted crumpets and honey, or watch the bartenders mess with a brandy alexander by adding Coco Pops and Nesquik.

Pantry.

Manly Wine

8-13 South Steyne, Manly (8070 2424, manly wine.com.au). Manly ferry. **Open** 7am-late daily. **Map** p151 ⑪

Ladies who lunch, hungover heads and midnight winos are all welcome at this beachside bar, which offers specials most nights of the week – Double Burger Thursdays come complete with a $20 beer jug.

Shops & Services

★ Manly Surf School

North Steyne Surf Lifesaving Club, Manly (9932 7000, www.manlysurfschool.com). Manly ferry. **Open** *Classes* 9am, 11am, 1pm, 3pm. **Rates** $70-$160. **Map** p151 ⑫ **Surfing**

This is the ultimate, the king, the numero uno of surf schools – literally. Voted number one by Surfing Australia, this is also the only Manly surf school to actually perform its classes in Manly. Surf's up.

McLean & Page

11-27 Wentworth Street, Manly (9976 3277, www.mcleanandpage.com). Manly ferry. **Open** 9.30am-5.30pm daily. **Map** p151 ⑬ **Fashion**

This high-end fashion boutique stocks Australian designers such as Josh Goot, Therese Rawsthorne and Camilla & Marc. The stock is beautiful but pricey.

Shop Next Door

48-50 Pittwater Road, Manly (9977 5569, theshopnextdoor.com.au). Manly ferry. **Open** 10am-6pm Mon-Wed, Fri; 10am-7pm Thur; 9am-6pm Sat, Sun. **Map** p151 ⑭ **Surfing**

This little gem stocks more than 150 surfboards made by craftsmen from around the world, as well as a host of on-the-up clothing brands, art and music.

FRESHWATER TO WHALE BEACH

North from Manly, the beaches become less crowded and more spectacular, with names such as Freshwater, Curl Curl, Dee Why, **Collaroy** (*see p174*), Narrabeen, **Newport** (*see p174*) and Avalon slipping off the tongue like a surfer off the crest of a wave. You're now entering serious surfing territory. Here, the air smells of sea salt and coconut oil, and it seems as if every second teenager hides under a mop of matted bleached blond hair, surfboard in tow.

The best way to explore is by car, allowing you to stop, take in the view and swim at leisure at whichever beach you fancy. Otherwise, the L90 bus from Wynyard will take you all the way to Palm Beach – about 90 minutes if you don't stop – calling in at various beaches en route. The road becomes steeper and more winding after you've passed Newport and the views are breathtaking. Visitors with a car can take a detour to **Garigal National Park** (www.nationalparks.nsw.gov.au),

which links Sydney's north shore suburbs with the northern beaches. Further north is the much larger **Ku-ring-gai Chase National Park**.

The final community before Palm Beach is **Avalon**, once something of a secret but now a thriving village with boutiques and hip cafés. **Avalon Beach** (*see p174*) was once considered as a possible location by the makers of *Baywatch*, but the locals weren't having any of it, and Avalon surfers still jealously guard their waters; they're in their combies from dawn until dusk, waiting for that perfect wave. The lookout point on Bilgola Head is well worth a stop – it offers stunning views down the coastline towards Bondi and up to Barrenjoey Lighthouse at Palm Beach.

There's one more treasure to be seen before you reach Palm Beach, the end of the northern beaches road. For many locals, **Whale Beach** (*see p174*) is closer to paradise than glitzier Palm. Its inaccessibility helps, making it a definite 'those in the know' bolt-hole. You can get there by bus – the 193 from Avalon Parade in Avalon – or by walking from the L90 bus stop on Careel Head Road. From there, turn left on to Whale Beach Road and continue until you reach the beach itself; it's roughly a half-hour hilly trek along roads lined with wonderful beach houses, but it's worth the effort. The pink sand, rugged surf and rocky headland have a quality all of their own, and there's an oceanside swimming pool. Stop at **Jonah's**, for five-star food on a coastal hilltop; bring a change of clothes, though – beachside gear won't cut it here.

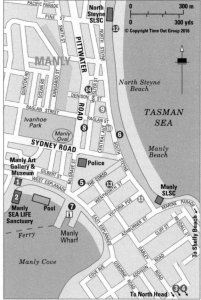

EXPLORE

Papi Chulo. See p150.

Restaurants & Cafés

★ Jonah's

69 Bynya Road, between Norma & Surf Roads, Whale Beach (9974 5599, www.jonahs.com.au). Bus 193, L90. **Open** 7.30am-late daily. **Set meal** $85 2 courses, $105 3 courses. **Contemporary Australian**

The Palm Beach area is to Sydney what the Hamptons are to New York: an exclusive weekend playground for the rich and famous. And if you want somewhere suitably decadent but discreet to eat (and stay), then Jonah's is top of the A-list. Bring a friend and tuck into the $220 fruits de mer sharing platter.

Pilu at Freshwater

Moore Road, Freshwater (9938 3331, www.pilu atfreshwater.com.au). Bus 139. **Open** 6-10pm Tue; noon-3pm, 6-10pm Wed-Sat; noon-3pm Sun. **Main courses** $45-$47. **Italian**

Giovanni and Marilyn Pilu's Sardinian restaurant is one of the most beautiful in the area, with panoramic views of the beach. But you may be too distracted by the likes of suckling pig terrine, chickpea focaccia and salsa verde, or spaghettoni, pecorino, watercress and smoked eel to notice. The wine list is extensive, with a focus on southern Italy.

Smalltown

1/21-23 Old Barrenjoey Road, Avalon (9443 2286). Bus 191. **Open** 7.30am-2pm. **Main courses** $14.50-$22. **Café**

Not only is the vibe here everything a beachside café should be – laid-back and family-friendly, with plenty of outdoor seating – but the food is genuinely exciting. Everything is cooked with thought and sensitivity, from trout fillet with grilled asparagus to posh bacon-and-egg rolls, and the plates are a visual treat. Oh, and the flat white is one of the best in the area.

Bars

Harbord Beach Hotel

29 Moore Road, Freshwater (9905 3434, www.harbordhotel.com.au). Bus 139. **Open** 10am-midnight daily.

Being a beachside haunt means this old watering hole doesn't go in for dark, cosy corners. Afternoon sun streams through the windows, glinting off framed caricatures, sporting memorabilia and freshly poured glasses of VB and Reschs. Perfect for a low-key lager by the seaside.

JB & Sons

1-3 Moore Road, Freshwater (www.jbandsons. squarespace.com). Bus 139. **Open** 4pm-late Mon-Fri; noon-late Sat, Sun.

JB & Sons is the latest venture from the team that opened Hemingway's (*see p150*). But this new venue narrows the focus to US food, a snappy drinks list and the relaxed vibes essential for coastal boozing.

Stowaway Bar

24 Lawrence Street, Freshwater (9905 2038, www.stowawaybar.com). Bus 139. **Open**

Don't mistake Palm Beach Wharf, on the western side of the peninsula, for the main beach. Palm Beach proper is on the eastern, ocean side. At the southern end of the beach – the safest place to swim – the colonial-style buildings of the Palm Beach Surf Club and private Palm Beach Pacific Club sit majestically, their picturesque wooden balconies surrounded by stately palms.

Soap fans might want to head further up to North Palm Beach, where, if you're lucky, the kids from *Home and Away* will be filming by the North Palm Beach Surf Club (ironically, one of the easiest surf clubs to join, as it's at the unfashionable end of Palmy). When the 'Summer Bay SLSC' sign is hanging on the side of the building, the Seven Network crew are in business and you may well spot wily old Alf Stewart (aka actor Ray Meagher) ordering a latte from the kiosk, or younger cast members learning their lines.

For more on the beach at Palm Beach, *see p174.*

Restaurants & Cafés

Barrenjoey House
1108 Barrenjoey Road, opposite Palm Beach Wharf, Palm Beach (9974 4001, www.barrenjoey house.com.au). Palm Beach ferry or bus 190, L90. **Open** 11.30am-11.30pm daily. **Main courses** $27-$39. **Seafood**
The restaurant at this quaint guesthouse specialises in seafood – Sydney rock oysters, perhaps, followed by Catalan shellfish stew. Dine on the breezy terrace for some relaxed seaside charm.

Boathouse
Governor Phillip Park, Palm Beach (9974 3868, www.theboathousepb.com.au). Palm Beach ferry or bus 190, L90. **Open** 7.30am-4pm daily. **Main courses** $26-$39. **Café**
Boathouse isn't the cheapest café in town, but it's definitely one of the most beautiful, with wharfside seating and waterfront views from the front lawn. Mains range from fish pie or beer-battered flathead to beef carpaccio or spring salad. If you're up early enough, you can come for breakfast too.

Bars

★ Cranky Fins Holidae Inn
1 Beach Road, Palm Beach (9974 1159, crankyfins.com). Palm Beach ferry or bus 190, L90. **Open** noon-11pm Mon-Sat; noon-9pm Sun.
This place has a 1950s surf shack vibe – white-washed floors, cosy booths, hanging buoys – and the playlist features Buddy Holly, Elvis Presley and the Supremes. With a deeply refreshing Kool Your Melon cocktail in hand – Hendrick's gin, watermelon, grapefruit and lime – it's hard to feel too stressed.

5-11pm Mon-Thur; 3pm-midnight Fri; 1pm-midnight Sat; 1-11pm Sun.
The Stowaway is a vintage hideaway where you can kill a few hours tucking into hearty spare ribs and buffalo wings, a boilermaker cocktail or two, and some classic blues tunes.

PALM BEACH & AROUND

Palm Beach lounges at the well-heeled tip of the northern beaches, where you'll find more multi-million-dollar mansions than seagulls. The area makes a luxurious home for a high concentration of the rich and famous keen to escape Sydney's glaring limelight. It wasn't always thus. In 1900, all the land except Barrenjoey Headland (which had been purchased by the government in 1881) was divided into 18 large blocks and offered for sale. None sold. Today, the average price of a Palm Beach property is a cool $3 million and every ocean view is taken; as a result, there aren't as many cabbage tree palms around as there were when they gave the place its name.

Palm Beach is worth at least a day's exploration. The community itself is reserved and somewhat haughty, but there are lots of restaurants and cafés worth stopping in at and masses of watersports on offer. If you haven't got time for the road trip from the city, splash out and do it in style by seaplane. Planes fly from Rose Bay to Pittwater on the sheltered western side of the Palm Beach peninsula, and companies offer sightseeing and gourmet tours.

EXPLORE

The West

If you want to get to Sydney's multicultural heart, you'll need to head west. Although the area is not on the typical Sydney tourist trail, it's still well worth a wander. Back in the 19th century, the area now called Greater Western Sydney was a series of rural farming communities, which is why some of the oldest white settlement buildings can be found there. These days, however, the 'settlement' story is very different: the western suburbs cover more than two-thirds of the metropolitan area and house a third of the city's population, with a mix of blue-collar Aussies, Asians, Eastern Europeans, Latinos and others making up the numbers. The melting pot of the west also attracts three-quarters of the 50,000 people who migrate to Sydney each year, making it the fastest growing area of the city (and Australia). The spread of cultures that is represented in these suburbs – which sprawl out from the inner city to the foothills of the lush Blue Mountains – underlines the reality of modern Sydney and Australia in general.

Old Government House.

Don't Miss

1 **Skyline Drive-in** Sydney's drive-in cinema (p158).

2 **Banh Cuon Kim Thanh** Try the famous Vietnamese breakfast, *banh cuon* (p159).

3 **Rouse Hill House & Farm** A sprawling traditional Aussie farm estate (p158).

4 **Circa Espresso** Pull up a milk crate at this hipster café (p157).

5 **Old Government House** Go on a ghost tour at Australia's oldest public building (p157).

EXPLORE

EXPLORE

PARRAMATTA

Parramatta – the 'capital' of the west – boasts a historic importance that rivals any area in Sydney, and is also home to the city's second business district. It's a sedate, friendly hub that is forging an identity for itself in the arts with council grants for artists and its **Riverside Theatres** complex (*see p215*), three venues that host stand-up comedy, various arts events and part of the Sydney Festival each January, as well as plays from all over Australia.

Parramatta's heritage as Australia's second-oldest white settlement makes it a popular stop for historically minded visitors. You can learn more about the area at the **Parramatta Heritage & Visitor Information Centre** (*see p293*), on the north bank of the river next to Lennox Bridge, which was built by convict labour in the 1830s. The centre is a short stroll from the ferry wharf via the **Riverside Walk**, designed by Aboriginal artist Jamie Eastwood and exploring the story of the Parramatta river and the traditions of the Burramatta people, Parramatta's first inhabitants.

Once known as the 'cradle city', Parramatta is the site of many Australian firsts: its first jail, land grant, successful farm (which saved the First Fleet from starvation in 1788), orchard, train line to Sydney and wool mill. Many of the first settlers were buried in **St John's Cemetery**, on O'Connell Street between St John's Cathedral and Parramatta Park.

Parramatta is a dynamic mix of old and new, with towering skyscrapers next door to heritage-listed huts. **Elizabeth Farm**, built in 1793 by wool pioneer John Macarthur and named after his wife, is the oldest colonial home still standing in Australia. Also open for viewing is **Old Government House**, the oldest public building in Australia.

Those seeking retail therapy during their tour of the west should head to the gargantuan **Westfield Parramatta** mall on Church Street, near the station. Pretty much everything is here – there are 528 outlets – including an 11-cinema complex popular with local teens.

Sights & Museums

Elizabeth Farm
70 Alice Street, between Arthur & Alfred Streets, Rosehill (9635 9488, www.hht.net.au). Parramatta or Rosehill rail. **Open** 9.30am-4pm Fri-Sun. **Admission** $4-$8.

Elizabeth Farm.

Elizabeth Farm is notable both for being the birthplace of the Australian wool industry – John Macarthur imported merino sheep for breeding at the site – and for the farm's main building. With its deep, shady verandas and stone-flagged floors, it became the prototype for the Australian homestead.

Old Government House

Parramatta Park (9635 8149, www.nsw.national trust.org.au). Parramatta rail or RiverCat ferry. **Open** 10am-4pm Mon-Fri; 10.30am-4pm Sat, Sun. **Admission** $6-$9.

Set in 105 hectares (260 acres) of parkland, Old Government House was built between 1799 and 1818 on the foundations of Governor Phillips's 1790 thatched cottage, which had collapsed, and is Australia's oldest public building. The building has been restored to its former glory by a multi-million-dollar revamp, boasts the nation's most important collection of Australian colonial furniture, and hosts great ghost tours.

Restaurants & Cafés

Chocolateria San Churro

287 Church Street (9633 1566, www.sanchurro. com). Parramatta rail. **Open** 10am-11pm Mon-Thur, Sun; 10am-midnight Fri, Sat. **Café**
San Churro is a chocolatier serving Spanish-style thick hot chocolate with Spain's greatest contribution to carb lovers the world over: churros. Cakes, shakes and ice-cream round out the menu. **Other locations** throughout the city.

Circa Espresso

21 Wentworth Street (circaespresso.com.au). Parramatta rail. **Open** 7am-4pm Tue-Fri; 8am-3pm Sat. **Main courses** $12-$19. **Café**
Circa Espresso is bringing some village vibes to Sydney's geographic centre with great coffee and tasty breakfast treats. Being the only café of its ilk in the vicinity means that things can get pretty busy here, so you may need to wait for a table.

Emporium

51 Phillip Street (9687 1955, theemporium parramatta.com.au). Parramatta rail. 7am-11.30pm daily. **Main courses** $18-$36. **Café/contemporary Australian**
It almost feels wrong to label the Emporium a restaurant. Because it's so much more: a two-floor, 150-seat eaterie with indoor and outdoor seating, a wine bar, a bakery and an on-site coffee roastery with a 25-kilo monster of a German bean machine. The fare is modern Australian with a hint of Mediterranean flair, all complemented by a rustic, Italianesque interior. You might find grilled calamari with chorizo and corn purée; pan-fried gnocchi with green peas, ricotta and broad beans, or overnight-cooked beef short rib with a maple and paprika glaze and chimichurri.

Bars

Albion Hotel

135 George Street (9891 3288, www.albionhotel. com.au). Parramatta rail. **Open** 10am-late Mon-Sat; 10am-midnight Sun.
The sprawling beer garden is a beaut: a leafy, shaded expanse that's easy to lose an afternoon in. The adjoining Garden Bar has a pavilion and banquettes and day beds to loll on. Catch live music, tune into sport on the big screen or simply idle time away after a day's sightseeing.

Bavarian Bier Cafe

2-8 Phillip Street (8836 1400, www.bavarian biercafe.com.au). Parramatta rail. **Open** 11am-midnight daily.
Sydney bars don't come more spectacular than this fully restored century-old church, now hosting hop-lovers and hearty-food fans. Pork knuckles and mega-schnitzels abound, best accompanied by torrents of excellent Bavarian amber.

Riverside Brewing Company

2 North Rocks Road, North Parramatta (www. riversidebrewing.com.au). Parramatta rail. **Open** 2-6pm Fri; noon-4pm Sat.
Parramatta's first craft brewery is a serious operation. Currently, staff are hard at work brewing batches of their 33 golden ale, 44 American amber, 55 pale ale, 69 summer ale, 77 India pale ale and 88 robust porter to sate Sydney's growing appetite for craft beer. Head here for the freshest brews in town on Friday and Saturday afternoons.

EXPLORE

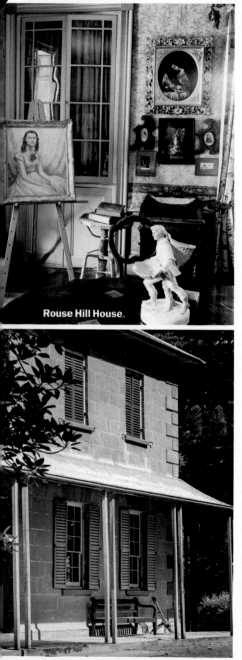

Rouse Hill House.

BLACKTOWN & AROUND

Blacktown, located 11 kilometres (seven miles) north-west of Parramatta, earned its name from being home to the Native Institution, established by the early colonial authorities to educate Aboriginal children. Today, 2.3 per cent of the local population is Aboriginal – that's just over 7,000 people.

For a unique insight into Australian taste through the years, head north of Blacktown to **Rouse Hill** and the historic **Rouse Hill House & Farm**. And if you want to see native wildlife, including a face-to-face encounter with a koala, visit the excellent, family-run **Featherdale Wildlife Park**, home to strange-looking cassowaries and scary-looking owls. Cinephiles should make a stop at Sydney's only drive-in cinema, **Skyline** (*see p187*), done out in a 1950s America theme.

Sights & Museums

Featherdale Wildlife Park
217-229 Kildare Road, Doonside (9622 1644, www.featherdale.com.au). Blacktown rail or bus 725. **Open** 9am-5pm daily. **Admission** $12.50-$23.
Kangaroos, koalas and Tasmanian devils all feature in this well-kept wildlife park, which houses one of Australia's largest collections of native animals. The huge diversity of birds includes the bizarre cassowary, which usually lives in the rainforests in the tropical far north.

Rouse Hill House & Farm
Guntawong Road, off Windsor Road, Rouse Hill (9627 6777, www.hht.net.au). Riverstone rail or bus 741R. **Open** *Tours* 9.30am-4.30pm Wed-Sun. **Admission** $4-$8.
This two-storey Georgian sandstone house, set in a 15-hectare (37-acre) estate, was the home of the Rouse family for six generations. Free settler Richard Rouse built the original house between 1813 and 1818, and his last direct descendant left in 1993. There are also some 20 outbuildings, ranging from a pretty Victorian summerhouse to a corrugated iron cottage annex, and a very early 'dry weather' garden.

Bars

Atura
32 Cricketers Arms Road, Blacktown (9421 0000, www.aturablacktown.com.au). Bus 724. **Open** 6.30am-late daily.
Atura Blacktown features bold styling and retro interiors. The place has a community feel – there's an open-mic night on weekends and an outdoor ping-pong table; the Miami-style pool has barbecues; and the bar boasts the largest collection of whiskeys west of Marrickville.

CABRAMATTA & BANKSTOWN

Further west is the Asian centre of **Cabramatta**, a food- and clothes-shopper's delight that draws visitors with its vibrant market life. Cabramatta, **Bankstown** and their neighbours comprise the country's multicultural heartland. Given Sydney's dominance over Australia's other state capitals, it's hardly surprising that it remains the most popular destination for immigrants entering Australia, and the vast majority of those that come to the city take up residence in the western suburbs. In some south-western suburbs, more than half the population was born overseas, with residents hailing from Italy, Greece, Vietnam, Cambodia, the Philippines, China, Serbia, Croatia, Poland, Latin America, Lebanon and the Pacific Islands.

One of the consequences of this multicultural mix is that there's high-quality, inexpensive dining to be had – Cabramatta in particular has developed a name for itself as the culinary centre of the western suburbs. It also suffers from a reputation as Sydney's heroin central thanks to the proliferation of Asian gangs, and tends to hit the headlines for drug- and gang-related deaths.

If you like dining and shopping, don't miss the area's exotic mix of Aussie suburbia. From Cabramatta station, cross over the road to Arthur Street and pass through the ornate Pai Lau Gate into **Freedom Plaza**, the main marketplace. It's like stepping into Asia itself, with the authentic flavours of Thai, Laotian, Cambodian, Filipino and Chinese cuisines on offer at numerous stalls. There are plenty of discount fabric, clothing and jewellery dealers too: on Park Road, John Street, Hughes Street and around the main plaza, direct importers and wholesalers ply their wares in typical bazaar fashion (haggling is the norm). Other attractions are nearby Buddhist temples **Tien Hau** (124 Railway Parade, Canley Vale) and **Kwan Yin** (2 Second Avenue, Canley Vale).

The best time to visit is when the Chinese and Vietnamese communities hold their New Year celebrations (around February), with wild dragon parades and more firecrackers than you can shake a match at. Some lucky visitors may experience the annual Moon Festival, held on the 15th day of the eighth lunar month – August or September, depending on the year.

Sport is a key feature of life in the west too. It's thanks to the high number of immigrants that soccer is a bigger sport than rugby in this part of the city. Sydney soccer fans follow their teams with a fiery passion based along ethnic lines, and the games can be boisterous and spectacular affairs. Local teams in the NSW premier league include the Parramatta Eagles, Marconi Stallions, Blacktown City Demons and Bankstown City Lions. Bankstown is also the hometown of the famous cricketing Waugh brothers, and boasts an

INSIDE TRACK GRITTY CITY

For a grittily honest portrayal of the lives of the homeless and disadvantaged in the Asian centre of Sydney, check out local director Khoa Do's no-holds-barred film *The Finished People* (2003); star-studded, downbeat drama *Little Fish* (2005), starring Cate Blanchett and Hugo Weaving; and *Cedar Boys* and *The Combination* (both 2009, both dealing with youthful Lebanese gang life in western Sydney).

impressive cricket team. Watch them on summer weekends at the **Bankstown Oval** (corner of Chapel Road South and Macauley Avenue).

Restaurants & Cafés

Banh Cuon Kim Thanh

Shop 7, 313 Chapel Road (south), Bankstown (9708 6661). Bankstown rail. **Open** 8am-6pm Mon, Wed-Sun. **Main courses** $8.50-$12. **Vietnamese**
Shake up your morning ritual with the northern Vietnamese breakfast of champions: *banh cuon* – slippery rice noodles served with slices of *cha lua* Vietnamese pork sausage, bean sprouts, cucumber and shredded lettuce. Save room for some deep-fried snacks: the *banh cong* shrimp and mung bean cakes are like a fried savoury muffin that you wrap in lettuce and dip in *nuoc cham* sauce; *banh tom* shrimp and sweet potato fritters are deliciously crunchy.

Battambang

15/73-79 John Street, Cabramatta (9754 2120). Cabramatta rail. **Open** 7am-6pm daily. **Main courses** $8-$10. **Pan-Asian**
Pork intestines, also known as chitterlings, aren't just a triumph of nose-to-tail eating, but a prized delicacy at this Cambodian eatery. You'll also find a good range of Khmer, Vietnamese and Chinese dishes – and the friendly staff are happy to provide you with an English menu.

Phounguen

148 Cabramatta Road East, Cabramatta (9727 2563). Cabramatta rail. **Open** noon-9.30pm daily. **Main courses** $10-$17. **Thai/Laotian**
Phounguen serves a mix of Laotian and Thai dishes – from green curry to pad thai to chicken feet salad – and a photo menu makes ordering a cinch. If you're after something different, there's Laotian dried beef – beef slices marinated in spices and then dried to a jerky, then deep fried so all the fatty bits get extra crispy before being tossed in a sticky syrup. But what this place is really known for is ox tongue, which is marinated and barbecued into a tender, smoky bundle of flavour. The decor is pretty basic but who cares when many dishes are ten bucks?

EXPLORE

The South

As Sydneysiders search for their own piece of beachside paradise, the south is coming into its own. Here, houses are bigger, prices are lower and there's more of a family vibe. The south technically starts at Greek community hub Brighton-le-Sands in the district of Rockdale, before extending into a very cliquey district known as 'the Shire', inhabited by people who call themselves 'the locals'. Cronulla is the stronghold of the Shire, championing a lifestyle of sun, sea, surf and anything (preferably motorised) that allows you to travel on water. It helps to have 'the look' when visiting Cronulla Beach: a tan, blonde hair and as little clothing as modesty will allow. If that's not you, you might be more comfortable with the multicultural Sunday crowd picnicking beneath the trees. And don't let the legacy of the 2005 riots put you off – the locals are a friendly bunch.

Languishing across Port Hacking from Cronulla is the former pirate's grotto turned artists' colonies of Bundeena and Maianbar. Here, inside the Royal National Park, life is full of private picnics, swimming spots and much home- and pool-building.

EXPLORE

Black Star Pastry.

Don't Miss

1 **Royal National Park** Swim or canoe at this vast nature reserve (p162).

2 **Grounds of Alexandria** Excellent coffee and great brunch (p163).

3 **Archie Rose** Beautiful industrial bar inside a distillery (p163).

4 **Cronulla Park Ice Creamery** Have a scoop on the beach (p162).

5 **Black Star Pastry** Heart-shaped biscuits like buttery love notes (p163).

CRONULLA

This beachside suburb in Sydney's Shire, immortalised in the coming-of-age novel *Puberty Blues* (and more recently its brilliant TV adaptation), has come a long way since the era of Chiko Rolls (an iconically Australian fast food that's like a spring roll) and surfie girls. Cronulla is a much longer beach than its more famous city counterparts Bondi, Coogee, Clovelly and Maroubra. It takes at least four hours to walk its length from South Cronulla northwards to Green Hills and beyond. There's also a walking track that starts at the end of South Cronulla and wends its way southwards around the cliff of **Port Hacking** and past sea pools to **Darook Park**, where you can swim in calm, clear water. Halfway along the track is **Bass and Flinders Point**: from here, you can stare across the water to Jibbon Beach in Bundeena on the edge of the Royal National Park.

Serious surfers like to head to the northern end, to **Eloura**, **Wanda** and **Green Hills** beaches, where there's often the background churn of 4WDs on the sand dunes behind the beach. Revs are big in these parts – especially on the water. Jet skis, speedboats and waterskiers create chaos in the otherwise sleepy arms of the Port Hacking estuary every weekend. For more water action, contact Cronulla Surf School (9544 0895, www.cronullasurf.com.au) for surfing lessons, or Pro Dive (9544 2200, www.prodivecronulla.com) to discover what lies beneath the waves.

Restaurants & Cafés

Beach Burrito Company
1 Kingsway (9544 3442, www.beachburrito company.com). Cronulla rail. **Open** 5-10pm Mon-Thur; 11.30am-10pm Fri, Sat; 11am-10pm Sun. **Main courses** $14-$20. **Mexican**
The *tacitos* served smack bang on the shores of Cronulla Beach are heaven in a basket. They're stuffed with cheese, pulled beef, chipotle chicken or chilli-roasted pork, then rolled, flash-fried and topped with lime and chilli salt.

Cronulla Park Ice Creamery
Shop 11, 20 Gerrale Street (9544 1592). Cronulla rail. **Open** 10am-7pm daily. **Ice-cream**
Sure, you can grab ice-cream and gelato here, but it also does coffee, which is great for your morning, pre-ice-cream needs.

Bars

Blind Bear Saloon
28 Cronulla Street (www.facebook.com/blindbear cronulla). Cronulla rail. **Open** 5-11.30pm Wed-Sat; 5-10pm Sun.

Want chicken wings and a pale ale? Then head to the 1920s-themed Blind Bear Saloon. Other pub classics here include burgers, hot dogs and hoagies.

Northies
Corner of Kingsway & Elouera Road (9523 6866, www.northies.com.au). Cronulla rail. **Open** 10am-11.30pm Mon-Wed; 11am-12.30am Thur-Sat; 10am-10pm Sun.
When the sun goes down on Cronulla's star attraction, things start to ramp up at Northies. This sprawling, single-storey venue tucked under a shiny new apartment complex faces right on to Cronulla Beach, ready to dole out beers and burgers as people migrate from the waterline to the nearest watering hole.

BUNDEENA

A ferry across Port Hacking estuary delivers you to Bundeena, a small township (population 2,300, of which about a quarter is under 18 years old) that spreads out along the top of the north-eastern section of the **Royal National Park**. Established in 1879, this was Australia's first national park – and only the second in the world after Yellowstone in the US. Covering 150 square kilometres (58 square miles) on the southern boundary of the Sydney metropolitan area, it offers stunning coastline, rainforest, open wetlands and heath.

Bundeena, which means 'noise like thunder' in the local Aboriginal language, was named after the sound of the surf pounding on the east coast. The Aboriginal Dharawal people used the area as a camping ground, and were sometimes joined by other large clans for feasting and ceremonies. In the 1820s, white settlers arrived in 'the Village', as locals call Bundeena, to build a few fishing shacks. More came during the 1930s Depression, but it was only after World War II that a substantial number of permanent houses and holiday homes began to appear.

There are three main beaches, two of which fall within the national park. The main strip of sand is **Hordens Beach**, which you'll see to your right as you approach by ferry. At its far end, hop up the rocks and take the track through the bush to **Jibbon Head**, about 20 minutes away, where there are awe-inspiring views out to sea. A sign en route points to Aboriginal rock carvings of whales and fish. From Jibbon Head, you can walk further down the coast on a well-worn track; it's about a three-hour return walk to Marley Beach, or six hours to Wattamolla. Take plenty of water, sunscreen and insect repellent in summer.

Sights & Museums

★ Royal National Park
9542 0648, www.nationalparks.nsw.gov.au. **Open** *Park* 7am-8.30pm daily. *Visitor centre*

EXPLORE

9.30am-4.30pm Mon-Fri; 8.30am-4.30pm Sat, Sun. **Admission** free; $11 per vehicle.
You can get to the Royal by following walking paths from various nearby Sydney Train stations – Engadine, Heathcote, Loftus, Otford, Waterfall – but driving is the easiest way to explore its vast expanse. The park's nerve centre is at Audley, on the Hacking river, once the heart of the park's Victorian 'pleasure gardens'. Here, you'll find the main visitor centre, spacious lawns, an old-fashioned dance hall and a causeway. You can hire canoes, take hikes and find secluded swimming spots too.

ROSEBERY

Away from the beach, but south of the CBD, you'll find what was once a cluster of metal workshops and furniture warehouses, and is now an industrial-chic neighbourhood with funky cafés, restaurants and shopping districts.

Explore minimalist design store **Koskela**, and sample the wares at the local outpost of Newtown stalwart **Black Star Pastry** (hot crumbly pies and the famous watermelon and strawberry cake). Pizza addicts can go all in for gooey cheese and crisp, charred bases at local pizza/pasta bar **Da Mario**, and caffeine fiends should grab a seat at **Allpress Espresso**. Sydneysiders have neglected Rosebery for far too long – now that it's cool, everybody's keen to join the club.

Restaurants & Cafés

Allpress Espresso

58 Epsom Road (9662 8288). Bus 309, 310, 370, M20. **Open** 7am-3pm Mon-Fri; 8am-2pm Sat. **Café**
All the heavy artillery – roasters, grinders, packers – is out back, yet all of it is visible from the sleek café frontage on Epsom Road. Italian-style sandwiches fly out the door as fast as the coffee and there's constant hustle on the banquettes and booths inside.

Black Star Pastry

C1 85-113 Dunning Avenue (blackstarpastry. com.au). Bus 309, 310, M20. **Open** 8am-3pm Mon-Fri; 8am-4pm Sat, Sun. **Café & bakery**
The coffee is good, but oh, the cakes! Top pick is lemon myrtle chiffon cake covered in toasted coconut – so light and spongy it looks like it's going to float off. **Other location** 277 Australia Street, Newtown (9557 8656).

Da Mario

36 Morley Avenue (9669 2242, damario.com.au). Bus 309, 310, 343, M20. **Open** noon-3pm, 5pm-late Tue-Sun. **Main courses** $16-$26. **Pizza**
Pizza fans, rejoice – this new joint makes pies the classic Italian way, with thin doughy bases and minimal ingredients that go a long way. Service is swift, the small wine list goes from Italy to Mudgee without topping $63 a bottle, and it's abuzz most nights.

Bars

Archie Rose

61 Mentmore Avenue (8458 2300, archierose. com.au). Bus 343. **Open** noon-10pm daily.
A beautiful bar inside a distillery, in the same compound as ace pastries, pizza and designer homewares.

Shops & Services

Koskela

85 Mentmore Avenue (9280 0999, www.koskela.com. au). Bus 309, 310, 343, M20. **Open** 9.30am-5pm Mon-Fri; 9am-4pm Sat; 10am-4pm Sun. **Homewares**
This warehouse space showcases a mix of vintage and new furniture and homewares selected by owners Russel Koskela and Sasha Titckosky, who curate each space to reflect a different room in the home. Koskela Kitchen is open for breakfast, coffee and lunch.

ALEXANDRIA

The suburb previously known for its trucks and warehouses has been invaded by great cafés of late and is billed as a potential successor to Surry Hills and Redfern as the next 'it' hood. Which means it's also been invaded by brunchers – so watch for queues.

Restaurants & Cafés

Cafe Sopra

Corner of Mitchell Road & Buckland Street (8399 4777, www.fratellifresh.com.au). Erskineville rail or bus 308, 355. **Open** noon-3pm, 6-10pm daily. **Main courses** $18-$26. **Italian**
A fruit-and-veg-shop-cum-Italian-restaurant, where fresh ingredients are simply cooked; pizza and pasta are to the fore. What's more, the wine list is a steal.

Don Campos

Shop 1, 21 Fountain Street (9690 0090, www. camposcoffee.com/new-south-wales). Erskineville rail or bus 308, 355. **Open** 6.30am-4pm Mon-Fri; 8am-4pm Sat, Sun. **Coffee shop**
Drink your fill of the Campos espresso in this restored warehouse space, or try a different single origin brew, a colddrip or filter coffee at the pour-over station.

Grounds of Alexandria

Building 7, 2 Huntley Street (9699 2225, www. groundsroasters.com). Bus 348. **Open** 7am-4pm Mon-Fri; 8am-3pm Sat, Sun. **Café**
First and foremost, this place is about coffee. There are two separate espresso stations – one for in-house and one for takeaways – which churn through huge bags of the beans that are roasted a few feet away. There are great eats, too, both for breakfast/brunch and lunch (sirloin steak sandwiches, pumpkin risotto, chargrilled marlin). The Grounds also has a leafy garden.

EXPLORE

Sydney's Best Beaches

Beaches are where Sydneysiders head to cool off and get zen. There are more than 50 beaches along Sydney's coastline, from upmarket Palm Beach in the north to family-magnet Cronulla in the south, each with its own character. The protected harbour beaches inside the Heads (the headlands forming the two-kilometre-wide entrance to Sydney Harbour) are smaller and have no surf, but are great for views and picnics. After heavy rain, however, they're not ideal for swimming, as pollution floats in through the storm pipes. Instead, locals take their daily dip in the outdoor seawater pools cut into the rocks – both harbour and ocean. The bigger, bolder ocean beaches attract surfers and serious swimmers.

Cronulla.

Don't Miss

1 **Parsley Bay** Part of a wildlife-filled nature reserve (p168).

2 **Chinamans Beach** A quiet paradise hidden beyond dunes (p169).

3 **Maroubra Beach** Huge waves make this a top surf spot (p172).

4 **Cronulla Beach** Six kilometres of sand and lots of surf breaks (p172).

5 **Collaroy Beach** Honey-coloured sand and a large ocean pool (p174).

Surf lifesavers.

BEACH RULES

From September to May, nearly all of Sydney's ocean beaches are patrolled at weekends by local volunteer lifesavers and during the week by lifeguards – hours vary with the beach and time of year. The famous surf lifesavers wear red and yellow uniforms and an unmistakeable skullcap. The council-paid lifeguards (who are sometimes also hired on harbour beaches) wear different colours – usually a more sober blue or green – and in surfing hotspots such as Bondi and Manly work 365 days a year, their exploits frequently the subject of reality television shows such as the high-rating *Bondi Rescue*.

Rules on Sydney's beaches are stringent: alcohol and fires are banned; and on many beaches, ball games, skateboards, in-line skates, kites and frisbees are also illegal. Smoking is also forbidden on many beaches, including Bondi, Tamarama, Bronte, Coogee and Maroubra in the south, at Manly and the northern beaches up to Palm Beach, and the beaches on the north side of the harbour. Beachgoers can be fined $110 for smoking and $200 for disposing of their cigarette butts, although most councils do not as yet force their rangers to issue fines, and offenders will generally be politely asked not to smoke on the beach again. Locals love to fish on the beach, but these days you need a licence and there are catch and size limits. Dropping rubbish is also an offence – 'Don't be a tosser, take your rubbish with you!' is the motto – and recycling

is a must in the bins provided. Don't expect to find deckchair touts, donkeys or even an ice-cream seller, because Sydneysiders are fiercely protective of the fact that their beaches are unspoilt – and they intend to keep them that way.

WATER TEMPERATURES

The water at Sydney beaches can turn icy without warning, so take the following as a guide only. As a general rule, the water temperature lags a couple of months behind the air temperature. So when the weather is warming up in October and November, the ocean is still holding its winter chill of 16-17°C (61-63°F). Only in December does the sea become a nicely swimmable 18-19°C (64-66°F). The ocean is a balmy 20-21°C (68-70°F) from February to April, sometimes until May. It can even reach 23-24°C (73-75°F) if there's a warm current running from the north. The bronze-skinned, barrel-chested beach bums who lounge along the coast like human iguanas tune out then.

Below are Sydney's best beaches: the harbour beaches are listed from east to west; the northern ocean beaches heading north; and the southern ocean beaches heading south.

For more information on many of the beaches listed here and their surrounding areas, see the relevant Explore chapters. For information on the latest surfing conditions, visit www.coastalwatch.com.

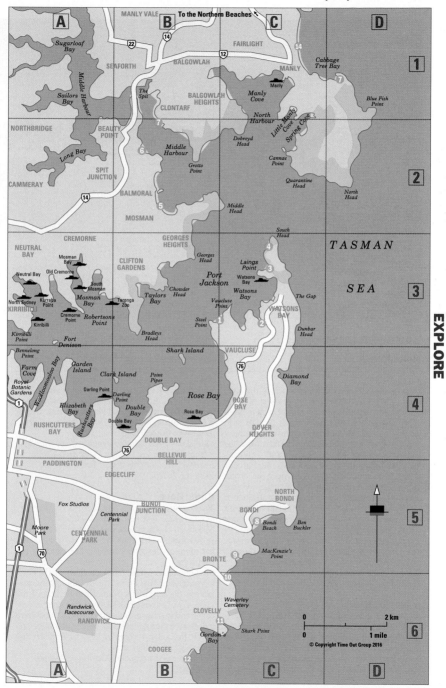

Camp Cove.

EXPLORE

HARBOUR BEACHES

Shark Beach
Nielsen Park, Vaucluse Road, Vaucluse. Bus 325.
Map 167 B3 ❶
Locals swim in the smooth warm waters of this sheltered harbour inlet all year round. In summer, it's as packed as an Australian beach can get, with families swarming the narrow 300m beach or picnicking in the shade of the Moreton Bay fig trees on the grassy slopes. Part of leafy Nielsen Park, the beach also has fabulous views of Manly, Shark Island (hence its name) and, from the upper parklands, the Harbour Bridge. If you don't swim, you can watch the ferries, yachts, kayakers, seaplanes and oil tankers vie for space in the harbour, or you could just grab a bite to eat. Nielsen Park (9337 7333), an Italian restaurant that's been serving since 1914, offers trattoria fare when it's not booked for a wedding. Less formal is its licensed café next door, which serves pizzas, wraps, ice-cream and excellent coffee and be prepared to queue. *Café. Changing rooms. Child-friendly. No dogs. Parking. Picnic area. Restaurant. Shade. Shark net (Sept-May). Showers. Toilets.*

★ Parsley Bay
Horler Avenue, Vaucluse. Bus 325. **Map** p167 C3 ❷
It's the grass, not the tiny beach, that is the big draw here. Nestled at the foot of a steep (and sometimes treacherous) road of million-dollar mansions, the bay is part of a 5.7-hectare nature reserve with an abundance of birds, fish and insects. It's great for

small children, who can play safely on the lawns and in the well-equipped recreation area, and there are excellent walks through the bush and even across a rickety suspension bridge over the water. The small crescent-shaped beach (roughly 70m long) leads into what are often murky waters: after heavy rain, rubbish floats into the bay from storm pipes. Nevertheless, the millpond-like swimming area is popular with snorkellers and scuba divers thanks to its array of tropical fish. *Café (closes 4pm). Changing rooms. Child-friendly (play area). No dogs. Parking. Picnic area. Shade. Shark net (removed for repairs 1mth winter). Showers. Toilets.*

Camp Cove
Victoria Street, Watsons Bay. Watsons Bay ferry or bus 324, 325, 380, L24. **Map** p167 C3 ❸
Serious sun-seekers love this 200m strip of bright yellow sand, which runs in a thin curve against a backdrop of designer cottages. The beach is not particularly great for surfing, but it's a fine place for a dip and provides fabulous views of the city's skyscrapers. At the southern end of the upper grasslands is the start of the South Head Heritage Trail. Camp Cove has one small kiosk serving sandwiches, coffee and ice-cream. Although the beach does have a dedicated parking area, spaces are at a huge premium; far better to come by ferry to Watsons Bay and walk around the corner. *Café (Oct-May). Lifesavers (Oct-May). No dogs. Parking. Toilets.*

EXPLORE

Lady Bay Beach

Victoria & Cliff Streets, Watsons Bay. Watsons Bay ferry or bus 324, 325, 380, L24. **Map** p167 C3 ❹
Sydney's first nudist beach, Lady Bay is just below South Head and a short walk along the South Head Heritage Trail from Camp Cove. Steep iron steps lead down to the 100m beach, which is reduced to virtually nothing when the tide comes in: you're better off sunbathing on one of the rocks. It's popular as a pick-up place for gay men, but Lady Bay offers scenic as well as sexual thrills, including spectacular views of the city and, if you walk around the headland to Hornby Lighthouse, the open sea to the east (it's actually the last southern beach inside the harbour).
No dogs. Toilets (located on the clifftop above beach).

North

Balmoral Beach

The Esplanade, Balmoral. South Mosman (Musgrave Street) ferry then bus 233 or Taronga Zoo ferry then bus 238. **Map** p167 B2 ❺
Home to Sydney's seriously rich, Balmoral has been a popular bathing spot since the late 1900s. Its beach promenade and Bathers' Pavilion (9969 50504, The Esplanade) were both built in the late 1920s and retain a genteel air from that era. Hundreds of families flock here at weekends to enjoy the sheltered waters of its two large sandy beaches, which together stretch for about a mile. The beaches are separated by Rocky Point, a tree-covered picnicking island accessible by a footbridge. To the south, Balmoral Beach has an enclosed swimming area surrounded by boardwalks and is excellent for children; to the north, Edwards Beach is bigger and less protected, but has interesting rock pools with shells, fish and anemones. You can hire boats from Balmoral Boathouse. The white rotunda which is often used for weddings also acts as a stage for Shakespeare by the Sea (www.shakespeare-by-the-sea.com).
Boat hire. Cafés. Changing rooms. Child-friendly (play area). Danger: underwater rocks. No dogs. Parking. Picnic areas. Restaurants. Shade. Shark nets. Shops. Showers. Toilets.

★ Chinamans Beach

McLean Crescent, Mosman. Bus 175, 178, 185, 229, 249. **Map** p167 B2 ❻
A real Sydney secret, Chinamans Beach in Middle Harbour is stumbled upon through dunes on the edge of the Rosherville bushland reserve. It's a quiet paradise, with 300m of beautiful sand, gently lapping waters and huge, strikingly designed homes perched on the hills above. Located right opposite busier Clontarf Beach (*see p170*), Chinamans has plenty of recreational facilities – a play area, picnic tables nestled under pepper trees and rolling lawns where you can play ball games – but no shop, café or restaurant. Children love the mass of barnacle-encrusted rock pools at the southern end, but it's prohibited to take any crustaceans home.
Changing rooms. Child-friendly (play area). No dogs. Parking. Picnic area. Shade. Showers. Toilets.

Clontarf Beach

Sandy Bay Road, Clontarf. Bus 171, E71.
Map p167 B1 ⑦

With around 600m of sand, a large grassy picnic area, an excellent playground, outdoor netted pool and all the facilities you might need, Clontarf is a very popular beach for families. It's right opposite the Middle Harbour Yacht Club, so there are good views of the Spit Bridge, with boats sailing underneath and cars racing over the top. It's worth stopping at Balgowlah Heights en route to pick up a picnic – the fantastic Balgowlah Heights Deli on Beatrice Street (no.122, 9949 3969) is open from 7am to 7pm daily.
Barbecues. Café. Changing rooms. Child-friendly (play area). No dogs. Parking. Picnic area. Pool. Restaurant (closed July). Shade. Shark net (Sept-May). Showers. Toilets.

OCEAN BEACHES

East

Bondi Beach

Campbell Parade, Bondi Beach. Bondi Junction rail then bus 380, 381, 382, 333, X84 or bus 222, 380, 389. **Map** p167 C5 ⑧

Australia's most famous beach, Bondi is believed to have been named after an Aboriginal word meaning 'the sound of breaking waves'. Today, its crashing breakers attract a huge fraternity of urban surfies as well as ubiquitous Britpackers and new-generation hippies strumming guitars on the sand. At the height of summer, the beach draws up to 40,000 people per day, but – and you'll find this hard to imagine if you arrive when it's crowded – there are times in the week when it's relatively empty. The elegant Bondi Pavilion, built in 1929 as a changing area, houses showers, toilets, a community centre and cafés. Two lifesaving clubs patrol the half-mile beach – 'Ready Aye Ready' is the motto of the North Bondi Surf Life Saving Club. The central area near the Pavilion is the safest swimming area; surfers favour the southern end, with its strong rips. Also at this end is a skateboard ramp and the famous Bondi Icebergs' pool and club. Be vigilant: 'Thieves go to the beach too', warn big NSW police signs. Lockers are available in the Pavilion – use them. For a local area map, *see p105.*
Barbecues. Cafés. Changing rooms. Child-friendly (play area). Lifeguards/savers. No dogs. Parking. Picnic area. Pool. Restaurants. Shark net (Sept-May). Shops. Showers. Toilets.

Tamarama Beach

Pacific Avenue, Tamarama. Bondi Junction rail then bus 361. **Map** p167 C5 ⑨

Bronte Beach.

A 100m sheltered cove, Tamarama Beach is neither easy to get to by public transport nor to park at should you decide to drive there. Not only that, once you arrive, it's not particularly accessible either: you have to climb down 40 steep steps to reach the water. And with its tricky surf and deep rip, it's not a swimming spot. That said, it's got a serious fan base of macho surfers who like to live dangerously and equally dedicated sun-seekers (there's absolutely no shade to be found on the sand). Britpackers play Sunday soccer matches on the large grassy picnic area and volleyball is the sport on the beach itself. The small children's play area with swings and a slide is within eyeshot of the excellent Tamarama Kiosk (9130 2419), which serves wonderful gourmet vegetarian and non-vegetarian sandwiches as well as refreshing power juices and coffee.
Barbecue. Café. Changing rooms. Child-friendly (play area). Danger: underwater rocks. Lifeguards/ savers (Sept-May). No dogs. Parking. Picnic area. Shark net (Sept-May). Showers. Toilets.

Bronte Beach

Bronte Road, Bronte. Bondi Junction rail then bus 378. **Map** p167 C6 ⑩
Bronte Beach is absolute bliss for local parents – pack the kids, the swimsuits and the boogie boards, and this 300m stretch of sand (complete with cute kids'

train) will babysit all day long. Though the water has a strong rip and is great for surfing, the outdoor Bronte Baths at the southern end – and the adjacent community centre – are the preserve of kids. There's plenty of shade under the sweeping sandstone rocks and scores of covered picnic benches (some with inlaid chessboards) on which to enjoy the traditional Aussie tucker served at the Bronte Kiosk on the beach – meat pies and hot chips aplenty. For more sophisticated dining options, there's a stretch of decent eateries behind the beach along Bronte Road, which run the gamut from sushi to gourmet salads, and from fish and chips to Mediterranean treats.
Barbecues. Cafés. Changing rooms. Child-friendly (play area). Danger: underwater rocks. Lifeguards/ savers (Sept-May). No dogs. Parking. Picnic area. Pool. Restaurants. Shade. Shark net (Sept-May). Shops. Showers. Toilets.

Clovelly Beach

Clovelly Road, Clovelly. Bondi Junction rail then bus 360 or bus 339, X39. **Map** p167 C6 ⑪
Once known as Little Coogee, tucked as it is around the corner from the more famous Big Coogee (which is now simply Coogee Beach; *see below*), Clovelly is an idyllic spot, swathed in natural beauty. The tiny square of sand slopes into a long inlet of calm water, surrounded by a boardwalk and a concrete promenade with chic barbecue pavilions and picnic tables. It's a favourite with scuba divers and snorkellers, but it's the wheelchair access that weaves the real magic. The Clovelly Bay boardwalk boasts specific entry points to the water with locking devices for a submersible wheelchair, on loan from the Beach Inspector's office (weekdays) or the SLSC (weekends). On the south promenade sits a chic 25m, three-lane lap pool. There's also a good café, Seasalt (9664 5344), which serves fish and chips at the takeaway kiosk and more exotic fare at the tables.
Barbecues. Café. Changing rooms. Child-friendly. Lifeguards/savers (Sept-May). No dogs. Parking. Picnic area. Pool. Restaurant. Shade. Showers. Toilets. Wheelchair access.

South

Coogee Beach

Beach Street, Coogee. Bondi Junction rail then bus 313, 314 or bus 372, 373, 374, X73, X74. **Map** p167 B6 ⑫
This excellent family swimming beach is 400m long, with old-fashioned pools carved into the rocks at both ends. In 1929, when nets were introduced, it was declared Australia's first shark-proof beach. It's not great for surfing, but at least you don't have to worry about getting hit by boards. There are fast-food restaurants aplenty, cafés and places to picnic, and it's very much a tourist attraction. In 2003, the northern headland was renamed Dolphin Point in memory of the six Coogee Dolphins rugby league players who were killed in the Bali bombings. Two

EXPLORE

BARBECUE ETIQUETTE
Even casual dining has its own rules.

Aussies are well known for worshipping the fiery altar, throwing snags (sausages), chops (pork, lamb), prawns and bugs (crustaceans), snapper or 'barra' (fish) along with vegetables (onions, aubergine, capsicum) and even fruit (pineapple and bananas) on the hallowed coals. Sydneysiders are no different, and while the universal barbie may seem the most casual of dining events, there is a

certain etiquette to every occasion, plus some rules that must be obeyed.

At public electric or gas barbecues (those in picnic areas, by beaches and in parks), first check you haven't jumped a queue – you'll usually know from the primal roar emanating from the milling throngs you'd hardly noticed. After use, always clean down your barbecue surface – and this means clean, no burnt offerings, no slimy grease spots, and absolutely no rubbish. Then retire to a nearby spot leaving the barbecue for the next person.

If you're invited to a home barbie, always turn up with chilled tinnies, stubbies or chardy, and a plate. No, not a plate to eat off… a plate of meat/fish/vegeburgers to be barbecued, preferably marinated, or a substantial salad for the table. And on no account touch the tongs without permission. An Aussie man's machismo is ruled by his Weber – keep a respectful distance.

If you fancy lighting up your own portable barbie on the roadside, in a park or on a beach, first check the signs. Many beaches and parks do not allow barbecues. Next check if there's a fire ban in place – which there often is in the hot summer months.

Be ready to participate in barbecue games however full/tired/drunk/bored you are. Best of the bunch is a gentle game of boules – worst is spin the (empty) bottle!

---

memorial plaques, plastered with photographs, list the 26 victims from the local community (from a total Australian death toll of 88).
Barbecues. Cafés. Changing rooms. Child-friendly. Lifeguards/savers. No dogs. Parking. Picnic area. Pools. Restaurants. Shade. Shark net (Sept-May). Shops. Showers. Toilets.

★ Maroubra Beach
Marine Parade, Maroubra. Bondi Junction rail then bus 317, 353 or bus 376, 377, 395, 396, X77, X96.
Maroubra Beach was chosen as the new headquarters for Surfing NSW back in 2003 – which didn't come as much of a surprise, since the waves are huge and it's long been a top surf spot. All the organisation's coaching, judging, and educational and safety programmes are conducted at the kilometre-long beach. The Safe Surf School (9365 4370, www.safesurfschools.com. au) is a perfect place for children to learn how to surf away from all the crowds. Much less touristy than neighbouring Coogee, it's also a favourite with beach

sprinters, who run through the shallows in their Speedos. There are a few local shops, showers and toilets, a well-equipped kids' play area and a sizeable skateboard park (which is packed when school's out) located next to the beach's windswept dunes.
Barbecues. Cafés. Changing rooms. Child-friendly (play area). Lifeguards/savers. No dogs. Parking. Picnic area. Pool. Restaurants. Shark net (Sept-May). Shops. Showers. Toilets.

★ Cronulla Beach
Mitchell Road, Cronulla. Cronulla rail.
A vast sandy beach more than 6 kilometres (4 miles) long, Cronulla had a flash of worldwide notoriety in December 2005 as a battleground between groups of white and Middle Eastern Australians. To Sydneysiders, though, it has long been the south's most popular surfing and swimming spot. Cronulla isn't actually one beach but a whole series, running from Kurnell on Botany Bay at the northern end through Wanda, Elouera, North Cronulla, South

Cronulla and on down to Shelly and Port Hacking in the south. On the surfing front, Cronulla Point has lots of breaks off three reef ledges, and experts like to attempt Shark Island, the area's most notorious break. It has the feel of a big Queensland resort with its high-rise apartments and hotels, bars, steakhouses and carloads of young rev-heads. The southern end, a half-moon patch of sand around 100m long, is patrolled by a lifeguard all year round; with less of a rip, this is family territory for bathing, messing around in the rock pools or swimming indoors at the Cronulla Sports Complex (located next to the lifesavers' hut). The much longer northern end of the beach has a fiercer undertow and views of a not-so-pretty oil refinery. There's a huge grassy picnic area with plenty of tables and an esplanade walkway. Getting to Cronulla from the city takes about 50 minutes by train or an hour by car.
Cafés. Changing rooms. Child-friendly (play area). Lifeguards/savers (south all year round; north Sept-May). No dogs. Parking. Picnic area. Pools. Restaurants. Shade. Shark net (Sept-May). Shops. Showers. Toilets.

North

★ Shelly Beach
Marine Parade, Manly. Manly ferry. **Map** p167 D1 ⑬

A ten-minute stroll south of Manly, small Shelly Beach is a family delight with yellow sand, gentle waters and a grassy picnic area. As you stroll south along the promenade from Manly, don't miss the Fairy Bower ocean pool, an excellent outdoor rock pool with spectacular views of the coastline and its famous sculptures (*Sea Nymphs* by Helen Leete). Set in Cabbage Tree Bay, Shelly Beach is best known for its good swimming conditions, but it is also popular with novice scuba divers and for seekers of quality surf; Shelly is the paddle-out spot for the Bower – one of Australia's better big wave locations.
Barbecue. Café. Changing rooms. Child-friendly. No dogs. Parking. Picnic area. Restaurant (closed Mon, Sun in winter). Shade. Showers. Toilets.

Manly Beach
Manly. Manly ferry. **Map** p167 C1 ⑭

Jumping aboard a Sydney ferry is a must and a trip to Manly is the perfect excuse. Take one of the trusty old yellow-and-green giants from Circular Quay to Manly Wharf in Manly Cove, where there's a small harbour beach (about 250m long) and a netted swimming area. To reach the open sea, head across the busy pedestrianised street, the Corso, to the 1.5km crescent of sand known as Manly Surf Beach, but actually comprising Queenscliff in the north, followed by North Steyne, South Steyne and Manly

Cronulla Beach.

Beaches. A magnet for mums, surfies and international tourists, Manly has all the facilities of a big resort and on a hot day attracts up to 50,000 visitors. It also has plenty of history: in 1903, it was one of the first beaches to permit daylight swimming, but the crowds didn't understand the danger of the surf – there are rips along the entire length of the beach – and so fishermen Eddie and Joe Sly set up Manly's first lifesaving patrol. It's not all about surf: you can snorkel, dive, sail and fish, and the beach volleyball nets are in almost constant use. Cyclists and in-line skaters can enjoy the bike track along the shore, from Burnt Bridge Creek to Shelly Beach. For a local area map, *see p151*.
Cafés. Changing rooms. Child-friendly. Lifeguards/savers. No dogs. Parking. Picnic area. Pool (at Queensdiff). Restaurants. Shade. Shark net (Sept-May). Shops. Showers. Toilets.

★ Collaroy Beach
Pittwater Road, Collaroy. Bus 188, 190, E83, E84, E86, E87, E88, E89, L88, L90. **Map** p148.
North of Manly lies a stretch of magnificent surfing beaches with wonderfully ludicrous names, such as Curl Curl, Dee Why, Long Reef and Narrabeen. At Collaroy, which lies directly south of Narrabeen, there's a kilometre stretch of honey-coloured sand pounded by huge waves. It's also got an excellent, large ocean pool, plus a toddler pool at its southern end. The Bruce Bartlett Memorial Playground to the rear is shaded and has masses of fun equipment. The Surf Rock Hotel is right on the beach. Its deck is the place to be for alfresco beers and light meals, right on the sand with the waves in front of you. This is a true local hangout; be prepared for the whole area to get thumping at night.
Barbecues. Cafés. Changing rooms. Child-friendly (play area). Danger: underwater rocks. Lifeguards/savers (Sept-May). Parking. Picnic area. Pools. Restaurants. Shark net (Sept-May). Shops. Showers. Toilets.

Newport Beach
Barrenjoey Road, Newport. Bus 188, 190, E88, E89, L88, L90. **Map** p148.
This half-mile of windswept beach offers good surf with easy access to a busy main road of shops, cafés and restaurants. Its accessibility makes it very popular with locals keen to catch a quick wave. There's a well-equipped, fenced-off play area in the grassland to the rear, but at dusk the beach can get rowdy and is no place for youngsters.
Barbecues. Cafés. Changing rooms. Children's play area. Danger: underwater rocks. Lifeguards/savers (Sept-May). No dogs. Parking. Picnic area. Pool (south end). Restaurants. Shark net (Sept-May). Shops. Showers. Toilets.

Avalon Beach
Barrenjoey Road, Avalon. Bus 188, 190, E88, E89, L88, L90. **Map** p148.

This sandy and sophisticated half-mile beach gets pretty busy in the summer, especially with surfers, who arrive by the carload to tackle the generous waves. There's also good swimming and an excellent ocean pool at the southern end, and the whole beach is backed by grassy sand dunes.
Barbecues. Changing rooms. Children's play area. Lifeguards/savers (Sept-May). Parking. Picnic area. Pool. Shark net (Sept-May). Showers. Toilets.

Whale Beach
The Strand, Whale Beach. Bus 190, L90 to Avalon then bus 193. **Map** p148.
Approached via a precariously steep road, this 700m stretch of salmon-pink sand offers big surf and a rugged coastline. There's a 25m ocean pool at the southern end: take care when the tide comes in as the waves crash over the pool and surrounding rocks. Unlike nearby Palm Beach (*see below*), Whale tends to remain crowd-free and is something of a local hideaway. There's a kiosk on the beach serving freshly made rolls, juices and hot food, while more elaborate cafés and restaurants turn a trade back up Whale Beach Road: the Olive & Rose café (9974 1383, closed Mon & Tue) is well worth a visit.
Barbecues. Café (closed July). Changing rooms. Child-friendly (play area). Danger: underwater rocks. Lifeguards/savers (Sept-May). Parking. Picnic area. Pool. Restaurants. Shade. Shark net (Sept-May). Showers. Toilets.

Palm Beach
Barrenjoey Road, Palm Beach. Bus 190, L90. **Map** p148.
Situated at the northernmost tip of the northern beaches peninsula, Palm Beach is a local paradise. Don't be fooled by Palm Beach Wharf, a busier beach on the west side that you come to first. Keep on driving up the hill and around the bend to get to the real deal on the east side: you won't be disappointed. Palm Beach is home to Sydney's rich and famous; colonial-style mansions set on the hillside possess breathtaking views of foaming ocean and more than a mile of caramel-coloured sand. The southern end, known as Cabbage Tree Boat Harbour, is the safest spot to swim and surf. If you find the sea too daunting, there's the excellent Jack 'Johnny' Carter outdoor pool, named after the man who spent 50 years teaching local kids to swim. The Sugar Palm Restaurant on Ocean Road (no.24, 9974 4410), right in the heart of Palm Beach proper, is a popular addition to the many eateries here: try to catch the evening wine and tapas served from 4pm to 9pm for a taste of the local high life. Further back on North Palm Beach, keep an eye out for young Aussie actors on a tea break – this is where the hit soap *Home and Away* is filmed.
Barbecues (in the play area). Café. Changing rooms. Child-friendly (play area is in the adjacent Governor Phillip Park). Lifeguards/savers (Sept-May). Parking. Picnic area. Pool. Restaurant. Shade. Shark net (Sept-May). Shops. Showers. Toilets.

EXPLORE

SEA SAFETY

How to cope with surf, sharks and stingers.

TO THE RESCUE

Each year, Sydney's famed surf lifesavers carry out countless rescue operations. A disproportionate number of these rescues are of foreigners who have underestimated the 'rips' (currents) in the surf. Waves at Sydney's ocean beaches can be up to four metres (13 feet) high and conceal powerful rips. More often, they are less than one metre; at Bondi and Manly, they're somewhere in between.

To be safe, always swim between the red and yellow flags that the lifesavers plant in the sand each day. If you stray outside the flags, the lifesavers will blow whistles and scream through megaphones at you. And don't think shallow water is completely safe. 'Dumpers' are waves that break with force, usually at low tide in shallow water, and can cause serious injury. Waves that don't break at all (surging waves) can knock swimmers over too and drag them out to sea. Finally, remember that alcohol and water don't mix – most of the adults who drown in New South Wales are under the influence.

If you do get caught by a rip and you're a confident swimmer, try to swim diagonally across the rip. Otherwise, stay calm, stick your hand in the air to signal to a lifeguard and float until you're rescued: don't fight the current by trying to swim towards the shore.

SHARK THINKING

Shark attacks are very rare – the last fatal attack in Sydney Harbour was back in 1963, although four occurred in New South Wales between November 2013 and February 2015. It's true that there have been more sharks seen in recent years, but this is because better sewage methods have made the beaches much cleaner and so more palatable to sharks. That said, the closest most people get to a shark is in an aquarium.

A lot of Sydney's beaches are shark-netted. The nets are usually around 150 metres long, seven tall and are anchored to the sea floor within 500 metres of the shore. You won't spot them because they are always dropped in ten metre-deep water, ensuring three metres (ten feet) of clearance for swimmers and surfers. The nets are meant not so much as a physical block to sharks but to prevent them establishing a habitat close to shore. They are moved from time to time to keep the sharks guessing.

If by some quirk of fate you do see a shark while swimming, try not to panic: just swim calmly to shore. Easier said than done, yes, but sharks are attracted to jerky movements. 'However,' say the experts at Taronga Zoo, 'if a shark gets close then any action you take may disrupt the attack pattern, such as hitting the shark's nose, gouging at its eyes, making sudden movements and blowing bubbles.'

STINGERS

Two kinds of jellyfish are common in summer. The jimble (a less potent southern relative of the deadly box jellyfish) is box-shaped with four pink tentacles. It is often found at the harbour beaches. On the ocean beaches, you're more likely to come across bluebottle jellyfish (aka Portuguese man-of-war), which has long blue tentacles and tends to appear only when an onshore wind is blowing.

Jimbles can deliver a painful sting but are not dangerous; bluebottles are nastier, causing an intense, longer-lasting pain, red, whip-like lesions and, occasionally, respiratory problems. Even dead bluebottles on the beach can sting, so don't touch them.

Treatment for each is different. If stung by a jimble, wash the affected area with vinegar (lifeguards and lifesavers keep stocks of it) – or, if you can, pee on it – gently remove any tentacles with tweezers or gloves, and apply ice to relieve the pain. If stung by a bluebottle, leave the water immediately, don't rub the skin and don't apply vinegar; instead use an ice pack or anaesthetic spray.

The tentacles should be wiped off with a towel, not pulled off with your fingers.

EXPLORE

Arts & Entertainment

Children

Sydney is a natural wonderland for kids, so small wonder that local 'grommets' (that's an Aussie surfing term for ankle-biters) have no trouble making their own fun. At most of the city's beaches there are coves and rock pools to explore on foot or by boat or canoe. And the cornucopia of gardens, parks and bushland all teem with wildlife, ready for walks and with rangers to guide you. In fact, there's very little in the city that's not open to children, which makes it family-holiday heaven.

For more information on children's activities, pick up a copy of the monthly *Time Out Sydney* magazine or visit timeout.com/sydney.

ARTS & ENTERTAINMENT

BEACHES

Beaches both with and without surf co-exist at **Manly** (*see p148* and *p173*), which also has lovely walks and plenty of cheap places to eat, as well as **Manly Sea Life Sanctuary**, full of sharks, turtles and amazing marine life. North of here, there are great playgrounds at **North Steyne** and **Queenscliff**, while south along Fairy Bower, the waterfront path leads to a paddling pool and safe swimming at **Shelly Beach** (*see p173*); older kids may like to take a surf lesson, and families should look out for the resident colony of little penguins.

The surf at **Bondi Beach** (*see p170*) is usually too strong and the sand too crowded for little ones, but there's a natural rock pool and playgrounds at the north end, and lots of space for in-line skating. At the south end is a challenging skateboarders' ramp. South of Bondi, sheltered **Bronte Beach** (*see p171*) has a large park with barbecue facilities, a fantastic playground and a superb fish and chip shop, **Fishy Bite** (491 Bronte Road, 9387 7956). While the sea is too dangerous here for youngsters, there's a great natural 'bogey hole' rock pool that was once a fertility pond for the Gadigal tribes and which today fills up at high tide and hosts darting schools of translucent fish. Next door, **Clovelly Beach** (*see p171*) is one of the safest and most tranquil in Sydney, with lots of colourful fish awaiting snorkellers. On land, there are barbecue pavilions, a playground, rock pools and surrounding grassy cliffs for the perfect picnic.

Balmoral Beach (*see p169*) on the North Shore is also good for picnics, and you can sip a drink in the café while the kids enjoy the playground or swim in a netted area. Further south, just before Maroubra, you'll find **Mahon Pool**, with a rock platform filled with starfish, sea anemones and crabs. Of the northern beaches, the best are **Dee Why Beach**, with its cool playground and host of child-friendly eateries, and **Collaroy Beach** (*see p174*), which has a paddling pool, large playground and barbecue facilities. Secluded **Clareville Beach** is a safe swimming beach on the Pittwater (western) side of the peninsula; the water's too shallow for adults, but is ideal for little kids.

MUSEUMS

As well as animal skeletons, the **Australian Museum** (*see p63*) has interactive exhibits, an indoor play and discovery area for under-sixes, and is free for under-16s. The **Australian National Maritime Museum** (www.anmm. gov.au) in Darling Harbour has a playground, plus ships to be explored. In Ultimo, the **Powerhouse Museum** (*see p75*) has regular exhibitions and interactive spaces; the **Ian Thorpe Aquatic Centre** (www.itac.org.au) is adjacent.

PARKS & PLAYGROUNDS

For wet and wild adventures without the beach, head to **Manly Waterworks** (corner of West

Esplanade and Commonwealth Parade, 9949 1088, www.manlywaterworks.com); sluicing down the gullet of the Insane Earthworm is an experience never to be forgotten.

Darling Harbour (*see p74*) is touristy, but has lots for kids of all ages. There's a giant playground at **Tumbalong Park**, conveniently surrounded by cafés, and a fun water play area, paddle-boats and a merry-go-round – not to mention the **Sea Life Sydney Aquarium** (*see p75*), an **IMAX** cinema (*see p187*) and **Wild Life Sydney Zoo**. At weekends and during school holidays, you'll see lots of street entertainers and perhaps an open-air concert or dusk firework display. Look for the whale-watching fleets that gather at nearby Cockle Bay – so adept at tracking these gentle behemoths, they will guarantee you a whale sighting.

In Kirribilli, you'll find **Luna Park** (*see p139*), the famous fun park perched right on the harbour, which celebrated 80 years of thrilling Sydney kids in 2015.

For older children, lovely **Centennial Park** (*see p98*) is big and buzzy: in-line skates, bikes and pedal cars can be hired from **Centennial Park Cycles** at Parkes and Grand Drives, and for horse riders there's the **Centennial Parklands Equestrian Centre** (114-120 Lang Road, next to Entertainment Quarter, 9360 5650, www.centennialstables.com.au). Alternatively, just find a shady spot and set out your picnic rug.

SERVICES

Dial an Angel
1300 721 111, www.dialanangel.com.
Open phone enquiries 8.30am-8.30pm daily.
A 24-hour nanny or babysitting service.

WILDLIFE

Shark fans should head to **Sea Life Sydney Aquarium** (*see p75*) and **Manly Sea Life Sanctuary**. Both offer close encounters with sharks and stingrays, as well as hands-on experiences with starfish and sea urchins. Manly Sea Life Sanctuary also has sleepover nights for kids and a Shark Dive Xtreme for over-14s. Sydney Aquarium offers an incredible range of marine life, including fairy penguins and the celebrated dugong duo, Pig and Wuru. Harbourside, **Taronga Zoo** has an incredible array of both native Australian and exotic animals on show. The most scenic way to get there is by ferry – from the dock, you can catch a cable car up the hill to the zoo and work your way back down to the ferry.

For more home-grown creatures, head west to **Featherdale Wildlife Park** (*see p158*) near Blacktown, where kids can hand-feed a wallaby, kangaroo or emu and have their photo taken with a koala. More koala cuddling is on offer at the **Koala Park Sanctuary**. The **Royal Botanic Gardens** (*see p67*) on the harbour is an ideal picnic spot, and kids love the tour by 'trackless train'.

IMAX.

ARTS & ENTERTAINMENT

Australian Reptile Park.

attractions are joined here by emus, kangaroos, echidnas, dingoes and wombats, plus ten acres of lush rainforest, eucalyptus groves and native gardens to explore.

Manly Sea Life Sanctuary
Western Esplanade, Manly, Northern Beaches (1800 199 742, www.manlysealifesanctuary. com.au). Manly ferry. **Open** 9.30am-5pm daily. **Admission** $17.50-$25; $12-$20 reductions. **Map** p316.
Shark Harbour's enormous aquarium has an underwater tunnel for viewing residents, including stingrays, grey nurse sharks and marine turtles. The brave can even dive with the sharks, or you can learn about the animals on daily tours. Penguin Cove is home to a colony of little penguins, while Underwater Sydney allows children to learn more about sea life with an interactive rock pool that's home to sea snails, hermit crabs, sea urchins and more. There's more for young children in Shipwreck Shores, with a soft play area, a splash play area and all sorts of fun activities; the crawl-through sea cave, complete with colourful corals and fossils, impresses across generations. Tickets are cheaper if bought online.

If you want to get out into the bush, there are several easy walks in and around Sydney, in particular at **Berry Island Reserve** (www. northsydney.nsw.gov.au), where you'll find a short track with informative plaques about the area's Aboriginal heritage. **Manly Dam Reserve**, off King Street, Manly Vale (catch a bus from Wynyard or Manly Wharf), has easy and very scenic walks, and you can swim safely. The **NSW National Parks & Wildlife Service** runs Discovery walks, talks and tours for children (1300 361 967, www.nationalparks. nsw.gov.au).

Taronga Zoo
Bradleys Head Road, Mosman, North Shore (9969 2777, www.zoo.nsw.gov.au). Taronga Zoo ferry or bus 247. **Open** 9am-5pm daily. **Admission** $21-$43. **Map** p316.
The 'zoo with a view' covers 17.5 hectares (43 acres) on the western side of Bradleys Head, and is home to some 2,600 animals of more than 340 species. Best of all, especially for foreign visitors, are the native species, including koalas, kangaroos, platypuses, echidnas, Tasmanian devils and lots of colourful, screechy birds.

★ Wild Life Sydney Zoo
1-5 Wheat Road, Darling Harbour, Central Sydney (1800 206 158, www.wildlifesydney.com.au). Town Hall rail or Darling Harbour ferry. **Open** *mid Apr-Sept* 9.30am-5pm daily (last entry 4pm). *Oct-mid Apr* 9.30am-6pm daily (last entry 5pm). **Admission** $28-$40; $19-$31.50 reductions. **Map** p308 D6.
This zoo recreates classic Australian animal habitats. There are koalas at Gum Tree Valley and wallabies in the rocky environs of Wallaby Cliffs, while enormous Kakadu Gorge replicates one of the world's most diverse ecosystems – the monsoonal Top End of the Northern Territory. Residents include saltwater crocodile Rex, one of the world's largest crocodiles. There's lots of fun for kids and adults: koala encounters at Koala Rooftop let you have your photo taken with the adorable creatures; Kangaroo Walkabout lets you get up close with Australia's national icon and Wild Flight is a self-propelled flight on a wire in the attraction's aviary. Tickets are cheaper if bought online.

Australian Reptile Park
Gosford exit off Pacific Highway, Somersby (4340 1022, www.reptilepark.com.au). Gosford rail then 10min taxi ride. **Open** 9am-5pm daily. **Admission** $33; $17-$20 reductions.
An hour's drive north of Sydney lives this collection of cold-blooded critters, creepy-crawlies and native animals including koalas, echidnas, wombats and Tasmanian devils. There are lots of noisy, colourful birds too. Interactive exhibits include Spider World and the Lost World of Reptiles.

Koala Park Sanctuary
84 Castle Hill Road, West Pennant Hills (9484 3141, www.koalaparksanctuary.com.au). Pennant Hills rail then bus 632, 636. **Open** 9am-5pm daily. **Admission** $27; $15 reductions.
Koalas are Australia's most laid-back animal, so who wouldn't want to chill out with one? The main

Film

In Sydney, going to the movies is almost as popular as surfing, barbecues or the Test series. Locals love the silver screen and observe with pride the success of many Sydney actors in international movies. The list is formidable, including huge players such as Russell Crowe, Nicole Kidman, Hugh Jackman and Naomi Watts. While local talent is supported in long-running Sydney film festivals, it's the blockbusters that cinemagoers flock to. Reflecting this boom is the nature of cinema-going itself. Watching movies outdoors with harbour and park backdrops has become a Sydney passion, with OpenAir Cinema and Moonlight Cinema leading the fray. Indoors, where once there was a series of independent cinemas dotted about town, now there are very few. Inevitably bowing to the teen-targeted multiplexes, the heritage-listed Ritz Cinema Randwick and Hayden Orpheum Picture Palace both screen mainstream fare.

ARTHOUSE FILM AND FESTIVALS

Despite the homogenisation, Sydney still has a healthy appetite for arthouse cinema, with the **Palace**, **Dendy** and **Chauvel** theatres showing independent films. And the giant institutions offer a luxurious touch (at a price), with **Hoyts'** LUX and **Event Cinemas'** Gold Class options.

Film festivals are an important part of Sydney's screen culture. In addition to the annual **Sydney Film Festival** (*see p188*), there are festivals dedicated to short films as well as more than a dozen annual festivals dedicated to the cinemas of specific countries, including France, Germany, Spain, Italy, Japan, Korea and Russia. For more on film festivals, *see p187*.

TICKETS AND INFORMATION

First-run movies open on Thursdays, with around four premières a week. Unless it's a blockbuster, you can usually get a ticket without a problem. Prices are around $16 to $19.50 for adults ($19 to $23 for 3D movies), with reductions for children, senior citizens, students and the unemployed. Public holidays usually involve a $1 'surcharge', while Monday and Tuesday are traditionally bargain nights, when tickets are reduced to as little as $8. The major chains – Hoyts,

Event Cinemas, Greater Union, Palace and Dendy – have websites with screening times, plus there are cinema ads in the entertainment sections of the *Sydney Morning Herald* and *Daily Telegraph*.

CINEMAS
First-run

The multiplexes typically offer Hollywood blockbusters and kids' movies. Christmas, September school holidays and the Easter long weekend are key periods for distributors, who often hold back movies for that all-important opening weekend at these times.

Event Cinemas Bondi Junction

Level 7 & 8, Westfield Shopping Town, 500 Oxford Street, Bondi Junction (9300 1500, www.event cinemas.com.au). Bondi Junction rail or bus 333, 352, 378, 380. **Screens** 13. **Tickets** $20; $14.50-$16.50 reductions. **Map** p315 P11.

This ultra-modern complex has digital surround sound, comfy seating, two 20m Vmax screens (great for 3D), its own bar, a 'fine dining' food court right on its doorstep and harbour views to boot. Programmes feature a mix of blockbusters and the mainstream

ASIAN CINEMA
China, Japan and Korea come to Sydney.

Of all of Australia's cities, Sydney has by far the biggest Asian demographic – 19 per cent of Sydney's population in 2011 – with the largest settlement being in the CBD and Haymarket. The highest concentration of Asian Australians in Sydney are Chinese, but Korean communities have grown tenfold in 25 years, with the greatest concentration of the country's 60,000 population being in Sydney.

Unsurprisingly, then, Sydney has a busy calendar of Asian film festivals. Event Cinemas George Street (*see right*), in Chinatown, hosts the **Korean Film Festival** in August. There's more Korean film at **Cinema K** at the Korean Cultural Centre (255 Elizabeth Street, 8267 3400, www.koreanculture.org.au).

As well as regular screenings of Asian films throughout the year at all 17 Hoyts cinemas, Hoyts Broadway (*see right*) rolls out the red carpet for the **International Chinese Film Festival** every November.

The **Japanese Film Festival** (www.japanesefilmfestival.net; *pictured*) is held at Event Cinemas George Street, Event Cinemas Parramatta (Westfield Shopping Centre, 159-175 Church Street, 9407 2777, www.eventcinemas.com.au) and the Art Gallery of NSW (*see p63*) in October.

If you want to browse for Asian films to take home, including Japanese, Korean and Chinese *anime*, your one-stop shop is **Media Asia** (50 Dixon Street, Chinatown, www.media-asia.com.au), where you'll find a good selection with English subtitles.

Ritz Cinema Randwick.

end of arthouse, and there are regular 'bring your baby' sessions. There's free parking in the Westfield car park for up to two hours, plus cinema patrons get an extra hour by validating their parking ticket. The two Gold Class cinemas ($30) offer a separate lounge and plush armchairs that recline until you're almost horizontal. If you opt for the $155 Gold Class option, you'll also be served dinner and wine.

Event Cinemas George Street
505-525 George Street, CBD (9273 7300, www.eventcinemas.com.au). Town Hall rail.
Screens 17. **Tickets** $20; $14.50-$16.50 reductions; $13 Tue. **Map** p311 E7.
This sprawling cinema complex shows virtually every new commercial movie release as soon as it opens. Located in the heart of George Street's garish entertainment strip, it attracts throngs of noisy kids and can get a little edgy at night, so guard your valuables. The state-of-the-art auditoria with digital surround sound and comfortable (if rather narrow) seats are especially popular with teens and out-of-towners. Includes Gold Class and Vmax options.

Hoyts Broadway
Broadway Shopping Centre, corner of Bay Street & Greek Streets, Glebe (9003 382 0211, www.hoyts.com.au). Bus 370, 412, 431, 432, 433, 434.
Screens 12. **Tickets** $20; $13-$17 reductions; $13 Tue. **Map** p310 C9.
At the top of a major shopping mall, this huge complex (the largest auditorium has 379 seats) often wilts under the pressure of sheer numbers, particularly at weekends when the rowdy teen crowd descends.

Three of the theatres are 'CinemaxX' standard, with high-backed seats, perfect sight lines, super-large screens and digital surround sound. 'Mums and Bubs' sessions for movie-craving carers and their infants run twice a month. Over-18s can go for the LUX package ($34), with free popcorn and soft drinks, plus a gourmet food menu and wine list for an extra price tag. And, of course, the comfiest seats in the house.

★ Hoyts EQ
Bent Street, Entertainment Quarter, Driver Avenue, Moore Park (9332 1300, www.hoyts.com. au). Bus 355, 371, 372, 391, 392, 393, 394, 395, 396, 397, 399, 890. **Screens** 12. **Tickets** $20; $13-$17 reductions; $13 Tue. **Map** p314 K12.
Located in the Entertainment Quarter, part of the Fox Studios complex, this vast pseudo-retro cinema boasts huge screens, stadium seating (total capacity 3,000) and smart facilities, and is a nice change from the pushing, shoving and traffic-choked thoroughfare of George Street. The LUX experience costs $34.

★ Ritz Cinema Randwick
43-47 St Paul's Street, Randwick (9399 5722, www.ritzcinema.com.au). Bus 314, 316, 317, 372, 373, 376, 377, 394, M50. **Screens** 6. **Tickets** $15; $9-$13 reductions; $9 Tue.
With a distinctive art deco design restored to its former 1930s glory and an impressive sound system, the six-screen Ritz cinema is both a local landmark and an excellent venue for catching the latest mainstream releases. Signs explain the regulations – no alcohol, bare feet, smoking or skateboards – which make sense if you hit the place in the afternoon after school's out. In the evening, the place attracts a different crowd, including film geeks who seek out the Ritz for its great acoustics and old-fashioned flair. Upstairs, the inimitable Bar Ritz has a marble bar and balcony – perfect for pre- and post-film drinks.

Arthouse

Both the **Dendy** and **Palace** cinema chains have great-value membership schemes, which are well worth the investment if you plan to go to the cinema regularly.

Chauvel
Paddington Town Hall, corner of Oxford Street & Oatley Road, Paddington (9361 5398, www. palacecinemas.com.au). Bus 333, 352, 378, 380. **Screens** 2. **Tickets** $18.50; $9-$14.50 reductions; $11 Mon.* **Map** p314 J10.
Named after the Australian film pioneer Charles Chauvel – of *Jedda* fame – this much-loved local cinema is now part of the Palace chain and has taken up the slack from the closure of the Palace Academy down the road. Its proscenium arch brings true grandeur to the art of film and the staff really know their stuff. There are Cinématèque and late-night cult-movie screenings. Check out the lovely upstairs bar.

Cinema Paris
Bent Street, Entertainment Quarter, Driver Avenue, Moore Park (9003 3870, www.hoyts. com.au). Bus 355, 371, 372, 391, 392, 393, 394, 395, 396, 397, 399, 890. **Screens** 4. **Tickets** $20; $13-$17 reductions; $13 Tue. **Map** p314 K12.

An unassuming arthouse cinema within Fox Studios' Entertainment Quarter, with a total seating capacity of 600. The Paris also hosts several film festivals, including the Polish Film Festival and Serbian Film Festival.

Dendy Newtown

261-263 King Street, Newtown (9550 5699, www. dendy.com.au). Newtown rail. **Screens** 4. **Tickets** $19.50; $11-$16 reductions; $10-$12 Tue. **Map** p316
Matching its Opera Quays sister (*see below*) for style if not setting, the Dendy Newtown offers quality first releases, 562 super-comfortable seats, big screens, Dolby digital surround sound and a bar. There are lots of special events, limited release flicks and Q&As.

Dendy Opera Quays

2 East Circular Quay, Circular Quay (9247 3800/ www.dendy.com.au). Circular Quay rail or ferry. **Screens** 3. **Tickets** $18.50; $9-$15.50 reductions; $10.50-$11.50 Tue. **Map** p309 G3.
A stone's throw from the Opera House, with great views to the Harbour Bridge, this luxurious complex (with a total capacity of 579) usually offers a mix of middlebrow and arthouse fare, and is fully licensed. There's also disabled access to all screens.

Golden Age Cinema

80 Commonwealth Street, Surry Hills (9211 1556, ourgoldenage.com.au). Central rail. **Screens** 1. **Tickets** $20; $15 reductions. **Map** p311 F8.
The heritage-listed Paramount Pictures building is in what was once known as the Hollywood Quarter. Its art deco elegance has been restored by Golden Age – a team of architects, designers and film fans – and the former screening room now shows arthouse flicks. The lovely bar is open to non-cinemagoers too, and serves fancy toasties, cheese and charcuterie.

IN THE KNOW AUSSIE OSCARS

Australia's answer to the Oscars is the Australian Academy of Cinema & Television Arts Awards. ('AACTA' sounds quite like 'actor', doesn't it? What a glorious coincidence.) Formerly known as the Australian Film Institute Awards, this institution has been doling out shiny baubles to champagne-flushed actors since 1958, when the local industry was still in its infancy. Winners of the Best Film Award include *My Brilliant Career*, *Breaker Morant*, *Gallipoli*, *Strictly Ballroom*, *The Piano*, *Muriel's Wedding*, *Shine*, *Lantana* and *Samson and Delilah*. Broadcast on TV since 1997, the AFI Awards were generally held in Melbourne, but –hurrah for Sydneysiders – since 2011 they've been a Sydney win, held at the Opera House. Where else?

Govinda's

112 Darlinghurst Road, Darlinghurst (9380 5155, www.govindas.com.au). Kings Cross rail. **Screens** 1. **Tickets** $15.50; (with meal) $29.80. **Map** p312 J8.
Adored by its twenty- and thirtysomething regulars, this Krishna-operated restaurant-cum-arthouse-cinema is a must-visit film experience. After you've loaded up on the generous vegetarian buffet, sit (or lie) back on the cushions and bean bags and enjoy arty films, documentaries and classics in 35mm. You can watch and not eat, but diners are given entry preference and since there are only 65 seats in the cinema – roughly half the restaurant's capacity – it's best to buy your ticket early.

★ Hayden Orpheum Picture Palace

380 Military Road, Cremorne (9908 4344, www. orpheum.com.au). Bus 143, 144, 151, 228, 229, 230, 243, 246, 247, 257. **Screens** 6. **Tickets** $20; $13-$16.50 reductions; $11.50-$13.50 Tue.
Without doubt the grandest cinema in Sydney, Cremorne's art deco picture palace is a stunning step back in time. Built in 1935 by George Kenworthy, the top theatrical architect of the period, today's version is even glitzier than the original thanks to a $2.5-million restoration some years back. The 744-seat Orpheum is the true star of the show. It even has a genuine Wurlitzer cinema organ, which rises out of a stage pit on weekend evenings complete with flashing lights and a grinning organist. Expect a mix of mainstream US, British and Australian fare, with some arthouse, special presentations and the occasional cabaret show.

Mu Meson Archives

Corner of Parramatta Road & Trafalgar Street, Annandale (9517 2010, www.mumeson.org). Parramatta Road buses. **Open** varies. **Admission** up to $10.
Don't be surprised if you come out a slightly altered human after watching one of the seriously obscure cult films on offer at this underground movie house. The venue, run by Sydney legends Jay Katz and Miss Death, is full to the brim with ancient videotapes and 16mm oddities. The entry price usually includes supper.

Palace Norton Street

99 Norton Street, Leichhardt (9564 5620, www.palacecinemas.com.au). Bus 435, 436, 437, 438, 440, 445, L38, L40. **Screens** 4. **Tickets** $19.80; $12-$16 reductions; $11 Mon.
Located in the heart of Little Italy, the sleek and stylish Norton Street cinema is the cream of the Palace chain. The air-conditioning keeps you cool, the seats are plush and comfortable, and the sound and sight lines are uniformly excellent. There's not much else you could ask for from a cinema. You'll find an intelligent mix of offbeat Hollywood releases, foreign movies and Australian arthouse fare. The Babes in Arms sessions on Thursday mornings are popular.

Hayden Orpheum Picture Palace.

★ Palace Verona

*17 Oxford Street, Paddington (9360 6099, www.
palacecinemas.com.au). Bus 333, 352, 378, 380.*
Screens 4. **Tickets** $19.80; $12-$16 reductions;
$11 Mon. **Map** p314 H9.

The Verona is a home from home for Paddington's
intellectuals, gays and arthouse fans. The four
screens are on the small side and the seats aren't
quite as soft as you'd expect, but the movies are an
enticing blend of quirky commercial, sexy foreign
and Australian.

Underground Cinema

Locations vary (www.undergroundcinema.com.au).

The wild card of moviegoing, Underground Cinema
is a roving, immersive film experience based around
secret screenings. Those who sign up are given clues
as to what the film is, a dress code and a rendezvous
point. When punters are led to the site of the film,
they're met by an extravagantly dressed set – right
down to fine details – and a cast of actors in the roles
of the movie's characters. For instance, *Wall Street* had
a 1980s 'power dress to impress' theme and required
attendees to broker some deals on the retro phones in
a high-powered office. *28 Days Later* dropped attendees into the midst of a zombie apocalypse. There are
two or three Sydney events per year, but you'll have to
be on the mailing list to hear about them.

DIGITAL DREAMS IN THE HARBOUR CITY

The production houses behind the cinematic hits.

Sydney is not just home to world-famous directors and actors, but also several major production companies. Many are at the forefront of digital imaging technology and create computer-animated sequences for Hollywood movies as well as their own full-length films.

Based at Fox Studios in Moore Park, Sydney special-effects house **Animal Logic** has contributed CGI to some of the biggest blockbusters in movie history. These include *The Matrix*, *The Lord of the Rings* trilogy and *300*. The company produced the design, effects and animation of *The LEGO Movie* in 2014, which proved to be another worldwide smash.

See-Saw Films, based in Sydney and London, was founded by producers Emile Sherman and Iain Canning. Recently, it produced John Curran's *Tracks* (starring Mia Wasikowska) and Anton Corbijn's *Life* (starring Robert Pattinson). Baz Lurhmann's

Bazmark, meanwhile, last produced the gaudy adaptation of F Scott Fitzgerald's *The Great Gatsby* and is branching out with a record label. The company has the motto 'A life lived in fear is a life half lived' and its emblem – an emu and kangaroo – is one shared with Australia itself.

In 2013, George Miller, director of the *Mad Max* movies, shut down his digital and animation production house, Dr D Studios – a partnership with Omnilab Media – to pile his energy back into **Kennedy Miller Mitchell**, his production house that has been in operation since 1978. We'd love to have picked through the fire sale he held for Dr D, at which he offloaded paraphernalia including railway carriages that had been refitted as meeting rooms. If that cash went towards finishing the excellent *Mad Max: Fury Road* (given five out of five stars by *Time Out*) after the production floundered 'in development hell' for 25 years, we're very happy he made the sacrifice.

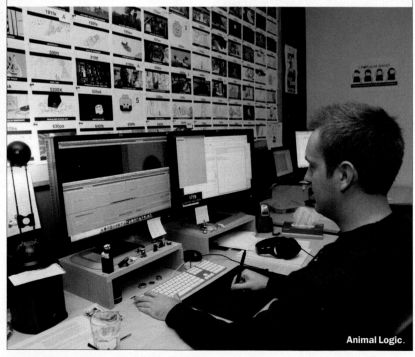

Animal Logic.

IMAX

IMAX Sydney
*31 Wheat Road, Darling Harbour (9281 3300,
www.imax.com.au). Town Hall rail, Darling
Harbour ferry, or Convention light rail.* **Tickets**
$23-$33.50; $17-$29.50 reductions. **Map** p309 E6.
The giant, eye-shaped IMAX cinema sticks out on
the water in touristy Darling Harbour. The 540-seat
theatre claims to have the world's largest screen,
some eight storeys high, and shows around eight
films a day from 10am to 9pm. Expect a mixed
bag of 2D and 3D affairs, with documentaries and
45-minute shorties a common feature. Hardly essential viewing, although the sheer impact of seeing a
film on a giant screen makes it a worthwhile stop for
the experience.

Open-air

Given the climate, it's hardly surprising that
Sydneysiders flock outdoors whenever they
can. Open-air screenings are a firm fixture on
the summer social calendar, with three main
inner-city offerings: a picnic-on-the-grass affair
in Centennial Park, a similar set-up in North
Sydney Oval (with seats and cover if desired)
and a sensational harbourside experience in the
Domain. Weather permitting (screenings are
cancelled only in gale-force conditions), all are
great nights out. You may have to pay booking
fees on top of the prices quoted below.

Bondi Openair
*Bondi Pavilion, Queen Elizabeth Drive, Bondi
Beach (9130 1235, www.openaircinemas.com.au).
Bondi Junction rail then bus 333, 380, 381, 382,
or bus 222, 333, 380.* **Tickets** $20-$25; $15-$20
reductions. **Date** Jan-Feb. **Map** p316.
Like the beach that hosts it, Bondi Openair cinema
is wonderfully unpredictable and offers myriad
forms of entertainment. Outside the beautiful Bondi
Pavilion, the bar offers drinks and dinner near the
ocean, plus a local DJ and bands. When it's time for
the main feature, grab a beanbag and head to the
lawn or sit in the amphitheatre – and all this with
the ocean roaring in the background. Every Sunday,
there's a Sundae Session with free Ben & Jerry's ice-
cream and games on the lawn, pre-screening.

Moonlight Cinema
*Belvedere Amphitheatre, Centennial Park,
Woollahra (1300 511 908, www.moonlight.com.
au). Bus 333, 378, 380.* **Tickets** $19; $14.50-
$16.50 reductions. **Date** early Dec-mid Mar.
Map p315 N11.
The Moonlight's programme focuses heavily on cur-
rent and recent mainstream releases, with classics
Grease and *Breakfast at Tiffany's* (on Valentine's Day)
popular fixtures. Entry is via Woollahra Gate (Oxford
Street) only, and films kick off at sunset. Bring a

picnic, cushions and insect repellent, and arrive early.
Limited Gold Grass tickets (at $32 a pop) guarantee a
prime spot, a 'bean bed' and a glass of wine.

★ OpenAir Cinema
*Mrs Macquarie's Chair, the Domain, CBD
(1300 366 649, www.stgeorge.com.au/openair).
Circular Quay rail or ferry, or Martin Place rail.*
Tickets $33; $31 reductions. **Date** early Jan-mid
Feb. **Map** p312 J3.
This is the ultimate outdoor moviegoing experience,
with the Harbour Bridge and Opera House in the
background. Sydney premières of mainstream movies happen here, and you'll also find a pick of current
and classic film fare. Films start at 8.30pm but the
gates open at 6.30pm – as do the stylish on-site bar
and restaurant. Capacity is around 1,700.

Sunset Cinema
*North Sydney Oval, Miller Street, North Sydney
(1300 438 849, www.sunsetcinema.com.au).
North Sydney rail.* **Tickets** $18; $12-$15 reductions.
Date mid Jan-mid Mar.
The Sunset offers a mix of blockbusters, family
favourites and Oscar contenders to a friendly local
crowd. There's an on-site bar and food, with beanbags
and deckchairs for an additional fee (book online to
avoid missing out).

Drive-in

Skyline Drive-In
*Cricketers Arms Road, Blacktown (9622 0202,
www.eventcinemas.com.au).* **Admission** 1 car
(2 people) $20.
Sydney's only drive-in underwent its first renovation
in more than 50 years not long ago, one that gave the
cinema a 1950s-in-America theme (*Happy Days* was
the inspiration, naturally). It's equipped with the
latest digital technology and an upgraded sound
system, and diner food such as hamburgers and hot
dogs is served by staff in era-appropriate costume.

FESTIVALS

See also p182 Asian Cinema.

Flickerfest
*Bondi Pavilion, Bondi Beach (9365 6877,
www.flickerfest.com.au). Bondi Junction rail
then bus 333, 380, 381, 382, or bus 222, 333,
380.* **Tickets** $18; $16 reductions. **Date** early Jan.
Map p316.
Running for nine days after the New Year madness
has subsided, Flickerfest is the only short-film festival in Australia to be recognised by the American
Academy of Motion Picture Arts & Sciences as an
Oscar-qualifying event. As a result, it's not only a serious event on the world film calendar, it's also one of
the few forums in which local short-film makers can
directly compare their work with international fare.

ARTS & ENTERTAINMENT

Mardi Gras Film Festival & Queer Screen Film Fest

Information: Queer Screen, PO Box 1081, Darlinghurst, NSW 2010 (9332 4938, www. queerscreen.com.au). **Dates** *Mardi Gras* Feb; *Queer Screen Film Fest* Sept.

Part of Sydney's month-long gay and lesbian jamboree, the festival is hosted at the Dendy Newtown (*see p184*) and other venues. In September, Queer Screen puts on the Queer Screen Film Fest.

▶ *For more on Mardi Gras, see p193.*

Sydney Film Festival

Information: Suite 102, 59 Marlborough Street, Surry Hills, NSW 2010 (9318 0999, sff.org.au). **Date** early June.

A slick, high-profile, intensive two-week orgy of international and Australian film (with up to 150 movies showing), opening on the Queen's Birthday weekend in early June. Regular highlights include major retrospectives and meet-the-film-maker forums, and the main venues are the grand State Theatre (*see p217*) and the Dendy Opera Quays (*see p184*). Off season, you can catch monthly Sydney Film Festival flicks at the Casula Powerhouse (www.sff.org.au/sff-events/sff-casula-powerhouse).

Sydney Underground Film Festival

Information: PO Box 202, Summer Hill, NSW 2130 (9797 9428, www.suff.com.au). **Date** Sept.

A three-day festival held in the Inner West, SUFF champions experimental, outrageous and politically inflammatory shorts, features and documentaries from around the world. It reached its 10th year in 2016.

Tropfest

Information: 62-64 Riley Street, East Sydney, NSW 2010 (9368 0434, www.tropfest.com.au). **Date** Sun in late Feb.

Instigated by actor-turned-director John Polson (*Swimfan, Hide and Seek*), this free outdoor festival of short films is held every February, and was originally held at Polson's old hangout, the Tropicana café in Darlinghurst. Now, the films are simulcast on giant screens in the Domain to an audience that runs into the tens of thousands, and also to other cities around Australia. The festival is heavily frequented by actors, directors and writers, and its judging panel usually includes A-list celebs who are working in town: Samuel L Jackson, Russell Crowe and John Woo have all performed judging duties in the past. All films are under seven minutes, made specially for the festival and have to contain a reference to the year's Tropfest Signature Item (past items have included a bubble, an umbrella, a kiss, a coffee bean and dice).

World of Women Film Festival

Chauvel Cinema, 249 Oxford Street, Paddington (9357 1490, www.wift.org). **Date** Oct, biennial.

Women in Film & Television (WIFT), a non-profit outfit committed to improving the lot of women in film, organises this festival of short and feature-length work by new and established female talents. The next festivals run in 2017 and 2019.

Tropfest.

ESSENTIAL SYDNEY FILMS

The city sparkles in these screen classics.

The Adventures of Priscilla, Queen of the Desert.

STONE SANDY HARBUTT (1974)

This 'Ozploitation' thriller about a cop infiltrating a bikie gang features some of the most memorable images of Sydney on film: a biker funeral procession powering down the F3 Motorway; a sniper on the roof of the Art Gallery of NSW; brawls outside the (now closed) Forth & Clyde Hotel in Balmain; and the gang's improbable lair in the former gunnery tunnels of Middle Head.

THE LAST WAVE PETER WEIR (1977)

Australia's greatest director has made just one feature film set in Sydney: an apocalyptic thriller about a lawyer (Richard Chamberlain) who has premonitions of a world-ending tsunami while defending an Aboriginal man (David Gulpilil). A metaphor for white Australia's relative ephemerality, the film would these days cause an outcry for exploiting Indigenous culture.

PUBERTY BLUES BRUCE BERESFORD (1981)

A novel written by two 15-year-old girls about sex, drugs and surfing in the southern beachside suburb of Cronulla became a popular coming-of-age film from the director of *Driving Miss Daisy*. Regarded affectionately for its outdated teenage slang – if someone tells you to 'rack off, moll', it's an insult, by the way – it was remade as a TV series in 2012.

LANTANA RAY LAWRENCE (2001)

Interconnected lives of Sydneysiders converge around the disappearance of a psychotherapist (Barbara Hershey) in this admired psychodrama starring Anthony LaPaglia, Kerry Armstrong and Geoffrey Rush. Sydney areas Balmain, Narrabeen, Pittwater, Paddington and the Rocks feature as locations in the movie, which is based on an award-winning play.

THE ADVENTURES OF PRISCILLA, QUEEN OF THE DESERT STEPHAN ELLIOTT (1994)

Three Sydney drag artists (Hugo Weaving, Terence Stamp and Guy Pearce) set off on a road trip to Alice Springs, experiencing homophobia and making unexpected friends on the way. The Imperial Hotel in Erskineville, until recently the home of drag in gay Sydney, is where the movie memorably begins, with Weaving lip-synching the (hilariously awful) song 'I've Never Been to Me'.

FINDING NEMO ANDREW STANTON, LEE UNKRICH (2003)

Pixar's beloved animated tale of a clownfish who traverses the Pacific Ocean to find his kidnapped son climaxes in a gloriously rendered version of Sydney Harbour. Several Australian actors voice sharks, pelicans, crabs and a dentist, including Barry Humphries, Geoffrey Rush, Eric Bana and Bill Hunter.

Gay & Lesbian

Sydney is one of the most vibrant, open and safest queer destinations on the map. What the city lacks in same-sex marriage reform it makes up with a welcoming out-and-proud queer culture that offers diversely bent scenes right across the city and its fringes.

Darlinghurst, centred on Oxford Street, is the queerest neck of the Sydney woods, with most of the city's gay and lesbian bars and clubs. Nearby in Surry Hills, the bars in lively Crown Street tend not to be exclusively gay but few drinkers would blink at same-sex affection. Potts Point and Kings Cross are two more inner-city areas that have more than a smear of queer of their name, while Erskineville in the Inner West deserves a special mention as home to the late-lamented Imperial Hotel, where many scenes from *The Adventures of Priscilla, Queen of the Desert* were shot.

THE SCENE

Many of the clubs on the Oxford Street strip in **Darlinghurst** have been serving up Cock-Sucking Cowboys and Screaming Orgasms for 30 years and counting. Oxford Street is also the landing strip for the **Sydney Gay and Lesbian Mardi Gras** (*see p193* **Hurrah for Mardi Gras!**), which turns the whole 'burb into a raucous, all-inclusive street party with 10,000 parade participants and 200,000 cheering spectators, every March.

A mere swerve away from Darlinghurst lies **Surry Hills**. This inner-city area has enjoyed a well-deserved renaissance after the mayor's small bar bill allowed for a number of quaint wine bars to open within its laneways and backstreets. Crown Street is always abuzz with foodies on the prowl for Sydney's next great dish and art lovers who frequent local small galleries.

Potts Point and **Kings Cross** are two more inner-city suburbs that have more than a smear of queer to their name. While Kings Cross is Sydney's infamous red-light district, you can always see local gay boys meandering through the streets on their way to work, the gym or the sauna. Some fabulous shopping can be found on Macleay Street in Potts Point.

The inner west houses popular queer-friendly, arty hoods such as **Newtown**, **Erskineville** and **Enmore**. The Imperial Hotel in Erskineville, well known as the spot where many Sydney drag queens got their first break, as well for its role in *The Adventures of Priscilla, Queen of the Desert*, had sadly closed at the time of writing – but perhaps it's not gone for good. And right beside Newtown train station is the **Bank Hotel**, which never fails to pull in a great catch of queer folk, particularly on a Sunday afternoon, as most Aussies have a total disregard for the words 'school night'.

INFORMATION

If you're in the area, drop into the **Bookshop Darlinghurst** (207 Oxford Street, 9331 1103, www.thebookshop.com.au) for a chinwag about what's going on. Alternatively, check the queer press, available in gay bars and clubs, bottle shops, newsagents, music venues and cinemas around town. The city's two free weekly gay newspapers, *Sydney Star Observer* (www.star observer.com.au) and *SX* (www.gaynewsnetwork. com.au) have full, up-to-the-minute 'what's on' and venue guides. Dykes will find the free monthly news magazine *Lesbians on the Loose* (www.lotl.com) required reading. You can find the latest events listed at www.au.timeout.com/sydney/gay-lesbian.

THE LAW

Gay, lesbian, bisexual and transgender people in New South Wales are legally protected against discrimination, as are those living with HIV or AIDS. Gay sex is legal (the age of consent is 16 for everyone) and the State Government recognises same-sex partnerships. Homophobia exists everywhere, of course, and Sydney is no exception, but it's monitored by the ACON Anti-Violence Project. The Surry Hills Police Station is your nearest port of call in an emergency when in the inner city (151-241 Goulburn Street, Surry Hills, 9265 4144). Emergency is accessed by dialling 000.

SAFE SEX

While safe-sex campaigns have hugely reduced the incidence of new infection, the dangers are still out there. The AIDS Council of NSW (ACON) is the government department at the forefront of the HIV/AIDS awareness issue. It spearheads a number of exciting and engaging projects that inspire the local community and beyond to play safe (www.acon.org.au).

WHERE TO STAY

It can safely be said that any 'international' hotel in Sydney (glass front, big lobby, expensive cocktails) will be gay-friendly. A large chunk of staff at any of these places will be 'family', so you should have no hassles. You can also search for accommodation through the International Gay & Lesbian Travel Association (www.iglta.org) and Gay & Lesbian Tourism Australia (www.galta.com.au).

NIGHTLIFE
Bars & pubs

Bank Hotel

324 King Street, Newtown (8568 1900, www.bankhotel.com.au). Newtown rail.
Open 11am-late daily. **Map** p316.
One of Newtown's most popular pubs, the three-level venue includes great outdoor areas, with a large beer garden. There are casual bars, a quality cocktail lounge, DJs at night and new bands upstairs at Waywards. The Bank is a place for everyone but it attracts a good smattering of queer folk throughout the week.

Beresford

354 Bourke Street, Darlinghurst (8313 5000, www.merivale.com.au/upstairsberesfordevents). Bus 311, 333, 352, 373, 377, 378, 380, 392, 394, 396. **Open** noon-1am daily. **Map** p311 G9.
Head to the Beresford on Sundays and you'll find a fair portion of Sydney's gay scene making the most of $6 pints, house wines and spirits from 6pm to

Bank Hotel.

Slyfox. See p194.

ARTS & ENTERTAINMENT

8pm, along with tunes from killer DJ talent to help them stave off the oh-crap-I-gotta-go-back-to-work-tomorrow blues. After night falls and everyone's had a few, they start to migrate upstairs for a rousing dance party featuring house tunes, diva classics and current EDM favourites played by the likes of DJs Alex Taylor, Kate Monroe and more.

Colombian Hotel
117-123 Oxford Street, Darlinghurst (9360 2151). Oxford Street buses. **Open** 9am-6am daily. **Map** p311 G8.
This is the gay pub that more gay pubs should try to be like. Inside are two levels of fun, both decorated in an 'art deco meets Aztec' design theme that succeeds against all the odds. The ground-floor bar opens on to the street, and is excellent for people-watching, while the upstairs cocktail bar is more sedate, although boogie fever breaks out later, with retro disco on Friday nights and soulful house on Saturday nights. Both floors get crowded pec-to-pec at weekends.

Oxford Hotel
134 Oxford Street, Darlinghurst (9331 3467, www.theoxfordhotel.com.au). Oxford Street buses. **Open** 10am-late daily. **Map** p311 H8.
It's fair to say that the Oxford is a little Sally-Field-in-*Sybil*. The basement of the iconic gay bar, known as Undergound, is a boutique bar and club. One level up, you'll find the main (street level) bar, with an open floorplan and outdoor deck. On level two sits Ginger's – dedicated to showcasing cabaret and live music. Lounge away, or prop yourself up at the bar, which is always well staffed and efficiently run, but can burn a hole in your hot pants price-wise. Climb the stairs to the top level, and the Polo Lounge – a chi-chi room of chesterfields and marble – awaits you.

Slide
41 Oxford Street, Darlinghurst (8915 1899, www.slide.com.au). Oxford Street buses. **Open** 7pm-late daily. **Map** p311 G8.
Slide is the Shirley Bassey of Oxford Street – camp, yet classy. The former bank is one of the most

HURRAH FOR MARDI GRAS!
Sydney's biggest party.

You'd have to be living under a rock not to know that Sydney is host to the world's largest queer parade, with the annual Sydney Gay and Lesbian Mardi Gras parade and party. The parade contains hundreds of floats and thousands of participants chanting, singing and dancing their message of freedom and liberation while huge crowds of spectators cheer them on. This stand-out event pulls in bent punters from every nook of the globe and has attracted celebs including George Michael, Margaret Cho, Kylie Minogue and a myriad of other queer and queer-loving A-listers. When the five-hour parade winds up, the post-parade party kicks off at the Entertainment Quarter. This 12-hour dance fest unfurls across a variety of venues, with regular spectacular performances staged throughout the night. It's by far the biggest queer party in the southern hemisphere, if not the world.

WHAT AND WHEN
The Mardi Gras festival takes place over three or four weeks, ending on the last weekend in February or the first weekend in March (dates move a little, so check near the time). Although it's the parade and party on the final Saturday that get the publicity, it's worth joining the locals at as many of the pre-parade events as you can fit in.

Things kick off with the Festival Launch (usually on a Saturday): many bring a picnic and make a night of it. Entertainment comes in the form of speeches and a few snippets from Mardi Gras festival shows.

Other celebrations include the Mardi Gras Film Festival, art exhibitions, themed parties and nightly cabaret and stage shows in venues all over Sydney. The Fair Day in Victoria Park, Camperdown (held on the Sunday a fortnight before the final weekend), attracts more than 60,000 people and features an excellent high-camp pet show.

The parade itself begins at sunset. It starts at the corner of Hyde Park and Whitlam Square, heads up Oxford Street to Flinders Street and finishes at the party venue, the Entertainment Quarter in Moore Park. Crowds have been estimated at up to half a million. Many stake out their territory at least six hours before the parade starts, while hotels and restaurants along the route sell seats at ticket-only cocktail parties. Another comfortable option is the Bobby Goldsmith 'Glamstand', which seats several thousand (for tickets and information, visit www.bgf.org.au or call 9283 8666); all proceeds go to assist men, women and children living in poverty with HIV/AIDS.

After the parade comes the party. Attracting some 17,000 revellers, it features top DJs and performers whose identities are usually kept secret until the night. As well as the crammed dance halls and outrageous drag shows, there are plenty of places in the Entertainment Quarter complex for drinking, eating and chilling out. There's also a hefty medical presence, in case things go wrong.

INFORMATION AND TICKETS
To keep abreast of what's going on, contact New Mardi Gras (9383 0900, www.mardigras.org.au) or get the excellent free programme, available from January from gay-friendly venues around Oxford Street and Newtown. You'll need to book accommodation and tickets (at least for the major events) months ahead. Tickets for the main party are available from mid December and can sell out quickly (13 28 49, www.ticketek.com.au).

Arq Sydney.

beautifully decked-out bars on the strip,. There's a creative bill of cabaret shows, live performances by local and touring singer-songwriters and spoken-word nights. Slide's signature serving is its dining and entertainment night, El Circo, where guests enjoy a nine-course meal in front of a cavalcade of entertainment with a different act for every course – the likes of trapeze artists, contortionists and even full-body shadow puppetry. After midnight, the venue scrubs up nicely as a cool little discotheque.

Slyfox
199 Enmore Road, Enmore (9557 2917, www. theslyfoxhotel.com). Bus 423, 426, 428. **Open** noon-late daily. **No credit cards**.
From the outside, the Slyfox looks like an average spit-and-sawdust Aussie pub, but inside you'll find one of Sydney's most established queer bars. With the joint jumping until 6am at weekends, the Funktion1 sound system is put to good use, and there's a solid roster of parties. You'll find regular queer nights, band gigs, and the legends from Bad Deep doing a bimonthly, themed venue takeover. *Photos p192.*

Clubs

Arq Sydney
16 Flinders Street, Darlinghurst (9380 8700, www.arqsydney.com.au). Bus 311, 333, 352, 373, 377, 378, 380, 392, 394, 396. **Open** 9pm-late Thur-Sun. **No credit cards. Map** p311 H9.

Arq is the busiest club on the Sydney scene, and the most obvious port of call for many a gay tourist. Its big nights are Saturday and Sunday, when it draws a very Oxford Street crowd of bare-chested pretty boys. With two levels and a mezzanine walkway, it holds around 900 people when full – which it always is at weekends. Head for the upper floor for sensational lighting and up-tempo house and trance music, delivered via an ultra-crisp sound system; the lower floor is more chilled, with lounges, pool tables and more funky music. Shows are a speciality, whether drag or song-and-dance numbers from pop stars (both aspiring and actual). The club goes into overdrive on long weekends, and its recovery parties are hugely popular. Look out for the Fomo foam parties in summer.

Palms on Oxford
124 Oxford Street, Darlinghurst (9357 4166). Oxford Street buses. **Open** 8pm-midnight Thur, Sun; 8pm-3am Fri, Sat. **No credit cards. Map** p311 H8.
It's unassuming and basic but always fun. Palms makes cheap and cheerful go a long way with its low budget sound system, tacky dancefloor and '80s lighting, but there is always a smile on everyone's face at this popular little nook of a club. The sounds spinning off the decks are as camp as a purse full of rainbows so if you don't like Donna Summer, Kylie, or Steps remixes, go someplace else. Palms is a great night out with not a whiff of attitude to be found

★ Shift Bar & Club

85 Oxford Street, Darlinghurst (9358 3848,
www.themidnightshift.com.au). Museum rail
or bus 311, 333, 352, 373, 377, 378, 380, 392,
394, 396. **Open** 4pm-late daily. **No credit cards.**
Map p311 G8.

One of the oldest gay palaces in Sydney, the
Midnight Shift underwent a bit of a nip/tuck in
2015, and the upstairs dance club retained the
name. Downstairs, meanwhile, is something
entirely different. After years of what felt like rud-
derless stops and starts, she's been given a fresh
overhaul and a new direction. Whereas there were
once dancefloors, two bars and a row of pool tables
for the blokes, now there's a large, pink-hued room
featuring a bar, plenty of seating and a wall covered by photographs of denizens past and present
– a salute to the generations who've made this a
stalwart of the strip. What looks like the smoking
balcony outside is actually a ciggie-free zone –
instead, it's meant to be a patio for hanging out and
watching the crowds walk by.

Stonewall Hotel

175 Oxford Street, Darlinghurst (9360 1963,
www.stonewallhotel.com). Oxford Street buses.
Open noon-6am Mon-Fri; 9am-6am Sat, Sun.
No credit cards. Map p311 G9.

If you're looking for a bar that's gayer than a Cher-
and-Dolly Parton tour with Liza as the support act,
then Stonewall is the place. What it lacks in decor
it more than makes up for in 'Hey, Miss Thang'
greetings, served up by the peroxided twinks who
parade here. Yes, Stonewall attracts a fairly young
crowd: over-35s might start to feel like worn-out
Bridgestone tyres. While the venue spills across
three levels, most of the action can be found downstairs at the main bar, where Tuesday's queer karaoke night and Thursday's Boys Bar Up – scantily
clad men dancing on the bar – occur. Friday and
Saturday nights never (and we mean ever) fail to
pull in a packed house. Hourly drag shows from
11pm onwards make this an absolute corker of a
night out.

Dance parties

★ Apollo the Party

www.apollotheparty.com.au.

March's Mardi Gras ain't over till the last queen
can't dance no more – which means it's still going
strong the day after the official event is over. You
probably won't have slept, so what are a few more
hours on another dancefloor then, you party animal? Apollo the Party is held at the Metro (624
George Street, CBD) and guarantees a final round
of happy-making tunes that will help revive your
spirits (and maybe even your serotonin levels) as
you throw your hands in the air and wave goodbye
to another successful Mardi Gras. Expect the entire
room to be jumping to 'YMCA' and confetti settling
in hard-to-reach places.

Bags packed, milk cancelled, house raised on stilts.

You've packed the suntan lotion, the snorkel set, the stay-pressed shirts. Just one more thing left to do – your bit for climate change. In some of the world's poorest countries, changing weather patterns are destroying lives.

You can help people to deal with the extreme effects of climate change. Raising houses in flood-prone regions is just one life-saving solution.

**Climate change costs lives.
Give £5 and let's sort it *Here & Now***

www.oxfam.org.uk/climate-change

Oxfam is a registered charity in England and Wales (No.202918) and Scotland (SCO039042). Oxfam GB is a member of Oxfam International.

Be Humankind Oxfam

Heaps Gay.

ARTS & ENTERTAINMENT

★ Bad Dog

www.baddog.net.au. Also check local gay press.
Organised by a group of DJs and artists dismayed
by the stodgy sameness of Sydney's gay clubs, the
Bad Dog events, which happen every few months,
are a refreshing alternative to the norm. The venues
tend to be away from the Oxford Street golden mile,
while the parties are renowned for drawing a crowd
that's high on friendliness and low on attitude.

Heaps Gay

www.heapsgay.com.
The queer kids from Heaps Gay used to take over
Chippendale's Gladstone Hotel, transforming the
grungy corner pub from workers' favourite to gay/
lesbian/hipster/hetero/anything goes extravaganza
with admirable aplomb. Now they've expanded to
the Oxford (*see p192*), on the third Saturday of every
month. The vibe at Heaps Gay is always just the
right mix of shaggy and shit-stirring, with a rowdy
crowd that's an equal mix of guys and girls – and you
can definitely bring your straight mates. Prepare
to boogie down to an awesome mix of '90s classics,
current favourites and oddball tunes that'll bring out
your inner dag – hey, 'Time Warp'! Heaps Gay also
showcases queer artists of every genre.

GYMS, SPORT & FITNESS

As in all large gay cities worthy of that mantle,
there is a thriving culture of the body in Sydney.
Try a gym that's a popular haunt with the queer
crowd or join an active club that'll get you meeting
like-minded queer folk.

City Gym

*107 Crown Street, East Sydney (9360 6247,
www.citygym.com.au). Kings Cross rail or bus
323, 324, 325, 389.* **Open** 5am-midnight Mon-
Thur; 5am-10pm Fri; 6am-10pm Sat; 8am-10pm
Sun. **Rates** $25 (day). **Map** p311 G8.
A legendary venue, popular with gay men and the
serious bodybuilding crowd. Full fitness facilities,
an extensive programme of classes and, for the
men, a notoriously cruisy changing area (with steam
room) and long, long hours.

Fitness First Darlinghurst

*Level 2, 63 Oxford Street, Darlinghurst (8116
4200, www.fitnessfirst.com.au). Museum rail or
Oxford Street buses.* **Open** 6am-11pm Mon-Wed;
6am-9pm Thur, Fri; 7am-7pm Sat; 8am-7pm Sun.
Rates $22 (day). **Map** p312 J7.

SEXY SHOPPING
Toys for boys (and girls).

Sydney has almost as many sex shops as it has Turkish *pide* takeaway joints. The myriad underground stores dotted throughout the CBD and occasional suburban retail strip are lined with enough designer dildos, varying vibrators and faux fists to feed a starving nation of porn stars.

One of Sydney's best and most aptly named adult stores, the **Toolshed** (1/81 Oxford Street, Darlinghurst, 933 22792, www.toolshed.com.au) serves up some of the most creative and imaginative objects destined for the orifice or appendage of your choice. From Mould Your Own Pussy kits and deluxe double-ended dildos, through to porn classics on DVD, the Toolshed is bringing Sydney's sexy back. If your slant is resolutely kinky, the delightful den that is **Sax Fetish** (110 Oxford Street, Darlinghurst, 9331 6105, www.saxfetish.com) caters for both newbies and old hands to the fetish game and carries some seriously sexy wear from studded harnesses, chaps and codpieces for the boys, through to latex leggings, rubber skirts and chrome bras for the gals. Don't forget your accessories: cock slings, lube, bondage rope, gauntlets and gloves. The friendly, skilled team there will soon allay any fears.

From hunky bear calendars featuring a furry fella for each month, through to saucy lesbian erotica, the **Bookshop Darlinghurst** (*pictured*; *see p190*) has been stocking its shelves with some of the sexiest queer literature available in this fair city. The Bookshop also has a great porn section that has proved to be a popular cruising zone with both queer bookworms and regular fans of titles such as *Inches* and *Honcho*.

Three cheers for Fitness First, which now sponsors Mardi Gras. Even better: if you go and work the weights there you'll be able to simultaneously check the talent down on Oxford Street and perv on a parade of buff guys en route to the showers or solarium. No wonder it's busy.

Freezone Volleyball
Sydney Boys High Gym, corner of Cleveland Street & South Dowling Road, Moore Park (www.freezone volleyball.org). Bus 339, 374, 376, 391. **Rates** $15. **Map** p311 H11.
Freezone offers a welcoming environment for gay, lesbian and transgender folks to meet up, tone up and compete. Participation by players of all levels is allowed at the Sunday training sessions (3-6pm) but membership (from $40 via the website) is encouraged. The first Sunday of the month is for newcomers.

Sydney Convicts
Centennial Park Reservoir Playing Fields, Paddington (www.sydneyconvicts.org). Bus 311, 333, 352, 373, 377, 378, 380, 392, 394, 396. **Map** p314 K13.
Australia's first gay rugby team proved that they're made of tough stuff by winning the international Bingham Cup Championship. They're always looking for new members, so if you're an aspiring footy champion and you're sticking around, it could be your lucky break. Either go along to a late-afternoon training session (see website for details), or join in on one of their touch matches (great for those wanting to cheer along, too) on Sundays at Centennial Park.

Sydney Spokes
www.sydneyspokes.com.
This club will get you out in the thick of cycle-mad Sydney, no matter your experience level. Gay and lesbian cyclists can sign up to bike tours galore, including coffee-trail and gay-heartland routes. There are even overnight trips, mountain-bike rides, and most other things you could possibly think of. Rides takes place most Sundays and odd Saturdays. Annual membership is $30.

Sydney Underwater Bushwalking Society
www.gaydive.org.au.
Gay snorkelling is not a euphemism. Or is it? Anyhow, this club makes monthly excursions to dive sites around Sydney and the coasts beyond. It's open to gay men, lesbians and their friends. The club's over 20 years old so you can bet they know some sweet spots. Join the Facebook group to find out about membership (www.facebook.com/groups/SUBSDiving).

Unbiased Bowling
Marrickville Bowling & Recreation Club, 91 Sydenham Road, Marrickville (9557 1185, www. marrickvillebowlingclub.com.au). Marrickville rail.

Sydney Convicts.

It may not be the world's most strenuous sport but lawn bowls does promise to improve your coordination, boost your mental health and… expand your social circle. Unbiased Bowling welcomes everybody, especially those in the gay and lesbian, bisexual and transgender communities. They run games every Sunday from 1pm at friendly Marrickville Bowls. Free lessons are available too.

SAUNAS & SEX CLUBS

When it comes to getting it on, Sydneysiders are anything but shy, and the city has a number of great sex-on-premises venues. Most have signed up to a code of practice organised by the AIDS Council, meaning they distribute free condoms and lube to customers. Over-18s only.

357

357 Sussex Street, CBD (9267 6766, www.357.com. au). Town Hall rail. **Open** 10am-6pm Mon-Thur; 24hrs 10am Fri-6am Mon. **Admission** $25; $18 10am-2pm Mon-Fri; $15 reductions. **Map** p311 E8.
Gay-owned and -run, 357 features four floors of action. The crowd runs from Asian to mature men, but if you are looking for buff, beefy gym types it may not be the place for you. It's all very clean and modern, and facilities include a spa, steam room, sauna, two cinema spaces and various 'fantasy rooms', plus a coffee shop and internet kiosk.

Bodyline Spa & Sauna

10 Taylor Street, Darlinghurst (9360 1006, www. bodylinesydney.com). Bus 311, 333, 352, 373, 377,

378, 380, 392, 394, 396. **Open** noon-7am Mon-Thur; 24hrs noon Fri-7am Mon. **Admission** $23; $16 gym members Mon-Thur; $12 reductions. **Map** p311 H9.
Bodyline was the first legal sex-on-premises gay venue in NSW, and is still gay-owned and -operated. It has a huge spa, steam room and sauna on the lower ground floor; a coffee lounge and cinema on the ground floor; private rooms and a video room on the first floor; and a great sun deck on the second floor. It's kept very clean and tends to attract the buff party crowd from the nearby nightclubs.

HeadQuarters on Crown

273 Crown Street, Darlinghurst (9331 6217, www. headquarters.com.au). Bus 311, 333, 352, 373, 377, 378, 380, 392, 394, 396. **Open** 5pm-5am Mon-Thur; 24hrs 3pm Fri-7am Mon. **Admission** $10-$18. **Map** p311 G9.
HeadQuarters specialises in 'fantasy play areas', including a pig pen, a jail room and enough mazes to get (happily) lost in. It holds frequent fetish nights, as well as the occasional all-nude evening. There's a coffee lounge and full air-con – thank goodness.

Signal

Corner Riley Street & Arnold Place, Darlinghurst (9331 8830, www.signalhouse.com.au). Bus 311, 333, 352, 373, 377, 378, 380, 392, 394, 396. **Open** 11am-3am Mon-Thur; 24hrs 11am Fri-3am Mon. **Admission** $12-$15. **Map** p311 G8.
There's no other way to say this: show them what you've got at the door and if you err on the greater side of eight inches, you're in for nix! Inside are padded benches, beds, glory-hole booths and movie lounges.

Nightlife

Whether it's mainstream hangouts such as Home, or late-night haunts like Club 77, Sydney's club scene is alive and thriving, with a wealth of local and big-name international DJs filling their stages on a regular basis. A boom in venues has seen established nightspots – including Ivy and Chinese Laundry – working hard to keep their crowds content, while venues such as Goodgod concentrate on young talent and keeping-it-indie.

Sydney has a history as a hub of musical creativity. It's had its challenges over the years, from the gentrification of the inner city replacing sweaty venues with fancy housing through to the rise and (thankfully) fall of poker machines, but nothing has stopped Sydney from being one of the greatest places to make and experience music.

See also **Jam Gallery** (*see p103*).

Bars & clubs

Cargo Bar
52-60 The Promenade, King Street Wharf, Darling Harbour (9262 1777, www.cargobar.com.au). Wynyard or Town Hall rail, Darling Harbour ferry, or bus 412, 413. **Open** 11am-late daily. **Admission** varies. **Map** p308 D6.
Fifteen years young, Cargo Bar is a bar most of the time, but as the sun sets over the harbour, the music – a blend of piano house and top 40 hits – is turned up. Cargo attracts a lot of corporates looking to loosen their ties after a long week, so if you're wanting to take a turn on a packed dancefloor, best visit on a Friday after five. There are DJs from 8pm Thursday to Sunday.

Chinese Laundry
Corner of Sussex & King Streets, CBD (8295 9999, www.chineselaundryclub.com.au). Town Hall or Wynyard rail. **Open** 10pm-6am Mon-Thur; 9pm-3am Fri; 9pm-4am Sat. **Admission** free Mon-Thur; $15-$20 Fri; $15-$25 Sat. **Map** p309 E6.
The Laundry is one of Sydney's biggest and most respected clubs. The top-notch sound system in

'the cave' has attracted heavyweight internationals James Holden, Gui Boratto and Sasha, and the outdoor dancefloor is a summer clubbing staple.

Civic Underground
388 Pitt Street, CBD (8080 7000, www.civichotel. com.au). Town Hall rail. **Open** 10pm-5am Fri, Sat. **Admission** $10-$25. **Map** p311 F8.
Despite a recent tightening-up in late-night licensing, a few venues are putting on the kind of nights that would make their European counterparts proud. With possibly the city's best sound system, this small, underground club attracts big internationals for all-night techno, deep house and filthy electro parties.

★ Cliff Dive
16-18 Oxford Square, Darlinghurst (www.thecliff dive.com.au). Oxford Street buses. **Open** 6pm-late Wed-Sat. **Admission** free. **Map** p311 G8.
The tiki bar and nightclub that began filling its dancefloor in late 2013 took a bit of a hit just a few months later when Sydney's new liquor licensing laws came into play, thwarting the post-3am serving of the Cliff Dive's famous pina coladas. It was touch and go there for a minute: Sydney's only under-the-sea-themed Papua New Guinean

dancehall almost flat-lined. But never say die, and never surrender – that's the tiki motto. The room's been given a bit of sparkle; the school of paper fish that swim above the dancefloor has been joined by a large crop of seaweed and bobbing jellyfish. The DJ booth has new speakers and the Gauguin-style murals by local artist and bartender Max Berry, along with the newly woven seagrass, add depth and texture. It's a bar you'll want to drink in early and dance in late.

El Topo Basement

Level 2, 500 Oxford Street, Bondi Junction (9387 7828, www.theeastern.com.au/eltopobasement). Bondi Junction rail. **Open** 6pm-4am Wed-Sat. **Admission** free. **Map** p315 P11.
This band room and club lies beneath top Mexican eaterie El Topo, which itself backs on to Bondi Junction Westfield. Following a good meal, chilli-eating competition or tequila masterclass in the restaurant upstairs, head down to the dancefloor and open-air courtyard for a Latin American vibe and shows from the likes of the Delta Riggs. Just make sure you take a breather to capitalise on the great margaritas and tacos.

Exchange Hotel

34-44 Oxford Street, between Riley & Liverpool Streets, Darlinghurst (9360 1375, www.exchange sydney.com.au). Museum rail or Oxford Street buses. **Open** 9pm-late. **Admission** free-$30. **Map** p311 G8.
Home to several of the city's favourite venues, the Exchange is the seedy after-party joint for anyone and everyone. At Q Bar, there's a dancefloor that swirls with funk and house; Spectrum (*see p209*) has a consistently impressive live music line-up; Phoenix, the underground indie lair, has a killer sound system and an up-for-anything crowd and 34B is home to the best burlesque acts in town. The only downside is deciding which to visit first.

Freda's

109 Regent Street, Chippendale (8971 7336, www.fredas.com.au). **Open** 6pm-midnight Tue-Sun. **Admission** free. **Map** p311 E10.
All-rounder is not an insult, especially when it's describing Freda's, a neighbourhood party bar that knows how to keep things cruisey in the early part of the week and ramp it up for a blowout at the pointy end. Head here on a school night, when gentle disco and house mixes are kept at comfortable chatting volume – put this on your first-date bar list – and a wood-fire image is projected behind the decks to give the industrial space a cosy vibe. From Thursday through to Saturday it's a whole other story. You could find yourself at a night of Italo pop, or maybe some psychedelic synth pop. You might catch a Madonna-themed rager, or a line-up of 1990s R&B anthems that will see you shake out that desk-bound hump. It's a licensed lucky dip.

GETTING AROUND AFTER MIDNIGHT
Don't get stranded.

Buses? Sydney Buses run late in all directions to compensate for the railway closures, so if you're stranded in the city, head to Town Hall and jump on an 'all nighter'.

Trains? The last train usually leaves around midnight and services don't start again until 4.30am. During this period Night Ride Bus services take over, departing from Town Hall station on George Street (near Woolworths).

Taxis? Beware the 3am changeover time. Around this point of the night, it can be near impossible to find a driver willing to pick you up unless you're headed in their direction. If things are looking particularly dire, head to one of the secure taxi ranks or try calling one of the following: Taxis Combined (13 3300); Silver Service Taxis (13 3100); Legion Cabs (13 1451).

Stranded? Armed with an iPhone but without a way of getting home? Get your hands on the TripView app, which can tell you the next departing bus, train or ferry from anywhere in Sydney, with the option to search directly by route or just by suburb if you're completely lost. The best part is, it's free. But if you're going to be using it a lot, we recommend downloading the full version for $2.49, which saves all your routes and information for easily accessible convenience.

ARTS & ENTERTAINMENT

Goodgod Small Club
*55 Liverpool Street, CBD (www.goodgodgoodgod.
com). Town Hall rail.* **Open** 5-11pm Wed, Thur;
5pm-3am Fri; 6pm-3am Sat. **Admission** free-$15.
Map p311 F8.
This alternative fixture started life as Good Good
Small Club, a dungeon at the rear of a very shabby
Spanish restaurant. The restaurant went under,
Goodgod spread out and got a makeover, and the
rest is clubbing history. The club now has popular
indie, retro, tech and hip hop nights on rotation,
and gets its fair share of big names too. If it's cool
enough for the Yeah Yeah Yeahs' Karen O, it's cool
enough for you.

Home
*Cockle Bay Wharf, Darling Harbour (9266 0600,
www.homesydney.com). Town Hall rail or Darling
Harbour ferry.* **Open** varies. **Admission** varies.
Map p310 D7.
Home is one of Sydney's few old-school, large-scale
clubbing experiences. It sprawls over three levels and four bars, with chill-out areas, space-age
lighting, a great sound system and an unrivalled
view over Darling Harbour. On various nights the
DJs will play trance, deep house and drum 'n' bass,
but save your dollars for the infamous Sash parties
on Sundays.

Ivy
*330 George Street, CBD (9240 3000, www.
merivale.com.au/ivy). Wynyard rail.* **Open** noon-
late Mon-Fri; 6pm-late Sat. **Admission** $15-$25.
Map p309 E5.

Merivale, Sydney's clubbing juggernaut, built
this answer to Soho House a few years back – and
it's been a central player in the newspapers' social
pages ever since. Costing a mammoth $160 mil-
lion, the complex has 13 individual venues including the super-exclusive rooftop Pool Club, stylish
cocktail bar and pick-up hotspot Ivy Lounge, and
Changeroom, the city's most popular hetero pseudo-
sex club (wallflowers take note: don't make direct
eye contact).

Kings Cross Hotel
*244-248 William Street, Kings Cross (9331
9900, www.kingscrosshotel.com.au). Kings Cross
rail.* **Open** noon-late daily. **Admission** free.
Map p312 J1.
The Kings Cross Hotel is a pub at heart, but it's one
that spans a six-storey building, from the rooftop
down to a subterranean dive bar, in the very heart
of Sydney's red-light-and-dancefloor district. In
keeping with the hard-won reputation of the area,
you can't get a middy of beer here. If you're drinking
at the Kings Cross Hotel, then you're committed to a
big night and you're expected to use the big glasses.
They're pumping Crowded House, Paul Simon and
the Chili Peppers early on and heavier bangers as the
night progresses. The security gets stricter the later
the hour, so be on your best behaviour.

Marquee
*80 Pyrmont Street, Pyrmont (1800 700 700,
www.marqueesydney.com). Pyrmont light rail.*
Open 10pm-4am Fri, Sat. **Admission** $20-$120.
Map p308 C6.

Tokyo Sing Song.

Part of the Star Casino's $870 million redevelopment is a super club that is anything but subtle. Marquee has played host to Avicii, Afrojack and will.i.am, and offers a true clubbing spectacle. It's a tried and tested formula – Marquee also has venues in New York and Las Vegas. The sound system is an absolute ripper; the LED screens and go-go dancers add to the drama. There are plenty of rooms to explore too. The main room dancefloor is where you'll find the most excitement, but you can get a good view of the action from an alcove behind the stage, or have a conversation and a cocktail in the book-lined library off to the left of it. We wouldn't recommend it for a laid-back late-night boogie or if you're keen to catch some cutting-edge electronic music. Instead, it's a place to be seen, hear a banger after banger and get a taste of the celebrity lifestyle. Basically, if you're feeling the need to pull on a skinny mini, drop some serious dosh and spend the night with your arms in the air, Marquee may well be what you're looking for.

Standard Bowl

Level 3, 383 Bourke Street, Surry Hills (9331 3100, www.thestandardbowl.com.au). Bus 311, 371, 373, 377, 378, 380, 392, 394, 396, 397, 399, 890. **Open** 9pm-2am Wed, Thur; 6pm-3am Fri, Sat. **Admission** free. **Map** p311 H9.

Modelled after the legendary Brooklyn Bowl, the Standard Bowl is a bar and venue with a miniature bowling alley, bleachers from which to watch the live (usually indie) action, DJ booth and dancefloor. The fun doesn't stop there, with pinball machines and pool tables on the mezzanine levels.

Tokyo Sing Song

145 King Street, Newtown (www.tokyosing song.com.au). Newtown rail. **Open** 11pm-4am Wed-Sun. **Admission** free. **Map** p310 A12.

Super offbeat entertainment is the order of the day at this late-night basement bar on King Street. Each month, a new curator takes over the venue and programmes a bunch of pretty crazy stuff – it might be a band, it might be DJs, but it more likely will be an experimental artist determined to mess with you, big time. The venue itself is a mishmash of Japanese pachinko parlour (you know, those joints with the endless rows of pokies – aka poker machines), Lower East Side speakeasy and the diviest bar your filthy mind could imagine (joy!). Tokyo Sing Song also offers punters a hidden disco, edamame beans (if you must), and just a general helping of weird.

World Bar

24 Bayswater Road, Kings Cross (9357 7700, www.theworldbar.com). Kings Cross rail. **Open** 3pm-late daily. **Admission** free. **Map** p312 K7.

This Kings Cross stalwart remains a favourite night-time destination for indie kids, university students and partygoers. Housed in a sprawling terrace, the World Bar is probably best known for serving kitsch cocktails in teapots, as well as offering a stage to up-and-coming indie bands and DJs playing everything from drum 'n' bass, electronic and indie to jazz. The venue is delightfully pokie machine-free – well, mostly. There's just one vintage machine, and it serves as a charity donation box.

Music
ROCK & POP

The genesis of Australian pub rock – and the scene that gave birth to every great Australian artist, from Johnny O'Keefe to Powderfinger – was the rise of feminism. No, really.

You see, most of the great Australian pubs were built in the early decades of the 20th century, when the capital cities and large country towns were really taking shape. These cornerstones of Australian life were built with a saloon bar or lounge area where women – who were naturally too delicate of constitution to tolerate the rough 'n' tumble atmosphere and salty language of the front bar – could enjoy a drink in private with their sensibilities un-offended. During the 1950s and early '60s, however, women began drifting into the front bar, just at the same time the first of the post-World War II baby boom generation were reaching legal drinking age. Pubs were starting to fill with teenagers of both sexes who wanted to be entertained, and these same pubs were starting to wonder what to do with their increasingly superfluous saloon bars. It's unknown who was the first far-sighted publican to say 'let's stick a band in there',

but whoever they were, they unwittingly started a cultural movement that's still going strong today.

The live scene has ebbed and flowed over the decades, and while Melbourne possibly has the greater claim on being Australia's premier live-music city, Sydney's been no slouch: while internationally it's probably best known for spawning Johnny O'Keefe, the Easybeats, Rick Springfield, AC/DC, INXS and Midnight Oil (while Silverchair were born just 150-odd kilometres north-east in Newcastle), it's had a rich and storied history as the hometown of decades of stars: Col Joye, the Atlantics, Rose Tattoo, Icehouse, Divinyls, X, Noiseworks, Radio Birdman, the Reels, Air Supply, Human Nature, the Sunnyboys, Celibate Rifles, Natalie Imbruglia, Youth Group, the Whitlams, Sarah Blasko and, perhaps most excitingly, the Wiggles are all products of Sydney's fertile creative scene.

It's also been a place to move to try something new: Billy Thorpe became a star here after stints in Brisbane and Melbourne, the Hoodoo Gurus was formed by former members of Perth punks the Hitmen, while Ed Kuepper formed the Laughing Clowns here after quitting the Saints and moving from London. Bands such as the

Allphones Arena.

Church and the Hummingbirds were quick to leave Canberra for the brighter lights of the bigger city.

It's been an inspirational place for songwriters too: James Reyne wrote Australian Crawl's masterpiece 'Reckless' after gazing over Sydney Harbour, and many of Paul Kelly's best-loved songs have been inspired by his time in Sydney, though not always entirely affectionately ('From St Kilda to Kings Cross', 'Randwick Bells', 'Darling It Hurts' – a pun on Darlinghurst). Adelaide immigrants Cold Chisel decamped to Sydney and ended up celebrating it in song (most notably on 'Breakfast at Sweethearts', named after a Kings Cross café), and Tim Rogers found poetry under the Glebe Point Bridge in You Am I's 'Purple Sneakers'.

The rise of poker machines in the 1990s, accompanied by increasingly restrictive licensing laws, threatened to spell the end of Sydney's rich musical heritage. However, thanks to the hard work of a handful of dedicated individuals, the laws were changed in 2009, pokies began to vanish into back corners and a new crop of young artists emerged: Angus & Julia Stone, Art vs Science, Sparkadia, PVT and Cassette Kids are some of the most high-profile products of the Sydney scene, while the Holidays and

Cloud Control are from the surprisingly fertile environment of the nearby Blue Mountains. Of course, that couldn't have happened without the venues that kept the faith in the bleak times, and the new blood that took advantage of the changes.

Radio is also vital to the lifeblood of Sydney's local scene. The national youth broadcaster Triple J (105.7) is based in Sydney, but the key stations to listen to for what's going on at ground level are the excellent community stations FBi (94.5 FM) and 2SER (107.3 FM), both of which are staffed by enthusiastic volunteers.

Ticketing is handled by a few major providers: **Ticketmaster** (www.ticketmaster.com.au), **Ticketek** (premier.ticketek.com.au) and **Moshtix** (www.moshtix.com.au) – but most venue websites will provide links straight through to their preferred provider.

Major venues

Sydney's generally the most important stop for any international touring act, simply because it's normally the biggest audience an act will play to in Australia. In fact, many tours will be 'east coast only' (Sydney, Melbourne, Brisbane), plugging the gap between the New Zealand visit and the Japanese leg of the world tour. These are the venues those big acts play: the stadiums, the big theatres, the largest clubs. Tickets generally sell quickly in the first day, but then tail off precipitously, so it's always worth checking, even if you're sure such-and-such would be a sell-out. And remember: you'll need ID to drink, so bring your passport to the bar.

Allphones Arena
Olympic Boulevard, at Edwin Flack Avenue, Sydney Olympic Park, Homebush Bay (8765 4321, www.allphonesarena.com.au). Olympic Park rail, or Lidcombe rail then bus 401. **Tickets** vary.
Built for the 2000 Olympics, the Allphones Arena (previously called the Acer Arena, and prior to that the Sydney SuperDome) boasts a whopping 21,000-seat capacity. It's where the biggest acts play, and extra services from Lidcombe to the Olympic Park are generally put on when events are taking place. While the venue houses everything from monster truck and extreme sports showcases to motivational speaker appearances, it's mainly used for gigs by arena-filling international acts. But it's also witnessed many significant moments in Australian music: Powderfinger's final ever Sydney show took place here, as did the ARIA Awards for many years.

Big Top
Luna Park, Milsons Point (9033 7600, www.bigtopsydney.com). Milsons Point rail or ferry. **Tickets** vary.

ARTS & ENTERTAINMENT

Sitting in the middle of Luna Park is what amounts to a mighty shed called the Big Top. That might sound like a negative description, but it's actually the venue's great strength since it means that it can accommodate everything from festival shows to metal bands and big indies: the Pixies played their first Sydney show here, while the likes of Nine Inch Nails and My Chemical Romance also graced its stage. It's been regularly used as a venue since 2004 and has the undeniable advantage of being one of the few venues conveniently adjacent to a rollercoaster.

★ Enmore Theatre
118-132 Enmore Road, Newtown (9550 3666, www.enmoretheatre.com.au). Newtown rail. **Tickets** vary. **Map** p334.
It's possibly Sydney's best-known venue, not to say the most loved. The art deco theatre was built in 1908 and has operated as a venue continuously since its 1920 remodelling (it's listed in the Heritage Buildings Register, which is remarkable for an active venue). The 1,600-seat theatre plays host to large national and international bands and stand-up acts, as a cursory glance of the poster-covered walls of the street-level snug bar will demonstrate.

Factory Theatre
105 Victoria Road, Enmore (9550 3666, www. factorytheatre.com.au). Newtown rail then bus 423, 426. **Tickets** vary.
Since opening in 2006, this custom-built venue has fired up the scene with shows by local and international musicians, plus dance, cabaret and film events – and since 2009 it's been the hub of the annual Sydney Comedy Festival, a role it's also taken for the Sydney Fringe Festival thanks to its large main room, good-sized courtyard/bar area and rabbit warren of small to medium-sized spaces perfect for multiple performances per night.

Hordern Pavilion
Driver Avenue, Moore Park (9921 5333, www. playbillvenues.com.au). Bus 339, 373, 374, 376, 377, 393, 395, 396. **Tickets** vary. **Map** p314 J12.
It's where the big acts play and dance events take place (many of the more DJ-oriented festivals base themselves around Moore Park, with the Hordern as their centrepiece). Despite looking like an airline hanger with raked seating, it offers surprisingly good sightlines and sound. If an act's in the upper echelons of a festival's line up, chances are it'll be doing its headline sideshow here.

★ Max Watt's
Errol Flynn Boulevard, Entertainment Quarter, Moore Park (www.maxwatts.com.au). Bus 339, 373, 374, 376, 377, 393, 395, 396. **Tickets** vary. **Map** p314 J12.
Formerly known as the Forum and the Hi-Fi in its various incarnations, Max Watt's is the Hordern's little brother, sitting across the road from it in the Entertainment Quarter. The great sound system, sunken dancefloor and three tiers of viewing (with bars on each) makes it a great band venue particularly, as well as a popular location for touring DJs and club nights.

★ Metro
624 George Street, at Central Street, CBD (9550 3666, www.metrotheatre.com.au). Town Hall rail. **Tickets** $20-$150. **Map** p311 E7.
The Metro is still the key rock venue of the CBD: it's where damn near everyone has played (or will play), it boasts one of the city's best live rooms in terms of sound quality, atmosphere and sightlines – there's staggered seating as well as a dancefloor. There are bars at the back and sides, very conveniently, and a small sub-venue (the Lair) for smaller events.

State Theatre
49 Market Street, between Pitt & George Streets, CBD (9373 6655, www.statetheatre.com.au). St James or Town Hall rail. **Tickets** $40-$250. **Map** p309 F6.
Bands here tend towards the more heritage end of the spectrum – performers that suit a seated audience paying rapt attention rather than a boozy general admission crowd. The State Theatre is a gorgeous building, mixing rococo and art deco with playful abandon, and is more often used for recitals and theatrical performances than gigs – but there are still plenty of music and comedy acts who get to perform on that gorgeous stage each year.

★ Sydney Opera House
Bennelong Point, Circular Quay (9250 7111, www.sydneyoperahouse.com). Circular Quay rail or ferry. **Tickets** vary. **Map** p309 G3.
Once upon a time the Opera House was home only to the highbrow, but now the only Sydney venue that can genuinely be called 'iconic' plays host to a wide range of performers on all of its stages. The Concert Hall is still home to the class acts (although its also where many of the acts for the Vivid festival perform, meaning that the unexpected likes of Battles, Melt Banana and Ladytron have played that stage), while the Opera Theatre is still mainly for orchestral, theatrical and operatic seasons. Meawhile, the Studio has seen everything from rock to cabaret, and the Drama Theatre has become increasingly popular as a venue for comedy.

Music pubs & clubs

Sydney's pub scene took a major hit in the 1990s, when band rooms were gutted to make room for pokies (poker machines), but things have been on the up since the restrictive Place of Public Entertainment (POPE) laws were scrapped in 2008, allowing venues to have live entertainment without having to double their security or build extra fire exits and other expensive amendments.

Beach Road Hotel.

Many of these venues are the ones that weathered the hard times, but new spaces have opened in recent times and more pubs are adding live music to their entertainment mix – so here's hoping that Sydney's about to recapture her 1980s reputation as a live-music town, not to mention developing the next wave of great Australian talent. A word of warning for travellers, though: since all of these venues are licensed, you'll need to be over 18 and have photo ID for entry unless the performance specifies that it's all ages. Keep your passport with you.

In addition to the venues listed below, **Basement** (*see p209*), principally a jazz venue, is also a favourite stop for any act that wants to play to an audience that actually listens – which makes it a particular favourite for acoustic acts.

Beach Road Hotel
71 Beach Road, Bondi Beach (9130 7247, www.beachroadbondi.com.au). Bondi Junction rail then bus 380, 381, 333, or bus 380, 333. **Open** 10am-11pm Mon, Tue; 10am-midnight Wed-Fri; 9am-midnight Sat; 10am-10pm Sun. **Map** p105.
Immense in scale, this one-stop pub has something for almost everyone. Hipsters, students and trashbags (Aussie slang for heavy partiers) find solace upstairs in the cavernous band room offering an often impressive line-up of DJs and Australian indie bands most nights of the week, many for free. Our advice? Go

along for Sosume Wednesdays – an indie and EDM celebration that'll make you forget it's a school night.

Gaelic Club
64 Devonshire Street, Surry Hills (9212 1587, www.gaelicclub.com). Central rail or light rail. **Open** varies. **Tickets** free-$80. **Map** p311 F10.
The Gaelic's a bit of a funny one: despite having one of the better live rooms of any venue in Sydney and being a key venue in the 1990s, it was woefully underused for much of the following decade. However, it appears to have got its mojo back with a healthy roster of big local and touring acts – and if the balcony's open, grab a drink and head up there: the sightlines are astonishing.

Hero of Waterloo
81 Lower Fort Street, Millers Point (9252 4553, www.heroofwaterloo.com.au). **Open** 10am-11pm Mon-Thur; 10am-11.30pm Fri, Sat; 10am-10.30pm Sun. **Map** p309 E3.
The Hero was built in a no-frills era, and none have been added in the intervening 170 years. Timber floors, convict-hewn sandstone walls and lantern light create the shell in which Guinness is to be drunk and songs sung by the fireside. Time your visit for Friday nights and Sunday arvos, when bands play, so you can holla along to a Kenny Rodgers tune, or hatch a plan to get into the Hero's cellars – where there's a tunnel to the Harbour that was once used for smuggling rum and drunken patrons to waiting clippers.

Newtown Social Club.

Lewisham Hotel & Live House

794-796 Parramatta Road, Lewisham (9560 8755, www.lewishamhotel.com.au). **Open** 11.30am-11.30pm Mon-Wed; 11.30am-3am Thur, Fri; noon-3am Sat; noon-10pm Sun.

If you're hankering for a good, honest dose of punk or metal, the Lewisham will cater to your needs. It's a friendly pub in the heart of Sydney's alternative Inner West that's got a band room and beer garden, as well as a bistro for that vital refuelling between beers.

Newtown Social Club

387 King Street, Newtown (9550 3974, www.newtownsocialclub.com). Newtown rail. **Open** 4pm-midnight Mon-Thur; noon-2am Fri, Sat; noon-10pm Sun. **Tickets** $10-$35.

The best possible scenario following the closure of a grungy rock pub such as the Sandringham Hotel is that it gets reborn as another music venue, albeit one too upmarket for some of the old locals. Venue Collective, the group behind Melbourne institutions the Corner Hotel and the Northcote Social Club, took over the space, reopening the ground floor as a winsome pub, with a band room upstairs hosting mainly Australian bands. The dining room out the back has a Nordic warehouse vibe thanks to the chipped brick, vertical gardens and sleek booths. They've spruced up the front bar and shoehorned a cocktail lounge under the stairs.

★ Oxford Art Factory

38-46 Oxford Street, Darlinghurst (9332 3711, www.oxfordartfactory.com). Oxford Street buses. **Tickets** $5-$70. **Map** p311 G8.

This Oxford Street venue seemed a pretty risky proposition in a strip better known for nightclubs than live music and entertainment, but it's proved itself with a steady mix of cult internationals, big locals, CD launches, label nights, art exhibitions and more. It also looks great, its brushed concrete industrial look a sly nod to the legendary Manchester nightclub the Haçienda (owned by Factory records – geddit?). It also does a great line in house cocktails.

★ Red Rattler

6 Faversham Street, Marrickville (9565 1044, www.redrattler.org). Newtown rail then bus 423, 426. **Tickets** $5-$40.

Marrickville's industrial past has opened the way for a number of short-lived (and technically illegal) venues in empty warehouse spaces – the Pitz and Quirkz had short, colourful lives in the suburb's backstreets – but the Rattler is totally legit, run by a collective of queer artists as a venue and art space. With a 200-capacity room filled with overstuffed sofas and other mismatched furniture (and a bar that serves it's own Rat's Piss microbrew), the place gives off the vibe of the coolest shared house you could ever wish you lived in, with the added bonus of great Australian – and, increasingly, international – bands, solo performers, cabaret and drama.

Spectrum

Exchange Hotel, 34-44 Oxford Street, Darlinghurst (9360 1375, www.spectrum.exchangesydney.com. au). Oxford Street buses. **Tickets** $5-$30. **Map** p311 G8.

The Exchange Hotel (*see p201*) has many rooms – 34B, Vegas, Q Bar – but Spectrum is its main live venue. It's got a reputation as the indiest of indie rooms, where the next generation of up-and-comers (and, to be fair, down-and-goers) join multi-band bills in a room with a good stage and a decent PA, and genuinely terrifying toilets. It's also a nightclub with a regularly rotating range of club nights, mainly when the bands finish around 11pm.

JAZZ

In recent years, jazz has moved further into the mainstream. More and more of today's stars are coming not from the sweaty pub stages but universities: rising chart stars Kate Miller-Heidke and Megan Washington are alumni of Brisbane's Conservatorium of Music, for example. Meanwhile, the relaxing of the restrictions around live music in Sydney coincided with an explosion in the number of small bars and venues that may not be appropriate places for a rock band to be blasting out, but are perfect for something a little quieter.

That being said, it's not simply the change in the laws that has led to the jazz renaissance – the city has long had a hunger for it. When illegal venues were springing up around Sydney before the POPE laws (*see p206*) were struck down, jazz was as important as rock music. Qirkz and 505 were both jazz venues, operating illegally out of a warehouse in Marrickville and an apartment building in Surry Hills, respectively. While Qirkz was shut down, **505** has made the leap to legitimacy.

In 2013, the long-running Darling Harbour Jazz & Blues Festival was axed, amid much protest, by the Sydney Harbour Foreshore Authority, which has new plans for the precinct, but fans can still flock to the **Manly Jazz Festival** – approaching 40 years old – which happens in early October over the Labor Day long weekend, and the annual **Newtown Jazz Festival** in November.

There are also two key organisations without which the Sydney scene would have withered and died. Jazzgroove has long been instrumental in keeping Sydney's jazz community furnished with gigs (for a long time, it ran a night at the now-defunct Excelsior Hotel and has now found a home with fellow travellers 505); and the Sydney Improvised Music Association (SIMA), has remained dedicated to providing an environment that encourages experimentation and musical exploration – and in so doing has seeded future generations of punters and performers alike.

Venues

★ 505

Corner of Cleveland & Perry Streets, Surry Hills (www.venue505.com). Central rail or light rail. **Tickets** free-$25. **Map** p311 F11.

There were stories about a room somewhere in Surry Hills where, on a Monday night, you bought a bottle from the nearby takeaway, ascended an unmarked stairwell and watched live jazz. Of course, sooner or later word got around (though it took five years to happen) – but unlike most illegal venue owners, the team behind 505 decided to go straight, moving the venue and opening it as a bar and restaurant. Musicians of a jazz, blues, world or roots persuasion play here six nights a week.

Basement

29 Reiby Place, off Pitt Street, Circular Quay (9251 2797, www.thebasement.com.au). Circular Quay rail or ferry. **Tickets** $15-$100. **Map** p309 F4.

Sure, plenty of acts play the Basement – but, as the below-street-level vibe, and walls covered in posters and photos of the likes of Miles Davis make clear – at its heart the Basement is all about jazz. Many acts choose to record their live DVD or album here, not least because the sound system's well tuned, the sightlines are good (with a sunken dancefloor and dining area, and bars to the back and side) and because it attracts the sort of audience who like to listen to good music. You won't need your jacket, though: it gets pretty warm in here, especially in the summer months.

ARTS & ENTERTAINMENT

★ Sound Lounge

Corner of City Road & Cleveland Street, Chippendale (9351 7940, www.sima.org.au). Bus 370, 422, 423, 426, 428. **Tickets** $10-$30. **Map** p310 C11.

The influence of SIMA on the development of Sydney's scene cannot be understated: as a breeding ground for new artists and as a meeting place for national and international performers, the Sydney Improvised Music Association has nurtured the existing scene while remaining dedicated to expanding the brief. Its home venue, the Sound Lounge in the Seymour Centre, is one of the most acoustically superb rooms in Sydney and is a frequent home for Sydney's jazz elite: Tina Harrod, Mike Nock and the Catholics are some of the regular performers you'll find here.

Sydney Opera House

Bennelong Point, Circular Quay (9250 7777, www.sydneyoperahouse.com). Circular Quay rail or ferry. **Tickets** vary. **Map** p309 G3.

Sydney's high-profile centre of culture has always been partial to jazz. It's where the big names play, and the Concert Hall stage has some of the best acoustics on the planet. It sounds even better now, actually, with the Opera House spending tens of thousands of dollars on an exquisite new Steinway piano. There are also regular jazz and funk performers playing for drinkers and diners at the Opera Bar, which may not have quite the acoustics of the Concert Hall, but wins hands-down for the Sydney Harbour view.

Vanguard

42 King Street, between Queen & Fitzroy Streets, Newtown (9557 9409, www.thevanguard.com.au). Newtown rail or bus 352, 370, 422, 423, 426, 428. **Tickets** $14-$24 ($49-$59 incl meal). **Map** p316.

A beautiful, beautiful venue – think 1920s bordello – The Vanguard's long been a welcome home for jazz and blues, with a solid line-up of touring acts and local favourites. These days the entertainment mix includes more cabaret/burlesque acts too. Like the Basement (*see p209*), it's a favourite with those who like to enjoy music and a meal.

COMEDY

Go to any comedy festival in the world and chances are that there'll be a horde of Australians in the line-up. Australia has always loved its comedy and – despite the relatively small population when compared with the UK or US – there are some major regional variations, which can be broadly summed up as 'Sydney style' and 'Melbourne style'.

In Melbourne, the comedy tradition was more theatrical: there were dedicated comedy clubs in the city and comedy developed as its own art form with a very specific, comedy-savvy audience. Sydney was slower to embrace that

model, and comedy developed as part of the entertainment mix in RSLs (servicemen's clubs) and pubs, jostling for space alongside bands, strippers and meat raffles. Well-known Sydney comedian and television presenter Wil Anderson believes that the influence of these two different gestations is still visible today: Melbourne comics are more likely than Sydney comics to perform in character and deliver monologue-style pieces, as befits comedy's theatrical heritage. Sydney comics, on the other hand, are more likely to be solo stand-ups, delivering quick-fire gags – the legacy of distracting a rowdy audience in a noisy venue.

Of course, it's not as clear cut as that. Sure, Sydney's been home to many classic, working-man stand-up comedians, but Sydney comedy is far from unsophisticated. Among the NSW comedy community are such august names as UK favourite Julia Morris, US star Joe Avati, former *Big Brother* host Gretel Killeen, Billy 'The 12th Man' Birmingham and master stand-ups Tom Gleeson and Kitty Flanagan, while US comic and writer Tommy Dean also calls Sydney home these days. Improv Australia was born here too, and every year the Enmore Theatre (*see p206*) plays host to the best improvisational comedy teams in the nation as they compete for the Cranston Cup.

Television's been well represented here too. Host, producer, writer and comedy renaissance man Andrew Denton is a Sydney boy, as is Chris Lilley (the writer/performer behind *We Could Be Heroes* and *Summer Heights High*). The arch-satirists Drew Forsyth, Phillip Scott and Jonathan Biggins (best known for their ABC show *Three Men and a Baby Grand* and their annual touring show *The Wharf Review*) also call the Harbour City home, while satirical comedy troupe the Chaser began at Sydney University before taking over print, radio and ABC television. Similarly, Channel Ten's *The Ronnie Johns Half Hour* might have been short-lived, but it did launch the comedy careers of Felicity Ward, Heath 'Chopper' Franklin, satirist/presenter Dan Illic and Jordan Raskopoulos, who's now perhaps best known as a member of the internationally acclaimed musical-comedy trio the Axis of Awesome. SBS's cult hit *Pizza* also began life in Sydney, launching the comedy careers of Paul Fenech, Rebel Wilson, Tahir Bilgiç, Ahn Do and Jabba.

The fact that national youth broadcaster Triple J (which also runs the annual Raw Comedy national stand-up competition) is based in Sydney has also helped Sydney comedy considerably: aside from launching careers for locals such as Wil Anderson, Adam Spencer, John 'Rampaging Roy Slaven' Doyle, Mikey Robins, Tim Ross, Merrick Watts and Lindsay MacDougall, Sydney has pinched the odd interstate gem for its on-air talent, including South Australians Sam Simmons and Greig 'HG Nelson' Pickhaver and Melburnians such as Corinne Grant, Alex Dyson and Tom Ballard.

The future for Sydney's next generation of comics is looking bright: stand-ups such as Jacques Barrett and Rhys Nicholson are breaking through to the bigger leagues, as is the unhinged, surreal Nick Sun, writer-turned-performer Dave Bloustien and arch-impressionist Jackie Loeb, while Jennifer Carnovale and Madeleine Culp have been winning critical plaudits as Cloud Girls.

The **Sydney Comedy Festival** (*see p36*) has been running annually since 2005. While it's not quite the size of Melbourne's annual event, it has been growing steadily, attracting headliners of the calibre of Dylan Moran, Ross Noble, Steven Wright, Henry Rollins, Julian Clary, Tom Green, Steve Coogan, Danny Bhoy and Pablo Francisco.

Venues

In addition to the venues listed below, **Sydney Opera House** (*see p210*) regularly has comedy shows, mainly in the Studio and the Drama Theatre: most are one- or two-week seasons from large Australian acts and international performers doing festival runs.

Many of Sydney's community clubs offer comedy as part of their entertainment mix. Acts such as Kevin Bloody Wilson and Stephen K Amos have done sets at **Revesby Worker's Club** (2B Brett Street, Revesby, 9772 2100, www.revesbyworkersclub.com.au), while Jimeon and Akmal have recently graced the stage of the **North Sydney Leagues Club** (12 Abbott Street, Cammeray, 9245 3000 www.norths.com.au).

The big-name touring acts play the same venues as bands: occasionally the **Metro** (*see p206*) will hold a comedy gig, but more often performers will be at the **Enmore Theatre** (*see p206*), the **State Theatre** (*see p206*). The **Factory Theatre** (*see p206*) doesn't usually run comedy as part of its day-to-day operations, but it acts as the hub of the annual Sydney Comedy Festival thanks to its warren of smaller rooms around the main stage.

Comedy Store

Entertainment Quarter, Corner of Lang Road & Driver Avenue, Moore Park (9357 1419, www.comedystore.com.au). Bus 339, 373, 374, 376, 377, 393, 395, 396. **Tickets** $10-$40. **Map** p314 J12.

It's had a colourful history, but since becoming part of the Century Venues family (along with the Factory, the Enmore and the Metro), the Comedy Store has settled into offering a solid five nights of

comedy a week. It generally hosts one- or two-week seasons of touring international comics and solid Australian headliners, with two or three support acts. It's the home of the NSW heats for Triple J's Raw Comedy contest and also stages showcase multi-comic bills. The Store can be a little tricky to find in the Entertainment Quarter, but if you head along the parking garage toward the cinemas, you should be fine. Snacks are available, and there's table service so you're not disrupting the performers by running around the joint.

Friend in Hand

58 Cowper Street, Glebe (9660 2326, www.friend inhand.com.au). Bus 431, 436, 438. **Tickets** $10-$15. **Map** p310 B9.

It only has comedy once a week, but Mic in Hand is the must-see Sydney open mic night. Every Thursday from 8pm, around ten newcomers will try their luck upstairs at the Friend in Hand, with an experienced MC and a headline act that is often a big name trying out new material ahead of a tour or festival. The room, with couches and chairs scattered around, fills early; the audience is notoriously comedy-savvy and encouraging. For a performer, it's one of the best rooms in Sydney – even Sam Simmons, 2015 winner of Best Show at the Edinburgh Comedy Awards – has appeared from time to time. For a punter, it's a great way to see the newest acts on the circuit.

★ Giant Dwarf

199 Cleveland Street, Redfern (www.giantdwarf. com.au). Central or Redfern rail. **Tickets** $20-$25. **Map** p311 E11.

The privately owned Cleveland Street Theatre was leased – quietly – by TV satire team the Chaser, or at least their production company, in 2013. It now hosts their Empty Vessel talks series as well as the comedic Erotic Fan Fiction night and the Chaser-produced Story Club. First Tuesday Comedy Club plays it relatively straight – an old-school formula of MC, opener, feature set and headliner. Appearance-wise, the venue has a kind of shabby-chic vibe that perhaps belies the amount of hard labour (and cash) that went into the art deco refurb.

Star Bar

600 George Street, CBD (9267 7827, www.star bar.com.au). Town Hall rail. **Tickets** $10-$20. **Map** p311 E7.

It's hidden in the back of a bustling CBD bar in the George Street entertainment precinct (close to the Metro and the Event Cinema complex), but once you've negotiated your way through the after-work throng, you'll find an odd little custom-built comedy theatre. There are armrest buttons for voting in the weekly Comedy Court every Friday night, when an experienced MC marshals a group of hopefuls trying their luck. On Saturdays, the voting stops, but the Quick Comedy still promises multiple comics doing short, punchy sets.

ARTS & ENTERTAINMENT

Performing Arts

For the best in Sydney theatre, you have to start off with the 'big three': Griffin Theatre Company is the theatre of choice for edgy and daring new Australian work; Belvoir tends to be all about reworking Australian classics and giving life to new ones; while the Sydney Theatre Company offers a diverse range of theatre and theatre styles in several different venues, but the 'big night out' theatre experience is its particular speciality.

Dance in Sydney is on the brink of a cultural revolution, with some offerings drawing on ancient traditions and others firmly steeped in the here and now. And, with fresh young artistic director Rafael Bonachela heading up the Sydney Dance Company, the future looks bright.

Sydney also has a very enthusiastic classical crowd that flocks to concerts – especially when they're laid on in an outdoor picnic-style setting.

Theatre

The big three major theatre companies – the **Griffin Theatre Company**, **Belvoir** and **Sydney Theatre Company** – may represent the biggest and best of Sydney theatre, but each of them offers cheaper and chancier options: Griffin in its independent theatre programme; Belvoir in its Downstairs Theatre; and STC in its Wharf Theatres. But for true underdog theatre and the authentic fringe experience, head to the **Old Fitzroy** and **Darlinghurst** theatres.

At the other end of the spectrum and the other side of the bridge (the Sydney Harbour Bridge, that is), the **Ensemble Theatre** tends to cater to an audience of loyal subscribers who aren't getting any younger. And it's perhaps not surprising that the best international productions and stars tend to crop up on the stages of the **Sydney Opera House**.

INFORMATION & TICKETS

For detailed, up-to-date information about what's happening on stage in Sydney, have a look at the 'Performing Arts' section of the monthly *Time Out Sydney* magazine or the Spectrum supplement in Saturday's *Sydney Morning Herald*.

In general, tickets bought directly from theatre box offices offer the cheapest deal, and many theatres offer discounted tickets on certain nights. For some shows, you can use a booking agency such as **Ticketek** (13 2849, www.ticketek.com. au), **Ticketmaster** (13 6100, www.ticketmaster. com.au) or **MCA Ticketing** (1300 306 776, www. mca-tix.com.au), though all charge booking fees.

COMPANIES

Australian Theatre for Young People
9270 2400, www.atyp.com.au.

ATYP is primarily devoted to the nurturing and training of young people, staging mostly new and contemporary work starring aspiring thesps. There may be a whiff of star-factory fantasy about it, but the company has built a reputation for putting on worthwhile work for the young and young at heart. It's based within the arts precinct at Walsh Bay but performances take place in venues all over Sydney – many at Fort Street Primary School in the Rocks. Nicole Kidman is its patron, and film director Baz Luhrmann its ambassador – both trod the boards with the company as children.

Bell Shakespeare Company
8298 9000, www.bellshakespeare.com.au.
In 1970, actor-director John Bell founded the Nimrod company, widely regarded as spearheading the Australian theatre revival of that decade in Sydney. Today, he devotes his energies to the Bell Shakespeare Company, whose unofficial motto is 'Shakespeare with an Australian accent'. The company, which celebrated its 25th anniversary in 2015, is known for its innovative, utterly comprehensible and intelligent remountings of the canon (not limited to Shakespeare). Up until 2015, Bell himself often acted or directed. Based in Sydney, with regular seasons at the Opera House, Bell productions also tour the rest of Australia and internationally.

★ Belvoir
9699 3444, www.belvoir.com.au.
Belvoir specialises in bold readings of the classics and new Australian plays, with a strong history of exploring Indigenous voices and the Aboriginal experience in contemporary Australia. Many of the country's best actors and directors have created their strongest work in collaboration with the company – think Geoffrey Rush, Cate Blanchett, Deborah Mailman and Richard Roxburgh. As of 2016, Belvoir falls under the artistic leadership of one of its long-term directors, Eamon Flack, who's well used to the pace of putting on 13 productions a year across two stages. The company's home is the once shabby but now entirely respectable Belvoir Street Theatre (*see p214*).

Darlinghurst Theatre Company
9331 3107, www.darlinghursttheatre.com.
This not-for-profit company started in the 1990s on the smell of an oily rag. Production by production it grew, until by the late 2000s it was running 48 weeks per year with an annual audience of more than 20,000. Its offshoots include Milk Crate Theatre for the homeless and disadvantaged, and its touring arm, Critical Stages.

Ensemble Theatre Company
9929 0644, www.ensemble.com.au.
Founded in 1958 by American Hayes Gordon, the Ensemble is the oldest surviving professional theatre company in New South Wales. Sandra Bates was the artistic director for 30 years; Mark Kilmurry took over in January 2016. The company manages without government funding, though it treads a fine line between cosseting and challenging the legion of loyal subscribers on whom it depends. Its usual programme includes a combination of new plays and seasoned classics, and it has become the theatre of choice for new work from playwright David Williamson. The Ensemble has its own theatre on the water in Kirribilli (*see p215*).

Griffin Theatre Company
9332 1052, www.griffintheatre.com.au.

One of the essential engines of Sydney's theatre scene, Griffin is the city's only company solely dedicated to nurturing, developing and performing new Australian work. Founded in 1978, and under the artistic direction of Lee Lewis as of 2015, this not-for-profit venture produces four to six shows a year at the Stables Theatre (*see p217*) and has a strong independent theatre programme. It also tours its highly regarded Playwright's Residency programme. The annual Griffin Award for the best unproduced new Australian play is also an important event in the local calendar. Hit films *Lantana* and *The Boys* both started their lives as plays here.

Hayes Theatre Co
8065 7337, www.hayestheatre.com.au.
Named after Australian musical theatre legend Nancye Hayes, this theatre is home to a co-op of theatre companies going by the name Independent Music Theatre. The building was previously the home of the Darlinghurst Theatre Company and called the Darlinghurst Theatre, but changed hands in 2013 and re-opened as Hayes Theatre Co in February 2014. It's also a home-away-from-home for New Musicals Australia, and the venue for the brand-new Sydney Cabaret Festival. Recent productions include the musicals *Rent* and *High Society*.

New Theatre
9519 3403, newtheatre.org.au.
Established in 1932 as a workers' theatre, the New – like Newtown, the once blue-collar inner-city suburb in which it resides – has changed substantially over the decades. Although it's still committed to political and socially enquiring work, the company has moved away from simplistic agit-prop and now has a wide remit ranging across classics, neglected Australian repertoire, contemporary European and American work, gay theatre and musicals performed on its stage in King Street (*see p215*). Technically amateur (the actors are all unpaid), the New is at its best when mounting large-cast classics that are no longer considered economically viable anywhere else.

★ Sydney Theatre Company
9250 1777, www.sydneytheatre.com.au.
Sydney's official state theatre company stages new and classic Australian works as well as new international writing. In 2016, STC stages will show the final season by outgoing artistic director Andrew Upton, with British director Jonathan Church taking the programming reins for 2017. STC productions are staged in several venues – its home at the Wharf Theatres (*see p218*), the Drama Theatre at the Opera House (*see p218*), and the Roslyn Packer Theatre (*see p217*). STC also programs STC ED, an education season for school-age audiences, and makes a point of bringing overseas talent to Australian audiences.
▶ *For news of the 'greening' of the Sydney Theatre Company's Wharf complex, see p23.*

ARTS & ENTERTAINMENT

Urban Theatre Projects

9707 2111, www.urbantheatre.com.au.
Urban Theatre Projects' mission is to work with Sydney's diverse cultures to make challenging and relevant contemporary theatre. Based in western Sydney (Bankstown), its work is produced through collaboration between artists and local residents, with a focus on storytelling, geographical identity and multimedia. UTP can be found performing in warehouses, railway stations, schools, shopping centres, town squares, private homes, buses and occasionally even theatres.

VENUES

The plush, 1,200-seat **Theatre Royal** in the CBD (MLC Centre, King Street, 9224 8444) once hosted major productions on a regular basis, but, thanks to having Sydney's least-capacious foyer and the perennial rumble from nearby undergound trains, it has been used less in recent years. That's set to change, though, as in August 2015 its owners partnered with Ambassador Theatre Group. ATG is the UK company behind Australian productions of *Legally Blonde the Musical*; *Thriller Live*; *Guys and Dolls*; *West Side Story* and *The Rocky Horror Show*, so expect crowd-pleasers at the Theatre Royal once it has been refurbished.

The **National Institute of Dramatic Art** (215 Anzac Parade, Kensington, 9697 7600, www.nida.edu.au), Australia's most eminent drama school – and the alma mater of Mel Gibson and Cate Blanchett – also puts on shows throughout the year.

Belvoir Street Theatre

25 Belvoir Street, at Clisdell Street, Surry Hills (9699 3444, www.belvoir.com.au). Central rail or light rail. **Open** *Box office* 5-6.30pm Tue; 5-8pm Wed-Fri; 9.30am-8pm Sat; 2.30-6pm Sun. **Tickets** *Upstairs* $72. *Downstairs* $25-$68. **Map** p311 F11.
This one-time tomato sauce factory is now owned by Belvoir (*see p213*), a non-profit consortium of performers, actors, writers and their supporters. Belvoir stages productions in its intimate 350-seat Upstairs Theatre and its somewhat more intimate 80-seat Downstairs Theatre, attracting Sydney's most discerning and loyal theatregoers. Australia's most esteemed actors, including Robyn Nevin and Colin Friels, are to be seen here.

Capitol Theatre

13 Campbell Street, between Pitt & George Streets, Haymarket (9320 5000, box office 1300 723 038, www.capitoltheatre.com.au). Central rail or light rail, or Capitol Square light rail. **Open** *Box office* 9am-5pm Mon-Fri. **Tickets** $79-$180. **Map** p311 E8.
Completed in 1893, the interior of the Capitol (originally known as the Hippodrome) was designed by an American theatre specialist to create the illusion of sitting outdoors under the stars. Once reduced to being a too-big porn cinema and then nearly derelict for years, the Capitol was expensively and extensively restored just as the fashion for gargantuan long-running musicals peaked. It's thoroughly kitsch, and the perfect venue for such long-running shows as the worldwide hits *The Lion King*, *Les Misérables* and *Wicked*.

Darlinghurst Theatre Company
at the Eternity Playhouse.

Ensemble Theatre
*78 McDougall Street, Kirribilli (9929 0644,
www.ensemble.com.au). Milsons Point rail or
Kirribilli ferry.* **Open** *Box office* 9.30am-5pm
Mon; 9.30am-7.30pm Tue; 9.30am-8.15pm
Wed-Sat. **Tickets** $46-$62; from $22 reductions.
Hayes Gordon transformed an old boathouse into
Sydney's first in-the-round space in the 1950s, but
the theatre has since recovered from the fickle whims
of offshore trendiness, and the company (*see p213*)
is now consistently commendable. The place has
one of Sydney's most scenic foyers and a house
style of honest, no-nonsense work. Sandra Bates
ran the Ensemble from 1986 to January 2016; Mark
Kilmurry succeeds her.

Eternity Playhouse
*39 Burton Street, Darlinghurst (8356 9987,
www.darlinghursttheatre.com). Kings Cross rail
or bus 311.* **Open** *Box office* 9.30am-5pm daily.
Tickets $20-$37. **Map** p311 H8.
Home to the Darlinghurst Theatre Company (*see
p213*), which co-produces a variety of new work
and updated classics in collaboration with a range
of local and touring companies. The Eternity
Playhouse is a 128-year-old heritage-listed building with stained-glass windows – a space rather
wonderfully at odds with the modern, edgy performances inside.

New Theatre
*542 King Street, between Angel & Knight
Streets, Newtown (9519 3403, bookings 1300
306 776, www.ramin.com.au/online/newtheatre).*
*Newtown or St Peters rail, or bus 308, 370,
422.* **Open** *Box office* 10am-6pm Mon-Fri &
1hr before show. **Tickets** $28; $22 reductions.
Map p316.
An intimate 160-seat auditorium at the calmer
end of King Street is home to the New Theatre,
Australia's most committed continuously producing company. Cheap as chips and far more nourishing, the New is usually one of Sydney's best, and
best-value, theatre options.

Old Fitzroy Theatre
*129 Dowling Street, Woolloomooloo (9356 3848,
www.oldfitztheatre.com). Kings Cross rail or bus
200.* **Open** *Box office* 11am-midnight Mon-Fri;
6.30pm on show days. **Tickets** $15-$35. **Map**
p312 H7.
Founded in 1997 by a desperately hip yet talented
collective of Sydney actors called the Tamarama
Rock Surfers Theatre Company, and located under
an old backpacker's pub, the Fitz has a reputation for
hosting cutting-edge work, new talent and whatever's currently hip, hot or happening. It hosts up to 12
main productions a year and also puts on the work of
visiting companies.
▶ *The Old Fitzroy also has a popular bar and
restaurant.*

Parramatta Riverside Theatres
*Corner of Church & Market Streets, Parramatta
(8839 3399, www.riversideparramatta.com.au).
Parramatta rail or ferry.* **Open** *Box office* 9am-5pm
Mon-Fri; 9.30am-1pm Sat & 1hr before show.
Tickets $15-$50.

CHEAP THEATRE DEALS
Finding tickets that won't break the bank.

Theatre's expensive, but there are deals to be found for the thrifty culture-hound. **Bell Shakespeare** (*see p213*) offers discounted tickets of $35 for anyone under 30, and its previews are just $45. For groups of ten or more, the **Belvoir Street Theatre** (*see p214*) offers a $10 discount per Upstairs Theatre ticket or a $6 discount per Downstairs Theatre. In addition, there are student rush tickets at $39/$25 available for Tuesday and Thursday evening and Saturday matinee shows. You can book these at any time by calling the box office.

The **Ensemble Theatre** (*see p215*) has introduced $25 Last Minute Rush tickets for opening-night shows. Email boxoffice@ ensemble.com.au during the week leading up to opening night and put 'LAST MINUTE RUSH' in the subject line along with your name and contact number. At 6pm on opening night, Ensemble will call people on their Last Minute Rush list and offer them $25 tickets.

The **Griffin Theatre Company** (*see p213*) offers tickets at the bargain price of just $20 as part of its Monday Rush promotion at its home, the Stables Theatre (*see p217*). Simply turn up at the box office an hour before each Rush performance to purchase tickets. Get there early, though, as tickets can only be bought on the day, in person, with a limit of two tickets per person. There are more deals to be found at the **New Theatre** (*see p215*) in Newtown: as well as the usual $27 reductions, there's a student rush deal for

$17 tickets. The tickets are available half an hour before the show, are limited to one ticket per customer and subject to availability. In addition, New Theatre operates Thrifty Thursdays, where all tickets are $17.

Performance Space (*see p217*) always offers season passes, which are excellent value if you want to catch a handful of diverse shows that run the gamut from re-mounts of successful shows staged elsewhere to experimental new works. And the **Sydney Theatre Company** (*see p213*) has a cheap tix initiative called the Suncorp Twenties, which makes $20 tickets available for every STC performance (excluding opening nights). It also offers discounted tickets for under-30s (not available for previews or Saturday nights). With the under-30 discount, Main Stage shows are $58. And no, you can't cheat the system – all under-30 tickets need to be picked up from the box office, with valid proof of age.

Opera fans can find cheap deals too. **Opera Australia** (*see p219*) offers standing-room tickets for only $44, which are sold from 9am on the day of each performance. Tickets are limited, however, and there's always a queue – so get in early to avoid missing out. Staff also sell $44 balcony-box restricted-view seats from 9am on performance day – they're sometimes known as 'listening seats' – and $50 student rush tickets for any remaining available seats from one hour prior to the performance.

Griffin Theatre Company at the Stables Theatre.

A council-mandated multi-theatre complex, perched beside a dried-up patch of the Parramatta river. It gets shows touring from around Australia, including inner Sydney venues such as STC, Griffin and Ensemble, and hosts the annual Big Laugh Comedy Festival early in the year.

Performance Space (Carriageworks)
245 Wilson Street, Eveleigh (8571 9111, bookings 1300 723 038, www.performance space.com.au). Redfern or Macdonaldtown rail. Open *Box office* 10am-6pm Mon-Fri & 1hr before show. Tickets $20-$25; $15 reductions. Map p310 B12.
Part of the increasingly vibrant and happening Carriageworks complex, the Performance Space is contemporary and funky and has the only foyer in Sydney where banging on about 'post-performative practice' won't earn you instant derision. With a strong focus on experimental performance and installations, the Performance Space remains the city's finest escape from the stultification of the mainstream.

Riverside Theatres
Corner of Church & Market Streets, Parramatta (8839 3398, www.riversideparramatta.com.au). Parramatta rail. Open *Box Office* 9am-5pm Mon-Fri; 9.30am-1pm Sat & 1hr before show. Tickets vary.
This western Sydney cultural hub hosts an exciting programme of theatre, dance, opera, circus, musicals and solo shows.

Roslyn Packer Theatre
22 Hickson Road, opposite Pier 6/7, Walsh Bay (9250 1999, www.roslynpackertheatre.com.au). Circular Quay rail or ferry, then 15min walk. Open *box office* 9am-8.30pm Mon-Sat; 3-5.30pm Sun (show days only). Tickets $25-$70. Map p309 E3.
This theatre, seating nearly 900, is programmed by the STC (*see p213*), so it doesn't depend on the whims of commercial producers. It often features good drama (and good dance, courtesy of the Sydney Dance Company, *see p218*), though its seating plan makes skipping out before interval a nightmare. Also on site is the Hickson Road Bistro and Walsh Bay Kitchen, offering pre- and post-dining, drinks and coffee. It's fairly out of the way, so it may help to think of the walk through the Rocks and under the Bridge as part of a great night out.

Seymour Centre
City Road, Chippendale (9351 7940, www. seymour.usyd.edu.au). Bus 370, 422, 423, 426, 428. Open *Box office* 9am-6pm Mon-Fri; 11am-3pm Sat & 2hrs before show. Tickets $10-$60. Map p310 C11.
The Seymour Centre showcases a grab-bag of productions in three different theatres, including family entertainment, university revues, dance,

Roslyn Packer Theatre.

musicals and, in past years, Belvoir (*see p213*) and Ensemble Theatre Company (*see p213*) shows too large for their regular homes. The York Theatre, designed with Tyrone Guthrie's open-stage model in mind, can sometimes feel a little too open, while the Downstairs Theatre can sometimes feel like a classroom, but the outdoor barbecue gets a welcome work-out prior to many a performance.

★ Stables Theatre
10 Nimrod Street, at Craigend Street, Kings Cross (9361 3817, www.griffintheatre.com.au). Kings Cross rail. Open *Box office* 6-10pm Mon-Sat. Tickets $35-$55. Map p312 J8.
Renovated in 2010, the building retained the original 120-seat theatre with its kite-shaped stage – one of the best venues for getting close to the action. Seating a closely packed audience of 120, with people sometimes sitting on cushions on the stairs on busy nights, the Stables is home to the Griffin Theatre Company (*see p213*), the foremost champion of new Australian writing for the stage.

State Theatre
49 Market Street, between Pitt & George Streets, CBD (9373 6655, www.statetheatre.com.au). St James or Town Hall rail. Open *Box office* 9am-5pm Mon-Fri (until 8pm on show days). Tickets $50-$135. Map p309 F6.
Sydney's State Theatre is a monument to another age; with elements of Gothic, Italianate and art deco design, the theatre itself offers a spectacle to rival the on-stage action. Hosting every kind of show from theatre to comedy to film (the Sydney Film Festival,

see p39, takes over the venue in June) and music, there's something to suit every taste. For glorious nostalgia, pick something along traditional lines, so that venue and performance work together.

Sydney Lyric

Pirrama Road, Pyrmont (9509 3600, www.sydneylyric.com.au). Star City light rail, Darling Harbour ferry or bus 443. **Open** *Box office* 9am-5pm Mon-Fri (later on show days). **Tickets** vary. **Map** p308 C6.
Sydney Lyric (formerly the Lyric) is a state-of-the-art theatre that, like the Capitol, is generally the home of big-budget musicals (the likes of *Cats, Matilda* and *West Side Story*) and spectacular all-ages theatre. Sightlines are good and there are bars and restaurants aplenty in the complex – and you can try your luck in the casino afterwards.

★ Sydney Opera House

For listings, see p221.
Danish architect Jørn Utzon's difficult child, the Opera House is a wonderful piece of sculpture masquerading as an arts venue. Despite the fact that it's best appreciated from the outside, experiencing the weirdness of Sydney's best-known icon is a must. In addition to the Joan Sutherland Theatre and the larger Concert Hall, it contains three theatre spaces: the Drama Theatre (notoriously widescreen and distant), the smaller Playhouse (mid-sized) and the Studio (a late attempt to reclaim the funk). Regardless of the building's drawbacks, the work is up there with Sydney's best, with the Sydney Thetre Company (*see p213*) and the Bell Shakespeare Company (*see p213*) making regular appearances, Vivid Festival and Sydney Festival productions popping in annually and a spate of excellent touring shows throughout the year.
► *For the inside story on the tragedy and triumph behind the Opera House, see p262. For music productions, see p220. For visits and tours, see p58.*

Wharf Theatres

Pier 4/5, Hickson Road, Walsh Bay (9250 1777, www.sydneytheatre.com.au). Circular Quay rail or ferry, then 15min walk. **Open** *Box office* 9am-7pm Mon; 9am-8.30pm Tue-Fri; 11am-8.30pm Sat; 2hrs before show Sun. **Tickets** $48-$79; $42-$67 reductions (not Fri or Sat). **Map** p309 E2.
The Wharf Theatres is a converted wharf and warehouse on the western side of the Harbour Bridge, near the Roslyn Packer Theatre (*see p217*). Surrounded by swanky residential redevelopments, it houses the Sydney Theatre Company's artistic, managerial and production staff, rehearsal space and a lovely restaurant, as well as two theatres, Wharf 1 and Wharf 2. The Sydney Dance Company, Australian Theatre for Young People and Bangarra Dance Theatre also perform here. The complex also boasts Sydney's best foyer.

Dance

Australian Ballet

1300 369 741, www.australianballet.com.au.
With a repertoire that combines the contemporary and the classical, this company draws on Australian and international choreographers – the inventive and imaginative choreography of dance colossus Graeme Murphy (formerly artistic director of the Sydney Dance Company) being a particular highlight.

★ Bangarra Dance Theatre

9251 5333, www.bangarra.com.au.
Australia's leading contemporary Indigenous dance company, Bangarra has been artistically directed by Stephen Page since 1991. Its value is in its mix of contemporary style with ancient Aboriginal traditions of storytelling through movement. Consistently popular, Bangarra regularly tours the world and remains one of Australia's only distinctive arts exports. A performance is a unique experience.

Sydney Dance Company

9221 4811, www.sydneydancecompany.com.
With the appointment of new artistic director and self-described 'movement junkie' Rafael Bonachela in 2009, the Sydney Dance Company continues its commitment to bringing contemporary dance – from Australian as well as international choreographers – to wide audiences. That's not to say that it dumbs down – the company is renowned for exciting and challenging work that is both highly visual and highly emotional.

ARTS & ENTERTAINMENT

Classical Music & Opera

The **Sydney Festival** (*see p33*) alleviates post-Christmas blues by running musical events throughout January – including the Sydney Symphony's free **Symphony in the Domain**. The other main outdoor event, also free, is Opera Australia's **Mazda Opera in the Domain**, on a Saturday near the end of January. The orchestral and carol-singing sit-ins in the Domain pack in tens of thousands of families every year, although connoisseurs steer clear of such mainstream fare, which tends to favour well-worn classics. ABC's TV and radio stations often broadcast live relays of opera performances, usually at weekends.

ORCHESTRAS & GROUPS

Australian Brandenburg Orchestra

9328 7581, www.brandenburg.com.au.
Australia's first period-instrument group – baroque and classical periods, that is – has played to sell-out audiences from Tokyo to Germany. Formed by artistic director Paul Dyer in 1990, the orchestra now puts on regular seasons at the City Recital Hall (*see p221*). Its concerts are fashionable events – rich mixes of visual and musical experience.

Australian Chamber Orchestra

8274 3800, www.aco.com.au.

Under the flamboyant artistic directorship of high-profile violinist Richard Tognetti, the ACO has been praised as one of the most exciting classical ensembles worldwide. Formed in 1975, the Sydney-based touring orchestra is relatively youthful, and Tognetti's programming is always provocative. He likes to mix periods, offer rarely heard works and blend period-instrument soloists with contemporary instruments. The results are invariably startling.

★ Musica Viva

8394 6666, www.musicaviva.com.au.
Musica Viva is the world's largest chamber music organisation, organising tours of Australian and international groups around the country. The outfit, which turned 70 in 2015, covers a wide range, from classical to world music. A roll-call of the world's best ensembles, including the Emerson, Jerusalem and Tokyo Quartets and violinist Gidon Kremer and his band, have all appeared on its impressive calendar.

Opera Australia

9318 8200, www.opera-australia.org.au.
Australia may be far from the great European opera houses, but the country's divas have been disproportionately represented in the ranks of global opera stars, among them Nellie Melba, Joan Hammond, the late Joan Sutherland, Elizabeth Whitehouse and Yvonne Kenny. And Opera Australia has the third-largest programme (after Covent Garden and the Vienna Staatsoper) of the world's opera companies. It performs in the Sydney Opera House (*see p221*) for seven months of the year; from April to

ARTS & ENTERTAINMENT

Sydney Dance Company.

May and November to December, it ups sticks to Melbourne. In Sydney, the orchestra is shared with the Australian Ballet. The company's touring arm, OzOpera, performs year-round across Australia. Visitors can also go behind the scenes at OA's fascinating headquarters in Surry Hills. Tours (book about two weeks ahead) take in the costume, millinery and wig-making departments, the props and storage departments, set design and building, and rehearsal spaces for singers and musicians.

Sydney Symphony

8215 4600, www.sydneysymphony.com.au.
Under the artistic directorship of Vladimir Ashkenazy since 2009, the Sydney Symphony continues to be the flagship of a network of Australian state capital city orchestras. Established in 1932 as a radio broadcasting orchestra, it has grown into the biggest and best in the country, attracting the finest soloists from Australia and abroad. The orchestra presents more than 140 events a year.

Other ensembles

Look out for the **Sydney Philharmonia Choirs** (9251 2024, www.sydneyphilharmonia.com.au), which has been going strong for nine decades and continues to stun audiences with several big concerts each year of choral works famous and obscure. The **Sydney Chamber Choir** (1300 661 738, www.sydneychamberchoir.org) specialises in Renaissance music as well as works

from contemporary Australian composers. The acappella outfit the **Song Company** (8272 9500, www.songcompany.com.au), Australia's premier vocal ensemble, performs early operas and oratorios. Pianist Kathryn Selby is the artistic director of **Selby & Friends** (9969 7039, www.selbyandfriends.com.au), whose core ensemble is popular piano group TrioZ. **Goldner Quartet** (www.goldnerquartet.com) celebrated its 20th anniversary in 2015 and still retains all its original members. Its Sister City Project will take it to all six of Sydney's partnered cities: Portsmouth (England), Wellington (New Zealand), Guangzhou (China), Florence (Italy), San Francisco (USA) and Nagoya (Japan).

VENUES

The **Eugene Goossens Hall** – named after the British composer and conductor who first suggested the idea of the Opera House back in 1954, and housed in the ABC headquarters in Ultimo (700 Harris Street) – is often used by smaller ensembles playing contemporary music. **Sydney Town Hall** (*see p67*) also showcases contemporary music, plus free organ recitals, the Sydney Youth Orchestras, and Sydney Festival events. Free lunchtime concerts are held weekly at **St James's** (173 King Street, CBD, sjks.org.au), **St Stephen's Uniting Church** (197 Macquarie Street, CBD, www.ssms.org.au) and **St Andrew's Cathedral** (*see p62*).

Sydney Symphony.

★ City Recital Hall

2 Angel Place, CBD (8256 2222, www.city recitalhall.com). Martin Place or Wynyard rail. **Open** *Box office* 9am-5pm Mon-Fri; 3hrs 30 mins before show Sat, Sun. **Tickets** free-$90. **Map** p309 F5.

The 1,238-seat City Recital Hall in the centre of the CBD gives Sydney's orchestras room to roam, as well as hosting international names (including pianist David Helfgott). The three-level, shoebox-shaped hall has a colour scheme borrowed from a Latvian Baroque church (soft grey, soothing aubergine and twinkles of gold), and the architecture and acoustics have been designed for both chamber orchestras and solo performers. The acoustics are said to match Amsterdam's Concertgebouw.

Concourse

409 Victoria Avenue, Chatswood (9020 6968, www.theconcourse.com.au). Chatswood rail. **Open** *box office* 9am-6pm Mon-Fri; 9am-5pm Sat. **Tickets** vary.

This elegant grey steel-and-glass concert hall could be mistaken for the Guggenheim Museum Bilbao's straight-laced younger brother. Inside, you'll find a captivating programme of orchestral concerts, contemporary music gigs and theatre shows.

Sydney Opera House

Bennelong Point, Circular Quay (box office 9250 7777, www.sydneyoperahouse.com). Circular Quay rail or ferry. **Open** *Box office* 9am-8.30pm Mon-Sat; 2hrs before show Sun. **Tickets** *Opera Theatre* $70-$250; $70-$195 reductions. *Concert Hall* vary. *Drama Theatre & Playhouse* $35-$80; $30-$60 reductions. *Studio* $25-$50; $25-$40 reductions. **Map** p309 G3.

The largest shell of the Sydney icon houses the 2,700-seat Concert Hall (although it was first intended for opera productions). Thanks to its purpose-built acoustics, symphonic music can be heard with a full, rich and mellow tone. Eighteen adjustable acrylic rings (aka the 'doughnuts') are suspended above the orchestra platform to reflect some of the sound back to the musicians. The hall also has the largest mechanical tracker-action organ in the world, with 10,154 pipes. The smaller, 1,500-seat Joan Sutherland Theatre is used by Opera Australia, but its small pit and stage are a tight fit for grand opera. The Studio (capacity 350) showcases anything from rap to percussion bands and spoken-word shows. The Utzon Room hosts small ensembles and the Baby's Proms. Two other spaces are used for drama productions (*see p218*).

Verbrugghen Hall

Corner of Bridge & Macquarie Streets, CBD (9351 1222, www.cityrecitalhall.com). **Tickets** $20-$40. **Map** p309 G4.

The Conservatorium of Music's Verbrugghen Hall is a world-class concert hall seating 528 across several sections. The venue features a large stage accommodating a full symphony orchestra, Pogson organ and choir gallery, and has superb acoustic qualities.

Escapes

Escapes & Excursions

Escaping Sydney's urban sprawl only takes a couple of hours' drive in any direction. Inland, to the west, are the World Heritage-listed Blue Mountains, with breathtaking views across deep valleys, sheer cliffs, waterfalls and bushland. To the north is Hunter Valley, famous for its wineries, while a trip south leads to the historic villages of the Southern Highlands. Beautiful beaches, rainforests and national parks can be found up and down the coast, with plenty to see along the way.

INFORMATION

NSW TrainLink (central reservations 13 2232, www.nswtrainlink.info) operates trains and coaches in New South Wales, around Canberra, and in Queensland and Victoria. Visit its website for details of its good-value multi-day train and tour packages to destinations in NSW.

For general information on areas around Sydney, visit the Sydney Visitor Centre (*see p293*) or contact Destination New South Wales (9931 1111, www.destination.nsw.gov.au).

Heading West

BLUE MOUNTAINS

A mere two hours west of the CBD, the Blue Mountains is one of Australia's most popular natural playgrounds and a must-visit for any tourist. This spectacular wilderness covers over 10,000 square kilometres (almost 4,000 square miles) of breathtakingly beautiful and rugged country: in 2000, the **Blue Mountains National Park**, which covers nearly 2,700 square kilometres (1,050 square miles), was grouped together with six other nearby national parks to form the Greater Blue Mountains World Heritage Area. Most of it is so isolated from Sydney's urban sprawl to the east that it could hide a species of tree, the Wollemi pine, that was thought to have been extinct for 150 million years.

The Blue Mountains – in reality a maze of plateaus and dramatic gorges – is part of the Great Dividing Range, which separates the eastern seaboard and its cities from Australia's rural and desert heart. They only look blue from a distance, due to sunlight refracting through the eucalyptus oil that evaporates from the bush's legion of gum trees.

For decades after the first settlers arrived in Sydney, the Blue Mountains were thought to be impassable – but the very future of the colony depended on breaking through the dense bush and bridging its gaping canyons. With no sheep tracks to follow, and river paths ending in crashing waterfalls, it took until 1813 before its secrets were finally unlocked to give farmers access to the sprawling, fertile land beyond.

Today, the area is easily traversed by rail and car (thanks to the efforts of a group of prisoners who were offered pardons if they could complete the first road in a matter of months; they did).

The administrative region called the City of the Blue Mountains is a narrow strip of townships and villages snaking its way along a high plateau between vast tracts of virgin bush. The townships are usually deliberately picturesque, full of twee 'olde wares' shops and 'Devonshire' teas. Lavishly restored cottages sit amid English-style cold-climate gardens, though some residents are radically embracing native flora, often to the discomfort of older locals who like their conifers, rose beds and topiary hedges.

With nature the area's star attraction, the best way to explore is by taking one or several of the numerous well-signposted and maintained bushwalks. These range from hour-long quickies to camping treks of several days' duration. Good advice on walks can be found at the Blue Mountains Information Centre (*see p227*). More adventurous types can enjoy rock climbing, abseiling and the thrill of riding mountain bikes in actual mountains.

While most townships have their own bush trails, the centre of the action lies in the adjoining townships of Katoomba and Leura. **Katoomba** is the most popular township for visitors, thanks to its proximity to attractions such as the **Three Sisters** rock formation near Echo Point and **Scenic World**, where a range of gravity-defying vehicles grant spectacular views as you travel over and into the **Jamison Valley**. If you've got some time, descend the precipitous 841-step **Giant Staircase** next to the Sisters (only the genuinely athletic or masochistic should attempt to climb up it), and then do the two-and-a-half-hour easy walk through the Jamison Valley to the foot of the scenic railway for a sweat-free, mechanised ascent.

Katoomba is home to the Blue Mountains City Council, three pubs, a swathe of cafés and plenty of writers, artists and poets of steeply varying quality. Its chief built attractions are the 1880s **Carrington Hotel**, a popular wedding venue,

and the intimate and terribly 'heritage' **Paragon Café** (65 Katoomba Street, 4782 2928). There are also some excellent second-hand bookshops. The three best for dusty bibliophiles – all on Katoomba Street – are **Brian's Books** (no.44, 4782 5115), **Mr Pickwicks** (no. 86, 4782 7598) and **Blue Mountains Books** (no. 92, 4782 6700).

Linked to Katoomba by bus, train, a panoramic cliff drive or a half-hour walk is **Leura**, with its more upmarket guesthouses, vastly smarter shops and manicured gardens. One of the world's chintz capitals, Leura is a delight for all lovers of knick-knacks, baubles and ornamental flummery.

Further into the mountains beyond Katoomba, the **Hydro Majestic Hotel** – recently restored to its golden-age glory – in Medlow Bath is popular for pricey coffee with an expansive view. Rather more down to earth is the village of **Mount Victoria**, the starting point for many more fine mountain hikes.

On the northern side of the mountains, off the Bells Line of Road above the Grose Valley, is the quintessentially transplanted English hamlet of **Mount Wilson**. This charming village is best visited in spring or autumn, when some house-proud locals open their gardens for your viewing pleasure and herbaceous envy. It's also notable for **Withycombe** (corner of the Avenue and Church Avenue), the house where the parents of writer Patrick White lived for a time. For more natural splendour, try the hushed and

Blue Mountains

majestic remnant rainforest grandiloquently named the **Cathedral of Ferns**.

Also in the area are the magnificent **Mount Tomah Botanic Gardens** (4567 3000, www. bluemountainsbotanicgarden.com.au), which showcase cool-climate plants from around the world. A range of guided and self-guided tours – including bushwalks – is available, but bookings are essential.

You'll need to travel to the south-western edge of the Blue Mountains to reach the other main attraction in the area: the **Jenolan Caves** (1300 763 311, www.jenolancaves.org.au). A tangled series of extraordinary underground limestone caverns, complete with stalagmites and stalactites, within a large and peaceful nature reserve, the caves are open 9am to 5pm daily.

The cavern experience comes in two flavours – easy guided tours with walkways and steps, and various adventure caves requiring helmets, overalls and climbing (from $90). If you're on the less adventurous side, take a tour of **Lucas Cave** ($32, $22 reductions).

Scenic World

Corner of Cliff & Violet Streets, Katoomba (4780 0200, www.scenicworld.com.au). **Open** 9am-5pm daily. **Tickets** Unlimited Discovery Day Pass (includes Railway, Skyway, Cableway and Walkway) $35; $18 reductions.

Views and vertigo are the main features of this collection of tourist transports. The Scenic Skyway – a cable-car system over the Jamison Valley – was renovated a few years ago. The new cars have glass floors, so now you can see that it really is a long way down – 270m (890ft), in fact. The Scenic Railway features an old coal train reinvented as the world's steepest rail incline, which takes you down into the rainforested valley – as does the Scenic Cableway, another cable car ride. There's a two-kilometre boardwalk between the lower Railway and Cableway stations, so you can go down on one and come back on the other.

Where to stay & eat

Blue Mountains YHA

207 Katoomba Street, Katoomba (4782 1416, www.yha.com.au). **Rates** $28-$31 dorm; $74-$84 double; $103-$140 family.

The Blue Mountains outpost of the YHA empire is an excellent modern hostel in a historic 1930s art deco building right in the centre of Katoomba.

Carrington Hotel

15-47 Katoomba Street, Katoomba (4782 1111, www.thecarrington.com.au). **Rates** from $127 incl breakfast.

A gorgeous, rambling, old-style resort hotel with lots of antiques and oodles of 19th-century charm. Cocktails on the balcony are a must.

Hydro Majestic Hotel

Great Western Highway, Medlow Bath (4782 6885, www.hydromajestic.com.au). **Rates** from $259.

An upmarket, beautifully restored historic hotel with astonishing views and a Victorian feel, this establishment was once famous for its spa cures, hence the 'Hydro'. Even if you're not staying at the Hydro, it's worth a visit for its tea and scones.

Jenolan Caves House

Jenolan Caves (1300 763 311, www.jenolancaves. org.au). **Rates** full board from $81 midweek; $129 weekend.

Inside the caves complex, this dark, wood-panelled hotel with roaring fires has the feel of a grand English country house. Next door, the Gatehouse Jenolan offers four-bed dorms for $30 a head.

Lilianfels Blue Mountains

Lilianfels Avenue, Echo Point, Katoomba (4780 1200, www.lilianfels.com.au). **Rates** from $305.

This five-star pile perched just above Echo Point is the poshest accommodation in the heart of the mountains, with two famed restaurants (Darleys, serving modern Australian cuisine, and Tre Sorelle, serving Italian) plus great views.

Wolgan Valley Resort & Spa

2600 Wolgan Road, Newnes, (9290 9733, www. emirateshotelsresorts.com). **Rates** from $2,050.

Perhaps Australia's finest country hotel, Wolgan Valley Resort & Spa stands out not just for its stunning location deep in the Wolgan Valley, but also for its luxuriously appointed villas and all-inclusive price tag. The restaurant's menu changes daily and features only the finest local produce.

Getting there & around

By car
Springwood, Faulconbridge, Wentworth Falls, Leura, Katoomba & Mount Victoria
Take the Great Western Highway (Route 32) and/ or Western Motorway (Route 4). It's 109km (68 miles) from Sydney to Katoomba; journey time is around 2hrs.

Kurrajong & Mount Tomah
Take the Great Western Highway (Route 32) or Western Motorway (Route 4); turn off to Richmond via Blacktown; then Bells Line of Road (Route 40). Mount Wilson is 6km off Bells Line of Road.

Jenolan Caves
Take the Great Western Highway (Route 32) via Katoomba and Mount Victoria; then turn south at Hartley; it's another 46km (29 miles) to the caves.

By train
Trains (Sydney Trains, 8202 2200, www. sydneytrains.info) depart hourly from Sydney's

Central Station for the upper mountains, with stations at Springwood, Faulconbridge, Wentworth Falls, Leura, Katoomba and Mount Victoria; journey time to Katoomba is around 2hrs.

By bus

Almost all Sydney-based tour companies offer a one-day bus trip for a quick look around. One easy sightseeing option is the **Blue Mountains Explorer Bus** (4782 1866, 1300 300 915, www.explorerbus.com.au). It's a double-decker (for some reason painted in the livery of a red London bus) departing just across from Katoomba train station 15 times a day between 9.45am and 4.45pm ($40 adults, $20-$35 reductions). It stops at 30 attractions, including galleries, tea rooms and scenic spots around Katoomba and Leura. You can get off and on as often as you like, and tickets are valid for up to seven days. Sydney Trains also offers a combined train plus Explorer Bus ticket (ExplorerLink).

Tourist information

The websites www.katoomba-nsw.com and www.bluemts.com.au also have information.

Blue Mountains Information Centre *Echo Point Road, Katoomba (1300 653 408, www.visitblue mountains.com.au)*. **Open** 9am-5pm daily.

Heading North
HAWKESBURY RIVER

If you've ever wondered what the west coast of Scotland would look like without the rain, mist and midges, head to Hawkesbury River. Skirting the outer edges of Australia's biggest city for much of its length, the great greenish-brown giant licks over 1,000 kilometres (620 miles) of foreshore as it curls first north-east and then, from Wisemans Ferry, south-east towards the sea, emptying into an estuary at Broken Bay. The river's fjord-like saltwater creeks and inlets are ideal for exploring by boat, and houseboating holidays are popular.

The town of **Windsor** retains many of its original buildings as well as its waterwheel. Among the stalwarts is the oldest inn in Australia still being used for its original purpose (the **Macquarie Arms**, built in 1815, 99 George Street); Australia's oldest courthouse (1822); **St Matthew's Anglican Church** (1 Moses Street), built by convict labour from a design by convict architect Francis Greenway (also in 1822); and the oldest Catholic primary school still in use (1836). Also of note is **John Tebbutt's house and observatory** (Palmer Street), with its outsized telescope. It's worth taking a tour with **Hawkesbury Valley Heritage Discovery**

Mount Tomah Botanic Gardens.

Ebenezer.

Tours (4577 6882), as you'll get the enthusiastic low-down on the area's history from a local guide.

Within easy reach of Windsor, there's more colonial architecture at **Richmond**, a tree-lined garden town whose railway station dates back to 1822, and **Ebenezer**, with Australia's oldest church (on Coromandel Road, built 1809).

The Hawkesbury's change of course is marked by an S-bend at **Wisemans Ferry**, another of the river's historic villages. It has Australia's oldest ferry service, which still runs 24 hours a day (and is one of the few remaining free rides in New South Wales). On the far side of the ferry is a section of the convict-built Great Northern Road, once 264 kilometres (164 miles) long, which shows just what sweat and toil really mean.

Up the road in the Macdonald River Valley, in the secluded hamlet of **St Albans**, is another colonial inn, the **Settlers Arms** (1 Wharf Street, 4568 2111). A couple of kilometres from here, in the **Old Cemetery** on Settlers Road, lies the grave of William Douglas, a First Fleeter who died in 1838. Rumours also suggest that St Albans was Windsor magistrates' preferred venue for illicit nooky over the years.

The lower reaches of the Hawkesbury are its most spectacular, with steep-sided forested banks and creeks branching off its wide sweep. Near the end of Berowra Creek (west of the Pacific Highway), at the foot of two deep, bush-covered hills, is beautiful **Berowra Waters**. There's not much here apart from a small car ferry, a cluster of bobbing boats and a few restaurants offering fine cuisine (including Hawkesbury oysters).

Much of the remainder of the river, as it makes its way to the sea, is equally tranquil – notably the slender fingers of water that make up **Cowan Creek** (east of the Pacific Highway). It's here, in the sweeping expanse of the **Ku-ring-gai Chase National Park**, that many people choose to cruise or moor for a spot of fishing.

If you haven't got time for houseboating, Australia's last riverboat postman may be the answer. The four-hour cruise from **Brooklyn** allows you to participate in the delivery of mail while taking in the scenery. The boat leaves Brooklyn Wharf at 10am weekdays, excluding public holidays: for details, call 9985 9900 or 0400 600 111. Otherwise, you could hike from Berowra railway station down to Berowra Waters along a fascinating, well-marked bush track (part of the Great North Walk). A round trip takes about four hours.

Where to stay & eat

Able Hawkesbury Houseboats

3008 River Road, Wisemans Ferry (4566 4308, www.hawkesburyhouseboats.com.au). **Rates** from $510 (2 days, 1 night).

Choose from seven different sizes of boat, from 26ft up to 52ft in length. Facilities include shower, toilet, fridge, TV, barbecue, cutlery and crockery.

Berowra Waters Fish Café

199 Bay Road, Berowra Waters (9456 4665). **Open** 9am-4pm Mon-Thur; 9am-8pm Fri; 8.30am-8pm Sat, Sun. **Main courses** $14-$21.

Berowra Waters.

A great setting with views across the water. Serves fish and chips in various guises. BYO.

Court House Retreat
19 Upper Macdonald Road, St Albans (4568 2042, www.courthousestalbans.com.au). **Rates** from $160.
B&B accommodation in a historic sandstone building that once housed a courtroom, police station and lock-up. Booking essential.

Retreat at Wisemans
5564 Old Northern Road, Wisemans Ferry (4566 4422, www.wisemans.com.au). **Rates** from $144.
Comfortable rooms with views of the golf course or river. The Riverbend restaurant, serving Mod Oz food, is recommended (about $45 for two courses).

Ripples Houseboat Holidays
87 Brooklyn Road, Brooklyn (9985 5555, www. ripples.com.au). **Rates** from $750 for 2 nights.
Two kinds of boat, sleeping up to four or ten.

Getting there

By car
Richmond & Windsor It's 59km (37 miles) from Sydney to Windsor; journey time 60-90 minutes.
   Via Hornsby: take Pacific Highway (Route 83) to Hornsby; Galston Road; then Pitt Town Road.
   Via Pennant Hills: take Epping Road (Route 2) to Pennant Hills; then Route 40.
   Via Parramatta: Western Motorway (Route 4) to Parramatta; then Route 40.

Wisemans Ferry & St Albans Pacific Highway (Route 83) to Hornsby; Galston Road; then Old Northern Road.

Berowra Waters Pacific Highway (Route 83); 12km (7 miles) north of Hornsby, look out for the Berowra turn-off. The Brooklyn turn-off is 12km (7 miles) further north.

By train
Richmond & Windsor There's a regular train service to Windsor and the upper Hawkesbury River area on the Richmond line (via Blacktown) from Sydney's Central Station. Journey time is around 1hr.

Berowra Waters The main Sydney–Newcastle line from Central Station goes to Berowra Waters (via Berowra Station) and Brooklyn (via Hawkesbury River Station). Journey time is around 40mins (note that not all trains stop at both stations).

By bus
For details of bus and coach services to the Hawkesbury region, contact the local tourist office (*see p230*) or NSW TrainLink (13 2232, www.nswtrainlink.info).

Tourist information

Hawkesbury River Information Centre
5 Bridge Street, Brooklyn (9985 7064). **Open** 9am-5pm Mon-Fri; 9am-4pm Sat; 11am-3pm Sun.

ESCAPES & EXCURSIONS

HUNTER VALLEY

The second most-visited region in New South
Wales after the Blue Mountains, the **Hunter
Valley** is the state's main wine-growing region
– and that is the reason to visit. The area around
the main town of **Pokolbin**, two hours north
of Sydney, boasts more than 75 wineries (from
the smallest boutiques to the big boys, such as
Lindemans), which offer tastings and cellar-door
sales of wine ranging from semillon and shiraz
to chardonnay. Mingled among the vineyards are
award-winning restaurants and luxury hotels,
but there are plenty of cheaper options too.

While such wine-based indulgence has put
the Hunter firmly on the tourist map, the area's
personality is, in contrast, also bound up with
coal mining. The very waterway from which the
region gets its name was originally known as the
Coal River (it was renamed in 1797 after the then
NSW governor, John Hunter), and the founder of
the Hunter's wine-making industry, Scottish civil
engineer James Busby, arrived in Australia in
1824 partly to oversee coal-mining activities in
nearby Newcastle. But while the Hunter Valley
once boasted the largest shaft mine in the
southern hemisphere, which held the world
record for coal production in an eight hour shift
(**Richmond Main Colliery**, now a museum
with tours and steam train rides on the first,
second and third Sunday of the month), all
but two of its mines have now closed.

The wine industry sprouted from humble
beginnings in the 1830s, but has fared rather
better. The original vines were cuttings taken
from France and pre-dated the phylloxera disease
that tainted European wine. Thus it's claimed
that Australian grapes make wine that's more
authentic than modern-day French wines, which
use roots from American vines. Seeing out the
tough 19th century, then the Depression of the
1930s and later fighting off competition from
other antipodean wine regions, such as South
Australia, the Hunter made it to the 1970s wine
rush and since then it has done little but flourish.

Despite its small area – the main vineyard
district north of the town of **Cessnock** is only
a few kilometres square – the sheer number of
wineries in the Lower Hunter Valley can present
the wine tourist with a problem: where to start?
Inevitably, familiarity leads many to the bigger,
more established vineyards – which is a good
way of gaining an insight into wine-growing
traditions. Large family companies in Pokolbin,
such as **Tyrrell's** (Broke Road, www.tyrrells.
com.au, 4993 7000) and **Tulloch** (Glen Elgin

Estate, De Beyers Road, www.tullochwines.com/
cellar-door, 4998 7580) have been producing
wine in the area for more than a century, while
at **Lindemans** (McDonalds Road, 4993 3700)
– in existence for 150 years – there's a museum
exhibiting old wine-making equipment. Other
big wineries, such as **McGuigan Simeon**
(corner of Broke and McDonalds Roads, www.
mcguiganwines.com.au, 4998 7700), offer the likes
of galleries, museums, restaurants and cafés.

But it would be a shame to miss out on the
smaller enterprises. Places such as **Oakvale**
(set against the Brokenback Range, Broke Road,
4998 7088, www.oakvalewines.com.au) and
Petersons (Mount View Road, 4990 1704, www.
petersonswines.com.au) offer the time and space
for a more individual tasting experience. Many of
these boutique wineries are set within picturesque
surroundings. **Hungerford Hill** (Broke Road,
4998 7666, www.hungerfordhill.com.au) –
formerly housed in a beautiful tiny converted
church, and recently moved into a new landmark
designer building – has some of the best 'stickies'
(dessert wines and rich ports) in the area. The
grounds of **Pepper Tree Wines** (Halls Road,
4909 7100, www.peppertreewines.com.au)
incorporate a former convent – the area's swishest
guesthouse (*see p231*) – which was moved lock,
stock and barrel to the Hunter for the purpose.

Further afield, in **Lovedale**, the **Wandin
Valley Estate** (Wilderness Road, 4930 9888,
www.wandinvalley.com.au) has accommodation
in villas and its own cricket ground. Talking of
which, visit **Brokenwood** (McDonalds Road,
4998 7559, www.brokenwood.com.au) to enjoy its
always cracking Cricket Pitch and Graveyard
wines. And yes, they do come from vines grown
on cricket pitches and graveyards.

Look out for the vintages that were produced
during 1988, 2000 and 2003: these were the best
years in the Hunter Valley for decades.

Since the Hunter is reasonably flat and compact,
and the wineries never far apart, it's a good place
to ditch four-wheel transport. Bikes are available
from some guesthouses for a small charge, while
Grapemobile (4998 7660) hires out bikes and
also runs enjoyable day and overnight cycling
and walking tours of the wineries from Cessnock.

Finally, if you're not high enough already, see
the regimented rows of vines from above with
a sunrise balloon flight: try **Balloon Aloft**
(*see 233* **Enjoy the Ride**).

There's plenty of good accommodation in the
area, but a unique place to base yourself is the
award-winning **Eaglereach Wilderness
Resort** (*see p231*). Perched on a mountain
top with vistas in all directions, and set in 400
hectares of raw bushland, this is a place to
experience nature at close hand. Expect to see
kangaroos at the window and giant lizards on
your doorstep.

Wine tours

While many Hunter Valley vineyards offer tastings at the cellar door, the local cops rightly take exception to drink driving, so the best idea may be to take an organised tour. You can travel in old-fashioned style in a horse-drawn carriage: **Pokolbin Horse Coaches** (0408 161 133) offers regular tours and can custom design a tour (minimum four) to suit your needs. The **Hunter Valley Wine Country Visitor Centre** (*see p232*) has details of other outfits.

Activity Tours Australia
4227 9902, 1800 990 457, www.activitytours. com.au. **Rates** (with wine and cheese tasting) $125.
Day trips from Sydney to the Hunter Valley, taking in five wineries, a tour to see how wine is made and a cheese factory. Maximum 19 people.

Hunter Vineyard Tours
4991 1659, www.huntervineyardtours.com.au. **Rates** from $70; $99 with lunch.
Full-day tour in 12- or 22-seat buses, taking in five wineries (lunch optional) in the Cessnock area. Pick-up is from local hotels.

Trekabout Tours
4990 8277, www.hunterweb.com.au/trekabout. **Rates** from $70.
Half- or full-day winery tours for up to six people. The shorter tour visits four to five wineries. Pick-up is from hotels in the Cessnock/Pokolbin area.

Where to stay & eat

Most Hunter Valley guesthouses won't take bookings for less than two nights, particularly over weekends. Rates drop considerably midweek. There are more (and cheaper) options in Cessnock.

Eaglereach Wilderness Resort
Moonabung Road, Vacy (4938 8233, www. eaglereach.com.au). **Rates** from $280.
A mountain-top retreat set in 400 hectares (1,000 acres) of raw bushland, with wraparound vistas and nature up close. Accommodation is in luxury log cabins.

Peppers Convent Guest House
Grounds of Pepper Tree Wines, Halls Road, Pokolbin (1300 987 600, www.peppers.com.au). **Rates** from $300.
The ultimate indulgence, surrounded by vineyards and with lots of antiques. One of the country's classiest restaurants, Robert's, is also here.

Tallawanta Lodge
Hunter Valley Gardens, next to McGuigan Winery, corner of Broke & McDonalds Roads, Pokolbin (4998 2000, www.hvg.com.au). **Rates** from $373 incl breakfast.

Hunter Valley.

A pleasant place to lay your head, right in the heart of the wine area. The associated Harrigan's Irish Pub also has decent rooms from $269.

Wandin Valley Estate
Wilderness Road, Lovedale (4930 9888, www. wandinvalley.com.au). **Rates** from $190.
Winery accommodation in six self-contained, well-appointed villas and studios just five minutes from Pokolbin. Great restaurant too.

Getting there

By car
Sydney-to-Newcastle Freeway (Route 1) to Freemans Interchange; then turn off to Cessnock (Route 82). Alternatively, leave Route 1 at Calga; head through Central Mangrove towards Wollombi; then turn off to Cessnock (Route 132). Journey time is 2hrs. The main wine-growing district around Pokolbin and Rothbury is about 12km (7 miles) north-west of Cessnock.

By train

Dungog, just south of Barrington Tops, is served by a few daily trains from Sydney (journey time just over 3hrs) via Newcastle (90mins). Some guesthouses will pick up from Dungog.

By bus

Rover Coaches (4990 1699, www.rovercoaches. com.au) runs a daily service to the Hunter Valley from Sydney, plus day and weekend tours of the region; call for departure points.

Tourist information

Hunter Valley Wine Country Visitor Centre
455 Wine Country Drive, Pokolbin (4990 0900, www.winecountry.com.au). **Open** 9am-5pm Mon-Fri; 9.30am-5pm Sat; 9.30am-3.30pm Sun.

BARRINGTON TOPS

Although it's less than an hour's drive north of the Hunter Valley, the **Barrington Tops** is as different from the wine-growing district as it's possible to be. A national park with a World Heritage listing, its upper slopes are thick with subtropical rainforest containing thousand-year-old trees, clean mountain streams and abundant wildlife. With its swimming holes, camping and bushwalking, the Barrington Tops is a domain for outdoor enthusiasts. The area can also be explored with mechanical help: try eco-specialist **Bush Track Tours** (0419 650 600, www.bushtracktours.com).

Further south are green hillocks and greener valleys, the sort of landscape that insists you jump out of bed straight on to the back of a horse or a mountain bike. If you have your own transport and three or four days to spare, you might consider visiting the triangle of attractions in this area – the Hunter Valley (*see p230*), Barrington Tops and Port Stephens (*see right*).

Where to stay

Barringtons Country Retreat
1941 Chichester Dam Road, Barrington Tops (4995 9269, www.thebarringtons.com.au). **Rates** (min 2 nights) from $130.
If you like to flirt with rural surroundings safe in the knowledge that all modern comforts are close at hand, try this place. Log cabins overlooking the valley, spa baths and imaginative cooking at moderate rates. It's about 15 minutes drive from Dungog.

Getting there

By car

Direct route: Sydney-to-Newcastle Freeway (Route 1) to the Maitland turn-off on New England Highway (Route 15); Paterson Road; then turn

right for Dungog approx 5km beyond Paterson. Journey time is 4hrs.
From Hunter Valley: follow signs from Cessnock to Maitland (via Kurri Kurri), then as above.

By train

Dungog, just south of Barrington Tops, is served by a few daily trains from Sydney (journey time is just over 3hrs) via Newcastle (90mins). Some guesthouses will pick up from Dungog.

Tourist information

Gloucester Visitor Information Centre
27 Denison Street, Gloucester (6558 1408, www.visitnsw.com). **Open** 8.30am-5pm Mon-Fri; 8.30am-3pm Sat, Sun.

PORT STEPHENS

The third point in a triangle of northern attractions that includes the Hunter Valley and Barrington Tops, **Port Stephens Bay** is a beautiful stretch of water most famous for its whale and dolphin cruises. Two pods of dolphins – around 70 individuals – inhabit the bay, and your chances of getting up close to them are very high. Whales come into the calmer waters of the bay on their migration route from Antarctica.

The main town in the area is **Nelson Bay**, on the northern bank of the harbour, where you'll find hotels, restaurants and takeaways. Several operators run good dolphin- and whale-watching tours. Highly recommended is a cruise on *Imagine* (5104 Nelson Bay Road, Nelson Bay, 4984 9000, www.imaginecruises.com.au), a luxury catamaran operated out of Nelson Bay Marina by Frank Future and Yves Papin. All year except June and July they offer a daily one-and-a-half-hour dolphin trip departing at 10.30am ($28, $15-$25 reductions), and a range of longer cruises departing from d'Albora Marina. There's a boom net on board, which is lowered over the edge for thrill-seekers to lie in and get really close to the dolphins. They also operate humpback whale cruises from June to mid November. You can also go looking for dolphins in a kayak with **Ocean Planet** (4342 2222, www.kayaktours.com.au).

Another option for nature lovers is a visit to the **Tomaree National Park** (4984 8200, www.nationalparks.nsw.gov.au) on the southern shore of the inner harbour. Here, you can see low-flying pelicans skidding in to land on the water, and there's a large breeding colony of koalas at Lemon Tree Passage. And if you have access to a four-wheel-drive, you can't miss **Stockton Beach**, a 32-kilometre (19-mile) expanse of sand starting at Anna Bay, where you can drive through the waves or even take a shot at dune-bashing over the towering silica

ENJOY THE RIDE

Different ways to reach and explore the Hunter Valley.

Rather than spending two hours in a car getting to the Hunter Valley, fly up with **Sydney Seaplanes** (1300 732 752, 9388 1978, www.seaplanes.com.au). Departing from Rose Bay, the seaplane takes off over Sydney Harbour and then traces the coast past the northern beaches and Central Coast, before landing at Cessnock Airport, where you can be met by a tour bus or hire a car.

    Balloon Aloft (1300 723 279, 4990 9242, www.balloonaloft.com) offers hot-air balloon rides; rendezvous an hour before dawn. The relaxing flight takes in the spectacular landscape of vineyards, rivers, forests and the rolling hills of the valley, followed by a champagne reception back on land. For an even slower place, travel in style by horse and carriage. **Hunter Valley Wine & Dine Carriages** (0410 515 358, www.hunter valleycarriages.com.au) can pick you up from your hotel and tailor a tour of wineries, including lunch. Tours are also available in a chauffeur-driven Cadillac with **Hunter Valley Cadillac Tours** (0429 346 759, www. huntervalleycadillacs.com.au). Or if you're feeling guilty about all the wine and cheese you've consumed, then hire a bicycle and burn off some of those calories. Contact **Hunter Valley Cycling** for hire or tours (0418 281 480, www.huntervalleycycling.com.au).

ESCAPES & EXCURSIONS

hills (providing you have someone to help tow you out when you get stuck – or overturn).

    Also worth a visit is **Fighter World** (Medowie Road, Williamtown, 4965 1810, www.fighterworld.com.au, $15, $12 reductions). An offshoot of the RAAF Williamtown airbase, it celebrates Australia's fighter-plane history with a wide variety of exhibits and aircraft.

Where to stay & eat

Peppers Anchorage Port Stephens

Corlette Point Road, Corlette (4984 2555, www.anchorageportstephens.com.au). **Rates** (min 2 nights) from $300 midweek.
This is a top-class resort right on the water. Private balconies offer sweeping views across the bay.

Port Stephens Motor Lodge

44 Mangus Street, Nelson Bay (4981 3366).
Rates from $99.
A motel-like place located a short stroll from the main township. It has a swimming pool.

Salamander Shores

147 Soldiers Point Road, Soldiers Point (4982 7210, www.salamander-shores.com). **Rates** from $109.
A pleasant hotel featuring lovely rooms with sea views, a pretty garden and a good restaurant.

Getting there

By car

Take the Sydney-to-Newcastle Freeway (Route 1). Journey time is around 2.5hrs.

By train

Trains run almost hourly from Sydney's Central Station to Newcastle. Buses connect with the trains for transfers to Port Stephens.

By bus

Port Stephens Coaches (1800 045 949, 4982 2940, www.pscoaches.com.au) runs a daily service to Nelson Bay, departing Eddy Avenue, Central Station, Sydney, at 2pm. It leaves Nelson Bay for the return trip daily at 9am. Journey time is around 3.5hrs.

Tourist information

Port Stephens Visitor Information Centre
Victoria Parade, Nelson Bay (4980 6900, www. portstephens.org.au). **Open** 9am-5pm daily.

Heading South

SOUTH COAST

According to most of the people who live there, particularly residents of the Shoalhaven region (which stretches 160 kilometres/100 miles south of the town of Berry), this is the area of New South Wales that has it all: wilderness galore, including large tracts of national park and state forest; beaches so long and white they make Bondi look like a house party at a sewage dump; some of the cleanest, clearest water in Australia; a bay 82 times the size of Sydney Harbour, with pods of crowd-pleasing dolphins; easy access to magnificent mountain vistas; heritage and antiques; 'surfing' kangaroos at Pebbly Beach, just to the south of Ulladulla; and the best fish and chips in the country at Bermagui (head for the marina and just follow the seagulls).

If you're driving from Sydney along the Princes Highway (Route 1), take a quick detour towards Stanwell Park and drive along Hargrave Road between Coalcliff and Clifton to marvel at the spectacular **Sea Cliff Bridge**, which twists and turns as it hugs the rocky coastline below and the ragged cliffs at your side. Back on the Princes Highway and beyond the Royal National Park, the first region you encounter is **Illawarra**, the administrative centre of which is the city of **Wollongong**. It's perhaps unfair to view Wollongong as one of the two ugly sisters on either side of Sydney (the other being Newcastle), but as you approach its smoking industrial surroundings, it's hard not to.

The road then begins to slide prettily between the coast on one side and the beginnings of the Southern Highlands on the other (Illawarra comes from an Aboriginal word meaning 'between the high place and the sea').

The first seaside town worthy of a stop is **Kiama**. The town's main attraction is the **Blow Hole**, which spurts spray up to 60 metres (200 feet) into the air from a slatey, crenellated outcrop next to a comparatively tranquil harbour. Also by the harbour is a fresh fish market, while on the way into town there's a block of 1885 quarrymen's cottages that have been renovated and turned into restaurants and craft shops. On the way out, don't miss the wonderful sign: 'Stan Crap – Funeral Director'.

Kiama is a good base for exploring the subtropical **Minnamurra Rainforest**, the **Carrington Falls** and nearby **Seven Mile Beach**, an undeniably impressive caramel arc, backed by a hinterland of fir trees.

An alternative base is the tree-lined inland town of **Berry**, a little further south. It's an entertaining hybrid of hick town and quaint yuppie haven, where earthy locals mix with weekending Sydneysiders in search of antiques and fine dining.

Jervis Bay.

Jervis Bay

Undoubtedly the Shoalhaven region's greatest attraction, and the one that drives normally restrained commentators to reach for their superlatives, is Jervis Bay. A huge place, it encompasses the wonderful **Booderee National Park** and 56 kilometres (34 miles) of shoreline. It also has a history of close shaves.

First, in 1770, Captain Cook sailed straight past it on the way towards Botany Bay, recording it only as 'low-lying wetlands' and missing entirely its deep, wide natural harbour (which made it an ideal alternative to Sydney as fulcrum for the new colony). Later, this ecologically sensitive beauty spot was mooted as a possible port for Canberra and the ACT. And in 1975, Murrays Beach, at the tip of the national park, was chosen as a site for a nuclear reactor (a project thankfully defeated by public protest).

These narrow escapes and a fortuitous lack of population growth around Jervis Bay

mean that this coastal area remains one of the most undisturbed and beautiful in Australia. Divers testify to the clarity of its waters; swimmers are sometimes literally dazzled by the whiteness of its sands (**Hyams Beach** is said to be the whitest in the world). It's not just popular with people: among its regularly visiting sea and bird life are fur seals, giant rays, whales (southern right, pilot and killer), sharks, sea eagles, penguins and many, many more.

A good way to get a feel for Jervis Bay and meet its resident bottlenose dolphins is to hook up with **Dolphin Watch Cruises** (50 Owen Street, Huskisson, 4441 6311, www.dolphin watch.com.au), which also runs whale cruises. **Huskisson**, the launching point for the cruises, is one of six villages on the shores of the bay. It's got a couple of accommodation options, a dive shop, **Deep6Diving** (64 Owen Street, 4441 5255), wonderful fish and chips, and a pub with a bistro, the Husky Pub – real name the **Huskisson** (4441 5001) on Owen Street. Just south of Jervis Bay there is excellent sailing,

ESCAPES & EXCURSIONS

snorkelling and swimming at **St George's Basin**, and fishing at **Sussex Inlet**.

You could stay in Huskisson, but it's worth bringing a tent to get a proper feel for the **Booderee National Park** (4443 8302), which is jointly managed by the local Aboriginal community. The best place to camp is at **Caves Beach**, where you wake up to the calls of birds and eastern grey kangaroos. **Green Patch** has more dirt than grass, but better facilities and can accommodate camper vans as well. The Christmas/New Year period sees a ballot for places. Book through the park's visitor centre (*see p237*).

Ulladulla

Despite all the stunning scenery around Jervis Bay, it can be worth venturing further south to the sleepy fishing town of Ulladulla for somewhere to stay. Ulladulla's protected harbour may not quite recall Sicily, but the town has a sizeable Italian fishing community (guaranteeing decent local pizzas and pasta), and the Blessing of the Fleet is an annual event on Easter Sunday. From here, it's easy to access wilderness areas to the west and further south – **Budawang** and **Murramarang National Parks** – plus yet more expansive beaches, such as **Pebbly Beach** (which is actually sandy) with its resident kangaroos.

Where to stay & eat

Berry Inn
122 Queen Street, Berry (4464 2064).
Rates from $140.
A National Trust-classified former bank with 13 individually styled rooms, one with a four-poster bed. There's also a swimming pool.

Huskisson Beach Tourist Resort
Beach Street, Huskisson (4406 2040, 1300 733 027, www.huskissonbeachtouristresort.com.au).
Rates from $40 camping (2 adults); $95-$450 cabin.
This resort has various cabins (including self-catering ones) as well as plenty of camping spots right opposite the beach. There's a pool too.

Jervis Bay Guest House
1 Beach Street, Huskisson (4441 7658, www. jervisbayguesthouse.com.au). **Rates** from $145.
This guesthouse opposite a beach has just four rooms, with balconies overlooking the sea and the sunrise, and is a short walk to the shops and restaurants of Huskisson. All this makes it very popular, so book well ahead.

Booderee National Park.

Ulladulla Guest House
39 Burrill Street, Ulladulla (1800 700 905, 4455 1796, www.guesthouse.com.au). **Rates** from $248.
A popular luxury option with great service and ten lovely rooms. Ulladulla also has self-catering units, a pretty saltwater pool, a sauna, a hot tub, a small gym, an art gallery and an excellent restaurant serving European and Australian mezze. A variety of in-room massages is available.

Getting there

By car
Take Princes Highway (Route 1). Allow at least 2hrs to Jervis Bay, 3hrs to Ulladulla and slightly longer to Pebbly Beach.

By train
There are regular trains from Central Station to Wollongong, Kiama, Gerringong, Berry and Bomaderry (for Nowra and Ulladulla), via the South Coast line, changing trains at Dapto. It's 3hrs to Bomaderry; from there, a limited coach service operated by **Premier Motor Service** (13 3410/4423 5233, www.premierms.com.au) continues on through Nowra as far as Ulladulla.

By bus
Interstate coaches travelling the Princes Highway between Sydney and Melbourne stop at many of the towns mentioned above. There are also local bus and coach services along the coast. Contact the local tourist offices for more details.

Tourist information

Booderee National Park Visitor Centre
Jervis Bay Road, Jervis Bay (4443 0977, www.parksaustralia.gov.au/booderee/plan/visitor-centre). **Open** 9am-4pm daily.

Shoalhaven Visitor Centre *Corner of Princes Highway & Pleasant Way, Nowra (1300 662 808, 4421 0778, www.shoalhavenholidays.com.au).* **Open** 9am-5pm daily.

Tourism Kiama *Blowhole Point, Kiama (1300 654 262, 4232 3322, www.kiama.com.au).* **Open** 9am-5pm daily.

Ulladulla Visitors Information Centre *Princes Highway, Civic Centre, Ulladulla (4444 8819, www.ulladulla.info).* **Open** 10am-6pm Mon-Fri; 9am-5pm Sat, Sun.

TAKE A TOUR
Climb high, get wet, go wild.

Plenty of tour operators run interesting and entertaining day trips in and around the Blue Mountains. Some tours start in Sydney, while others leave from Katoomba. The following outfits are recommended.

Based in Katoomba, the **Australian School of Mountaineering** (4782 2014, www.asmguides.com) has provided outdoor training and guiding for more than two decades. It runs a range of canyoning, rock climbing and abseiling trips.

Also operating out of Katoomba, **Fantastic Aussie Tours** (4780 0700, www. fantasticaussie-tours.com.au) offers day tours to the Jenolan Caves. Prices start at $80, including cave entrance. Cheaper tickets are offered for bushwalkers who just want a bus service to the caves.

Canyoning expeditions involving swimming, wading and squeezing through tight spaces, as well as other outdoor activities including bushwalking, snow- and ice-climbing, mountain biking and abseiling, are offered by **High 'n' Wild** (4782 6224, www.high-n-wild.com.au). Prices are from $120.

For something slightly more relaxed, a packed day trip from Sydney from **Oz Trek Adventure Tours** (9666 4262, www.oztrek. com.au) includes a visit to the Olympic site at Homebush, a tour of the major Blue Mountain sites and a one- to two-hour bushwalk. The tours cost $69.

SOUTHERN HIGHLANDS

The Southern Highlands, known by wealthy 19th-century Sydneysiders as the 'sanatorium of the south' for its cool climes and fresh air, has recently experienced something of a renaissance as a tourist destination. It's easy to see why – just a two-and-a-half-hour train ride from Sydney, the area has well-preserved villages such as Berrima (founded 1831), fading stately homes such as Ranelagh House in Robertson and a range of cosy accommodation, all set in a gently undulating landscape so easy on the eye that it evokes a different country (even before the area was first settled, Governor Macquarie said it reminded him of England).

There's some truth to the local saying that the Southern Highlands are mostly for 'the newlyweds and the nearly-deads', but there is something here for most tastes: the highlands encompass tropical and subtropical rainforest, the second-largest falls in New South Wales and the edge of Morton National Park.

Of the many pleasant approaches by car, two leading from the main coastal road (Princes Highway) stand out. The first is to take the Illawarra Highway (from Albion Park) through Macquarie Pass National Park; the second is to take the tourist drive from just beyond Berry. The route from Berry – rising, bending and finally dropping towards the Kangaroo Valley – is often romantically thick with mist, but on even a partly clear day it affords luscious views of the countryside.

Kangaroo Valley Village, despite its iron roofs and sandstone-pillared **Hampden Bridge** (built in 1897), is a little disappointing, but the walking and camping nearby are excellent, as are canoeing and kayaking on the Kangaroo river (contact Kangaroo Valley Tourist Park near the bridge, 1300 559 977, www.kangaroo valleytourist.asn.au).

Leaving Kangaroo Valley, the road rises and twists once more before leading to the **Fitzroy Falls**. A short saunter from the impressive **Fitzroy Falls Visitor Centre** (4887 7270, open 9am-5.30pm daily) and you are amid scenery that's as Australian as Paul Hogan. There are five falls in the vicinity, but Fitzroy is the nearest and biggest, plummeting 81 metres (266 feet) into **Yarunga Valley**. Take any of the walks around the falls and you could encounter 48 species of gum tree, lyre birds and possibly a wombat.

Another way of exploring the top end of underrated **Morton National Park** is to use the town of **Bundanoon** as a base for bushwalking and cycling. Bundanoon, which means 'a place of deep gullies', is as Scottish in flavour as its name sounds. Every year, in the week after Easter, the town transforms itself into Brigadoon for a highland gathering, featuring traditional games, Scottish dancing and street parades. Bundanoon was also once known as the honeymoon centre of the Southern Highlands – in its heyday it had 51 guesthouses – but these days the bedsprings rarely squeak, as it has largely fallen out of fashion.

Slightly north of the forgettable town of Moss Vale is **Berrima**, considered Australia's finest example of an 1830s village. This is the town the railways forgot, so many of its early buildings remain in pristine condition. A highlight is the 1838 neoclassical **Court House** (corner of Wilshire and Argyle Streets, 4877 1505, www. berrimacourthouse.org.au) with its sandstone portico and curved wooden doorways. Don't miss the reconstruction of the 1843 trial of the adulterous Lucretia Dunkley and her lover: particularly good is the judge's sentencing of the pair for the murder of her dull husband. Other historic buildings include **Harper's Mansion** (9 Wilkinson Street, 4877 1508, harpersmansion. com.au, open 10.30am-4pm Sat, Sun, $7, $3 reductions) and Australia's oldest continually licensed hotel, the **Surveyor General Inn** (*see right*), both built in 1834.

An unexpected delight on the long road to Bowral is **Berkelouw's Book Barn** (Old Hume Highway, 4877 1370, open 9.30am-5pm daily), containing some 200,000 second-hand books. **Bowral** itself is attractive enough, especially during the spring Tulip Festival, but its biggest claim to fame is as the town that gave Australian cricket the late Donald Bradman. The great man is honoured in the **Bradman Museum** (St Jude Street, 4862 1247, www.bradman.org.au, open 10am-5pm daily, $20, $15 reductions; includes International Cricket Hall of Fame). The museum is on the edge of the lush Bradman Oval, opposite the old Bradman home. If cricket doesn't captivate you, then take a trip up **Mount Gibraltar**, overlooking the surrounding countryside, and the view surely will.

About 60 kilometres (37 miles) west of the town of **Mittagong** (via part-dirt road), the mysterious and beautiful **Wombeyan Caves** feature a number of unique encrustations and deposits. You can take a guided tour, and there's on-site accommodation and camping: contact the **Wombeyan Caves Visitor Centre** (Wombeyan Caves Road, Taralga, 4843 5976, www.jenolancaves.org.au, open 8.30am-5.30pm daily) for details.

Destined to become the area's most famous village, and all because of a talking pig, is the sleepy hollow of **Robertson**, where the film *Babe* was shot. On the way back to Sydney, be sure to take the road out of Robertson to the **Princes Highway** for some spectacular sea views as you twist and turn your way down the hillside.

Where to stay & eat

Briars Country Lodge & Inn
Moss Vale Road, Bowral (4868 3566, www.briars.com.au). **Rates** from $130.
A country retreat with 30 garden suites set in beautiful parkland. Adjacent to the lodge is the Georgian Briars Inn (built around 1845), which has a true country atmosphere, with cosy bars and bistro food.

Bundanoon Hotel
Erith Street, Bundanoon (4883 6005, www. bundanoonhotel.com.au). **Rates** (per person) from $50.
This creaky old hotel boasts a wonderful billiards table and the occasional poetry reading. In addition to rooms with shared bathrooms there are some with en suite facilities.

Fountaindale Grand Manor
Illawarra Highway, Robertson (4885 1111, www.fountaindale.com.au). **Rates** from $155.
The best place in the area to enjoy a leisurely cream tea. It also offers a 'country-style' lunch and has a good dinner menu.

Surveyor General Inn
Old Hume Highway, Berrima (4877 1226, www.surveyorgeneral.com.au). **Rates** from $75.
The rooms are simple, with brass beds and shared bathrooms, but the inn oozes historical charm.

Getting there

By car
The inland route (120km/75 miles) via Hume Highway (Route 31) takes just under 2hrs. The coastal route is via Princes Highway (Route 60); then turn inland on Illawarra Highway (Route 48) by Albion Park. It's slightly longer (130km/80 miles) and slightly slower (just over 2hrs).

By train
Trains to the Southern Highlands depart from Sydney's Central Station every day. Most stop at Mittagong, Bowral, Moss Vale and Bundanoon. The journey takes about 2.5hrs.

By bus
Several bus companies serve the Southern Highlands area, among them **Priors Scenic Express** (1800 816 234, 4472 4040) and **Greyhound** (1300 473 946, www.greyhound. com.au).

Tourist information

Tourism Southern Highlands *62-70 Main Street, Mittagong (1300 657 559, 4871 2888, www.southern-highlands.com.au).* **Open** 9am-5pm Mon-Fri; 9am-4pm Sat, Sun.

In Context

History

Reconciling the past.

TEXT: JULIET RIEDEN & JENNY VALENTISH

People have inhabited the area now known as Sydney for tens of thousands of years. When Captain James Cook turned up in 1770 with orders that he should 'with the consent of the natives take possession of convenient situations in the name of the king,' he noted that those natives 'appear to be the most wretched people on earth. But in reality they are far happier than we Europeans.' Not surprisingly, the first words the Europeans ever heard from the Aboriginal inhabitants of the Sydney area were 'Warra! Warra!' – meaning 'Go away!'

STEPS TO SETTLEMENT

On 29 April 1770, Captain James Cook landed at Botany Bay, which he named after discovering scores of plants hitherto unknown to science. Turning northwards, he passed an entrance to a harbour where there appeared to be safe anchorage. Cook called it Port Jackson after the Secretary to the Admiralty, George Jackson. Back in Britain, King George III was convinced that the east coast of the island, which had been claimed for him and named New South Wales, would make a good colony. For one thing, it would help reduce Britain's overflowing prison population. For another, a settlement in the region would be convenient both as a base for trading in the Far East and in case of a war with the French or Dutch.

On 13 May 1787, Captain Arthur Phillip's ship, *Sirius*, along with three provisions ships, two warships and six vessels of convicts, set sail from Portsmouth. On board were some 300 merchant seamen, their wives, children and servants, and nearly 800 convicts. Some 36 weeks later, on 18 January 1788, after stops in Tenerife, Rio de Janeiro and the Cape of Good Hope, the *Sirius* arrived at Botany Bay. The rest of the First Fleet arrived a couple of days later. Fewer than 50 passengers had perished en route – not a bad rate for the period.

At that time of year, Botany Bay turned out to be a grim site for the new colony: there was little fresh water and it was exposed to strong winds and swell. One plus was that the naked 'Indians' seen running up and down the beach 'shouting and making many uncouth signs and gestures' turned out to be relatively friendly. Eager to make a good impression, Phillip and a small party of frock coats took a rowing boat to meet their new subjects. The meeting went well: the British exchanged a looking glass and beads for a wooden club.

Probably relieved that his first contact with the locals had not gone awry – when William Jansz of the Dutch East India Company had met Aboriginal people in 1606, he reported back that they 'killed on sight' – Phillip decided to search for Port Jackson. He returned with glowing reports: it was 'one of the finest harbours in the world, in which a thousand sail of the line might ride in perfect security.' This is one of the earliest descriptions of Sydney Harbour.

That same day, Phillip's men caught the improbable sight of two ships approaching from the sea. These were the French frigates *La Boussole* and *L'Astrolabe*, commanded by Jean-François de Galaup, Count de la Pérouse, who was on a voyage of discovery through the southern hemisphere. Surprised by the old enemy, Phillip decided to up-anchor the whole fleet the following morning and lead it to Sydney Cove – named after Viscount Sydney, the minister responsible for the colony.

The First Fleeters set to as soon as they arrived. Trees were felled, marquees erected, convict shacks constructed from cabbage palms, garden plots dug and a blacksmith's forge set up. On 7 February, the settlers gathered to hear Phillip declared the first governor of the state of New South Wales and its dependencies. It wasn't long, though, before convicts started to disappear. Several were found clubbed or speared to death, probably in revenge for attacks on the locals. Food ran dangerously low, scurvy took hold and the settlers' small herd of cattle began to diminish.

During the next few weeks, the animosity between the settlers and the Indigenous people came to a head, and the disappearance of several more convicts and a marine provoked Governor Phillip to try to capture some natives in a bid to force talks. Two boats were sent to Manly (named after the 'manly' nature of the undaunted Aborigines seen there). Following courteous overtures, the settlers suddenly grabbed an Aboriginal man, called Arabanoo, and rushed him to a boat under a hail of stones and spears. Arabanoo's hair was cut, his beard shaved and he was bathed and dressed in European clothes. But despite attempts by the settlers to persuade him to tell his compatriots that they meant no harm, no ground was gained on the path to friendship.

In those early days, capturing Aborigines to turn them into honorary white men was all the rage. Two such captives, Bennelong and Colbee, were rough-and-ready types, scarred from warfare and smallpox. Colbee soon bolted, but Bennelong stayed for five months and eventually, dressed in top hat and tails, travelled to London to have tea with the royal family. He gave his name to the point of land where a hut was built for him – and on which the Sydney Opera House now stands.

Early in 1789, the local Aborigines began to succumb to smallpox contracted from the British or from sailors on the French vessels that had put in at Botany Bay. Hundreds were soon dead, among them Arabanoo. The epidemics fuelled a belief among white settlers, then and later, that the Aboriginal peoples were ultimately doomed to extinction.

RISE OF THE RUM CORPS

If conditions were bad for the settlers at first, they soon worsened. Two years and two months after the First Fleet sailed, Britain sent its first relief to Sydney. Carrying a small stock of provisions, the *Lady Juliana* arrived in 1790 with more than 200 convicts. Most were women, and almost all were too weak to work.

This Second Fleet also brought a regiment known as the New South Wales Corps (NSWC), which had been formed to replace the marines. They found the settlement short of clothes, while rations had become so meagre that it was feared that everyone

might starve to death. Both soldiers and convicts were so frail through lack of food that the working day had to be shortened. Thefts became commonplace, and penalties for stealing increased. Meanwhile, the Aboriginal peoples were prospering on the food that grew, leaped or swam all around them, but the first settlers were so bound by the diet of the mother country that they would rather have starved than 'eaten native'.

By the end of June 1790, four more ships had sailed into Port Jackson, carrying convicts who were transported in abominable conditions. Some 267 people had died en route, and of the 759 who landed, 488 suffered from scurvy, dysentery or fever. Between 1791 and 1792, the death rate matched London's at the height of the Great Plague. Those remaining alive were forced to struggle on. Men faced a lashing from the cat-o'-nine-tails if they didn't work hard. The women were forced into long hours of domestic work or kept busy weaving in sweatshop conditions.

IN CONTEXT

Bennelong.

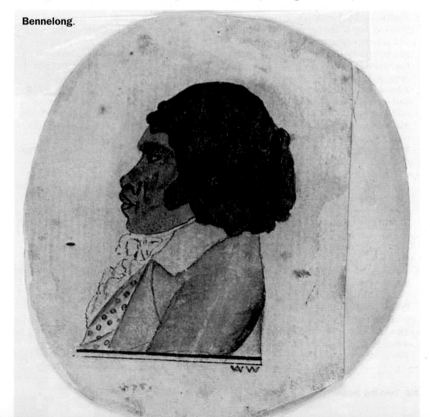

IN CONTEXT

HOW TO SPEAK CONVICT: AN A-Z
Learn some new words.

Aggranoy – vulgar merger of 'aggravate' and 'annoy'.

Bunko – a confidence trick.

Chiseller – a swindler; term used by 'crims' when a person takes them down.

Dangler – a prisoner convicted of obscene exposure.

Equaliser – a revolver, pistol, cannon or 'squirt'.

Fizgig – a police informer.

Gigglesuit – a straitjacket.

Heelie – the ballast in loaded dice, the brake on the crooked roulette wheel, the pea in the thimble game – any contrivance geared to give a pat result.

Ice – jewellery, particularly diamonds.

Jelly – gelignite for blowing a safe.

Kite – a forged or stolen cheque.

Lair – one who wears showy clothes and swaggers in them.

Motza – an abundance or excess of anything, particularly money.

Nod the nut – to plead guilty to a charge.

On the coat – to be on bad terms, a fact signalled by tugging the lapel as warning.

Pelideluxe – a superlative 'pelican' (idiot).

Rat – a betrayer or informer.

Saddling paddock – a popular site for alfresco *amours*.

Tiddly – not quite drunk but decidedly mellow.

Unstuck – brought to ruin.

Vagged – to be imprisoned for vagrancy ('lagged for vag').

Whack up – to divide the spoils prior to scarpering.

Yips – an affliction of nerves before a stick-up or other nefarious act.

Zac – money or gains; also 'bunts', 'chaff'.

Finally, though, the arrival of yet more transports from England, bringing with them convicts, free settlers and supplies, meant that life in the colony began to pick up. In October 1792, Phillip reported that nearly 5,000 bushels of maize had been harvested and around 1,700 acres were under cultivation. In December of that year, Phillip returned to England convinced the settlement would last. It was almost three years before another governor arrived to take Phillip's place. The commanders of the NSWC used this interim period to their own advantage by granting officers rights to work the land and employ convicts to do it for them. Thanks to a shortage of money, rum rapidly became common currency, and as the NSWC ruled the rum trade it became known as the Rum Corps.

Things progressed slowly until 1808, when Governor William Bligh (of mutiny on the *Bounty* fame) was deposed in a military coup. Bligh's evil temper and his attempts to deal with the corruption of the NSWC, which had bullied his predecessors through their control of the colony's rum, led to his downfall. The Rum Corps arrested the governor and imprisoned him for a year – the only time in Australian history when an established government has been overthrown by force.

The Corps ruled until Bligh was sent back to England and a new governor, Lachlan Macquarie, arrived. Macquarie later wrote that, on his arrival, he found the colony 'barely emerging from a state of infantile imbecility, and suffering from various privations and disabilities: the country impenetrable beyond 40 miles from Sydney.' A great planner, Macquarie oversaw the building of new streets and the widening of others. He named three of the largest streets: George Street, after the king; Pitt Street, after the prime minister; and the grandest of all he named Macquarie Street, after himself. With the help of convict architect Francis Greenway, he set about building a city to be proud of, with a hospital, several churches, a sandstone barracks and Macquarie Lighthouse (still on South Head) to guide ships into the harbour.

TAKING ROOT

With the discovery of the fertile hinterland beyond the Blue Mountains in 1813, the colony advanced in earnest. The flow of migrants increased after the end of the

Napoleonic Wars in 1815, and soon farms and settlements dotted the regions around Sydney and Parramatta. In 1822, Macquarie was forced from the colony by powerful landowners; he returned to Scotland and died in London in 1824.

There still remained the issue of defence: Sydney was seen as prey to any passing foe. The city's vulnerability and its isolation from the distant motherland were confirmed in 1830 when its citizens woke to find that, in the night, four American frigates had passed through the Heads and sailed up to Sydney Cove without anyone noticing. Since that day, Australia has been paranoid about attack, whether from the Russians during the Crimean War, Yankee privateers or the Spanish. Fear of an invasion from Asia has been a constant undertone of government policy in more recent times. Finding transportation of convicts ruinously expensive, the British government sought to have the infant colony subsidise the cost. Convict labour was increasingly used to generate income. As in all slave societies, the workforce was inefficient, and the colony soon became the dumping ground for England's unemployed working classes rather than her criminals. Most of these free immigrants were bonded to their colonial employers, their passage paid for by the sale of land. In 1840, transportation of convicts to New South Wales was abolished. A total of 111,500 convicts – of whom just 16,000 were women – had arrived in NSW and Tasmania. By 1849, the population of convicts was outnumbered by free settlers. A new type of vessel, the clipper ship, had cut the sailing time from England to Australia by 49 days, to just 91. In the 1850s, gold was discovered in New South Wales and Victoria, and prospectors rushed to Australia from all over the world. During the 1880s, more than 370,000 arrived, mostly British or Irish. Rich British businessmen poured money into the country and mine owners and farmers profited.

Governor Phillip had ensured as far back as 1790 that some physical distance was maintained between the government precinct (to the east of what is now known as Circular Quay), and the barracks and convict quarters to the west. Built into the steep sandstone cliffs, this no-man's-land – now known as the Rocks – quickly became as degenerate as the worst of London's slums. Tiers of narrow streets and sandstone stairs crammed with makeshift shacks led up from waterfront pubs and cheap lodging houses to comfortable terraced houses inhabited by sea captains and stevedores. The massive influx of immigrants in the mid 1800s meant that housing was scarce, a problem exacerbated by many inner-city homes being converted into storehouses and offices.

By the late 19th century, the Rocks was known as Sydney's worst den of iniquity. Prostitution, drunkenness, theft and street gangs were rife. Sailors ashore after months at sea were robbed of everything they owned or press-ganged straight on to another vessel.

The increasingly squalid goings-on and the build-up of rubbish, silt and sewage made conditions in the Rocks perfect for rats and the bubonic plague carried by their fleas. In the first nine months of 1900, the plague killed 103 people. Crowds stormed the Board of Health's offices demanding a share of the colony's meagre supply of anti-plague medicine. The Rocks and Darling Harbour were quarantined, and in 1902 the Sydney Harbour Trust was set up to clean up the harbour: it later announced that it had pulled from the water 2,524 rats, 1,068 cats, 283 bags of meat, 305 bags of fish, 1,467 fowl, 25 parrots, 23 sheep, 14 pigs, one bullock, nine calves and nine goats.

CIVILISING MISSIONS

In the 1880s, Sydney's remaining Aboriginal inhabitants were rounded up into a camp at Circular Quay and given government rations in a bid to keep them off the streets. In 1895, an Aboriginal reserve was set up at La Perouse, near Botany Bay – far from the centre of the city. By the end of the 19th century, most of the area's Indigenous inhabitants were restricted to reserves or in missions, where they were introduced to the supposed benefits of Christianity and European civilisation.

By this time, it was apparent that, though the Aboriginal population was in decline, the mixed-descent population was increasing. The fact that the latter group had some European blood meant that there was a place for them – albeit a lowly one – in society. Many children of mixed race were forcibly separated from their parents and placed in segregated 'training' institutions before being sent out to work.

IN CONTEXT

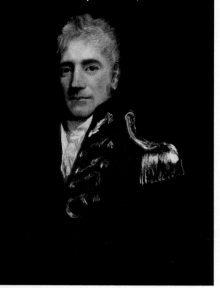

Lachlan Macquarie. *See p246.*

Girls were sent to be domestic servants to satisfy the nation's demand for cheap labour. It was also held that long hours and exhausting work would curb their supposed promiscuity.

The Commonwealth of Australia came into existence on 1 January 1901. The country had 3.8 million inhabitants, and more than half a million of them crowded on to the streets of Sydney to celebrate the inauguration of the nation. The Aboriginal peoples weren't recorded in the first census, however. They had to wait until 1967, when 90 per cent of the public voted to make new laws relating to Aboriginal people. This led the way for them to be recognised as Australian citizens, and to be included in the census of 1971.

POPULATE OR PERISH

After a lull following the 1890s depression, migration revived. In the years leading up to 1914, 300,000 mainly British migrants arrived, half of whom came on an assisted passage scheme. In 1908, a Royal Commission set up to advise on the improvement of Sydney concluded that workers should be moved out of the slums to the suburbs. Six years later, however, World War I broke out. Around 10,000 volunteers in

Sydney queued to go on the 'big adventure'. Most were sent to Gallipoli – a campaign that became synonymous in the Australian collective memory with British arrogance, callousness and incompetence.

By the time the Allied forces were withdrawn in January 1916, the combination of lacklustre Allied leadership and stiff Turkish resistance meant that casualties were well above 50 per cent, with little to show for thousands of lost lives. After the disaster of Gallipoli, Australia was not going to return to a subservient colonial role: the nation had come of age.

With the end of World War I, it was reasoned that to defend Australia properly the country needed more people. A further 300,000 migrants arrived in the 1920s, mostly from England and Scotland, a product of the policy known as 'White Australia'. The origins of the policy can be traced to the mid 19th century, when white miners' resentment towards Chinese diggers boiled over in violence. The 1901 Immigration Restriction Act placed 'certain restrictions on immigration' and provided 'for the removal from the Commonwealth of prohibited immigrants'. For example, applicants were required to pass a written test in a specific, usually European, language – with which they were not necessarily familiar. It was not until 1974 that Australia eliminated such official racial discrimination from its immigration policy.

Australia's vulnerability to attack came back to haunt it during World War II. On 31 May 1942, three Japanese midget submarines powered through the Heads and into Sydney Harbour. The first got tangled in a net across the harbour mouth, but the others slipped past. The third midget was spotted and attacked, but the second took the chance to fire two torpedoes at the US cruiser *Chicago*. Both missed, but one sank the depot ship HMAS *Kuttabul*, killing 19 Australian and two British naval ratings asleep on board. Except for Aborigines and settlers killed in early skirmishes, these 21 men have been the only victims of enemy action on home ground in Sydney's history.

After the war, Australia once again decided it needed to boost the size of its population. The slogan 'populate or perish' was coined, and a new immigration scheme organised. In 1948, 70,000 migrants arrived from Britain and Europe. By the late 1950s, most migrants were coming from Italy, Yugoslavia and Greece. In 1951, the concept of assimilation was officially adopted as national policy, with the goal 'that all persons of Aboriginal descent will choose to attain in a similar manner and standard of living to other Australians'.

Eradication of Aboriginal culture was stepped up during the 1950s and '60s, when even greater numbers of Aboriginal children were removed from their families. Many Aboriginal babies were adopted at birth and later told that their true parents had died. The removal of children from their parents was halted in the 1970s, but the scars remain. The 'Stolen Generations' became the subject of fierce debate in Australia. Expat director Phillip Noyce's 2002 film *Rabbit-Proof Fence* – the story of three stolen children who run away from a camp and attempt to walk home over 1,000 miles of inhospitable country – brought the story to the world.

In 1964, Australian troops joined their US counterparts in action in Vietnam. As in the States, anti-Vietnam War sentiment became a hot issue, and tens of thousands of Australians blockaded the streets of the major cities. A new Labor government, led by Gough Whitlam, came to power in 1972 after promising a fairer society and an end to Australia's involvement in the war. Within months, the troops were brought home. Not long afterwards, 'Advance Australia Fair' replaced 'God Save the Queen' as the national anthem, the Queen's portrait was removed from post office walls and her insignia on mailboxes painted out. Land rights were granted to some Aboriginal groups, and in 1974 the government finally put an end to the White Australia policy that had largely restricted black and Asian immigration since 1901.

Two years later, the official cord to Britain was cut when the Australian Constitution was separated from that of its motherland. Ties with Britain loosened further in 1975 during a messy political wrangle, when the Conservative opposition moved to block the government's supply of money in the upper house. Without a budget, Gough Whitlam's government was unable to govern, so the Queen's representative, Governor-General John Kerr, sacked it and made Opposition Leader Malcolm Fraser prime minister.

There was fury that an Australian-elected government could be dismissed by the monarch's appointee, and resentment towards Britain flared.

A THIRD CENTURY BEGINS

Immigration continued throughout the 1980s and '90s, but now there were quite a few new faces among the crowds hoping for a better life in the 'lucky country'. Hundreds of thousands of migrants began arriving from Asia. Today, on average, around 90,000 people emigrate to Australia each year, from more than 150 countries. Of settlers arriving in 2002/03, the biggest groups were those born in the UK (13.3 per cent), New Zealand (13.1 per cent), China (7.1 per cent), India (6.1 per cent), South Africa (4.9 per cent), the Philippines (3.4 per cent) and Indonesia (3 per cent).

With such a multicultural mix, you'd think it was time to reconsider the 'self-governing republic' option – but you'd be wrong. In a close-run national referendum in 1999, 55 per cent of the electorate voted to keep the Queen as head of state; of Australia's six states, only Victoria wanted a republic.

'Aboriginal life expectancy is 20 years lower than that of other Australians; the infant mortality rate is higher.'

Some 460,000 Aborigines and the ethnically distinct people from the Torres Strait Islands off northern Queensland live in Australia today, but a rift still exists between them and the rest of the population. Aboriginal life expectancy is 20 years lower than that of other Australians; the infant mortality rate is higher; the ratio of Aboriginal people to other Australians in prisons is disproportionately high; and many are still restricted to the fringes of society.

In 1992, the 'Mabo decision' marked a breakthrough in Aboriginal affairs: the High Court declared that Australia was not *terra nullius* ('empty land') as it had been termed

IN CONTEXT

Migrants on board ship, 1900-1910.
See p248.

followed by a 20-minute speech to Parliament about the need for such an apology.

LABOR IN VAIN

At the end of 2007, Australia entered what promised to be a new and exciting political era, but which turned out to be a dirty drama of leaks, spills and backstabbing.

It began with the landslide ('Ruddslide') victory of the 'Kevin 07' Labor Party that delivered the youthful, Mandarin-speaking Queensland farm boy Kevin Rudd to the leadership. Prime Minister Rudd wasted no time in righting what many considered to be Howard's errors, joining a host of other nations in ratification of the Kyoto Protocol for climate change and withdrawing troops from Iraq. The party enjoyed a period of high popularity in the opinion polls but cracks began to show in 2009, when leaks from within his own party portrayed him as a megalomaniac, whose centralist leadership style involved insulting treatment of staff and ignoring the counsel of his fellow ministers. By June, Rudd had lost the support of his party; he found himself deposed on 24 June by his deputy Julia Gillard. As Rudd stepped down as party leader and prime minister, the 49-year-old Welsh-born, flame-haired, proudly unmarried and avowedly atheist Julia Eileen Gillard became Australia's 27th prime minister and the first female to hold the office.

Keen to vindicate her decision to win public endorsement as PM, Gillard went to the polls 23 days later. In a closely fought race against the Liberal leader – the 'mad monk' former boxer turned triathlete and volunteer firefighter Tony Abbott – the two parties won 72 seats each of the 150 seat House of Representatives, resulting in Australia's first hung parliament since 1940. Australia was in flux for weeks as the two leaders wooed the six independent crossbench MPs who held the balance, Gillard ultimately prevailing for a 76-74 minority government. She was sworn in on 14 September 2010.

Two years into Gillard's tenure, she was accused by politicians and journalists alike of playing the 'gender card' when she called out the Leader of the Opposition, Tony Abbott, on misogyny in a speech delivered in Parliament and declared that she had been the victim of a sexist smear campaign. In 2012, Kevin Rudd challenged her leadership, to which Gillard

since the British 'invasion'. This decision resulted in the 1993 Native Title Act, which allowed Aboriginal groups and Torres Strait Islanders to claim government-owned land if they could prove continual association with it since 1788. Later, the Wik decision determined that Aboriginal people everywhere could make claims on government land that was leased to agriculturists. But Prime Minister John Howard's Liberal coalition government, under pressure from farming and mining interests, curtailed these rights.

In response, Aboriginal groups threatened (but did not mount) major demonstrations during the 2000 Sydney Olympics. The Olympic opening ceremony paid tribute to the country's Aboriginal origins, and the flame was lit by Aboriginal runner Cathy Freeman. To outsiders, it seemed that Australia was embracing its past rather than marginalising it, but Indigenous Australians themselves were less impressed. John Howard, in particular, came in for harsh criticism for his refusal to apologise for the actions of past generations during his 1996-2007 term as prime minister. It was his successor, the Labor Party's Kevin Rudd, who made an apology to the Stolen Generation in 2008, responded by announcing a leadership ballot on 27 February. She won the vote, but the challenge indicated a damning loss of faith on the part of senior members of the party.

Labor's standing in the polls continued to worsen, and on 26 June 2013, Gillard called a leadership spill on live television – an Australian political term for declaring the leadership to be vacant and open for reelection – pledging that the loser should retire from politics. She was defeated by Kevin Rudd and immediately tendered her resignation.

Rudd's victory was short-lived. With Labor voters largely having lost faith in the party and with dissent from within the party, he was defeated in the September 2013 federal election by the Liberal leader, Tony Abbott.

A NATION OF BOAT PEOPLE

Prime Minister Tony Abbott once declared that Australia was 'unsettled' when the First Fleet arrived in 1788 – completely disregarding the fact that Aboriginal culture can claim to be the oldest on Earth. Rightfully, there was public uproar. Indeed, the fact that the British invaded the country is often used as an argument in the thorny matter of border control policy.

For a nation built on immigration, Australia's treatment of refugees has been condemned on a global scale – in particular its policies of turning back boats and of offshore detention. To point the finger at any one government or political party would, however, be inaccurate. In August 2001 a Norwegian freighter, MV *Tampa*, rescued 438 asylum seekers from a stranded fishing boat. According to international law, shipwreck survivors should be taken to the closest suitable port, but the Howard government refused permission for the ship to enter Australia's territorial waters, threatening to prosecute Captain Arne Rinnan as a people smuggler if he disobeyed. Eventually, 150 of the refugees were granted asylum in New Zealand, while others were sent to an offshore processing camp on the island of Nauru. Captain Rinnan received the highest civil honour in Norway as a result of his determination to get the refugees to safety during this stalemate.

When another boat became stranded two months later, in a stirring bit of propaganda – which became known as the Children Overboard affair – the Australian public were shown news footage of children in the sea. It was claimed by the Howard government that the refugees had thrown their children into the water to blackmail the Australian Navy into rescuing them, however a Senate Select Committee inquiry found that the footage showed the rescue of children after their boat fell apart from the strain of being towed.

By this time, however, the practice of banishing asylum seekers to offshore detention centres was in full swing – and remains so at the time of writing. The 'Pacific Solution' saw the establishment of camps in Nauru, Manus Island and Papua New Guinea.

There was quite the contrast in policies when Labor initially came into power in 2007. Kevin Rudd was bold about his belief in a 'Big Australia', increasing the immigration quota and declaring an end to the Pacific Solution. The opposition capitalised on the fact that boat arrivals increased considerably during Rudd's tenure – and if there was ever any doubt, it was now clear that 'boat people' would become a major election issue for both parties.

When Julia Gillard took over the leadership of the Labor Party, she reintroduced offshore processing, and presented the 'Malaysian Solution', which would send people who had arrived by boat to Malaysia in exchange for refugees based in Malaysia who had been assessed as having genuine claims. However, the High Court ruled that this exchange – designed to deter 'queue jumpers' – was invalid.

Rules got even tougher when the Liberal Party's Tony Abbott came into power in 2013. The Border Force Act, introduced on 1 July 2015, forbids any person who has visited or worked at the detention centres to speak about what they have seen – with the threat of two years' imprisonment. In response to this, more than 40 medical and charity staff who had visited the camps wrote an open letter refusing to obey this decree.

As for the future, Opposition Leader Bill Shorten demanded at the ALP National Conference in July 2015 that if Labor comes into power at the next election, it should have the ability to turn back the boats and continue with offshore processing. Shorten may have added the caveat that asylum seekers would be treated more humanely, but even so, the future doesn't look bright for Australia's humanitarian record.

THE OTHER HISTORY
What happened to the people who were here first?

It's estimated that the first people arrived in Australia 50,000 to 70,000 years ago, travelling by foot from the north across land bridges and later by boat. Australian Aboriginals have one of the oldest continuous cultures in the world, but there was never a unified nation: instead, people grouped into an estimated 500 clans or tribes, speaking some 250 languages and living a mainly nomadic life.

One of the most difficult things for the individualist, capitalist Europeans to understand when they colonised Australia was the relation of land, spirituality and culture to Aboriginal people. According to Indigenous laws, no individual can own, sell or give away land. Land belongs to all members of the community, and they in turn belong to the land. Ownership of a particular region was established during the Dreaming or Dreamtime – the time of creation. The thread of creation stories tells of spiritual ancestors who came from the sky or earth, creating the world, giving life to animals and people, and establishing laws.

As the settlement of Sydney staggered through its first years, the local Indigenous population was almost wiped out by diseases such as smallpox. Those who survived were then caught in a cycle of dispossession, violence and armed resistance. The founding of the Commonwealth of Australia in 1901 ignored Aboriginal people, excluding them from the national census. This was not an oversight: from the early days of settlement it was widely assumed that Aboriginal people were doomed as a race.

By the 1930s, however, it became impossible to ignore that they were vigorously resisting extinction. In 1939, assimilation became federal government policy. Indigenous people were expected to abandon their own culture and fit into white society. The most heartbreaking and controversial aspect of this brutal policy was the forcible removal of children – now known as the 'stolen generations' – from their parents. These children were placed in institutions or fostered out to white homes as part of what has since been described as 'a policy of cultural genocide'. It is thought that 100,000 people were affected from 1910 to the 1970s, when the policy was halted.

The 20th century was marked by the growth of political activism, which led in turn to a slow process of reconciliation. In 1967, more than 90 per cent of Australians voted in a national referendum to empower the federal government to make legislation in the interests of Indigenous people and to count them as citizens in the census. On top of this, the Mabo and subsequent Wik court cases in the 1990s sent shockwaves through Australian society. The British had claimed Australia without treaty or payment because they categorised it as *terra nullius* – that is, as land that belonged to nobody. The court rulings recognised that Indigenous Australians were in fact the original inhabitants of the land, and that British settlement did not necessarily extinguish their native title.

Fear and uncertainty about potential land claims resulting from this decision grew until ultimately the Howard government stepped in and watered down the ownership rights, tying potential claims cases up in courts for years to come. In 1997, an enquiry into the stolen generations produced a controversial report that shamed white Australians, but Prime Minister John Howard refused to apologise (instead, he issued a statement of 'regret').

Nevertheless, a wave of reconciliatory activity ensued. In 2000, the People's Walk for Reconciliation saw an unprecedented 300,000 march across Sydney Harbour Bridge. In February 2008, Prime Minister Kevin Rudd delivered a formal official apology to Aborigines for 'past injustices', stating that the aim was 'to build a bridge of respect with Indigenous Australia.'

It was a start, but Australia's leaders face a long road ahead. The cold facts about the First Australians are positively chilling. Aboriginal people on average live 20 to 25 years less than the rest of the population.

They suffer persistent problems of economic disadvantage, substance abuse, domestic violence and discrimination, exacerbated by limited access to employment, education and health facilities in the remote areas where so many live.

Within the Indigenous community, there are contradictory views on the way ahead. Passively accepting government hand-outs is seen by some as perpetuating the problems. The emphasis now is on targeting money and finding innovative long-term social solutions while involving the Indigenous community fully in the decision-making process. Sydney is at the spearhead.

In September 2010, it was announced that the 'Block', a controversial 1970 Aboriginal housing development/slum in the inner-city heartland of Redfern, would be dismantled and the Pemulwuy Project built in its place. This $50 million development, however, had reached a stalemate in 2015, between the Aboriginal Housing Company (AHC) and the Redfern Aboriginal Tent Embassy (RATE), the latter having set up camp on the site to protest the fact that the project was turning into a commercial development, instead of a development of affordable housing.

It's now usual to preface public events with an acknowledgement of the 'traditional owners' of the area; the red, black and yellow Aboriginal flag is flown on public buildings; important sites, such as Uluru, have been handed back to Aboriginal ownership; and more and more Indigenous people are appearing in public life. None of this can make up for the lost centuries of repression, but it's a giant leap forward on the long path towards social harmony.

Protest outside Sydney Town Hall against the government's treatment of Aboriginal people, June 2015.

Architecture

*Sydney's skyline is an argument that
just keeps on getting more interesting.*

TEXT: ANGUS FONTAINE

The fever to chop and change, scrap and scupper,
is a decidedly convict ethic. From the moment the
ancient culture of the indigenous Gadigal collided
with the modern world of the British settlers, Sydney
has been a city determined to carve bold new futures
from humble beginnings with hard work, big vision
and a whatever-it-takes mentality.

Nature has been the defining factor in Sydney's
physical development – the city has come a long way
in its two centuries of modern settlement since trees
blunted axes and so were dynamited to make way for
the first homes. Ever since, Sydney has specialised
in sledgehammer development of its public spaces
– even the city's own view of its ethereal harbour
is bisected by an ugly stretch of highway, the Cahill
Expressway, which casts a shadow over the otherwise
glorious hurly-burly of Circular Quay and the Rocks.

Yet, despite planners, builders and architects,
it is the city's glorious geography that continues
to govern its design.

NATURAL LEANINGS

In many ways, Sydney's topography mirrors its natural framework – wild, ragged and epic. The city plan is based on an ancient pattern of campsites, protected from hot, dry westerly winds and chilly southern gales, yet capturing the fresh north-east breezes that sweep in from the same direction as the views and the mid-morning sun. Winding main roads such as King Street and Oxford Street lie on Aboriginal walking tracks.

The natural connection between land and sea is the essence of Sydney life. Surf beaches burst through bushland and into rivers, vast oceans snake deep into broken bays and western inlets, creeks trickle their contents into lake systems and swampy billabongs. Animals are everywhere – birds, insects, fish, beasts defying description – all cohabiting with mankind.

FIRST WESTERN ARCHITECTURE

It says much of Sydney that its first great architect was a convict and a forger (a forger later celebrated with a portrait on Australia's $10 note). Francis Greenway was in private practice in Bristol in England in 1812 when he was found guilty of forging a document and sentenced to death, a penalty later commuted to 14 years hard labour in the penal colony of Sydney.

In a city battling for survival, even convicts enjoyed certain freedoms. Greenway soon caught the attention of the colony's great visionary and emancipist, Governor Lachlan Macquarie. In 1817, Greenway was given a ticket-of-leave to build the **Macquarie Lighthouse** at South Head, and Macquarie was so pleased with the result that he called upon Greenway to design a new Government House (now the **Old Government House** in Parramatta; see p157). It was the first of many historic buildings Greenway bequeathed to the city. Others include **Cadman's Cottage** (110 George Street), **Windsor Courthouse** (see p227), the **Conservatorium of Music** (Conservatorium Road; originally constructed in 1821 as the Government Stables), **St James's Church** (173 King Street) and **Hyde Park Barracks** (see p63). Greenway's volatile behaviour later saw him

Macquarie Lighthouse.

WHEN HARRY MET SYDNEY
A Modernist visionary.

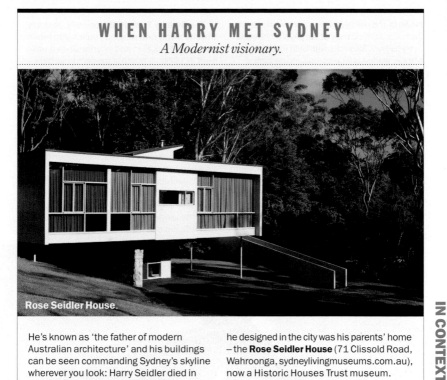

Rose Seidler House.

He's known as 'the father of modern Australian architecture' and his buildings can be seen commanding Sydney's skyline wherever you look: Harry Seidler died in 2006 aged 82, but his spirit lives on. The great man never got to see his last project, the **Ian Thorpe Aquatic Centre** (see p178), which opened to huge acclaim in late 2007. Its white, wave-shaped roof – with echoes of Utzon's Opera House (see p262 **Sydney Opera House**) – is striking enough, but it's inside that the real wonder starts, with the Olympic-sized pool appearing to have been caught in the curve of a huge rolling wave. It seems fitting that Seidler's last gift to Sydney should be a public space for locals to enjoy, not to mention one that embraces the city's growing commitment to green initiatives: it uses hydraulic roof vents for natural ventilation and harnesses rainwater for internal amenities such as toilets and sprinkler systems.

The inspirational architect was born in Vienna in 1923 and fled to England in 1938 to escape Nazi persecution. After World War II, he studied architecture at Harvard and arrived in Sydney in 1948. The first building he designed in the city was his parents' home – the **Rose Seidler House** (71 Clissold Road, Wahroonga, sydneylivingmuseums.com.au), now a Historic Houses Trust museum. With this building, Seidler started on an incredible journey that saw him creating ultra-modern architecture celebrating the optimism and energy of Australia and especially Sydney. This is most tellingly demonstrated in his **Horizon Tower** in Forbes Street, Darlinghurst, a glitzy 42-storey apartment block with curved balconies jutting out from a central column. The tower can be seen from all over central Sydney – a streak of bright white against the blue sky.

Seidler's buildings, however, have divided opinion, with critics labelling his architectural vision too narrow and single-minded. Other Seidler buildings include **Australia Square**, the **MLC Centre** and the contentious **Blues Point Tower**, at the bottom of Blues Point Road in McMahons Point. Seidler was known as a man of passion who took on bureaucrats and local councils with gusto, and his legacy to the city is a series of buildings that continues to help define the city to its citizens.

exiled by the colony. It was a portent of the fates that would befall many of the city's architects.

Hyde Park Barracks was built in 1819 – a huge, walled prison compound designed to cure night crime perpetrated by Sydney's roaming population of convicts. The three-storey main building included a cookhouse, bakery, cells and soldiers' quarters. Each floor had four large rooms divided by staircases, with rows of hammocks for 70 convicts per room – more than 800 in the barracks altogether. In 1887, the interior was rebuilt to house the District Law Courts of New South Wales, but thereafter the barracks fell into gross decay for over a century. They were later saved from demolition by Sydney's Historic Houses Trust, which sensitively blended glass and steel into the original fabric of stone.

The **Sydney Town Hall** (*see p67*), possibly the city's only non-religious building to retain its original function and interior since it was built in 1868, is another modern landmark typical of the city's turbulent architectural history. Built on the site of an old cemetery next to St Andrew's Cathedral, the Town Hall was to be Sydney's riposte to the lavish hall built by Melbourne during the gold rush. But things went awry early. The competition for its design was won by J H Willson, an unknown Tasmanian architect. Alas, his sudden death seemed to curse all who followed him.

City architect Albert Bond designed the chamber now known as the vestibule (open to the public), which served as the meeting hall until the larger Centennial Hall was built. This magnificent space, referred to in its day as the

Hyde Park Barracks.

Place of Democracy, was an engineering triumph, with a highly structured roof, lined with Wunderlich metal panels to protect patrons from falling plaster dislodged by the vibration of the immense organ (which still functions today). The building's large porte-cochère over the present (rebuilt) steps, and its own ring road inside a stone and iron palisade, was destabilised in 1934 during tunnelling for the underground railway and had to be demolished.

Off shore sits **Fort Denison** (see p83), also known as Pinchgut Island. Built from 8,000 tonnes of sandstone quarried near Kurraba Point in Neutral Bay, the ex-prison-fort features one of the last Martello towers built in the world. This harbour battlement (and ration-scarce prison – hence 'Pinchgut')

was built in 1841 to defend Sydney against an attack by Russian warships that never came. Ironically, when a Japanese submarine entered the Harbour in May 1942 (passing through anti-submarine nets), a salvo from the American cruiser USS *Chicago* hit the tower, causing still-visible damage. Today, tours reveal the tower's gunroom with its three eight-inch muzzle-loading cannons – weapons never fired and yet never to be removed without dismantling the stonework.

20TH-CENTURY CONTROVERSIES
The **Queen Victoria Building** (see p69) remains one of the great retailing success stories of Sydney. It was originally designed as a fresh produce market, and construction

Queen Victoria Building.

NEW SYDNEY ARCHITECTURE

These recent additions have changed the profile of the city.

One Central Park.

DR CHAU CHAK WING BUILDING, UTS

Designed by Canadian-American Frank Gehry, one of the world's most celebrated architects, the Dr Chau Chak Wing Building is the flagship project of University of Technology Sydney. It can be viewed in all its eccentric glory from a new pedestrian pathway, the Goods Line, which runs along the eastern border of the site (between Central Station and Darling Harbour) in the tracks of a former freight railway line.

Named after a Chinese-Australian businessman and philanthropist who donated $20 million to the project, the 12-storey Business School building has a focus on postgraduate and executive education and research.

Although the building's design is based on the idea of a tree-house structure, its façade, made of 320,000 custom-designed bricks, has been described as a 'squashed brown paper bag'. Says Gehry: 'Maybe it's a brown paper bag, but it's flexible on the inside, there's a lot of room for changes or movement.' Visitors are welcome, but should be mindful that classes may be in progress.

ONE CENTRAL PARK

One Central Park, well on its way to becoming one of Sydney's most acclaimed buildings since its 2012 opening, could almost represent the city's tech take on the Hanging Gardens of Babylon. Emporis has ranked its East Tower one of the world's best skyscrapers; the Chicago-based Council for Tall Buildings and Urban Habitat named it the best tall building in the world; and it was the overall winner of the 2014 LEAF (Leading European Architects Forum) award.

The first stage of a larger redevelopment, the 117-metre One Central Park residential tower designed by Jean Nouvel features 'vertical gardens' by Patrick Blanc and LED art by Yann Kersalé. Located opposite the UTS Tower, it's an apartment complex with a shopping centre (called Central) located on the lower levels. The design includes a cantilevered section with a heliostat to provide light to the parkland below. The main park is Chippendale Green, while the Balfour Street 'pocket' park was created by closing a section of that street to provide a connection between Central Park and the rest of Chippendale.

BARANGAROO

Set on the north-west edge of Sydney CBD and at the southern edge of the Harbour Bridge, Barangaroo was once an ancient Aboriginal site, and later the shipping and stevedoring heart of Sydney and the Hungry Mile, where men queued daily – and often in vain – for work on the wharves.

The redevelopment project – which began in 2012 and is expected to be completed in 2023 – divides into three precincts: Barangaroo South (an extension of Sydney's CBD, with office buildings, apartments, retail outlets, public spaces and a hotel); Barangaroo Central (which will accommodate James Packer's controversial casino and entertainment complex); and Barangaroo Reserve.

The newly opened six-hectare reserve will no doubt be the major draw – unless you're a high-stakes gambler, of course. The park features a reconstructed, naturalistic headland based around the pre-1836 shoreline. The site reconnects Millers Point – Sydney's first neighbourhood – to the waterfront, by way of grassed areas, lookouts, walking and cycle paths, a huge cutaway cavern beneath the park's hill for exhibitions and eateries, two new harbour coves, and tidal rock pools created from sandstone excavated directly from the Barangaroo site.

More than 6,500 blocks were placed to create the foreshore, while 75,000 native trees, plants and shrubs were used to landscape Barangaroo Reserve. Of the 84 species chosen, 79 are native to Sydney Harbour. Because many of the species could not be found in commercial nurseries, seeds and cuttings were collected from wild sites around Sydney Harbour and the Hawkesbury River.

Dr Chau Chak Wing Building.

Barangaroo.

IN CONTEXT

SYDNEY OPERA HOUSE

The city's most famous building is a tale of architectural alchemy.

Set in a heavenly harbour on a former Gadigal fishing site, its cream wings reminiscent of the sails of the First Fleet (or great white sharks devouring each other), the **Sydney Opera House** is the city's most famous asset. It took 14 troubled years and $102 million to build – a staggering $95 million more than was anticipated. In true Aussie style, the shortfall was met by lotteries. The cultural cathedral has never been visited by the man who conceived and largely built it, Danish architect Jørn Utzon, who resigned in 1966, halfway through the project, following a clash with the Minister of Public Works over rising construction costs. Despite a protest calling for his reinstatement, the government appointed three Australian architects – DS Littlemore, Peter Hall and Lionel Todd – to finish the job. On the night of the inauguration – 20 October 1973 – two small possums made an impromptu stage appearance.

The building's originality lies in its referencing neither history nor classical architectural forms. Here, the roof is infinitely more important than the walls, and all columns, divisions, windows and pediments are dispensed with. In 2007, the Opera House received World Heritage recognition as an architectural wonder of the world. Try to attend one of the 2,400 performances held each year – there's everything from comedy to theatre and dance, symphony and cinema. Or there's the annual Vivid Sydney festival every winter, with light from installations flashing in spectacular fashion across the Opera House sails. Otherwise, book one of the daily guided tours, which include a two-hour backstage tour and a one-hour 'essential' tour. It's not all performance: the building is also a wonderful place to while away a few hours. Eateries range from the universally acclaimed Bennelong inside the sails (with a great harbour outlook), to the stylish Opera Bar, with indoor and outdoor seating and live entertainment, and the family-friendly Sidewalk Café.

began in the economically disastrous year of 1893. Arguments raged from the get-go as to the style required. Renaissance? Gothic? 'American Romanesque' won out, but, beautiful as it was, the QVB fell into disuse and by the 1980s was listed for demolition, with a car park slated to replace it. Saved by a restoration proposal, the building is now hailed as one of the city's greatest architectural and commercial marvels.

East of the QVB sits the **Anzac War Memorial** (see p63), at the south end of Hyde Park. Ever egalitarian, Sydney's 1919 competition for tenders was won by C Bruce Dellit – a 29-year-old in just his second year of practice – with a radical anti-revivalist vision that caused uproar with civic fathers and venerated architects alike. Built in Bathurst granite, Dellit's building can be approached from four directions, with the north and south grand staircases climbing to a Hall of Memory, home to a unique wreathlike balustrade. The east and west ebb down to the Hall of Silence, and 'Sacrifice', a sculpture of a naked soldier, to whom visitors naturally bow in reverence.

The second half of the 20th century in Sydney is especially known for the architectural works of two men: Harry Seidler and Jørn Utzon. The former was one of the city's most prolific architects (see p257 **When Harry Met Sydney**), whose Modernist design principles (seen in the Rose Seidler House and Horizon Tower, among others) were widely praised but failed to garner universal popularity.

Utzon's **Sydney Opera House** (see p262 **Sydney Opera House**), meanwhile, is the city's most famous building. Completed in 1973, it is remarkable for many reasons, including its controversial beginnings. How did a former Gadigal fishing site unite an ambitious state premier (Joseph J Cahill), a visiting American architect (Eero Saarinen) and a young Danish architect (Jørn Utzon) in generating one of the world's most important modern buildings? And why did Utzon resign from the project halfway through completion?

MODERN ICONS

Utzon's influence on Sydney runs deep. Sitting on the site of the first Government House (the archaeological ruins of which are still visible through the glass flooring),

the tall, dark and handsome pair of **Governor Phillip Tower** and **Museum of Sydney** (see p63) was designed in 1995 by Richard Johnson who worked with Utzon on Opera House modifications.

'(An) Aussie architectural icon is Sydney-boy Glenn Murcutt, a Pritzker Prize winner whose motto is 'touch the earth lightly'.'

Italian superstar Renzo Piano is one of the few architectural virtuosos to dare establish a dialogue with the 'grand old lady down the road.' The soaring, ghost-white façades of his 44-level **Aurora Place** office tower (88 Phillip Street) and 17-storey apartment high-rise nearby (114 Macquarie Street) play mainsail to Utzon's billowing spinnakers. Italian-born Piano might be famous for a craftsman's sense of materials but he unveiled Aurora Place in 2000 as Australia's most expensive piece of real estate yet.

A more Aussie architectural icon is Sydney-boy Glenn Murcutt, a Pritzker Prize winner whose motto is 'touch the earth lightly' and whose fame stems from simple yet complex homes built from timber, corrugated iron and louvred glass. One of his early works (1976) is the **Berowra Waters Inn** (Berowra Waters, NSW), a flourishing restaurant still in operation today. Murcutt's influence pervades the breathtaking **Walsh Bay Finger Wharves**, a family of timber wharves and shore sheds recently reworked into a modern residential and cultural precinct by Bates Smart with the help of renowned French architect Philipe Robert. These romantic echoes of Sydney's maritime history were the first locations in Australia to be nominated as a World Heritage Site and today house the Sydney Theatre Company and Sydney Dance Company.

IN CONTEXT

Essential Information

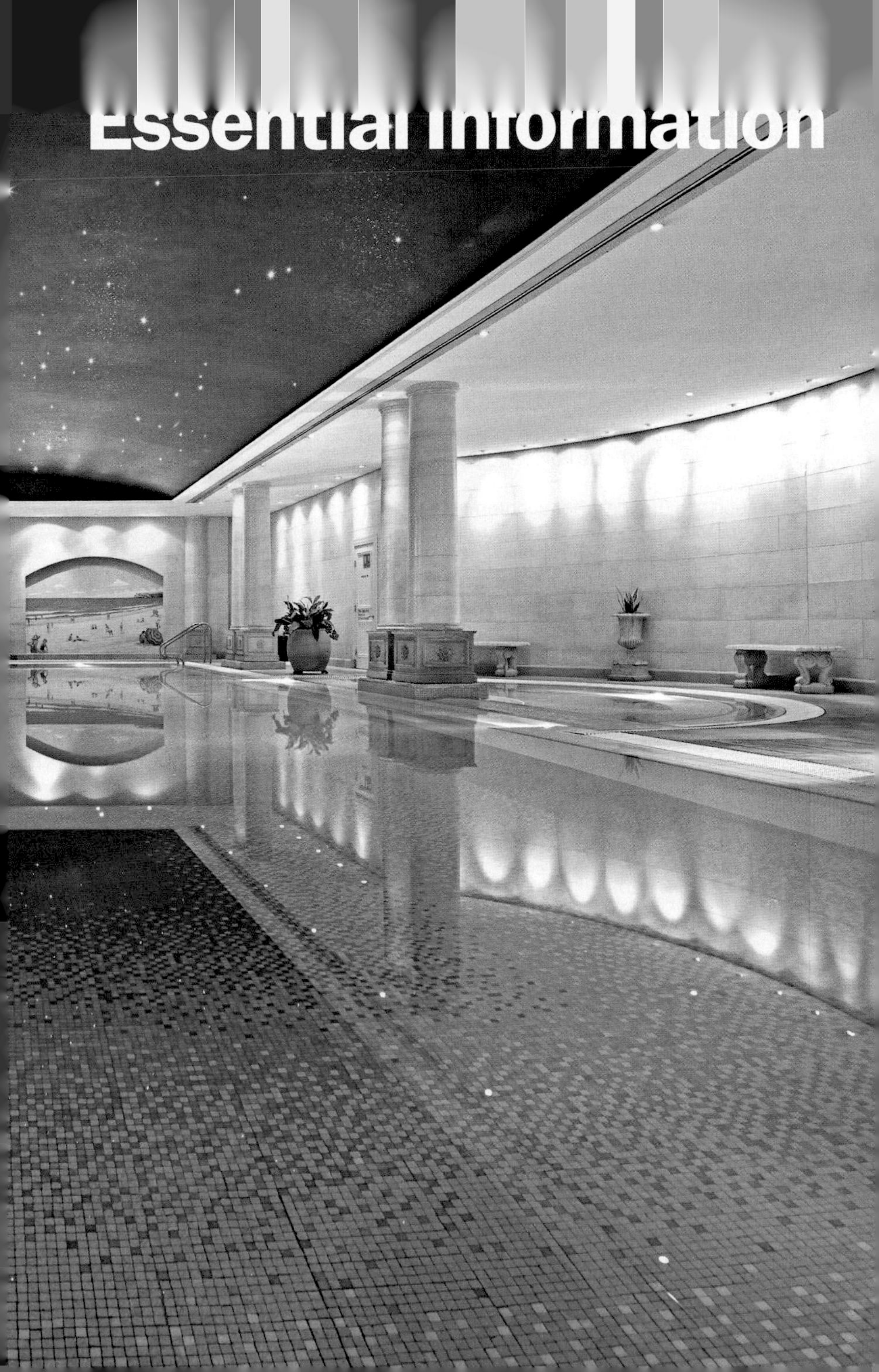

Hotels

The Harbour City offers everything from great backpacker digs to five-star luxury, from the CBD to Bondi and all areas in between. Hotels at the top end compete with those you'll find in any world city. In the centre, you'll find the luxury establishments in prime positions, many with fantastic harbour views. Other hotels are strung around the central sightseeing areas: the Rocks, Circular Quay, George Street, Hyde Park and Darling Harbour. Meanwhile, a group of backpacker joints congregates around Kings Cross, nearby Potts Point and Darlinghurst, and Elizabeth Bay.

The secret to finding great accommodation can often be to look outside the city centre and seek out unusual, independently run establishments. Standards are pretty high, wherever you go and whatever level of the market: Sydneysiders are used to their spaces being spic and span and this is reflected in hotels.

ESSENTIAL INFORMATION

WHERE TO STAY

Staying in central areas means you'll have the sights on hand. If you're in Kings Cross, Darlinghurst or Elizabeth Bay, you'll have plenty of restaurants and bars on your doorstep, but if you want to see the tourist sights you'll need to catch a train back into town. The Inner West areas, such as Newtown and Glebe, are likewise a short train or bus ride from the city centre, but have the advantage of good pubs and a student atmosphere. Newtown's bustling King Street can be noisy and traffic-polluted, but that's just part of its charm.

If you fancy staying near the beach, you can't go wrong with Bondi, Coogee or Manly. If you stay in Manly (a popular option with British visitors), you're limited by the (picturesque) ferry service from the city, which stops around midnight. For the full seaside experience, head for the northern beaches – Newport, Collaroy or the stunning but pricey A-listers playground of Palm Beach.

In the end, though, where you stay may depend on when you come. The busiest tourist times are between November and May. The beach areas are packed from mid December to late January, when the school holidays are in full swing. If you want a room during Mardi Gras (February or March) or a harbour view at New Year, you'll have to book well in advance. Serviced apartments, listed at the end of this chapter, are often a good option for long stays.

ABOUT THE LISTINGS

Most hotels are air-conditioned, but not all – check first if this is an important requirement. Rates quoted below are 'rack' rates, standard prices that are often higher than what you'll pay. It's always worth asking for standby prices, weekly rates or special deals – you may well get them, even in the peak season.

Top hotels also often offer discounts at weekends, when business people are sleeping in their own beds. A ten per cent Goods & Services Tax (GST) applies to all hotels and hostels (as well as tours, internal air fares and restaurant meals), and by law it has to be part of the advertised price.

Note that 1800 telephone numbers are toll-free, and 1300 numbers are always charged at a local rate – but these only work within Australia.

Circular Quay & the Rocks

Deluxe

Langham, Sydney

89-113 Kent Street, Millers Point, NSW 2000 (9256 2222, www.langhamhotels.com). Circular Quay rail or ferry. **Map** p309 E4.

A consistent favourite among the city's well-heeled visitors, the service-oriented Langham in Millers Point has the feel – and indeed some of the looks – of a typical contemporary European hotel, blended with the Langham's Asian touches. Tones are hushed as the army of staff attend to every need and whim of the guests. Rooms have original artworks, marble bathrooms and plush bespoke furnishings. Most have views of Walsh Bay or Observatory Hill. The hotel's renowned spa, which comes with an indoor pool complete with a sparkling night-sky ceiling, is quite something. Head to Palm Court, a fancy tearoom by day and swanky cocktail bar by night, and Kent Street Kitchen for contemporary Australian and European food. *Photos pp268-269.*

Park Hyatt Sydney

7 Hickson Road, the Rocks, NSW 2000 (9241 1234, www.sydney.park.hyatt.com). Circular Quay rail or ferry. **Map** p309 F3.

The Park Hyatt has played host to a steady stream of celebrities, heads of state and international jet-setters with money to burn. The jaw-dropping, close-up vista of the Opera House and the Harbour Bridge is a major selling point, but you get what you pay (a lot) for – the cheaper rooms offer just glimpses of what the more expensive suites have framed through their windows. A refurbishment has transformed the top-end suites into über-minimalist apartment-style hangouts. Extras include a rooftop swimming pool, deluxe spa and much-vaunted 24-hour butler service. There are also LCD TVs, CD/DVD players, high-speed internet connections and marble bathrooms. The chic Dining Room restaurant provides yet more amazing views (through floor-to-ceiling glass doors) and excellent food, while the Living Room offers casual bites and Aussie wines. The Bar caters to whisky, gin and vodka fans.

Shangri-La

176 Cumberland Street, the Rocks, NSW 2000 (9250 6000, www.shangri-la.com). Circular Quay rail or ferry. **Map** p309 E4.

Ideally located between the Opera House and the Harbour Bridge, this is another luxury spot with undeniably breathtaking views. And, what's more, every room has those views, which is one reason for its popularity. Rooms here are some of the largest in the city and there are lots of extra touches designed to maintain a loyal base of regulars. The Horizon Club executive lounge on the 30th floor, with its towering 18m (60ft) glass atrium, comes at a premium but offers complimentary breakfast and snacks, and business facilities. The swanky Blu Horizon cocktail bar is popular with city boys, while the Altitude restaurant on the 36th floor has unbeatable picture-postcard views of the the harbour, bridge and Opera House. Decor is a mix of modern eastern with classic hotel chic, but with views like these you won't be paying too much attention to the furniture. There's also a gym and indoor swimming pool.

Expensive

Pier One Sydney Harbour

11 Hickson Road, Dawes Point, the Rocks, NSW 2000 (1800 780 485, 8298 9999, www. pieronesydneyharbour.com.au). Circular Quay rail or ferry. **Map** p309 F2.

Another successful marriage of historic architecture and contemporary design, this sleek, chic boutique hotel on Walsh Bay has water views in the most unexpected places, including beneath your feet: the glass floor in the lobby is quite the showpiece. Located in a converted warehouse at the quiet end of the Rocks, the rooms feature much of the original timber and ironwork. Some rooms have telescopes, some have Walsh Bay or partial bridge views, and all have wireless internet connection and slick modern furnishings. The Gantry Restaurant & Bar provides alfresco dining and cocktails on the water, while the private pontoon is convenient for those travelling by water taxi or private yacht.

Moderate

Lord Nelson Brewery Hotel

19 Kent Street, Millers Point, NSW 2000 (9251 4044, www.lordnelson.com.au). Circular Quay rail or ferry. **Map** p309 E3.

Time marches on, but you wouldn't know it at the Lord Nelson, whose motto is: 'You've been praying, the Lord has delivered.' The clean and relatively spacious Victorian-style rooms with plantation shutters are air-conditioned, but the look and feel of the place is pure 19th-century colonial – the pub opened in 1841 and claims to be the oldest in the city. There are only nine guest rooms, all with original bare sandstone walls and, despite the antique feel, most come with en suite bathrooms. The laid-back downstairs

---

IN THE KNOW PUB OR HOTEL?

In Australia, pubs are also called 'hotels'. Many pubs do actually have rooms at reasonable prices, but standards are mixed, so ask to see the accommodation first. Also check that there is adequate soundproofing.

ESSENTIAL INFORMATION

brasserie, its walls hewn from convict-quarried sandstone, serves contemporary Australian cuisine, while the bar, serving ploughman's lunches, and the microbrewery draw a lively crowd.

Russell

143A George Street, the Rocks, NSW 2000 (9241 3543, www.therussell.com.au). Circular Quay rail or ferry. **Map** p309 F4.

With a great location in the middle of the Rocks, the Russell still somehow manages to feel more like a cosy country B&B than a city-centre hotel. Housed in a turreted 1887 building, rooms feature such period flourishes as ornate fireplaces, antique brass beds, marble washbasins, pine dressers and floral bedspreads and wallpapers. Some rooms are en suite, and some have portable air-conditioners and TVs. There's also the pleasant Acacia breakfast room on the ground floor, the historic Fortune of War pub and a tiny rooftop garden.

Central Sydney

THE CBD

Deluxe

Four Seasons Hotel Sydney

199 George Street, NSW 2000 (1800 142 163, 9238 0000, www.fourseasons.com). Circular Quay rail or ferry. **Map** p309 F4.

The former Regent Hotel was taken over by Canadian chain Four Seasons in the early 1990s and since then has been quietly delivering an extremely high level of service within very plush surroundings. The decor is expensive-looking in a modern way, with a restrained, pared-down opulence. All the rooms are spacious and have marble bathrooms; some overlook Walsh Bay, the Harbour Bridge and the Opera House, while the rest have city views. The 32nd-floor Executive Club caters to high-flying business types with its corporate concierge, separate check-in and added goodies such as meetings facilities and complimentary refreshments. Don't skip whisky cocktails at Grain off the lobby, or the farm-to-table Mod Oz cuisine at chef Mark Best's restaurant, Pei Modern.

Hilton Sydney

488 George Street, NSW 2000 (9266 2000, reservations 9265 6045, www.hiltonsydney. com.au). Town Hall rail. **Map** 309 F6.

Since its refurbishment back in 2005, the Hilton has reclaimed its position as one of the city's premier five-star hotels – quite an achievement without the usually obligatory harbour view. From the light-filled, four-storey-high lobby with its spiralling aluminium sculpture to the 31 'relaxation' rooms and suites, staying here is an undeniably classy experience. The design features limestone flooring, plush fabrics, mood lighting and (in the suites) open-plan spa bathrooms. Eating and drinking spots include Luke Mangan's Glass brasserie and wine bar, the Zeta cocktail bar and the historic Marble Bar (established 1893) in the basement, left untouched during the refurbishment. There are also extensive conference and business facilities, and a top-end health club with gym, indoor pool, saunas and steam rooms. Great views, too, from the higher floors over nearby Sydney Tower.

InterContinental Sydney

Corner of Bridge & Phillip Streets, NSW 2000 (1800 221 335, 9253 9000, www.sydney. intercontinental.com). Circular Quay rail or ferry. **Map** 309 G4.

Langham. See p267.

Housed in a building that dates from 1851, the InterContinental is now fully up to date, with high-speed internet access and digital TV in all rooms. These have a classic-contemporary feel and come with either harbour or city views. Book a table at 117 dining for upmarket contemporary Australian cuisine, the sandstone-arcaded Cortile café for traditional high tea, and Café Opera for a seafood buffet. The luxurious rooftop lounge, with its uninterrupted harbour views, is only accessible to Club InterContinental members, who pay extra for such privileges as a personal concierge service. The vistas from the top over Sydney Harbour are spectacular, and available to all guests from the indoor swimming pool on the 31st floor.

QT Sydney

49 Market Street, NSW 2000 (02 8262 0000, www.qtsydney.com.au). St James or Town Hall rail. **Map** p309 F6.

For a taste of inner-city luxury, you can't beat QT Sydney. It packs 200 individually designed rooms, a day spa (spaQ), barber, two bars, a café and restaurant into the heritage-listed Gowings building – and still feels boutique rather than behemoth. The place has been themed with a nod to the building's original use as a full-service men's department store, with vintage American barber shop chairs and a hammam-inspired steam room. A reception lounge channels midcentury modern through the prism of contemporary design. It's not all retro: Grant Stevens' large-scale video work *The Drift* provides a meditative vista in the public lounge and Daniel Boyd's digital-dot works grace the elevators. Each room is just a little different, whether it's the colour scheme, furniture or fittings, but the basics are the same: custom-designed 'gel' mattresses; flatscreen TVs; dark grey palettes for the bathrooms; fiery

colours for the rooms. On one side of the building you get original floorboards; the other side has carpet and dark-wood panelling retained from previous occupants. The Gilt Lounge is a good spot for pre-dinner drinks and retro-inspired snacks; while Gowings Bar & Grill is great for brasserie-style surf and turf, with a menu that's big on crustaceans, wood-fired meats and rotisserie fowl.

Sheraton on the Park

161 Elizabeth Street, NSW 2000 (1800 073 535, 9286 6000, www.sheraton.com). St James rail. **Map** p309 F6.

Overlooking bucolic Hyde Park, this huge hotel occupies a prime location in the central business and shopping district. The grand lobby screams luxury, with its massive black marble pillars and curved staircase, and the rooms have a refined, modern and quasi-nautical design theme (all stripes and circles), and feature black marble bathrooms. There's a spacious pool and fitness centre on level 22, the revamped Conservatory Bar on level one and a tea lounge off the lobby, which offers 'contemporary' high tea served by stylish black-clad waiters.

Westin Sydney

1 Martin Place, NSW 2000 (1800 656 535, 8223 1111, www.westin.com). Martin Place rail. **Map** p309 F5.

Here you get the best of both worlds – a sense of history married to some very contemporary design and deluxe service. Located in pedestrianised Martin Place, smack-dab in the middle of the CBD, the Westin is partly housed in what used to be the General Post Office, built in 1887. Rooms in the heritage-listed building feature high ceilings and period details, while rooms in the newer tower have floor-to-ceiling city views and a more contemporary look, with stainless steel and light wood. There is a renowned spa and a spectacular atrium as well as a selection of restaurants and bars in the GPO building. Exercise addicts take note: the 'workout rooms' come with treadmill, weights, a yoga mat and other fitness paraphernalia.

Expensive

Establishment

5 Bridge Lane, NSW 2000 (9240 3100, www. merivale.com). Circular Quay rail or ferry, or Wynyard rail. **Map** p309 F4.

Although it only has 31 rooms, including two penthouse suites, the Establishment's cool clout far outweighs its capacity. Exceedingly stylish, this place would be perfectly at home in the smarter districts of London or New York. Catering to celebrities, fashionistas and those with deep pockets, the complex incorporates two critically acclaimed restaurants – Sushi e and est. – the elegant cocktail bar den Hemmesphere, vintage speakeasy Palmer & Co and high-end Canto-palace Mr Wong. As for the guest rooms, half are all sharp angles, minimalist Japanese elements and flashes of bright colour, while the others are more subdued. Expect luxurious touches at every turn (Philippe Starck taps, Bulgari toiletries, Bose stereo systems).

Four Points by Sheraton Darling Harbour

161 Sussex Street, NSW 2000 (1800 074 545, 9290 4000, www.fourpoints.com). Town Hall or Wynard rail. **Map** 309 E6.

With 630 rooms (including 45 suites and several hundred more rooms on the way), this place caters to large tour groups, executives and the international conference crowd. The Sydney Convention Centre is a stone's throw away, and the hotel is within walking distance of several museums as well as Chinatown and the central business and shopping districts. All the expected facilities are provided, such as high-speed Wi-Fi, large work desks and cable TV. Some rooms have balconies overlooking Darling Harbour. There are high-tech conferencing facilities, a fitness centre and a shopping centre with a food court. The glassed-in Corn Exchange restaurant offers an elaborate seafood buffet; the historic Dundee Arms pub specialises in barbecued pub grub; and locally brewed beer and cocktails are served in the Lobby Lounge.

Grace Hotel

77 York Street, NSW 2000 (9272 6888, www. gracehotel.com.au). Martin Place or Wynyard rail. **Map** p309 E6.

This charming hotel is housed in an 11-storey corner block – a loose copy of the Tribune Tower in Chicago – that began life in 1930 as the headquarters of department store giant Grace Brothers. During World War II, General MacArthur directed South Pacific operations from here. A total refurbishment was completed a decade ago, but many of the

original features, such as the lifts, stairwells, marble floors and ornate ironwork, have been retained and restored to great effect. Rooms, however, are modern, large and comfortable, and all have bathtubs. The indoor heated lap pool is small, but there's also a sauna and a steam room, plus a sun-filled fitness centre and rooftop terrace. Grace Brasserie serves cocktails and innovative bar food.

Rydges World Square

389 Pitt Street, NSW 2000 (1800 838 830, 8268 1888, www.rydges.com). Central rail or light rail, or Town Hall rail. **Map** p311 F8.

Located in the shopping and entertainment precinct known as World Square, the Rydges features comfortable and spacious, if rather neutrally decorated, guest rooms with free Wi-Fi. Bathrooms all have full-sized baths. Since it is within easy walking distance of Darling Harbour, Chinatown and the Queen Victoria Building, this hotel is popular with business people and those seeking cheaper (relatively speaking), good-quality rooms. There's also a large fitness centre and a retail plaza that connects to the lower lobby. The Sphere restaurant serves Italian food, and there's a bar, the Cidery Bar & Kitchen, with an outside deck overlooking World Square.

Moderate

Park8 Hotel

185 Castlereagh Street, NSW 2000 (9283 5000, www.park8.com.au). Town Hall rail. **Map** p311 F7.

With its motto 'hip on a budget', Park8 is perfect for those who love to be in the heart of the action. Located on a busy city corner, this compact urban

Park8 Hotel.

hotel has standard en suite rooms, 'studios' with an additional double sofa bed and a spa bath, and seven airy, two-storey loft apartments that can sleep up to four people. Some rooms overlook Hyde Park. Perched above a busy bar, restaurant and gaming room complex, the noise is kept to a minimum with efficient soundproofing and window seals.

Budget

Nomads Westend

412 Pitt Street, NSW 2000 (1800 013 186, 9211 4588, nomadsworld.com/westend). Central rail or light rail. **Map** p311 F8.

Who says backpackers have it rough? Located just around the corner from Central Station, this clean and modern hotel is popular with anyone on a budget, including families. There are laundry facilities, a commercial-grade kitchen and a café, plus extras geared towards working holidaymakers, such as an in-house travel agency and jobs board. There's always something going on here, which is particularly helpful for lone travellers – at the time of writing, Friday is wine-and-cheese night and Saturday is barbie night. Rooms (most have air-conditioning) are either en suite or have an adjacent private bathroom. The reception is open 24 hours daily, breakfast is astonishingly good value at just $2 and airport transfers are offered to guests staying for three or more nights.

Pensione

631-635 George Street, NSW 2000 (1800 885 886, 9265 8888, www.pensione.com.au). Central rail or light rail. **Map** p311 E8.

The Pensione is part of the Eight Hotels group of affordable, stylish hotels in central Sydney. On the edge of Chinatown opposite World Square, budget accommodation really doesn't come much better than this (although you should choose your rooms wisely as it can get noisy). Yes, some rooms are very small, but they're all kitted out with a mini fridge, TV, air-con and phone, and feature modern tiled bathroooms that wouldn't look out of place in a glossy homes mag. There are around 15 family rooms, the largest sleeping up to six, so it's a good option for young families who want something urban and edgy. Other facilities include internet kiosks and Wi-Fi in the guest lounge, a kitchenette and a coin-operated laundry.

Sydney Central YHA

11 Rawson Place, NSW 2000 (9218 9000, www. yha.com.au). Central rail or light rail. **Map** p311 E9.

The largest of the YHA properties in Sydney, this place has it all. Deep breath: kitchen, laundry, separate games, dining and TV rooms, high-speed internet terminals, mini supermarket, café, underground bar and a rooftop pool, sauna and barbecue area with panoramic city views. Popular activities include pub crawls, big-screen movie nights and walking tours. All of this is housed in an imposing, heritage-listed building opposite Central Station. There are around 50 twin rooms, some en suite, and dorms that sleep up to eight.

Y Hotel Hyde Park

5-11 Wentworth Avenue, NSW 2010 (1800 994 994, 9264 2451, www.yhotel.com.au). Museum rail. **Map** 311 G8.

Run by the venerable old YWCA, this spot attracts all kinds (and both sexes), from budget-conscious business travellers to families and young singles. Deluxe rooms, corporate and studio rooms are all en suite and come with TV, fridge and high-speed internet connection. Family rooms have three beds, while backpacker rooms sleep four. All are clean and contemporary and have basic furniture. Rates include continental or light breakfast; laundry facilities, a café and a kitchen round off the services. The location, just south of Hyde Park, is fantastic.

HAYMARKET
Budget

Railway Square YHA
8-10 Lee Street, NSW 2000 (9281 9666, www.yha.com.au). Central rail or light rail. **Map** p311 E9.
This YHA hostel, built in a former parcels shed, is very near its Central counterpart (*see p271*). The design incorporates a real disused railway platform, with some dorms housed in replicas of train carriages (very Harry Potter), the bathrooms in the main building adjacent. Most dorms have between four and eight beds, and there are a couple of en suite double rooms. It's clean and bright, with a large openplan communal area dotted with sofas, a sizeable kitchen, laundry facilities and an internet café. Facilities include a fun small spa pool and air-conditioning. It's very popular, so book ahead.

wake up!
509 Pitt Street, NSW 2000 (1800 800 945/9288 7888, www.wakeup.com.au). Central rail or light rail. **Map** p311 E9.
Located opposite Central Station, this award-winning hostel is big, clean, efficiently run and has very proactive security, despite the party atmosphere. The common areas are like a twentysomething's dream, with circular sofas, a funky TV lounge, endless banks of computers, a street café, kitchen, laundry, ATMs and a travel agent to organise your trips and help you find work locally. The air-conditioned dorms sleep four, six, eight or ten, and some are women-only. There are also double and twin rooms, some with private showers. Bedlinen is provided and check-in is 24 hours.

DARLING HARBOUR & PYRMONT
Deluxe

Darling
The Star, 80 Pyrmont Street, Pyrmont, NSW 2000 (1800 800 830, www.thedarling.com.au). The Star light rail. **Map** p308 C6.
Yes, it's in a casino and it's in Pyrmont, but don't hold that against the Darling, which is all about contemporary design and the latest in-room technology.

Its prime position near Sydney Harbour, and panoramic views of the city skyline, Harbour Bridge and out to the Blue Mountains are other major assets. Part of the $870-million redevelopment and extension of the Star complex, the Darling is the first five-star hotel to open in Sydney's CBD since the 2000 Olympic Games. Although it's pretty new, it's already had a mini facelift, and guests can now look forward to new features at its spa, a fitness centre and a gleaming lobby upgrade. The Darling has four different kinds of suite – Penthouse, Stellar, Adored and Jewel – as well as 114 Darling Rooms. Luxury buffs take note: beds have 400-thread Egyptian cotton sheets and a hand-picked pillow menu; rooms have textured wallpaper and bespoke furniture. In addition to the spa, there's a eucalyptus-scented pool, and the hotel is also home to Sokyo Japanese restaurant.

Expensive

Novotel Sydney on Darling Harbour
100 Murray Street, Darling Harbour, NSW 2000 (1300 656 565, 9934 0000, www.novotel darlingharbour.com.au). Convention light rail. **Map** p308 D6.
Next door to the Sydney Convention & Exhibition Centre, the Novotel is aimed mainly at business travellers. Rooms come stuffed with communication features such as LCD TVs, mobile phone- and laptop-charging stations and – of course – Wi-Fi. The panoramic harbour and city views are lovely, and there's also a swimming pool, tennis court, gym and sauna. The hotel is home to Liquid – an average cocktail bar with a good outdoor terrace – and a restaurant, the Ternary.

Moderate

Ibis Sydney Darling Harbour

70 Murray Street, Darling Harbour, NSW 2000 (1300 656 565, 9563 0888, www. accorhotels.com.au). Convention light rail. **Map** 308 D6.

This is a no-frills, get-what-you-pay-for option in a good location. Rooms are modern, although on the small side, but the being in Darling Harbour makes up for it and the place is still good value for money. Some rooms have views of Darling Harbour and the city, while others look over Pyrmont.

DARLINGHURST

Expensive

Medusa

267 Darlinghurst Road, NSW 2010 (9331 1000, www.medusa.com.au). Kings Cross rail or bus 311. **Map** p311 H8.

What's not to love about a heritage-listed Victorian mansion that's been painted pink? Embodying a very Darlinghurst sense of urban chic, the Medusa is an ode to colour and design, all interesting angles and bright flourishes of imagination. The lobby is pink, too, with bulging floral mouldings and an oversized paper chandelier. All rooms have luxe touches like CD players, Aveda toiletries and fluffy bathrobes; they also have kitchenettes. The expansive Grand Rooms feature period fireplaces, groovy chaises longues and a sitting area. The recently added business suite, including generous desk space, can be rented hourly, while rooms around the diminutive courtyard are pet-friendly.

Moderate

Kirketon

229 Darlinghurst Road, NSW 2010 (1800 332 920, 9332 2011, www.kirketon.com.au). Kings Cross rail. **Map** p312 H8.

Built in the late 1930s and now part of the Eight Hotels group, which owns various budget boutique properties in Sydney, the Kirketon has nice touches in the rooms, such as chocolates and Kevin Murphy toiletries, and the overall design is contemporary minimalist, with rich colours and slick bathrooms with showers. The dining room and bar – where chef Eric Tan serves ultra-modern international cuisine – remain popular with locals.

SURRY HILLS

Moderate

Crown Hotel

589 Crown Street, Surry Hills, NSW 2010 (9699 3460, www.crownhotel.com.au). Bus 301, 302, 303, 352, 355, 372, 393, 395, M50. **Map** p311 G11.

This very hip yet thoroughly unpretentious complex opened ten years ago and there's nothing quite like it in Surry Hills, land of fab restaurants but very few hotels. On the ground floor is Players, an airy pub converted from an 1880s hotel, plus an upscale wine shop. Level two features Dome, a sexy cocktail bar complete with chandeliers, a glass bar and a huge mural based on François Boucher's baroque painting *Girl Reclining*. Last but not least are the hotel rooms, equally stylish and featuring deluxe extras such as L'Occitane bath products, Egyptian cotton bedlinen and wall-mounted 42-inch plasma screen TVs.

ESSENTIAL INFORMATION

Ovolo Woolloomooloo. *See p274.*

Eva's Backpackers.

CHIPPENDALE
Budget

Y Hotel City South
179 Cleveland Street, Chippendale (1800 300 882, 8303 1303, www.yhotel.com.au). Redfern rail. **Map** p316.

Close to Sydney University, Prince Alfred Park (with its great pool), Broadway, Glebe and Newtown, this architect-designed boutique hotel is quite a find. It's run by the YWCA and is a joy to stay in: its diverse clientele includes everyone from backpackers and families through to business people. In-room broadband, air-conditioning and chic contemporary decor make for comfortable surroundings, while a decent gym, outdoor terrace, rooftop garden, secure on-site parking and the usual laundry and kitchen facilities are added bonuses. The tranquil apartment, with two large bedrooms, two bathrooms, courtyards, and a fully equipped kitchen, living and dining area, is wonderful.

KINGS CROSS, POTTS POINT & WOOLLOOMOOLOO
Deluxe

Ovolo Woolloomooloo
Woolloomooloo Wharf, 6 Cowper Wharf Road, Woolloomooloo, NSW 2011 (9331 9000, www.ovolohotels.com). Kings Cross rail then 10min walk, or bus 311. **Map** p312 H6.

The former W hotel in the historic Woolloomooloo Wharf is now owned by Ovolo, Hong Kong's hip hotel chain. It's still a funky, alternative hotel with lots to offer those who like something a bit different from their five-star hangout. The plush rooms feature original elements from the old wharf building, and there's a fitness centre, an indoor pool and the very popular Water Bar. The hotel has no restaurant, but there's an array of high-class, high-priced eateries along the marina edge of the wharf (rooms on this side have the best views). The hotel occupies only part of the swanky wharf development; there's also a complex of exclusive apartments and the deluxe Spa Chakra, which is pricey but divine. *Photos pp272-273.*

Expensive

Larmont Sydney
14 Kings Cross Road, Potts Point, NSW 2011 (9295 8888, www.lancemore.com.au/larmont_sydney). Kings Cross rail. **Map** p312 J7.

This boutique hotel has the area's best accommodation. Rooms are comfortable and contemporary; a neutral colour palette is enlivened by splashes of colour or pattern, and bathrooms are spacious. All rooms have free Wi-Fi, large desks and 42-inch plasma TVs. Some have private patios with comfortable furniture.

Moderate

Simpsons Hotel Potts Point
8 Challis Avenue, Potts Point, NSW 2011 (9356 2199, www.simpsonshotel.com). Kings Cross rail. **Map** p312 J6.

A very elegant and charming place, combining the stylishness and comforts of a boutique hotel with the informal sociability of a B&B. Located at the quieter end of a tree-lined street, the lovingly restored mansion was built in 1892 and still retains many of its original Arts and Crafts details. The high-ceilinged rooms are old-fashioned, but elegantly so, and by no means dowdy. This is the life: sipping a free port or sherry by an open hearth in winter (OK, the fires are gas-powered imitations), tucking into a continental breakfast in the conservatory, thumbing through the hardbacks in the library… Book well in advance as Simpsons gets a lot of repeat business, and note that it doesn't have a licence to sell alcohol.

Victoria Court Hotel

122 Victoria Street, Potts Point, NSW 2011 (1800 630 505, 9357 3200, www.victoriacourt.com.au). Kings cross rail. Map p312 J6.

Leafy Victoria Street is an interesting mix of posh restaurants, ramshackle youth hostels and converted Victorian mansions – all just around the corner from the strip clubs and general sleaze of Kings Cross. This small hotel, formed from two 1881 terraced houses, is a celebration of Victorian extravagance, from the four-poster beds to the floral-printed everything (carpeting, curtains, wallpaper). All rooms are air-conditioned and have private bathrooms; some have marble fireplaces and wrought-iron balconies. Breakfast is served in the gorgeous plant-filled courtyard around a bubbling fountain.

Budget

Eva's Backpackers

6-8 Orwell Street, Kings Cross, NSW 2011 (1800 802 517, 9358 2185, www.evasbackpackers.com. au). Kings Cross rail. Map p312 J6.

With its friendly, laid-back atmosphere and reputation for being very clean and quiet (rare for a backpackers' hostel in this neighbourhood), Eva's has gained an enthusiastic following. There are twin, double and dorm rooms, some en suite, some with air-conditioning. Extras include free breakfast, a kitchen, a laundry room with free washing powder, wake-up calls, luggage storage facilities, internet access, and a rooftop terrace and barbecue area with fabulous views over Sydney. Located at the (less dodgy) Potts Point end of Kings Cross, it's on a quiet street, but close to everything.

Ibis Budget Sydney East

191-201 William Street, Kings Cross, NSW 2011 (9326 0300, www.ibis.com). Kings Cross rail. Map p312 H7.

This budget hotel provides no-frills, modern accommodation in air-conditioned rooms in various configurations: a double bed with room for one more person in an overhead bunk; rooms for four with two sets of bunks; and family rooms with a double and a bunk bed for two. All rooms have en suite bathrooms. Set on the busy part of William Street, it can feel as if you're on a racetrack at times, but everything you need is on the doorstep.

O'Malley's Hotel

228 William Street, Kings Cross, NSW 2011 (9357 2211, www.omalleys hotel.com.au). Kings Cross rail. Map p312 H7.

It may be attached to a popular Irish pub and music venue, and, yes, it's dangerously close to everything that's wrong with Kings Cross, but don't write off O'Malley's. The 1907 building's rooms are all en suite and feature lovely period touches along with old-fashioned charm. The location is convenient, too: just two minutes from the rail station. The Harbour View suite has a kitchen.

Original Backpackers Lodge

160-162 Victoria Street, Kings Cross, NSW 2011 (9356 3232, www.originalbackpackers.com.au). Kings Cross rail. Map p312 J7.

This sprawling hostel in a Victorian mansion may look a little on the lived-in side, but it has plenty of character – not to mention a lovely spacious courtyard, free bedlinen and towels, 24-hour check-in and complimentary airport pick-up. There are single, double and family rooms as well as ten-person dorms, some of which are women-only. All rooms have TVs and fridges, and some have balconies, although most bathroom facilities are shared. There's usually something going on in the courtyard, whether it's karaoke or an Aussie barbie. The kitchen is big and modern, with food lockers, and there are laundry facilities.

Eastern Suburbs

PADDINGTON & RUSHCUTTERS BAY

Moderate

Arts Hotel Sydney

21 Oxford Street, Paddington, NSW 2021 (9361 0211, www.artshotel.com.au). Oxford Street buses. Map p314 H9.

This friendly, family-run hotel has a great location in a modern building, with fabulous independent cinemas and shops nearby. Smart, contemporary rooms all have private bathrooms and free Wi-Fi; garden rooms face the tranquil courtyard. You can make the most of the weather with the solar-heated pool and garden courtyard, or just relax in the ground-floor breakfast room overlooking busy Oxford Street. The hotel's owners also rent out their alpine chalet (three beds, two baths) in the Blue Mountains. *Photos pp276-277.*

Vibe Rushcutters

100 Bayswater Road, Rushcutters Bay, NSW 2011 (13 8423, 8353 8988, www.vibehotels.com.au). Bus 324, 325. Map p312 H9.

The Vibe hotel chain tries to be many things at once – stylish, affordable, young – and, by and large, it succeeds. The contemporary rooms may be on the small side but they have air-conditioning and get

ESSENTIAL INFORMATION

lots of light. Facilities here include a spacious fitness centre with steam room. While the rooftop pool is a little exposed on windy days, its panoramic vista of Rushcutters Bay Park (great for jogging), the water and the city is superb. There's a cocktail bar, and a restaurant with a pleasant covered terrace. There are two other Vibes in town: one in North Sydney and one on Goulburn Street in the city. *Photos p278.*

DOUBLE BAY & WOOLLAHRA
Deluxe

InterContinental Sydney Double Bay
33 Cross Street, Double Bay, NSW 2028, (02 8388 8388, www.ihg.com). Edgecliff rail, or bus 323, 324, 325, L24. **Map** p313 N1.
In its previous incarnations, this hotel hosted US presidents, Australian prime ministers (Bob Hawke famously ran through the lobby in budgie smugglers), Princess Diana and – sadly – Michael Hutchence on the last night of his life. Now, it's back at its brilliant best after a huge renovation. There are 140 contemporary rooms and suites, a rooftop pool with cabanas, several restaurants, bars and retail spaces. Stillery, the bar off the lobby, has more than 60 gins and a list of signature cocktails (make ours a Four Pillars gin martini with olives) alongside ciders, wines and more spirits.

Moderate

Hughenden Hotel
14 Queen Street, Woollahra, NSW 2025 (9363 4863, 1800 642 432, www.hughendenhotel.com. au). Bus 389 or Oxford Street buses. **Map** p314 L11.
This boutique hotel was thought to be a lost cause when sisters Elizabeth and Susanne Gervay bought it back in 1992. But they transformed the crumbling, grand 1870s mansion into a popular hotel offering sophisticated modern accommodation with en suite bathrooms in comfortable old-world surroundings. There's also an attached four-bed terraced house that can be rented in its entirety. Elizabeth is an artist and Susanne an author, so literary events and art exhibitions take place regularly. There's a cosy lounge, an old-fashioned bar with a baby-grand piano and a sun terrace. Quaife's restaurant is named after the original owner, the founder of the colony's medical association, and serves bistro-style dishes in generous portions. Three rooms are designated as pet-friendly.

BONDI & COOGEE BEACHES
Moderate

Coogee Bay Hotel
Corner of Arden Street & Coogee Bay Road, Coogee Beach, NSW 2034 (9665 0000, www. coogeebayhotel.com.au). Bus 313, 314, 353, 372, 373, M50, X73.

The hotel has been operating on the same site since 1873 – though it's had a few facelifts in its lifetime. Not exactly a quiet beachside retreat, this complex is very big and very busy. The brasserie serves hearty fare for breakfast (included in the room price), lunch and dinner seven days a week, and there are several different bars, including a spectacular sports bar. Rooms come as 'boutique-style' – spacious, in neutral colours with sofas – and smaller 'pub-style', running from standard rooms with varied bed configurations to suites with access to beach-facing balconies. There are family rooms too.

Dive Hotel
234 Arden Street, Coogee Beach, NSW 2034 (9665 5538, www.divehotel.com.au). Bus 313, 314, 353, 372, 373, M50, X73.
A smart and elegant guesthouse, the Dive Hotel's contemporary design centres on bold colours and polished wood. Its cosy, sun-filled breakfast room looks out on to a bamboo-bordered garden, while views of the ocean from some of the rooms are equally wonderful. All rooms are en suite, with a microwave, fridge and TV, and while the bathrooms may be small, they are stylishly fitted out with mosaic tiles and stainless-steel sinks. The annex – a three-bedroom house

Arts Hotel. *See p275.*

two blocks from the beach – accommodates families. Dive is a disarmingly welcoming place; gracious owners Terry Bunton and Mercedes Mariano and their poodle (Babe), retriever (George) and cat (Bob), help take the sharpness off the style.

Ravesi's
118 Campbell Parade, Bondi Beach, NSW 2026 (9365 4422, www.ravesis.com.au). Bondi Junction rail, then bus 333, 380, 381, 382, or bus 333, 380. **Map** p316.
Ravesi's is known primarily for its noisy street-level bar, but upstairs is a chic boutique hotel. All rooms have private bathrooms and are impeccably furnished: the designs, by renowned abstract artist Dane van Bree, use a palette of Aboriginal colours – mainly black, copper and bronze. The split-level suites have private terraces and superb sea views.

Budget

Lamrock Lodge
19 Lamrock Avenue, Bondi Beach, NSW 2026 (9130 5063, www.lamrocklodge.com). Bondi Junction rail, then bus 333, 380, 381, 382, or bus 333, 380. **Map** 316.

A good bet for the more mature backpacker looking for somewhere not too raucous. The Lamrock is located on a quiet street 100m from Bondi Beach, and it's a very clean, well-maintained place, sporting funky bamboo flooring. All rooms have TVs, microwaves and fridges, and there are four-bed dorms with rates that get better the longer you stay. Decor is in typical hostel style (bedlinen, quilts and pillows are supplied), and there are plenty of vending machines in addition to the kitchen. There are also laundry facilities. Friendly, helpful staff and 24-hour security help to create a genuinely relaxed and easygoing vibe.

Inner West
GLEBE
Budget

Alishan International Guesthouse
100 Glebe Point Road, Glebe, NSW 2037 (9566 4048, www.alishan.com.au). Glebe light rail, or bus 370, 431, 433. **Map** p310 B9
Conveniently located among the cafés, bookshops and restaurants that line Glebe Point Road, this

ESSENTIAL INFORMATION

Vibe Rushcutters. *See p275.*

converted century-old mansion is a good Inner West option for those on a budget. The spacious lounge-diner sports a smart stone floor and rattan furnishings, and the very large commercial-grade kitchen is for guests to use (no meals are provided). There are dorms; simple single, double and family rooms; plus a Japanese-style twin room with low beds and tatami mats. Some of the rooms come with private bathrooms but note that none of them have air-conditioning or an in-room phone.

NEWTOWN
Budget

Australian Sunrise Lodge
485 King Street, Newtown, NSW 2042 (9550 4999, www.australiansunriselodge.com). Newtown rail. **Map** p316.
This friendly, family-run inn is cosy and surprisingly quiet, given its location on King Street – Newtown's main drag. Guest rooms have a TV, fridge, microwave, tea and coffee facilities, and kitchen utensils. Some have balconies overlooking a courtyard and are en suite, but none have a telephone or air-con (though there are ceiling fans). The lodge is recommended by Sydney University for off-campus accommodation, so expect a studenty vibe.

Billabong Gardens
5-11 Egan Street, Newtown, NSW 2042 (9550 3236, www.billabonggardens.com.au). Newtown rail. **Map** p316.
Bohemian, bright and arty, the decor at this Newtown hostel-motel is a patchwork of bright colours, exposed brick and crazy patterns. Set just outside the bustling environs of King Street, it attracts artists and musos, even offering special deals for visiting bands, including space to store their equipment. The place is clean and all rooms have ceiling fans and Wi-Fi. Some rooms have TVs and fridges, but note that none of them have air-conditioning. Other pluses include a large modern kitchen, laundry, solar-heated pool, TV room and a lovely, leafy courtyard. Staff are extremely friendly and more than willing to help guests with everything from organising tours to finding work on an organic farm via the World Wide Opportunities on Organic Farms association.

North Shore
Expensive

Rydges North Sydney
54 McLaren Street, North Sydney, NSW 2060 (1300 857 922, 9922 1311, www.rydges.com). North Sydney rail or Miller Street buses.
North Sydney, with all its office towers and corporate headquarters, means business. So it's no surprise that the Rydges caters mostly to business travellers.

All rooms have a private bath and shower, and many of the deluxe rooms and suites have beautiful views over the harbour. There are also 18 'iRooms' with a computer and unlimited internet access, as well as executive boardrooms, video-conferencing facilities and even a conference concierge service. The hotel has spent millions of dollars on its back-friendly 'dream beds', so at least there's a good night's kip to look forward to after a hard day at the office.

Budget

Glenferrie Lodge
12A Carabella Street, Kirribilli, NSW 2061 (9955 1685, www.glenferrielodge.com). Kirribilli ferry. **Map** p309 H1.
A swish, three-star, harbourfront B&B just seven minutes by ferry from Circular Quay, this pretty, rambling house boasts spotless facilities and ample bathrooms. Air-conditioning may not be installed in the guest rooms, but there are ceiling fans and there's a lovely harbour breeze to ensure that the nights never get too stuffy. The lounge offers cable TV and Wi-Fi, and the dining room serves dinner five nights a week. The pet-friendly policy means critters can come too.

Northern Beaches
Deluxe

Jonah's
69 Bynya Road, Palm Beach, NSW 2108 (9974 5599, www.jonahs.com.au). Palm Beach ferry.
You'll have a whale of a time at Jonah's – provided, that is, you can afford room rates that verge on the leviathan. All of the dozen suites (including the particularly luxurious penthouse) are plushly furnished in contemporary style and have stunning views over Whale Beach from their private balconies. King-sized beds, limestone bathrooms with whirlpool spas and Bulgari toiletries are just some of the pampering touches you can expect. Friday and Saturday rates include the unmissable dinner and breakfast at the renowned restaurant, and if you really want to put the rubber stamp of luxury on the whole experience, why not skip the car journey and fly up by seaplane from Rose Bay?

Expensive

Novotel Sydney Manly Pacific
55 North Steyne, Manly, NSW 2095 (9977 7666, www.accorhotels.com.au). Manly ferry. **Map** p316.
This large hotel overlooking Manly Beach has 213 guest rooms, all decorated in typical contemporary hotel style, many with beach views. A heated outdoor rooftop pool, plus fitness centre, sauna and spa ensure that guests get plenty of opportunities to burn off any of the calories they might have gained at the hotel's restaurant, Zali's, which

provides an upmarket café menu in the evenings and a Mediterranean buffet on Saturday evening and for Sunday lunch. Alternatively, the Corso, Manly's pedestrian shopping and café strip, is within easy walking distance, and central Sydney is only a half-hour ferry ride away.

Moderate

Barrenjoey House
1108 Barrenjoey Road, Palm Beach, NSW 2108 (9974 4001, www.barrenjoeyhouse.com.au). Palm Beach ferry.
The atmosphere at the Barrenjoey is relaxed and beachy, with white-painted walls, white furniture and the odd touch of rattan or bamboo, all punctuated by colourful sprays of fresh-cut flowers. A guesthouse since 1923, it has three en suite rooms and four with shared bathrooms – all are spotless and comfortable. The front rooms are best, as they overlook sparkling Pittwater. The café-restaurant, with its convivial terrace in summer and roaring fire in colder months, is a popular meeting spot. Unsurprisingly, given the decor of the hotel, the restaurant's speciality is seafood.

Newport Arms Hotel
Corner of Beaconsfield & Kalinya Streets, Newport, NSW 2106 (9997 4900, www.newportarms.com.au). Newport ferry or bus 188, 190, L88.
The Newport Arms is a firm favourite with local families for its child-friendly restaurant and playgrounds. On the shores of Pittwater, which is about a 40-minute drive from the CBD or 15 minutes from Palm Beach, the Newport is close, but thankfully not too close, to the action. There are eight doubles, all with basic furniture and private bathrooms, and one family room that sleeps six. The hotel also houses a very popular pub, with cheap drinks and live music. The waterfront beer garden features the Garden Bistro, two bars and an all-weather dining area.

Budget

Pittwater YHA
Morning Bay, Pittwater, NSW 2105 (9999 5748, www.yha.com.au). Halls ferry then 15min walk.
If you're looking for a real Australian bush experience within the city limits, then head here. Overlooking pretty Morning Bay, this stone-and-wood hillside lodge is hidden in the trees in Ku-ring-gai Chase National Park. You can't get here by car, but it's worth the arduous journey – an hour's bus to Church Point, a ferry to Halls wharf, then a steep, 15-minute climb through the bush – because the wildlife all around is breathtaking. Red and green rosellas, laughing kookaburras, wallabies, possums and goannas are just a few of the native Aussie animals you're likely to spot here. Guests can hire canoes and kayaks or swim in the bay, and there are women-only massage workshops once

BLINGPACKERS
A new breed of traveller.

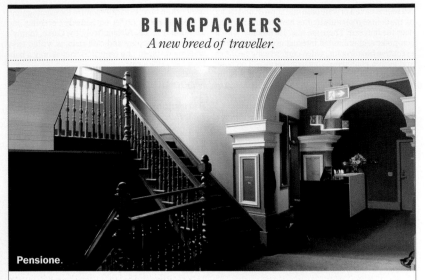

Pensione.

They wear designer shades and smart jeans, and they wouldn't be seen dead with a koala hanging off their backpack: meet the blingpackers, a growing tribe of urban travellers who are shaping the future of the budget hotel industry in the Emerald City. The 'BPs', as they're known to the hostels and boutique hotels who are falling over themselves to win their custom, are an eclectic group. More than just your average gap-year backpacker, BPs are twenty- and thirtysomethings taking a career sabbatical, couples with children who want to put a 'travelling' spin on the school hols, new partners cementing their relationship with a few months on the road... the list goes on. And in response to this new breed of tourist comes a new kind of low-rent but high-design accommodation. Exit bed bugs, rickety towering bunks, swirly carpets and bobbly blankets; enter slick, spotless hostels jostling for design kudos, with modern furniture, up-to-the-minute bathrooms, kitchens, plush pillows, freshly ground coffee and perfectly mixed cocktails. To name a few names: **Pensione** (*see 271*), **Railway Square YHA** (*see 272*), **wake up!** (*see p272*), **Billabong Gardens** (*see p278*) or **Y Hotel City South** (*see p274*).

or twice a year. It's BYO food (there are no shops) and bedlinen, or you can hire the latter subject to water availability; no sleeping bags are allowed. It's incredibly popular, so advance bookings are essential. There are also kitchen and laundry facilities and, of course, a barbie.

Sydney Beachhouse YHA
4 Collaroy Street, Collaroy, NSW 2097 (9981 1177, www.yha.com.au). Bus 151, 183, 184, 185, E83, E84, E85, E86, E87, E88, E99, L85, L90.
Who needs the glamour and glitz of Palm Beach when Collaroy's got charm to burn and much, much lower prices? This YHA hostel is one of the best budget options in the northern beaches, with bright, clean rooms and plenty of extras (check out the hilarious inflatable surf machine). There are four-person dormitories, twins and family rooms;

free surfboards, boogie boards and bicycles to borrow; and a compact, solar-heated outdoor pool. Other facilities include a kitchen, a barbecue area, arcade games, pool table and internet café.

The South
Expensive

Novotel Brighton Beach
Corner of Grand Parade & Princess Street, Brighton-le-Sands, NSW 2216 (1300 656 565, 9556 5111, www.novotelbrightonbeach.com.au).
The family-friendly Novotel Brighton Beach is full of extras that help to make up for its rather uninspiring decor: an overhead walkway to the beach; a pool with outdoor slide for the kiddies; tennis court,

fitness centre and a spa offering all the usual treatments. The Baygarden restaurant, on the third floor with a swanky terrace, has views over the bay and serves modern Australian cuisine; the cocktail bar also has a fine view. The hotel is five minutes from Sydney International Airport (25 minutes from the CBD), making it a convenient option for stopover travellers. All rooms have private bathrooms and balconies with views inland or over Botany Bay.

Rydges Cronulla
20-26 Kingsway, Cronulla, NSW 2230 (1300 857 922, 9527 3100, www.rydges.com). Bus 967, 987.
Overlooking Cronulla Beach and the picturesque sweep of Gunnamatta Bay, this mid-range option is good for the naturalist, being close to the great bushwalking trails and wildlife of Royal National Park. All rooms have en suite bathrooms and at least one balcony, plus a desk and TV. Other facilities include a pool, sauna, spa and beauty salon.

Serviced apartments

Somewhere between a hotel suite and a rented apartment, these used to be strictly the domain of the business traveller. But no more. These days, many holidaymakers can't get enough of the comforts of home – more space, more flexibility, in-built kitchens and other conveniences, such as washing machines.

Adina Apartment Hotel Sydney Central
2 Lee Street, Haymarket, NSW 2000 (8396 9800, www.tfehotels.com). Central rail or light rail. **Map** p311 E9.
Choose from one- and two-bed apartments, lofts and studios, most with full kitchens, housed in the Parcel Post building. There's a grocery delivery service and a bar and café. Laundry facilities too.

Apartment One
297 Liverpool Street, Darlinghurst, NSW 2010 (9331 2881, www.contemporaryhotels.com.au). Bus 389 or Oxford Street buses. **Map** p311 H8.
This gloriously hip two-level apartment is part of the Contemporary Hotels group. There are three outdoor terraces and lovely designer touches everywhere you look. Long-stay rates are available.

Harbourside Apartments
2A Henry Lawson Avenue, McMahons Point, North Shore, NSW 2060 (9963 4300, www. harboursideapartments.com.au). McMahons Point ferry. **Map** p309 E1.
The Harbourside's sweeping views of the Bridge and Opera House are fantastic (so make sure to ask for an apartment overlooking the water). The apartments have white walls, modern furniture and fully equipped kitchens.

Mantra 2 Bond Street
Corner of George & Bond Streets, CBD, NSW 2000 (1800 222 226, 9250 9555, www. mantra2bondstreet.com.au). Wynyard rail. **Map** p309 F5.
Located in the heart of the financial district, these apartments have full business services and well-equipped kitchens. There are three penthouses and a small rooftop pool.

Meriton World Tower
World Tower, 91-95 Liverpool Street, CBD, NSW 2000 (1800 214 822, 8263 7500, www. meritonapartments.com.au). Central rail or light rail, or Town Hall rail. **Map** p311 E/F8.
World Tower, part of the new World Square development, is the tallest residential building in the city. Studios and one-bed apartments are on levels 18-36, and two- and three-bed apartments on levels 62-74; the higher you go, the better the views.

Pullman Quay Grand Suites Sydney
61 Macquarie Street, Circular Quay, NSW 2000 (9256 4000, www.accorhotels.com.au). Circular Quay rail or ferry. **Map** p309 G4.
Near the Opera House, this five-star complex of one and two-bedroom apartments delivers the goods – spacious suites (twice the usual size) with balconies and views over the harbour, en suite bathrooms, well-equipped kitchens, two TVs and plenty more.

Regents Court Hotel
18 Springfield Avenue, Potts Point, NSW 2011 (9358 1533, www.regentscourt.com.au). Kings Cross rail. **Map** p312 J7.
This swish complex of studio suites is favoured by film and arty types. The rooftop terrace has great skyline views and there's free tea, coffee and biscotti at reception.

Seasons Darling Harbour
Corner of Harbour & Goulburn Streets, Darling Harbour, NSW 2000 (1800 888 116, www.kingparkhotels.com). Central rail or light rail, or Paddy's Markets light rail. **Map** 311 E8.
The immediate location may not be very inspiring, but this apartment block is conveniently sandwiched between Darling Harbour and Chinatown. The complex includes two restaurants, a nightclub and karaoke bar, an outdoor pool and a volcano-shaped jacuzzi.

Wyndham Sydney
Corner of Wentworth Avenue & Goulburn Street, Surry Hills, NSW 2000 (9277 3388, www.wyndhamap.com). Museum rail. **Map** p311 F8.
Apartments here range from studios to units with two bedrooms; all are well equipped and furnished in smart contemporary style. Wyndham is situated just south of Hyde Park.

Getting Around

ESSENTIAL INFORMATION

ARRIVING & LEAVING

By air

Sydney Airport (9667 9111, www.sydneyairport.com.au) is on the northern shoreline of Botany Bay, nine kilometres south-east of the city centre. Opened in 1920, it's one of the oldest continuously operating airports in the world. Since a swanky upgrade for the 2000 Olympics and another upgrade of the domestic terminal in 2005, it's now among the world's best – and quite proud of it.

There are three terminals: T1 is for all international flights on all airlines and for QF (Qantas) flights 001-399; T2 is a domestic terminal for Tiger, Virgin Australia, Regional Express and Jetstar (over 12 million passengers pass through T2 every year and a $20-million upgrade was recently completed); T3 is the Qantas terminal for QF domestic flights 400-1599 and QantasLink flights 1600 and above.

The international terminal is a great place to shop, with more than 120 outlets ranging from ordinary duty-free shops and international designer stores to Aussie gear such as Sportscraft, Ripcurl, UGG and RM Williams, plus souvenir outlets selling Aboriginal artefacts and kitsch mementos. There are also more than 40 food and beverage outlets.

To and from the airport

Built for the Olympics, the **Airport Link** (13 1500, www.airportlink.com.au) is an efficient **rail** service between Sydney Airport and Central Station. The line is a spur of the green Sydney Trains line, so serves all the main inner-city interchanges.

It takes ten minutes to reach Central Station from the domestic terminals and 12 minutes from international terminal T1. Trains run from T1 4.56am-12.54am Monday to Friday, and 5.06am-12.42am Saturday and Sunday. On weekdays, there are approximately six to eight services every hour from 6am to 10pm, and then four per hour until the last train. On weekends and public holidays there are four services per hour. A single fare from T1 to Central Station is $17.80 ($14 reductions); from the domestic terminals it's $17 ($13.60 reductions).

Tickets to airport stations are also available from any Sydney Trains

station. Return tickets allow you to travel to and return from one destination only. You have until 4am the next day to complete your journey. A station access fee applies at International Airport and Domestic Airport stations. If your ticket shows International Airport or Domestic Airport as the origin or destination, the access fee is included in the cost of the ticket. If your ticket does not include the access fee, simply buy a GatePass ($13, $11.60 reductions) when you exit at the airport stations.

The **KST Sydney Airporter** (9666 9988, www.kst.com.au) **shuttle bus** runs a door-to-door service to all hotels, major apartment blocks and backpacker joints in the city, Darling Harbour and Kings Cross. A single costs $15 ($28 return). Look for the white buses with a blue and red logo at the Meeting Point outside T1 and at the Horseshoe outside both T2 and T3. Book three hours in advance for hotel pick-ups and give yourself plenty of time to get to the airport, as the shuttle will take twice as long as a taxi.

Each terminal has its own sheltered **taxi** rank, with supervisors in peak hours to ensure a smooth and hassle-free flow of taxis. You never have to wait for long, even in the vast sheep-pen-style queuing system of the international terminal, where 190 vehicles are on call. If you have any special needs – wheelchair access, child seats or an extra-large vehicle – go to the front of the queue and tell the supervisor, who will call you a specially fitted taxi. It takes about 25 minutes to get into the city, depending on the traffic and time of day, and costs around $50.

The main car rental companies (*see p285*) all have desks at the airport.

Airlines

Around 40 airlines operate regular internationa flights into Sydney, including:

Air Canada
www.aircanada.com.
Air New Zealand
www.airnewzealand.com.au.
British Airways
www.britishairways.com.
Cathay Pacific Airways
www.cathaypacific.com.
Emirates
www.emirates.com.

Garuda Indonesia
www.garudaindonesia.com.
Japan Airlines
www.jal.com.
Malaysia Airlines
www.malaysiaairlines.com.
Qantas Airways
www.qantas.com.au.
Singapore Airlines
www.singaporeair.com.
Thai Airways International
www.thaiairways.com.
United Airlines
www.united.com.
Virgin Atlantic Airways
www.virgin-atlantic.com.

The following airlines operate domestic flights.
Jetstar Airways
www.jetstar.com.au.
Qantas
www.qantas.com.au.
Regional Express (Rex)
www.rex.com.au.
Tiger Air
www.tigerair.com.au.

By bus

Lots of bus companies operate throughout Australia; they all use the **Sydney Coach Terminal** located in **Central Station** as their main pick-up and drop-off point. **Greyhound** (1300 473 946, from abroad +617 4690 9850, www.greyhound.com.au) is one of the largest operators.

By rail

The State Rail Authority's **NSW TrainLink** (reservations 13 2232, www.nswtrainlink.info) operates out of Central Station with extensive user-friendly services to all main NSW and interstate destinations.

By sea

International cruise liners, including the *QE2*, dock at the **Overseas International Passenger Terminal** located on the west side of Circular Quay, or in Darling Harbour.

PUBLIC TRANSPORT

To get around Sydney, you'll probably use a combination of trains, ferries, buses and maybe the light rail. As well as the Sydney Buses network (run by the State Transit Authority, STA), there are Sydney Trains and Sydney Ferries. Other transport services, such as the Manly Fast Ferry, are privately run and therefore generally more expensive. The centre of Sydney is so small that, if you're in a large group, it's often cheaper to pool your money for a taxi. Look for Sydney's new (and clearly marked) network of bike lanes if you're on two wheels (see p286).

Transport Infoline

13 1500, www.transportnsw.info. **Open** Phone enquiries 6am-10pm daily.

A great, consumer-friendly phone line and website offering timetable, ticket and fare information for STA buses, Sydney Ferries and Sydney Trains, plus timetables (only) for cross-city private bus services.

Fares & tickets

There are several combination travel passes covering the government-run transit system, and they're worth buying if you plan to use public transport extensively. A fare structure called MyZone has made travelling on Sydney public transport much easier. MyZone tickets are accepted on the entire Sydney Trains, State Transit and Sydney Ferries network, as well as private bus services and some private ferries too.

MyMulti 1, 2 & 3

MyMulti tickets give you unlimited travel in one of three zones and unlimited bus and ferry travel across Greater Sydney. These tickets are available in weekly, monthly, quarterly or annual versions. To find the right MyMulti ticket for you, check www.sydneytrains.info or ask at any train station or bus information kiosk (where you can also buy them). Newsagents displaying a 'MyMulti Ticket Stop' sign, and ticket offices or vending machines at Circular Quay and Manly that also sell passes.

Note that these passes cannot be used on the STA premium Sydney Explorer and Bondi Explorer bus services, Sydney Ferry harbour cruises, JetCats or private buses.

MyMulti Day Pass

Perfect for one-day shopping binges or exploring Sydney's tourist attractions, the MyMulti Day Pass is an all-in-one ticket that gives you unlimited travel on buses, ferries, light rail and trains throughout Greater Sydney until 4am; excluded

from the ticket are some event buses, charter services, the Manly Fast Ferry and other private ferry services, and the NSW TrainLink Regional trains and coaches. It costs $24 ($12 reductions) and is available from station ticket offices, vending machines, Sydney Buses Transport Shops, Sydney Ferries ticket offices and other ticket outlets (including many newsagents and convenience stores).

Opal Card

This tap on/off card allows you to use all modes of public transport across Sydney, the Blue Mountains, the Central Coast, the Hunter Valley, Illawarra and the Southern Highlands. With this card, you only pay for the services you use on trains, buses, ferries and light rail. The smartcard ticket automatically deducts the correct fare for your journey as long as you tap on at your starting station and tap off once you reach your destination. (You will hear a ping if you've done it correctly.) Opal fares work out to be cheaper than traditional paper tickets, with a 30 per cent discount on off-peak travel on train services and a $2.50 cap on Sundays. Peak periods are 7-9am and 4-6.30pm on weekdays on Sydney Trains, and 6-8am and 4-6.30pm on weekdays on NSW TrainLink Intercity services.

Opal cards can be purchased at retailers across the city (newsagents, newsstands and convenience stores are your best bet). You can also order one online (www.opal.com.au) or by calling 13 6725. Your balance is displayed every time you tap on/off so you'll know when you are running low. To top up, visit an Opal retailer or use the machines at transport stations across the Sydney metropolitan area, including City Circle, Circular Quay and Sydney Airport stations. You can also set up an automated top-up service online if you plan to stay in the city for a while.

Rail

Sydney Trains (www.sydney trains.info) is the passenger rail service covering the greater Sydney metropolitan region (and the sister company to NSW TrainLink, which covers country and long-distance routes within NSW). The sleek, double-decker silver trains run underground on the central City Circle loop – Central, Town Hall, Wynyard, Circular Quay, St James and Museum stations – and overground to the suburbs (both Central and Town Hall stations

provide connections to all the suburban lines).

Trains are certainly quicker than the bus and are quite frequent, though a 15-minute wait is not uncommon during off-peak periods. For one of the best rides in Sydney, take the train from the city to the north shore – it crosses the Harbour Bridge and the views are spectacular. Tickets can be bought at ticket offices or vending machines at rail stations. Expect huge queues in rush hour and higher prices. A single ticket anywhere on the City Circle costs $3.30 ($1.60 reductions); an off-peak return costs $4.40 ($2.20 reductions). For more details of Sydney Trains services, call the Transport Infoline (see p282) or visit www.sydneytrains.info. For a map of the Sydney Trains city network, see p320.

Ferries

No trip to Sydney would be complete without clambering aboard one of the picture-postcard green-and-yellow ferries that ply the harbour and are used daily by hundreds of commuters. They're not only cute, they're useful, too. All ferries depart from Circular Quay ferry terminal, where Sydney Ferries operates from wharves 2 to 5. These stately vessels are a great way to explore the harbour: there's plenty of room to take pictures from the outdoor decks or just to sit in the sun and enjoy the ride.

Ticket prices vary, but a single from Circular Quay to destinations within the Inner Harbour (under 9km) costs $6.20 ($3.10 reductions); it's $7.60 ($3.80 reductions) for trips beyond 9km. Tickets are sold at ticket offices and vending machines at Circular Quay and Manly. Tickets for Inner Harbour services can also be purchased on board. For a map of the ferry system, see p319.

Sydney Ferries Information Centre

Opposite Wharf 4, Circular Quay (13 1500, www.sydneyferries.info). Circular Quay rail or ferry. **Open** 6.45am-6.15pm Mon-Sat; 7.15am-6.15pm Sun. **Map** p327 F4.

Light rail

Having once run the biggest and most successful (and sustainable) tram service in the world, Sydney finally caved to public demand and welcomed back its streetcars in 1997.

Currently, there is a 23-station service from Central Station via

ESSENTIAL INFORMATION

Darling Harbour, Pyrmont and the Star casino to the Inner West, ending at Dulwich Hill. It's useful for visiting Darling Harbour, Paddy's Markets, Sydney Fish Market, Glebe and the Powerhouse Museum. Extensions to the system are planned.

Trams today operate 24 hours a day, seven days a week, between Central and the Star stations, and from 6am to 11pm Monday to Thursday and Sunday, 6am to midnight Friday and Saturday, from Central all the way out to Lilyfield in the west. Trams run about every ten to 15 minutes from 6am to 11pm, and every 30 minutes outside these hours. A single journey on an Opal Card costs $2.10. There are touch-on and touch-off points at every station. Tickets are also available from Central Station or on board the train.

Buses

Buses are slow but fairly frequent, and offer a better way of seeing the city than the Sydney Trains, which operate underground within the centre. Buses are the only option for transport to popular areas such as Bondi Beach, Coogee and the northern beaches (beyond Manly), which aren't served by either train or ferry. Sydney is divided into sections, with each section equivalent to 1.6km. Sections are marked on all route maps and are shown on some bus stop signs.

The minimum adult fare is $2.40 ($1.20 reductions) for one to two sections, and the maximum is $4.70 ($2.30 reductions) for six or more sections. The bus driver will not stop unless you hold out your arm to request a ride. If you're in the suburbs, you'll probably be able to pay the driver in small change (big notes=big grimace). If you have a MyMulti pass, validate it in the green machines at the door.

The bus route numbers give you an idea of where they go. Buses 131-193 service Manly and the northern beaches; 200-296 the lower north shore (including Taronga Zoo) and the northern suburbs; 300-400 the Eastern Suburbs (including Bondi, Paddington, Darlinghurst and Sydney Airport); 401-500 the Inner South and Inner West suburbs, including Balmain, Leichhardt, Newtown and Homebush; and 501-629 the north-west, including Parramatta and Chatswood. In general, the 100s and 200s start near Wynyard Station and the 300s-600s can be found around Circular Quay.

Bus numbers starting with an 'X' are express services, which travel between the suburbs and major centres on the way into the city. Stops are marked 'Express'. Limited-stop or 'L' services operate on some of the longer routes to provide faster trips to and from the city (mainly for commuters). Buses in the central and inner suburbs run pretty much all night, but services from central Sydney to the northern beaches stop from around midnight until 4.30am.

'Nightride' buses operate hourly services to outer suburban train stations after the trains have stopped; they run until 5am and cost $3.80 ($1.90 reductions) for up to five sections and $4.70 ($2.30 reductions) for six or more sections.

The tourist-oriented **Sydney & Bondi Explorer** bus service (www.australianexplorer.com.au) is Sydney's only hop-on hop-off service. It takes in all of the city's major tourist destinations, including Darling Harbour, the Rocks, Chinatown, Kings Cross, Paddington, Bondi Beach and Rose Bay.

TAXIS

It's quite easy to flag down a taxi in Sydney and there are many taxi ranks in the city centre, including ones at Central, Wynyard and Circular Quay. Restaurant and bar staff will also call a taxi for you. A yellow light indicates the cab is free, and it's common to travel in the front passenger seat alongside the driver. Drivers will often ask which of two routes you want to follow, or if you mind if they take a longer route to avoid traffic. But there are drivers who don't know where they're going and will stop to check the map; if this happens, make sure they turn off the meter. Tipping is not expected, but passengers sometimes round up the bill and, for all the griping about Sydney cabbies that goes on, they are among the few taxi drivers in the world who'll round down fares for convenience sake. The standard fare is $2.19 per kilometre from 6am to 10pm (add an extra $0.44 per km from 10pm to 6am), plus a $3.60 hiring fee and, if relevant, a $2.50 telephone or network booking fee. If a cab takes you across the Bridge, the maximum $4 toll (less during off-peak hours) will be added to the fare, even if you travelled via the toll-free northbound route. If you've left something behind in a cab, *see p290.*

Taxi companies

Legion Cabs
13 1451, www.legioncabs.com.au.

Premier Cabs
13 1017, www.premiercabs.com.au.
RSL Cabs
9581 1111, www.rslcabs.com.au.
St George Cabs
13 2166, www.stgeorgecabs.com.au.
Silver Service Taxis
13 3100, www.silverservice.com.au.
Sydney's popular luxury taxi service; amazingly, the same price as a regular taxi, but often hard to book.
Taxis Combined Services
133 300, www.taxiscombined.com.au.
Zero200
8332 0200, www.zero200.com.au.
A wheelchair-accessible taxi service.

Taxi apps

GoCatch

GoCatch sticks to taxi bookings and claims to have the most registered drivers of any app in the country. You can see your cab approaching through the app and, unlike Uber, you can opt to pay with cash or via a PayPal account. Booking fee is $2.50, with a 5% credit card surcharge. Free download from iTunes and Google Play.

InGoGo

Another good option in a pinch, InGoGo allows for advanced taxi bookings, shows the taxi approaching via the app, and appears to have plenty of drivers. Another plus is that there's no fee hike during busy periods. Advanced bookings incur a fee of $2, with a surcharge of 5% on card payments. Free download from iTunes and Google Play.

Uber

Hail a nearby cab or try the UberX option, which gets you a private driver at roughly 30 per cent less than the cost of a regular cab. Pickups are quick and reliable, payments are cashless and pricing is clearly outlined, with fare splitting as an option. Beware of 'surge pricing' though – at times of high demand, Uber raises fees. Booking fee is $2 with a 5% Uber service fee. Free download from iTunes and Google Play.

Water taxis

These are great fun, but expensive. The cost usually depends on the time of day and the number of passengers, but the fare for two from Circular Quay to Doyles fish restaurant at Watsons Bay, which takes ten to 12 minutes, is anywhere from $100 to $150. The outfits below accept all major credit cards, and can be chartered for harbour cruises.

Beach Hopper Water Taxis
0412 400 990, 1300 306 676.
If you want to be dropped off at a beach – literally on to the sand – call Sydney's only beach-landing water-taxi service. It also operates a summer Beach Safari service: for $35 per person per day, you can hop on and off at any number of harbour beaches on its run.

Water Taxis Combined
9555 8888, www.watertaxis.com.au.
This company can pick you up from almost any wharf, jetty or pontoon, provided there is enough water depth, and, in the case of private property, there is permission from the owner. The limousine taxis take up to 21 passengers.

Yellow Water Taxis
1300 138 840, www.
yellowwatertaxis.com.au.
Claiming to be 'Australia's most experienced water taxi operator', Yellow offers instant quotes online and guarantees cheaper prices than its competitors (it will beat any rival written quote if challenged). Its standard craft can carry up to 16 passengers but the 'maxi-taxi' carries 28.

DRIVING

Driving in Sydney can be hair-raising, not so much because of congestion (Sydneysiders may complain, but it's not that bad for a major city), but primarily because of the fast and furious attitude of locals – this is not a city known for its patient drivers.

Under Australian law, most visitors can drive for as long as they like on their domestic driving licence without the need for any additional authorisation. A resident must apply for an Australian driving licence after three months, which involves a written test. You must always carry your driving licence and your passport when in charge of a vehicle; if the licence is not in English, you need to take an English translation as well as the original licence.

Driving is on the left. The general speed limit in cities and towns is 60kph (38mph), but many local and suburban roads have a 50kph (30mph) limit. A 40kph speed limit was introduced in the CBD and other parts of Sydney with a high level of pedestrians. However, note that the main thoroughfare of George Street in the CBD is currently closed for construction of the light rail extensions.

The maximum speed on highways is 100kph (60mph), and 110kph (70mph) on motorways and freeways. Speed cameras are numerous and there are heavy penalties for speeding.

The legal blood alcohol limit is 0.05 per cent for experienced drivers, zero for provisional or learner drivers. Seat belts are mandatory and baby capsules or child seats must be used for all children.

Car hire

Most of the major car rental firms are situated on William Street in Kings Cross, and also have outlets at Sydney Airport. Rates vary almost hourly and all offer discounted deals. What's given below is the rate for the cheapest hire car available for a one-day period quoted on a given day. Rates drop if the car is hired for a longer period. Those offering ultra-cheap deals should be approached with caution, though: always read the small print before you sign.

You will need to show a current driver's licence and probably your passport to hire a car. Credit cards are the preferred method of payment and are nearly always asked for to cover insurance costs. A few firms will rent to 18-year-olds, but usually you have to be over 21 and hold a full driving licence to rent a car in New South Wales. If you're under 25, you'll probably have to pay an extra daily surcharge, and insurance excesses will be higher.

Avis
200 William Street, Kings Cross
(9246 4600, www.avis.com.au).
Kings Cross rail. **Open** 7.30am-6pm daily. **Map** p312 H7.
Other locations Sydney Airport (8374 2847).

Budget
93 William Street, Kings Cross
(8255 9600, www.budget.com.au).
Kings Cross rail. **Open** 7-30am-5.45pm daily. **Map** 312 H7.
Other location Sydney Airport (9207 9165).

Hertz
65 William Street, Kings Cross
(9360 6621, www.hertz.com.au).
Kings Cross rail. **Open** 7.30am-5.30pm Mon-Fri; 8am-1pm Sat, Sun. **Map** 312 H7.
Other locations Pyrmont (9518 8450); Sydney Airport (0413 768 464).

Red Spot
Hyde Park Plaza, 38 College Street
(9356 8333, www.redspot.com.au).

Museum rail. **Open** 8am-6pm Mon-Fri; 8am-2pm Sat. **Map** p311 G8.
Other location Sydney Airport (9352 7466).

Thrifty
85 William Street, Kings Cross
(8374 6177, www.thrifty.com.au).
Kings Cross rail. **Open** 7.30am-5.30pm Mon-Fri; 7.30am-4pm Sat, Sun. **Map** p312 H7.
Other location Sydney Airport (9582 1762).

Petrol stations

Petrol stations are fairly plentiful, and easy to find on main roads, although you won't find so many in central Sydney. Try www.motormouth.com.au to find the cheapest fuel in your neighbourhood.

Parking

In central Sydney, parking is a pain and best avoided if possible. In some suburbs, such as tree-lined Paddington, the quality of the road surface is poor, and narrow one-way streets with parking on both sides compound the problem. Then there's the hyper-vigilant parking inspectors ('brown bombers' to locals, on account of their quick descent and staid uniforms). Note that you must park in the same direction as the traffic on your side of the road and display tickets on your dashboard. Many street meters accept credit cards. Rates at city-centre car parks range from $16 to $23 for one hour, with $20 to $62 the day rate. Early Bird special rates often apply if you park before 9am and leave after 3.30pm. Look under 'Parking Stations' in the *Yellow Pages* (www.yellowpages.com.au) for more car parks.

Secure Parking
60 Elizabeth Street, CBD
(8912 4900, www.secure parking.com.au). **Open** 24hrs daily. **Map** p309 F5.
Other location 137 Castlereagh Street, 1 Martin Place, entrance on Pitt Street, CBD.

Wilson Parking – St Andrews House
464 Kent Street, CBD (1800 727 5464, www.wilsonparking.com.au).
Open 6am-midnight Mon-Thur, Sun; 6am-1am Fri. **Map** p311 E7.
Other locations CitiGroup Centre, 271 Pitt Street, CBD; St Martin's Tower, entrance on Clarence Street, CBD.

ESSENTIAL INFORMATION

Tolls

The toll for the Harbour Bridge and Tunnel varies between a maximum charge of $4 for cars heading south (free for northbound cars) at peak-hour and as low as $2.50 off-peak. The toll for the 'eastern distributor' is $6.48 for northbound cars travelling into the city, free for those heading out or south. The Cross-City Tunnel (www.crosscity.com.au), running west to east, opened in 2005 to ease congestion in the CBD, but has proved much less popular than expected because of the toll fees – exclusively electronic and still considered extortionate for a trip of just over two kilometres. The toll fee depends on the size of your vehicle; most pay $5.19 for the Eastbound Tunnel (Darling Harbour to Eastern Distributor Exit or Rushcutters Bay), the same for the Westbound Tunnel (Rushcutters Bay to Darling Harbour), and $2.45 for Sir John Young Crescent Exit (from the East). For vehicles with a height exceeding 2.8m, or length exceeding 12.5m, it's $10.38 (for Eastbound and Westbound) and $4.90 for Sir John Young Crescent.

CYCLING

Sydney's steep hills, narrow streets and chaotic CBD make cycling a challenge, even for the most experienced of cycle couriers. But, gradients aside, that's all changed as councils have introduced cycleways and exclusive bike lanes to the city centre and CBD fringe. Both Centennial Park and Manly offer safe cycle tracks and there's a fantastic junior track (replete with traffic lights) at Sydney Park in St Peters.

Helmets are compulsory for all cyclists in Sydney, including children carried as passengers. During the day, a bicycle must have at least one working brake and a bell or horn. At night, you'll need, in addition, a white light at the front and a red light at the rear, plus a red rear reflector. There are lots of other road rules, and you are well advised to respect them, as bicycles are considered to be vehicles, so rule-breaking incurs heavy fines. For full details, go to www.cityof sydney.nsw.gov.au/explore/getting-around/cycling or check out *Time Out*'s series of bicycle features at www.au.timeout.com/sydney.

Cycling enthusiasts are becoming increasingly vocal in Sydney, and with good reason – the Bike Plan network of arterial cycleways now spans over 200 kilometres

(125 miles) and is growing apace. It has been accompanied by a boom in hipster bike shops (many centred on the Clarence Street strip in the CBD). The City of Sydney provides cycleways maps for the Sydney metropolitan area and also free cycling courses with bike-maintenance classes and cycling in the city 'confidence sessions'. View what's available online at www.sydneycycleways.net or call 9265 9333.

Centennial Park Cycles

50 Clovelly Road, Randwick (9398 5027, www.cyclehire.com.au). Bus 339, X39. **Open** 8.30am-5pm daily. **Rates** *Mountain bikes* from $15/hr. *Children's bikes* from $10/hr. **Map** 315 N14.
Family-run, Sydney's largest cycle and in-line skate hire shop has been in operation for more than 30 years. They have it all here, from tandems to tag-alongs, pedal cars and scooters. Staff also provide a bicycle pick-up and delivery service. Credit card details and photo ID are required to hire equipment.

Manly Bike Tours

Shop 6, 54 West Esplanade, Manly (8005 7368, www.manlybike tours.com.au). Manly ferry. **Open** 9am-6pm daily. **Rates** *Hybrid bikes* $21/hr; $36/day. **Map** p316.
Located across from Manly Wharf, this company offers self-guided tours around Manly and the northern beaches area. The company provides a great range of bikes for adults and children. Hire also includes a helmet, lock, map and bar bag. Credit card details and photo ID are required to hire equipment.

WALKING

Walking is often the most practical – and enjoyable – way of getting around central areas, though there can be long waits at pedestrian lights. There are a number of marked scenic walks that you can follow: enquire at the **Sydney Visitor Centre** (*see p293*) for details or check out www.sydney.com/things-to-do/nature-and-parks/walks for a few ideas. For central Sydney street maps, *see pp308-316* and individual Explore chapters.

Resources A-Z

TRAVEL ADVICE

For up-to-date information on travel to a specific country – including the latest on safety and security, health issues, local laws and customs – contact your home country government's department of foreign affairs. Most have websites with useful advice for would-be travellers.

AUSTRALIA
www.smartraveller.gov.au

CANADA
www.voyage.gc.ca

NEW ZEALAND
www.safetravel.govt.nz

REPUBLIC OF IRELAND
foreignaffairs.gov.ie

UK
www.fco.gov.uk/travel

USA
www.state.gov/travel

ADDRESSES

Addresses begin with the apartment or unit number, if any, followed by the street number, followed by the street name. For example, Apartment 5, 50 Sun Street would be written as 5/50 Sun Street. This is followed by the locality and then by the state or territory and postcode – for instance, Paddington, NSW 2021. Postcodes cover a much larger area than their UK equivalents. Many residents and businesses have post office box numbers instead of personalised addresses.

AGE RESTRICTIONS

It is legal to buy and consume alcohol at 18. A learner's driving licence can be applied for at 16. A driving test can be taken at age 17, and if passed, drivers must then show a provisional 'P' plate (red P for one year, green P for two years), before being eligible for a full driving licence. Both gays and heterosexuals can have sex at 16 in NSW (though be warned, laws vary from state to state). It is illegal to sell cigarettes to under-18s, but there is no legal minimum age for smoking.

CONSUMER

The excellent and practical website of the **NSW Office of Fair Trading** offers advice for consumers on how to avoid 'shady characters, scams and rip-offs' and for businesses on how to do the right thing by their customers. The excellent **Traveller Consumer Helpline** (1300 552 001) provides a rapid response (including access to translators) for travellers who experience unfair employment schemes, problems with car rental or accommodation, faulty goods or overcharging.

NSW Office of Fair Trading
4-8 Woodville Street, Hurtsville (13 3220, www.fairtrading.nsw.gov.au).
Open 8.30am-5pm Mon-Fri.

CUSTOMS

Before landing on Australian soil, you will be given an immigration form to fill out, as well as customs and agriculture declaration forms. You will pass through either the Green (nothing to declare) channel or the Red (something to declare) channel. Your baggage may be examined by Customs, regardless of which channel you use. Anyone aged 18 years or over can bring in $900 worth of duty-free goods ($450 for under-18s), 2.25 litres of alcohol and 50 cigarettes or 50 grams of other tobacco products. You must declare amounts of more than $900. Visitors can bring items such as computers into Australia duty-free, provided Customs is satisfied that these items are intended to be taken away again on departure.

UK Customs & Excise (www.gov.uk/uk-border-control/overview) allows travellers aged 18 and over returning from outside the EU to bring home £390 worth of gifts and goods, 200 cigarettes or 250 grams of tobacco, and one litre of spirits or two litres of fortified wine.

US Customs (www.cbp.gov) allows Americans to return from trips to Australia with goods valued up to US$800.

Quarantine

You must declare all food, plant cuttings, seeds, nuts or anything made from wood, plant or animal material that you bring into Australia. This includes many souvenirs and airline food. If you don't, you could face an on-the-spot fine of $340, or prosecution and fines of more than $66,000. Sniffer dogs will hunt out the tiniest morsel as they roam the airport with their handlers.

Quarantine officers use high-tech X-ray machines to check your luggage. Quarantine bins are provided at the airport for you to ditch any food and plants you may have about you before you reach immigration. Check the website of the **Australian Quarantine & Inspection Service** (agriculture.gov.au) for details.

Australia also has quite strict laws prohibiting and restricting the export of native animals and plants, and items deemed 'moveable cultural heritage'. These include birds and their eggs, fish, reptiles, insects, plants, seeds, fossils and rock art. Products made from protected wildlife, such as hard corals and giant clam shells, are not allowed to be taken out of the country. If in doubt, check with the **Department of the Environment & Heritage** (6274 1111, www.deh.gov.au).

If you need to carry medicine for yourself in or out of the country, it is advisable to have a prescription or doctor's letter. Penalties for carrying illicit drugs in Australia are severe and could result in a jail term. Check the **Customs National Information Line** (1300 363 263, www.customs.gov.au).

DISABLED

It was not until 1992 that building regulations required that provision be made for disabled people, so some older venues do not have disabled access. Restaurants tend to be better, as most of them have ramps.

New transport standards will require that people with disabilities have access to most public transport

ESSENTIAL INFORMATION

ESSENTIAL INFORMATION

within 20 years. For the time being, many Sydney streets are far from wheelchair-friendly. Constant construction upheavals and the city's hills aside, the standard of pavement surfaces in the inner suburbs leaves a lot to be desired. Poor street lighting compounds the problem.

For more information, check out the excellent website of the **Disability Information Resource** (www.australia.gov.au/people/people-with-disability), which provides details on wheelchair access throughout the city, from music venues and restaurants to museums and public toilets. Or contact the following:

Information on Disability & Education Awareness Services (IDEAS)
(1800 029 904, 4226 1597, www. ideas.org.au). **Open** 8.30am-5pm Mon-Fri.
Provides information and referral on all disabilities for the whole of NSW and has a great, up-to-date database on Eastern Suburbs services.

Spinal Cord Injuries Australia
1800 819 775, www.scia.org.au.
This organisation provides consumer-based support and rehabilitation services to help people with physical disabilities participate fully in society. Phone/internet enquiries only.

State Library of NSW Disability Information
(9273 1414, www.sl.nsw.gov.au/using/disability/docs/slnsw_accessibility_guide. pdf). **Open** 9am-5pm Mon-Fri.
A helpful information line that offers a great starting point for disabled visitors.

DRUGS

Cannabis and harder drugs are illegal in Australia, but that hasn't prevented a significant drug culture – and problem – from developing. High-volume imports from Asia ensure cheap and dangerously pure strains of heroin arrive on the streets, while cannabis, ecstasy, cocaine and ice (crystal meth) are the chosen poisons of the city's youth.

Kings Cross is the epicentre of drug dealing in Sydney and has been the target of a clean-up campaign by the local government. The future of the 'shooting gallery' safe injection room in the area hangs in the balance, as nay-sayers and project supporters argue over its success rates. Still,

come nightfall it's not uncommon for addicts to shoot up on the streets, in the parks and even on beaches. Needle disposal bins are everywhere. For helplines, *see p289.*

ELECTRICITY

The Australian domestic electricity supply is 230-240V, 50Hz AC. UK appliances work with a basic plug adaptor, but US 110V appliances need a transformer as well. The plug is Australasia-specific.

EMBASSIES & CONSULATES

Consulate General of Canada
Level 5, Quay West Building, 111 Harrington Street, CBD (9364 3000, visa information 9364 3050, (www.canadainternational. gc.ca). Circular Quay rail or ferry. **Open** 8.30am- 4.30pm Mon-Fri. **Map** p309 E4.

Irish Consulate
Level 26, 1 Market Street, CBD (9264 9635, www.dfa.ie). Town Hall rail. **Open** *Phone enquiries* 2-4pm Mon-Fri. *In person* 10am-1pm Mon-Fri.* **Map** 309 E6.

New Zealand Consulate-General
Level 10, 55 Hunter Street, at Castlereagh Street, CBD (8256 2000, nzembassy.com). Martin Place or Wynyard rail. **Open** 9am-4pm Mon-Fri. **Map** p309 F5.

South African High Commission
Rhodes Place, State Circle, Canberra (6272 7300, www.sahc.org.au). **Open** 8.30am-1pm, 2-5pm Mon-Fri.

United Kingdom Consulate
Level 16, The Gateway, 1 Macquarie Place, at Bridge Street, CBD (9247 7521, united-kingdom.visahq.com. au). Circular Quay rail or ferry. **Open** *Phone* 9am-5pm Mon-Fri. *Counter* 10am-12.30pm, 1.30pm-4pm Mon- Fri. **Map** p309 F4.

Consulate General of the United States
Level 59, MLC Centre, 19-29 Martin Place, CBD (9373 9200, sydney. usconsulate.gov). Martin Place rail. **Open** *Phone Enquiries* 8am-5pm Mon-Fri. *In person* 8am-11.30am Mon-Fri. **Map** 309 F5.

EMERGENCIES

For the fire brigade, police or ambulance, dial **000**. It's a free call from any phone. From a mobile phone, call **112** – which allows

your location to be pinpointed. For hospitals, *see p289.* For helpline numbers, *see p289.* You can contact the Poisons Information Centre (open 24hrs daily) at 13 1126.

GAY & LESBIAN

The quickest way to find gay-related information is via the popular website *Same Same* (www.samesame.com.au), weekly newspaper *SX* (gaynewsnetwork. com.au), free monthly magazine *Star Observer* (www.starobserver. com.au) or, for women, the excellent monthly mag *Lesbians on the Loose* (www.lotl.com). The last three are available free at newsagents, clubs and bars all over town.

For the entertainment scene, *see pp190-199.*

Help & information

For information on STDs, HIV & AIDS, *see p289.*

Gay & Lesbian Counselling Service of NSW
8594 9596, www.glcnsw.org.au. **Open** 5.30-10.30pm daily.
Information and phone counselling.

Gay & Lesbian Tourism Australia
0418 834 588, www.galta.com.au.
A non-profit organisation dedicated to the welfare of gay and lesbian travellers in Australia.

HEALTH

The universal government health-care system, Medicare Australia, has a reciprocal agreement with Finland, Italy, Malta, the Netherlands, New Zealand, Norway, Republic of Ireland, Sweden and the UK, entitling residents of those countries to get necessary medical and hospital treatment for free. This agreement does not cover all eventualities (for example, ambulance fees or dental costs), and only applies to public hospitals and casualty departments.

If you have travel insurance, check the small print to see whether you need to register with Medicare before making a claim; if not, or if you don't have insurance, you can claim a Medicare rebate by taking your passport with visa, together with the medical bill, to any Medicare centre.

For more information, phone or write to the Medicare Information Service (*see p289*).

Medicare Information Service
*PO Box 9822, Sydney, NSW 2001
(13 2011, www.humanservices.
gov.au).* **Open** 9am-4.30pm
Mon-Fri.

Accident & emergency

In an emergency, call **000** for
an ambulance.

Prince of Wales Hospital
*Barker Street, Randwick (9650
4000). Bus 373, 374.*

Royal North Shore Hospital
*Reserve Road, St Leonards
(9926 7111). St Leonards rail.*

Royal Prince Alfred Hospital
*Missenden Road, Camperdown
(9515 6111). Bus 412.*

St Vincent's Public Hospital
*Corner of Burton & Victoria Streets,
Darlinghurst (8382 1111). Kings
Cross rail or bus 333, 378, 380.*
Map p312 H8.

Complementary medicine

Australian Natural Therapists Association
1800 817 577, www.anta.com.au.

Australian Traditional Medicine Society
*(12/27 Bank Street, Meadowbank,
8878 1500, www.atms.com.au).*

Contraception & abortion

FPA Health (Family Planning Association)
*Clinics & advice 1300 658
886, www.fpnsw.org.au.*
Open 9am-5.30pm Mon-Fri.

Marie Stopes International
*1800 003 707, www.mariestopes.
com.au.* **Open** 7am-8pm daily.

Dentists

Dental treatment is not covered by
Medicare, and therefore not by the
reciprocal agreement (*see p288*). In
the absence of medical insurance,
be prepared for hefty fees. Check
the Yellow Pages (www.yellowpages.
com.au) for listings, though it's
a good idea to ask locals or hotel
staff to recommend a dentist they
know and trust.

Doctors

For listings of doctors, see the *Yellow
Pages* (www.yellowpages.com.au)
under 'Medical Practitioners'. If your

home country is covered under
the reciprocal Medicare agreement,
and your visit is for immediately
necessary treatment, you can claim
a refund from Medicare. Try to get
to one of the increasingly rare 'bulk
billing' medical practices, where
your trip will be free. Otherwise,
you will only get back a proportion
of the fee, which must be claimed
in person.

Hospitals

Hospitals are listed in the White
Pages (www.whitepages.com.au)
under 'Health NSW'. For hospitals
with 24-hour emergency
departments, *see left* **Accident
& emergency**.

Pharmacies

Standard opening times for chemists
are 9am-5.30pm Monday to Friday,
9am-5.30pm Saturday, and 10am
to 5pm Sunday. Many convenience
stores and supermarkets stock over-
the-counter drugs.

Prescriptions

In Australia, prescription costs
vary depending on the drugs being
prescribed. On the Pharmaceutical
Benefits Scheme (PBS) you shouldn't
have to pay too much – but to get
the best price you must have a
Medicare card or temporary
Medicare card, available to visitors
from nations with a reciprocal
health-care agreement from any
Medicare office, with your passport
and visa.

STDs, HIV & AIDS

AIDS Council of NSW (ACON)
*414 Elizabeth Street, Surry Hills
(9206 2000, www.acon.org.au).
Museum rail.* **Open** 9am-6pm Mon-
Fri. **Map** p311 F10.
ACON offers information, advice
and support.

HIV/AIDS Information
9332 9700, thealbioncentre.org.au.
Open 8am-6pm Mon-Fri.
Statewide information service.

Sydney Sexual Health Centre
*Sydney Hospital, 8 Macquarie
Street, CBD (1800 451 624, 9382
7440). Martin Place rail.* **Open**
Phone enquiries 9.30am-6pm
Mon-Fri. *Clinic* 8.15am-5.45pm
Mon-Fri. **Map** p309 G5.
Government-funded clinic aimed at
young people at risk, gay men and
sex workers.

HELPLINES

Alcohol & Drug Information Service
1800 198 024, 9442 5000.
Open 24hrs daily.
Crisis counselling, information,
assessment and referrals.

Alcoholics Anonymous
*9387 7788, www.alcoholics
anonymous.org.au.* **Open** 24hrs
daily.
Manned by volunteers who are
recovering alcoholics.

Child Abuse Line
*13 2111, www.community.
nsw.gov.au.* **Open** 24hrs daily.
For immediate help, advice and
action involving children at risk.

Domestic Violence Line
1800 656 463. **Open** 24hrs daily.
Phone 000 if in immediate danger.
Otherwise, this service offers expert
counselling and advice.

Gamblers Counselling Service
*1800 858 858, www.gamblinghelp
online.org.au.* **Open** 24hrs daily.
A face-to-face counselling service
plus 24-hour telephone helpline.

Kids Helpline
1800 551 800, www.kidshelp.com.au.
Open 24hrs daily.
Confidential support for children
and young people aged five to 18.
Counsellors available by email or
for real-time web counselling.

Law Access
*1300 888 529, www.lawaccess.nsw.
gov.au.* **Open** 9am-5pm Mon-Fri.
Advice and information on all
legal issues.

Lifeline
13 1114. **Open** 24hrs daily.
Help for people in crisis.

Rape Crisis Centre
1800 424 017, 1800 737 732.
Open 24hrs daily.
Rape counselling over the phone.

Salvation Army Salvo Care Line
1300 224 636. **Open** 24hrs daily.
Help for anyone in crisis or
contemplating suicide.

LANGUAGE

Despite the country's history,
contemporary vernacular Australian
owes more to US English than the
UK variety, and the mongrel tongue
that has emerged from the hybrid is
'Strine'. Words that have a peculiarly

ESSENTIAL INFORMATION

Australian flavour include: arvo (afternoon); bludger (scrounger, as in 'dole bludger'); daggy (nerdy or goofy); daks (trousers); doona (duvet); dunny (lavatory/loo/toilet); and thongs (flip-flops, not G-strings); as spoken by sheilas (ladies) or blokes (gents). Take special care when talking about your roots ('root' means shag/bonk/sexual encounter while 'I'm rooted' can imply extreme weariness or a dire situation – more so than your ancestry or the streaks in your hair). You will probably hear 'G'day, mate' and 'Fair dinkum', but often said with a knowing wink. *See p246*, **How to Speak Convict: An A-Z**, for more bonza examples of Strine, each more beaut than the last.

LEFT LUGGAGE

There is baggage storage by Smarte Carte in **Sydney Airport** (call 9667 0926 for information).

LEGAL HELP

For consulates, *see p288*. For information on the Law Access helpline, *see p289*.

LOST PROPERTY

For belongings lost on public transport, try phoning 131 500 (for property lost on the bus) or 9379 3341 (for property lost on the train). You can also visit www.sydneybusses.info/lost-property if you've lost property on a city bus. If you've left something behind in a cab, phone the relevant taxi company. For property lost on the street, contact the police on 9281 0000. For items lost at the airport, phone 9667 9583 or contact the relevant airline directly.

MEDIA

Magazines

Time Out Sydney magazine has a great feel for the pulse of the city. It has excellent coverage of the food and drink scene, as well as entertainment listings. The magazine launched in 2007, with *Time Out Melbourne* following in 2010. *Time Out Sydney* comes out on the last Wednesday of the month and is sold in all major newsagents and many bookshops. Check out the website au.timeout. com/sydney and subscribe to one of the weekly or daily newsletters at au.timeout.com/sydney/newsletter.

Newspapers: dailies

Sydney has two local papers, the broadsheet *Sydney Morning Herald* (www.smh.com.au, owned by Fairfax) and the tabloid *Daily Telegraph* (www.dailytelegraph. com.au). The *SMH* is an institution with an ego to match. Local stories prevail, with solid coverage of politics and events, but beware the comment columns. *The Daily Telegraph* is a true tabloid, with plenty of scandal splashes and bitchy celebrity news in its 'Sydney Confidential' spread.

There is also a freebie newspaper, *MX* (www. mxnet.com.au), handed out at Sydney Trains stations from Monday to Friday.

The two national newspapers, the *Australian* (www.theaustralian. news.com.au) and the *Australian Financial Review* (afr.com), are both based in Sydney, and carry that bias in their coverage. The *Australian* has been trying to shake out its starchiness, but the result has been a rather bizarre mishmash of armchair trendiness and what could be called a kind of 'gentle conservatism'. The *Review* offers excellent news coverage, plus business and politics.

Newspapers: weekend

The Saturday *Sydney Morning Herald* is a vast publication, mainly due to a surfeit of classified advertisements. The Saturday *Telegraph* is not as thick, but still has its fair share of supplements. The *Australian* aspires to stylish minimalism, with a slick, svelte weekend broadsheet on Saturday, accompanied by a print-heavy magazine. On Sundays, there is Fairfax's tabloid *Sun-Herald*, designed to compete with the popular *Sunday Telegraph*.

Radio

AM stations
2BL (ABC) *702 AM*
The Australian Broadcasting Corporation's popular and 2nd largest (after 2GB) talk station features non-commercial, nonranting, reasonably intelligent banter and news.
2CH *1170 AM*
Easy, yawn, listening.
2KY *1017 AM*
Racing, racing and more racing.
2UE *954 AM*
The place for controversial talkback shows.

NewsRadio (ABC) *630 AM*
Rolling news service with strong international content and daytime coverage of parliament.
Radio National (ABC) *576 AM*
Intelligent, provocative talk shows, arts and current affairs.
Radio 2GB *873 AM*
Veteran talk show radio station that feeds off local whingeing, humorous tirades and chatty hosts.
SBS Radio *1107 AM*
Ethnic, multilingual programmes for Sydney's diverse communities.

FM stations
ABC Classic FM *92.9 FM*
Classical music for non-purists, and some cool jazz.
FBi *94.5 FM*
Take a side-step from the mainstream and discover the groovin' underground.
KIIS ((MIX)) *106.5 FM*
An all-day mix of hits
Nova *96.9 FM*
Young, brash and cheeky.
SBS Radio *97.7 FM*
Special-interest ethnic programming.
Triple J *105.7 FM (ABC)*
Well respected as the station most devoted to the discovery and spread of new music.
2DAY *104.1 FM*
A playful mixture of current chart hits and old-school throwbacks.
2000 FM *98.5 FM*
Ethnic specialist with community driven shows and a range of multilingual programming.
2MMM (Triple M) *104.9 FM*
Rock, ads and then more rock.
Pure Gold WSFM *101.7 FM*
Classic hits from the 1960s to '80s.
smoothfm *95.3 FM*
Sydney's go-to station for relaxing tunes to put you at ease. We have a crush on morning drive DJ Bogart Torelli.

Television

The government-funded TV and radio networks are **ABC** (Australian Broadcasting Corporation) and **SBS** (Special Broadcasting Service).

ABC has strong links with the BBC and tends to get first dibs on new BBC series while maintaining a strong raft of home-grown shows. Its strengths are documentaries and current affairs and comedy considered too edgy for their commercial rivals. Recent Aussie international hits *Kath & Kim* and *Summer Heights High* both debuted on ABC before being picked up in global broadcasting deals. ABC also has a 24 hour news channel, **ABC News 24**.

SBS has a remit to support multicultural programming and is woefully underfunded, a dollar dearth it has of late supplemented with advertising. It features foreign films (subtitled), has good world news at 6.30pm every night and is renowned for its documentaries, many from independent Australian producers. It's also where you'll find comprehensive European football coverage and many HBO series considered too risqué for the commercial networks.

The other three networks – **Seven**, **Nine** and **Ten** – are commercial and, for the most part, populist, featuring a large dose of US TV, heaps of local lifestyle shows and ads seemingly every five minutes.

MONEY

The Australian dollar is rendered as '$' and cent 'c'. Paper money comes in $100, $50, $20, $10 and $5 denominations. Coins come in bronze $2 and $1 pieces, and silver 50c, 20c, 10c and 5c pieces.

ATMs

There are 24-hour ATMs all over town – outside banks, and increasingly in pubs, bottle shops and convenience stores. Most also accept debit cards linked to international networks such as Visa Debit, which will charge $3 for withdrawals.

Some ATMs accept credit cards – check the card logos displayed. Be aware that withdrawing money on your credit card usually incurs interest, starting immediately.

Credit cards

MasterCard, Visa and American Express are widely accepted. You can also use credit cards to get cash from any bank (take your passport), and some ATMs. To report lost or stolen cards, call (free) these 24-hour numbers:

American Express 1300 132 639.
Diners Club 1300 360 060.
MasterCard 1800 120 113.
Visa 1300 651089.

Tax & tax refunds

A ten per cent GST (Goods & Services Tax) is charged on some goods, food and services, including accommodation, and is included in the display price. Tourists can reclaim it on selected goods when they leave the country by using the **Tourist Refund Scheme** (TRS).

This scheme applies only to goods you carry as hand luggage or wear on to the aircraft or ship when you leave.

The refund can be claimed on goods costing a total of $300 or above (including GST) bought from one shop no more than 30 days before you leave. You can buy several lower-priced items from the same shop, either in one go or at different times, provided you've spent at least $300 total within the 30-day period. And you can reclaim tax for items bought from any number of shops, as long you've spent at least $300 in each one.

To claim a refund, you must get a tax invoice from the shop or shops in question. You then claim your refund at a TRS booth, after passport control. Here, you'll need to show the goods, the tax invoices, your passport and boarding pass. Refunds can be paid to a credit card, taking five business days.

Full details are on the Australian Customs website, www.border.gov.au – click on 'tourist refund scheme'.

NATURAL HAZARDS

With a dangerously thin ozone layer, the sun is Sydney's biggest natural hazard. The best way to avoid it is to 'slip, slap, slop' – slip on a T-shirt, slap on a hat, and slop on some sun cream, preferably SPF 30 or higher.

Australia's array of mini-creatures is legendary. And Sydney, being temperate and humid, is the perfect breeding ground for all things cold-blooded or with six or more legs. Most bugs, arachnids and reptiles are harmless, but there are a few nasties to look out for. The following are the critters you should be aware of.

Spiders

While many different types of spider tend to congregate in Sydney, there are two with a potentially fatal bite – the Sydney funnel web and the redback. The funnel web is a nasty, aggressive creature native to the Sydney bush. Black, sparsely haired and much-feared (despite not adding to its death toll of 13 since anti-venom was introduced in 1981), it lives in holes in the ground. Unlike most spiders, males are the more deadly of the species. If bitten, apply pressure and immobilise the wounded area, using a splint if possible, and get to a hospital (or dial 000) immediately. The redback, which is smaller and black with a red stripe on its pea-sized body, lives mainly outside. Apply ice if bitten and seek immediate medical help.

Snakes

Five of the ten most dangerous snakes in the world are said to live in Australia, with names like King brown, Taipan and Tiger. Most are more scared of you than you are of them, but a couple can be aggressive if cornered – so play it safe: always wear boots when hiking through the bush, don't put your hands in any holes or crevices, and watch where you're walking. If someone with you is bitten, assume that the snake is venomous. Wrap the limb tightly, attach a splint and keep the victim still and calm, then seek immediate medical help. Snake bites will not cause immediate death and antivenom is usually available from medical services.

Cockroaches

Despite being nasty to look at, cockroaches are harmless.

Flies and mosquitoes

Flies and mozzies are a fact of Aussie life, but besides imparting an itchy bump (mozzies) and an irritable disposition (flies), they're not dangerous. There are also a couple of flies that bite, such as the march fly – but their bite is not poisonous, just a tad painful. Personal repellents, such as Aeroguard or Rid, tend to be fairly effective, or you can buy coils to burn outdoors, or repelling candles. Mosquito nets and screens are a good idea in summer.

Bushland brutes

If you plan to go bushwalking anywhere on Australia's east coast, there are a couple of creatures you need to watch out for besides snakes. Ticks are very dangerous, if not removed immediately, as they excrete a toxin that can cause paralysis or, in extreme cases, even death. So each day after bushwalking, check your body for lumps and bumps – they tend to like hairy areas, skin creases and ears – and slowly pull or twist any ticks out with sharp-pointed tweezers. Leeches are common bushland suckers – literally. However, they aren't dangerous and can easily be persuaded to let go by applying salt or heat.

POLICE

To report an emergency, dial **000**. If it is not an emergency, call the police at **13 1444**. The **City Central Police Station** is at 192 Day Street, CBD (9265 6499). More info at www.police.nsw.gov.au.

POSTAL SERVICES

Australia Post (13 7678, www.
auspost.com.au) delivers once a
day Monday to Friday, with no
delivery on Saturdays or Sundays.
Post to Europe takes four to ten
days. Stamps for postcards to
Europe and the USA cost $2.75,
and for letters it's $2.65 (up to 50
grams). Letters within Australia
cost from 70c to $1.40, and $6.20
for express post.

Most post office branches open
from 9am to 5pm Monday to Friday,
but the GPO Martin Place branch is
also open on Saturdays. Stamps can
also be bought at some newsagents
and general stores. Suburban post
offices will receive post for you;
otherwise, have it sent Poste Restante
(general delivery) to GPO Sydney,
NSW 2000 – and collect it from the
address below.

General Post Office

*1 Martin Place, CBD (9229 7700).
Martin Place or Wynyard rail.* **Open**
8.15am-5.30pm Mon-Fri; 10am-2pm
Sat. **Map** 309 F5.

Poste Restante

*Level 2, Hunter Connection
Building, 310 George Street,
CBD (13 1318). Martin Place
or Wynyard rail.* **Open** 9am-5pm
Mon-Fri. **Map** p309 F5.

RELIGION

Look in the Yellow Pages (www.
yellowpages.com.au) under 'place
of worship' for places of worship.

SAFETY & SECURITY

Sydney is a fairly safe city, although
car theft, vandalism and burglary are
on the increase. That said, you will
frequently read about drug-related
shootings, and racial tension has
remained a problem since the Bali
bombings and the riots on Cronulla
Beach in 2005. And while the
stereotype of hot-blooded Aussie
males ending an alcohol-fuelled
evening with a pub brawl is not the
norm, it's not entirely unknown either.

In an emergency, dial **000**.

SMOKING

Smoking is banned on public
transport and in cafés, restaurants
and many enclosed spaces, such
as theatres, shopping malls and
community centres. Smoking in
pubs and clubs is now completely
banned. There are fines for tossing
cigarette butts out of car windows.

TELEPHONES

Dialling & codes

The country code for Australia is
61; the area code for NSW, including
Sydney, is **02**. You never need to
dial the 02 from within the state.
Numbers beginning 1800 are free
when dialled within Australia;
numbers beginning 13 or 1300
are charged at a 25c flat fee.

Making a call

To make an international call, dial
an international access code – either
0011 or **0018**, or + on a mobile –
followed by the country code, area
code (usually omitting any initial 0),
and then the number.

The different international access
codes have different pricing systems.
Telstra, the dominant Australian
phone company, offers a choice of
0011 Minutes or 0018 Half Hours.
The 0011 calls are for shorter chats,
charged per second. The 0018 calls
are for a long chat and you'll know
exactly how much your call will cost
up front. Warning beeps tell you
when your half-hour is almost up.

The country code for the UK is **44**,
for New Zealand **64**, for the USA and
Canada **1**, for the Republic of Ireland
353 and for South Africa **27**.

Standard local calls are untimed
flat-fee calls between standard fixed
telephone services within a local
service area. To check if local call
charges apply, call 13 2200.

STD calls (national long-distance
calls) are charged according to their
distance, time and day, plus a fee.
Each call starts with five pip tones.

Public phones

There are still a few working public
phones dotted around the city, as
well as in bars, cafés, railway
stations and post offices. You
can also make long-distance and
international calls at many internet
cafés. Most public phones accept
coins ($1, 50c, 20c, 10c). Some also
accept major credit cards. Cheap
international phonecards are
available from newsagents.

Directory enquiries

Dial **1223** to find a number within
Australia, and **1225** for international
directory enquiries.

Operator services

For operator-assisted national or
international calls, phone **1234**.

Mobile phones

Australia's mobile phone network
operates on dual-band 900/1,800 MHz
(megahertz). This means that if you're
coming from the UK you should be
able to use your own mobile phone –
but that's not as simple as it sounds.

If you keep your UK SIM card in
the phone, when you arrive your
phone will register itself with a local
network with which your UK service
provider has an agreement. If you
want to use this facility, check with
your service provider before you go,
as you may need to set your phone
up to work abroad. This is the easiest
method, but it can be potentially
expensive: calling numbers in
Australia will cost the same as
calling back to the UK – a lot –
and you'll have to pay to receive
calls as well as to make them.

Another simple option is to buy
or rent a phone. Plenty of Sydney
companies offer competitive mobile
phone rentals with local networks,
for a minimum of three days, billed
to your credit card. Or you could
just buy or rent a SIM card for an
Australian network and put it in your
UK phone (and top it up as required).
However, your phone may have been
'locked' so that it works only with your
UK service provider's SIM card. You're
entitled to get the phone unlocked, and
the service provider has to give you an
unlocking code – for free – if you ask
for it. Once you've unlocked your
phone you can put any SIM card in
it. In practice, service providers tend
not to make this easy, and the process
can be fraught with difficulties.
Alternatively, any mobile phone
repair shop will do it, for about $40.
If you're in Sydney for a year or more,
you could get a phone or SIM card on
a billed package. To get this kind of
plan – usually 12 months minimum –
you'll need an Australian credit rating,
and it takes six months to get one.

To investigate further, look under
'mobile phones' in the Yellow Pages
(www.yellowpages.com.au) or try
these places:

Paddington Phones

*381 Riley Street, Surry Hills
(9281 8044, www.paddington
phones.com.au). Central rail or
light rail.* **Open** 9am-5.30pm
Mon-Fri. **Map** p311 F9.
Rentals, prepaid phones and fixed-
term deals are available.

Vodafone Rentals

*Arrivals Hall, T1 International
Terminal near exit A, Sydney Airport
(9700 7788 , www.vodafone.com.au).*
Open 6am-10pm daily.

LOCAL CLIMATE

Average temperatures and monthly rainfall in Sydney.

	High (°C/°F)	Low (°C/°F)	Rainfall (mm/in)
Jan	26 / 79	19 / 66	89 / 3.5
Feb	26 / 79	19 / 66	102 / 4
Mar	25 / 76	17 / 63	127 / 5
Apr	22 / 72	15 / 58	135 / 5.3
May	19 / 67	11 / 52	127 / 5
June	17 / 61	9 / 49	117 / 4.6
July	16 / 61	8 / 49	117 / 4.6
Aug	18 / 63	9 / 49	76 / 3
Sept	20 / 66	11 / 52	74 / 2.9
Oct	22 / 72	13 / 56	71 / 2.8
Nov	24 / 75	16 / 61	74 / 2.9
Dec	25 / 77	17 / 63	74 / 2.9

Rent or buy a phone or SIM card as soon as you arrive.
Other locations 580 George Street (1300 650 410); Westfield Bondi Junction (1300 650 410).

TICKETS

You can book tickets for all major venues (music, theatre, dance and so on) through agencies **Ticketek** (13 2849, www.ticketek.com.au) and **Ticketmaster** (136100, www.ticketmaster.com.au). Also try **Tickets4me** (02 4730 6932, www.tickets4me.com.au) or **Moshtix** (1300 438 849, www.moshtix.com.au). All charge booking fees.

TIME

New South Wales operates on Eastern Standard Time (GMT plus 10 hours). Between October and March, Daylight Saving Time comes into operation, and the clocks go forward one hour. Australia has three time zones – the others are Western Standard Time (GMT plus 8 hours) and Central Standard Time (GMT plus 9.5 hours). Confusingly, Queensland doesn't recognise Daylight Saving Time.

TIPPING

Tipping is appreciated but not usually expected in restaurants and cafés, where ten per cent is the norm. Locals tend not to tip in taxis.

TOILETS

There are plenty of free, well-maintained public lavatories in Sydney – in department stores, shopping centres, rail stations, beaches and parks. It is frowned upon to use the toilet in a bar if you're not also buying a drink.

And a note for women: Sydney's sewage pipes are a lot narrower and so more prone to blockage than most of those elsewhere, and tampons and sanitary towels can easily block them. Always use a bin instead.

TOURIST INFORMATION

As well as the visitor centres below, the City of Sydney's website – at www.cityofsydney.nsw.gov.au – and Tourism NSW's site – at www.visitnsw.com.au – have lots of useful information. If you plan to travel elsewhere in the country, Australia's official website – www.australia.com – is packed with helpful ideas and information.

Sydney Visitor Centre
Level 1, corner of Argyle Street & Playfair Road, the Rocks (1800 067 676, www.bestof.com.au/nsw). Circular Quay rail or ferry. **Open** 9.30am-5.30pm daily. **Map** p309 F3.

33 Wheat Road, Darling Harbour (9240 8788). Town Hall rail or Darling Harbour ferry. **Open** 9.30am-5.30pm daily. **Map** p310 D7. The main official information resource for visitors, with two city-centre locations.

Sydney Harbour National Park Information Centre
13 1555, www.nationalparks.nsw.gov.au/Sydney-Harbour-National-Park). Online and phone info.

Manly Visitor & Information Centre
17 East Esplanade, Manly Wharf, Manly (9976 1430, www.manly australia.com.au). Manly ferry. **Open** 9am-5pm Mon-Fri; 10am-4pm Sat, Sun (until 5pm in summer). **Map** p316.

Parramatta Heritage & Visitor Information Centre
346A Church Street, next to Lennox Bridge, Parramatta (8839 3311, www.parracity.nsw.gov.au). Parramatta rail or ferry, then 10min walk. **Open** 9am-5pm daily.

VISAS & IMMIGRATION

All travellers, including children – except for Australian and New Zealand citizens – must have a visa or an ETA (Electronic Travel Authority) to enter Australia. An ETA is sufficient for tourists from EU countries – including the UK and Ireland, except holders of GBN (British National Overseas) passports – the USA, Canada and Japan (but not South Africa), who are intending to stay for up to three months.

ETAs, available for tourist and business trips, are the simplest to arrange: your travel agent or airline, or a commercial visa service can arrange one on the spot if you give them details or a copy/fax of your passport (no photo or ticket is required). You don't need a stamp in your passport: ETAs are confirmed electronically at your port of entry. You can also apply for an ETA online via www.eta.immi.gov.au. It costs $20, and you can be approved for entry in less than 30 seconds.

If your entry requirements are more complex or you want to stay longer than three months, you will probably need a non-ETA visa, which you apply for by post or in person to the relevant office in advance of your trip. For up-to-date information and details of the nearest overseas office where visa applications can be made, check www.border.gov.au.

WEIGHTS & MEASURES

Australia uses the metric system.

WHEN TO GO

Sydney has a moderate climate, with warm to hot summers, cool winters and rainfall all year round. Spring brings clear blue skies, with temperatures warm enough to shed the woollies, especially when the sun shines. In summer, Sydneysiders live in shorts. In January and February, the sun bakes the city, and temperatures can top 30°C (90°F) – and even go over 40°C (104°F). In autumn, the city is swept by strong winds, while winter mornings and nights mean low temperatures that can – but rarely do – dip down to 6°C (43°F). On occasion snow falls in the Blue Mountains.

Further Reference

BOOKS

Non-fiction

Birmingham, John *Leviathan*
Sydney's dark, seductive underbelly laid bare by the nation's pre-eminent gonzo author.
Carey, Peter *30 Days in Sydney: A Wildly Distorted Account*
Dual Booker Prize winner and ex-Balmain resident returns to Sydney after 17 years in NYC to pen a love letter told through many characters.
Clark, Manning *A History of Australia*
Six-volume history, with sympathy for the underdog.
Dalton, Robin *Aunts Up the Cross*
Dalton's affectionate memoir of life in Sydney's most raffish locale, Kings Cross.
Doyle, Peter *City of Shadows*
Mesmerising police mug-shots from 1920s to '50s Sydney tell of Sin City's desperate years.
Drewe, Philip *Sydney Opera House*
An incisive and intellectual examination of Utzon's building.
Dupain, Max & Rex *Inside Sydney*
Max Dupain's 1920s and '30s photographs reflected Sydney's emergence as a modern city.
Facey, Albert *A Fortunate Life*
Autobiography tracing Facey's life from Outback orphanage to Gallipoli, the Depression and beyond.
Falconer, Delia *Sydney*
A sultry, unflinching and violently loving paean to Sydney – sexy, gaudy and golden but full of melancholic rot and humour.
Foster, David et al *Crossing the Blue Mountains*
Accounts of journeys into the interior from Sydney, including that of Darwin in 1836.
Gill, Alan *Orphans of the Storm*
Shocking true story of the thousands of people who came to Australia in the 20th century as child migrants.
UBD Gregory's Sydney Compact Street Directory
A bit of a brick, but the best guide to Sydney's streets you'll find.
Halliday, James *Australia Wine Companion*
Good to take on a tour of vineyards.
Hughes, Robert *The Fatal Shore*
Epic tale of brutal early convict life; made into a TV series.
Hughes Turnbull, Lucy *Sydney, Biography of a City*

Authoritative tome from way back to now. Good reference material.
James, Clive *Unreliable Memoirs*
Achingly funny memoir of 'the Kid from Kogarah's' Sydney childhood by Britain's favourite Aussie.
Keneally, Thomas *The Commonwealth of Thieves*
History of the colony in the time of the first three fleets.
Moorhouse, Geoffrey *Sydney*
A fresh look at the city's history by a distinguished travel writer.
Morgan, Sally *My Place*
Bestselling autobiography of an Aboriginal woman from Western Australia.
O'Brien, Siobhan *A Life by Design: The Art and Lives of Florence Broadhurst*
The mysterious death and extraordinary life of the Sydney socialite and wallpaper queen.
Pilger, John *A Secret Country*
Passionately critical account of Australia by the expat journalist.
Tench, Watkin *Complete Account of the Settlement of Port Jackson*
The diary kept by the heroic Tench was Sydney's first bio: part thriller, travelogue and comedy.
Walsh, Kate *The Changing Face of Australia*
A pictorial chronology of a century of immigration, underlining the shift towards a multiculture.
Wheatley, Nadia *The Life and Myth of Charmian Clift*
Well-crafted biography of one of Australia's best writers.
Writer, Larry *Razor*
Sydney's badlands from the 1920s to the '50s, as controlled by two opposing but equally colourful madams, brought vividly to life.

Fiction

Carey, Peter *Bliss*; *Illywhacker*; *Oscar and Lucinda*; *The True History of the Kelly Gang*; *Theft*
Booker Prize-winning novelist whose *Bliss* (later a film and, in 2010, an opera) captures Sydney's charged sexuality.
Courtenay, Bryce *Brother Fish*; *Whitethorn*
Australia's bestselling writer, though he doesn't always stick to Oz-related subject matter.
Drewe, Robert *The Bodysurfers*
Brilliant collection of short stories captures the sex, swelter and gaudy kink of Sydney.

Franklin, Miles *My Brilliant Career*
Famous 1901 novel about a rural woman who refuses to conform.
Gibbs, May *Snugglepot and Cuddlepie*
Most famous of Gibbs's children's books about the gumnut babies.
Grenville, Kate *The Secret River*; *The Lieutenant*; *Sarah Thornhill*
Local author's acclaimed trilogy of Sydney as the final – and the first – frontier for black and white relations.
Keneally, Thomas *Bring Larks and Heroes*; *The Chant of Jimmy Blacksmith*
Two novels about oppression – of convicts in the former, Aboriginal people in the latter.
Lawson, Henry *Joe Wilson and His Mates*
Collection of short stories about mateship and 'larrikinism' by the first Australian writer to be given a state funeral (in 1922).
Lindsay, Norman *The Magic Pudding*
Splendidly roguish children's tale – as Australian as a book can get; made into a so-so movie.
Nowra, Louis *Ice*
Two British entrepreneurs tow an iceberg to Sydney in the 1920s with transformative effects on the city.
Park, Ruth *The Harp in the South*; *Poor Man's Orange*
Tales of inner-city struggle, written in the 1940s. Park also wrote the wonderful children's book *The Muddle-Headed Wombat*.
Porter, Dorothy *The Monkey's Mask*
Sydney-born poet who reinvented the verse novel with this mesmeric tale of a lesbian detective who falls for her suspect.
Slessor, Kenneth *Selected Poems*
Quintessential Sydney poet, famed for his haunting epic 'Five Bells'.
White, Patrick *Voss*; *Tree of Man*
The triumphs and travails of Sydney suburbia colliding with the wild Australia at its doorstep by Sydney's Nobel Prize winner.
Winton, Tim *Cloudstreet*; *That Eye, the Sky*; *In the Winter Dark*
The best novels from a two-time winner of the Miles Franklin award.

Travel

Bryson, Bill *Down Under*
Amusing travel writer Bryson dissects the Aussie character and explores the brown land.

Dale, David *The 100 Things Everyone Needs to Know about Australia* Essential background reading: covers everything from Vegemite to Malcolm Fraser's trousers.
Jacobson, Howard *In the Land of Oz* Parodic account of Jacobson's travels down under.

FILM

The Adventures of Priscilla, Queen of the Desert (Stephan Elliott, 1994)
Terence Stamp joins Guy Pearce and Hugo Weaving in high heels for this gritty high camp tale of Sydney drag queens on tour.
Blue Murder (Michael Jenkins, 1995)
Banned for over a decade in NSW, this explosive tele-movie tells of Sydney's blurring of cop and crim and 'the best force money could buy'.
Candy (Neil Armfield, 2006)
Heath Ledger is mesmerising as the cocky heroin addict in love with the beautiful Candy (Abbie Cornish). Set in Sydney and Melbourne, it's a depressing and deeply affecting tale, made even more poignant in the light of Ledger's death in 2008.
Cedar Boys (Serhat Caradee, 2009)
Restless Lebanese youths collide with suburban white girls in an artfully directed drug-heist thriller.
Dirty Deeds (David Caesar, 2002)
Set in '60s Sydney, this rollicking crime tale tells of the Mafia's arrival in Kings Cross. Stars John Goodman, Bryan Brown, Toni Collette and Sam Neill.
Finding Nemo (Andrew Stanton & Lee Unkrich, 2003)
Pixar family favourite finds two fish searching for a clownfish in Sydney Harbour. Bill Hunter stars as the dentist.
Godzilla: Final Wars (Ryuhei Kitamura, 2004)
For his 50th birthday, Godzilla battles a series of monsters across Sydney, decimating downtown Haymarket and blowing up the Sydney Opera House.
The Great Gatsby (Baz Luhrmann, 2013)
Baz's blockbuster adaptation uses Balmain, Waverley, Centennial Park, Glebe Island and Parramatta as locations.
Lantana (Ray Lawrence, 2001)
AFI award-winning thriller about marriage and relationships, set in Sydney. Stars Aussie actors Geoffrey Rush, Kerry Armstrong and Anthony LaPaglia.
The Last Wave (Peter Weir, 1977)
Hometown director Peter Weir's spine-tingling tale of a white lawyer haunted by mystical Aboriginal influences.
Little Fish (Rowan Woods, 2005)
A look at Sydney's underworld of drug dealing and addicts in Cabramatta, starring Cate Blanchett.
Looking for Alibrandi (Kate Woods, 2000)
An Italian-Australian battles with her identity in Sydney's western suburbs. Pia Miranda and Anthony LaPaglia excel.
Mad Max: Fury Road (George Miller, 2015)
Filmed in Namibia and Sydney's Fox Studios, this sequel to the '70s landmark sees Tom Hardy replace Mel Gibson in the title role.
Moulin Rouge! (Baz Luhrmann, 2001)
OTT love story from local boy Baz Luhrmann, filmed at Sydney's Fox Studios and starring north shore's Nicole Kidman.
Muriel's Wedding (PJ Hogan, 1994)
Toni Collette plays a young woman stifled by the tropics but liberated by Sydney's lunatic fringe.
Newsfront (Phillip Noyce, 1978)
A beautifully told and deftly written tale of rival news teams in 1950s Sydney.
Paper Planes (Robert Connolly, 2015)
A rare local hit, this kids' movie is about a boy who competes in the world paper plane championships.
Puberty Blues (Bruce Beresford, 1981)
A withering portrayal of teenage girls, alcohol and sex amid the surf culture of Sydney's Sutherland Shire. Now also a TV series.
Ruben Guthrie (Brendan Cowell, 2015)
A Sydney advertising executive (Patrick Brammall) gives up drinking for a year in this comedy exploring Australia's drinking culture.
Sirens (John Duigan, 1994)
Sirens follows hedonist painter Norman Lindsay and a clergyman (Hugh Grant).
Stone (Sandy Harbutt, 1974)
A trashy, brutal bikesploitation B movie filmed at Middle Head; Quentin Tarantino is a fan.
The Sum of Us (Geoff Burton & Kevin Dowling, 1994)
A youthful Russell Crowe plays a gay plumber looking for love in Sydney's Inner West.
Two Hands (Gregor Jordan, 1999)
Panania boy Bryan Brown plays an underworld Sydney crime boss, with Heath Ledger as the hapless lad who's entangled in his world.
The Wolverine (James Mangold, 2013)
Hugh Jackman reprised his role as the metal-infused Marvel mutant for this X-Men origin story. Shooting locales included Surry Hills and Sydney Olympic Park.

MUSIC

AC/DC Australia's greatest rock export. Latest album: *Rock or Bust*.
Angus & Julia Stone The brother/sister duo from Avalon bring drowsy appeal and earnest storytelling skills to the airwaves.
Beasts of Bourbon Revered Surry Hills-sired supergroup. Classic opus? *The Low Road*.
Blasko, Sarah This Sydney songbird won the ARIA for 'Best Female Vocalist' in 2009.
Cave, Nick Enigmatic, brooding vocalist from the Bad Seeds.
Crowded House The beautifully balladeering Neil Finn-led trio.
Easybeats, The Australia's first international rock stars.
Empire of the Sun Chart-topping glam rock duo fronted by Luke Steele.
Divinyls, The Punchy vintage rock outfit fronted by Chrissie Amphlett, who died in 2013.
Hirschfelder, David One of Australia's most successful modern composers.
Hoodoo Gurus A great singles band, still going strong more than three decades after forming in Sydney.
INXS Michael Hutchence fronted this globally successful outfit until his death in 1997.
Johns, Daniel The erstwhile frontman for Newcastle trio Silverchair released his long-awaited solo debut *Talk* in 2015.
Kelly, Paul A Melbourne troubador who came of age in Sydney, Kelly's paeans to the city include 'Randwick Bells' and 'From St Kilda to Kings Cross'.
Midnight Oil Northern beaches boys turned international rock stars. The band split in 2002 so that frontman Peter Garrett could concentrate on politics – he's the former Minister for Youth in the federal government.
One Day A collective of hip-hop groups hailing from the Inner West.
Preatures, The The Sydney five-piece got their start jamming at the Lansdowne Hotel, recorded their debut album in Surry Hills.
Presets, The A DJ duo who met at the Sydney Conservatorium of Music, their 2008 album *Apocalypso* won them a string of awards. They're a killer live act.
Sticky Fingers Local seven-piece playing a mix of reggae and indie.
Wiggles, The The super-successful Sydney-born 'Fab Four of kid rock'.
Wolfmother Grammy-winning rockers from Erskineville.
You Am I Definitive mod-rockers still going strong. Their *Hourly Daily* album captures Sydney like no other.

Index

10 William St 94
121BC 81
357 199
465 the Avenue 145
4A Centre for
   Contemporary
   Asian Art 71
505 209

A

A Tavola 105
A&Pasticceria 127
Able Hawkesbury
   Houseboats 228
ACME 111
Activity Tours Australia
   231
Addison Road Centre 131
addresses 287
Adina Apartment Hotel
   Sydney Central 281
Adriano Zumbo 122
Aesop 95
age restrictions 287
airport 282
Albion Hotel 157
Allianz Stadium 98
Allphones Arena 205
Allpress Espresso 163
Alishan International
   Guesthouse 277
Alpha60 95
American Apparel 79
Ananas 54
Anchor 109
Andrew 'Boy' Charlton
   Pool 62
Annandale 125-126
Annex 110
Anvil Coffee Co 139
Anzac Memorial 63
Apartment One 281
A.P.C. 82
Apollo 89
Apollo the Party 195
Aquabumps 110
Arcadia Liquors 86
Archie Rose 163
Argyle 56
Aria 59
Arida 91
Ariel 95
Arq Sydney 194
Art Gallery of New
   South Wales 63
Art Month 36
Arts Hotel Sydney 275
Artspace 89
Ashfield 127
Atura 158
Australian Ballet 218
Australian Brandenburg
   Orchestra 219

Australian Chamber
   Orchestra 219
Australian Heritage Hotel
   56
Australian Museum 63
Australian National
   Maritime Museum 178
Australian Reptile Park
   180
Australian Sunrise Lodge
   278
Australian Tattoo & Body
   Art Expo 35
Australian Theatre for
   Young People 212
Avalon Beach 151, 174

B

Bach Eatery 132
Bad Dog 197
Balloon Aloft 51
Balmain 120-123
Balmoral 140
Balmoral Beach 169
Banh Cuon Kim Thanh 159
Bang 80
Bangarra Dance Theatre
   218
Bank Hotel 191
Bankstown 159
Bankstown Oval 159
Barbecue 172
Barber Shop 69
Bar H 81
Bar Italia 126
Bar Zini 75
Barrel Bar & Dining 141
Barrenjoey House 153
Barrington Tops 232
Barringtons Country
   Retreat 232
Basement 209
Bassike 122
Batch Brewing Co 130
Bathers' Pavilion 169
Battambang 159
Bavarian Bier Café 157
Baxter Inn 69
beaches 164-175
Beach Burrito Company
   162
Beach Road Hotel 109, 207
Bear 71
Bearded Tit 86
Becker Minty 91
Bell Shakespeare
   Company 213
Belle Fleur 122
Belvoir 213
Belvoir Street Theatre
   214
Bennelong 59
Bennelong Bar 59

Bentley Restaurant & Bar
   67
Beresford 191
Berowra Waters Fish Café
   228
Berta 80
Berry Inn 236
Best Beaches 164-175
Biennale of Sydney 34
Big Top 205
Billabong Gardens 278
Bills 105
Billy Kwong 89
Birchgrove 120-123
Bistro Moncur 100
Bistrode CBD 67
Black Bar 76
BLACK by ezard 75
Black Star Pastry 163
Blackmores Running
   Festival 29
Blacktown & Around 158
Blind Bear Saloon 162
Bloodorange 111
Bloodwood 132
Blu Bar on 36 56
Blue Mountains 224
Blue Mountains YHA 226
Blue Sky Helicopters 51
Blue Spinach Recycled
   Designer Clothing 80
Boathouse 153
Bodyline Spa & Sauna 199
Bondi Beach 170
Bondi Beach to Coogee
   Beach 104-110
Bondi Bowling Club 109
Bondi Icebergs Club 104
Bondi Junction 101-104
Bondi Openair 187
Bondi Pavillion 104
Bonza Bike Tours 49
Botanist 139
Bourke Street Bakery
   129
Braza 126
Briars Country Lodge
   & Inn 239
Bridgeclimb 48
Brickfields 87
Bronte Beach 171
Bundanoon Hotel 239
Bundeena 162
Buon Ricordo 111

C

Cabramatta 159
Cabramatta Moon
   Festival 29
Café Nice 59
Café Sopra 163
Café Sydney 59
Camelot Lounge 130

Camilla Frank's Beach
   House Store 110
Camp Cove 168
Candle Factory 56
Capitol Theatre 214
Capsule 88
Cargo Bar 200
Carousel 110
Carriageworks Farmers
   Market 87
Carrington Hotel 226
Catalina 116
CBD, The 62-70
Centennial Park 98
Centennial Park Cycles
   286
Centennial Parklands
   Dining 99
Central Sydney 60-91
Chaco Bar 77
Chairmain Mao 117
Charing Cross Hotel 117
Chatswood 142
Chatswood Chase 145
Chauvel 183
Chester White 90
Chica Bonita 149
Children 178-180
Chinamans Beach 169
Chinatown 70-74
Chinatown Night Market 74
Chinese Laundry 200
Chinese New Year 33
Chinese Noodle
   Restaurant 71
Chinta Kechil 113
Chiosco 141
Chippendale 87
Chiswick 100
Cho Cho San 89
Chocolateria San Churro
   157
Christensen
   Copenhagan 114
Cinema Paris 183
cinemas 181-187
Circa Espresso 157
Circular Quay 52-59
City Gym 197
City Recital Hall 221
City2Surf 39
Civic Hotel 71
Civic Underground 200
Cliff Dive 78, 200
climate 293
Clontarf Beach 170
Clovelly Beach 171
Cockatoo Island 83
Cockatoo Island Ferry 49
Collaroy Beach 174
Collector Store 82
Coco Chocolate 139
Colombian Hotel 192
comedy 210-211

Comedy Store 211
Commons 78
Constellation Playground 120
consumer rights 287
Coogee Bay Hotel 109, 276
Coogee Beach 171
Coogee Pavillion 109
Concourse 143, 221
Corner Shop 95
Cornersmith 129
Corridor 133
Corroboree 31
Cottage 133
Court House Retreat 229
Courthouse Hotel 134
Craft Beer Week 30
Cranky Fins Holidae Inn 153
Cream on Crown 82
Cream on King 135
Cremeria De Luca 128
Cremorne 140
Cricketers Arms 82
Cronulla 162
Cronulla Beach 172
Cronulla Park Ice Creamery 162
Cronulla Surf Schoool 162
Cross Eatery 67
Crown Hotel 273
Crows Nest 145
Customs House 57
customs 287
cycling 286

D

Daiso 88
Daisy's Milkbar 130
Daniel San 150
dance 218
Da Mario 163
Da Orazio Pizza & Porchetta 105
Darling 272
Darling Harbour 74-76
Darling Harbour Ferry 50
Darling Point 112-114
Darlinghurst 77-80
Darlinghurst Theatre Company 213
Dawn Fraser Baths 120
Day Spa at the Langham Hotel 57
Dendy Newtown 184
Dendy Opera Quays 184
Dial an Angel 179
Din Tai Fung 143
disabled information 287
Dive Hotel 276
Dock 86
Don Campos 163
Double Bay 112-114
Dove & Olive 82
Downstairs 77
Drake Eatery 105
driving 285
Dr Faustus 80
drugs 288
Drugstore 128

E

Eaglereach Wilderness Resort 231
Earl's Juke Joint 134
Earth Food Store 110
East Side Ink 103
East Sydney 77-80
Eastern Suburbs 92-117
Eau de Vie 78
Edition Coffee Roasters 77
Efendy 120
electricity 288
Elizabeth Bay 111-112
Elizabeth Bay House 111
Elizabeth Farm 156
El Topo 102
El Topo Basement 201
embassies 288
emergencies 288
Emma's Snack Bar 132
Empire 126
Emporium 157
Enmore 131-135
Enmore Theatre 206
Ensemble Theatre 215
Ensemble Theatre Company 213
Entertainment Quarter 98
Erskineville 131-135
Establishment 270
Ester 87
Eternity Playhouse 215
Eva's Backpackers 275
Eveleigh 84-87
Eveleigh Farmers Market see Carriageworks Farmers Market
Event Cinemas Bondi Junction 181
Event Cinemas George Street 182
Excelsior Jones 128
Exchange Hotel 201

F

Factory Theatre 206
Featherdale Wildlife Park 158
Felix 68
ferries 144, 283
Ferrython 33
Festival of the Winds 29
film 181-189
   festivals 187, 188
Fine Foods Store 54
fireworks 37
Five Points Burgers 139
Fleetwood Macchiato 132
Flickerfest 32, 187
Fifties Fair 39
Fitness First Darlinghurst 197
Flying Fish 76
Football Grand Finals 29
Fountaindale Grand Manor 239
Four Ate Five 80
Four Frogs Creperie 117
Four in Hand 95
Four Points by Sheraton Darling Harbour 270
Four Seasons Hotel Sydney 268
Fourth Village Providore 142
Foxtrot 145
Freda's 87, 201
Freezone Volleyball 198
Freshwater Beach 151
Friend in Hand 211

G

Gaelic Club 207
Galeries Victoria 69
Garigal National Park 151
gay & lesbian 190-199
   nightlife 191-197
   help & information 288
   Mardi Gras 35, 193
   saunas & sex clubs 199
   sport & fitness 197
Gazebo 111
Gertrude & Alice 110
Giant Dwarf 211
Ginkgo Leaf 101
Glebe 123
Glebe Point Diner 124
Gleebooks 125
Glenferrie Lodge 279
Glenmore Hotel 56
Golden Age Cinema 184
Golden Century 71
Good Food Month 31
Goodgod Small Club 202
Govinda's 77, 184
Grace Hotel 270
Grand National 95
Grandma's Bar 69
Graphic Festival 31
Great Synagogue 63
Greenwich 145
Griffin Theatre Company 213
Grounds of Alexandria 163
Guillaume 94
Gunther's Dining Room 86

H

Haberfield 127
Harbord Beach Hotel 152
Harbourside Apartments 281
Harlequin Market 114
Hawkesbury River 227-230
Hayberry 145
Hayden Orpheum Picture Palace 184
Hayes Theatre Co 213
Haymarket 70-74
Hazy Rose 79
Head On Photo Festival 38
HeadQuarters on Crown 199
Heaps Gay 197
helplines 289
Hemingway's 150
Henson 131
Hero of Waterloo 207
Hilton Sydney 268
Hive Bar 133
Home 202
Hordern Pavilion 206
Hotel Centennial 101
hotels 266-281
House of Crabs 85
Hoyts Broadway 182
Hoyts EQ 182
Hughenden Hotel 276
Hunter Valley 230-232
Hunter Valley Wine Country Visitor Centre 232
Hunter Vineyard Tours 231
Huskisson Beach Tourist Resort 236
Hyde Park Barracks Museum 63
Hydro Majestic Hotel 226

I

Ian Thorpe Aquatic Centre 178
Ibis Budget Sydney East 275
Ibis Sydney Darling Harbout 273
Icebergs Dining Room 105
Ici et La 82
I'm Free Walking Tour of Sydney 48
IMAX Sydney 187
Incu 95
Inner West 118-135
InterContinental Sydney 268
InterContinental Sydney Double Bay 276
Italian Forum 126
Ivy 202

J

Jam Gallery 103
Jasmin1 126
JB & Sons 152
jellyfish 175
Jenolan Caves 226
Jenolan Caves House 226
Jervis Bay Guest House 236
Jimmy Liks 90
Jonah's 152, 279
Johnny Lobster 145
John Smith Cafe 85
Justice & Police Museum 57

K

Kazbah 120
Kensington 116-17
Kepos Street Kitchen 85
Kings Cross Hotel 202
Kings Cross 273
Kirketon 273
Kirribilli 138
Kirribilli Hotel 140

INDEX

INDEX

Kirribilli House 138
Kit & Ace 82
Koala Park Sanctuary 180
Koskela 163
Ku-ring-gai Chase
  National Park 151
Kwan Yin 159

L

Lady Bay Beach 169
Ladurée 101
Lamrock Lodge 277
Laneway Festival 34
Langham, Sydney 267
language 289
Larmont Sydney 274
left luggage 290
legal help 290
Leichhardt 125-126
Let's Go Surfing 110
Lewisham Hotel and Live
  House 208
Light Brigade Hotel 101
Lilianfels Blue Mountains
  226
Little Guy 125
Little Jean 113
Little Kitchen 108
Lobo Plantation 69
Local Taphouse 79
Lodge Bar 121
London 95
Longrain 80
Lord Dudley 101
Lord Gladstone 88
Lord Nelson Brewery
  Hotel 56, 267
Lord Raglan 86
Lord Wolseley 76
lost property 290
Lox Stock & Barrel 108
LP's Quality Meats 87
Lucio's 94
Lucio Pizzeria 77
LuMi 76
Luna Park 139

M

.M Contemporary 101
Madame Frou Frou 124
Madame Tussauds 75
Mamak 71
Manly 148
Manly Art Gallery &
  Museum 148
Manly Beach 173
Manly Bike Tours 286
Manly Ferry 50
Manly Sea Life Sanctuary
  180
Manly Surf School 151
Manly Wine 151
Mantra 2 Bond Street 281
Maple Store 135
Mardi Gras 35, 193
Mardi Gras Film Festival
  & Queer Screen Film
  Fest 188

Marigold 71
Maroubra Beach 172
Marrickville 129-131
Marrickville Pork Roll 130
Mary's 134
Marquee 202
Max Watt's 206
MCA Store 59
McLean & Page 151
McMahons Point 138
Mecca Espresso 76
media 290
Medusa 273
Melbourne Cup 31
Menya Mappen 71
Mercedes-Benz Fashion
  Week 35
Meriton World Tower 281
Messina 77
Metro 206
Michael Reid Gallery 112
Midnight Special 135
Milsons Point 138
Minskys Hotel 141
Mint Condition 122
Momofuku Seiobo 76
Moncur Cellars 101
money 291
Monopole 90
Moon Park 85
Moonlight Cinema 187
Moore Park 98-99
Mosman 140
Mosman Ferry 50
Moun Toma Botanic
  Gardens 226
Movida 80
Mr Crackles Carryout 77
Mr Wong 68
Mrs Sippy 113
Ms G's 89
Mu Mesen Archives 184
Museum of Contemporary
  Art 58
Museum of Sydney 63
Murray Rose Pool 113
Music 204-210
  classical & opera 219
  jazz 209
  rock & pop 204-209
Musica Viva 219
My Sydney Detour 49

N

N2 Extreme Gelato 71
Neighbourhood 110
Nelson Road Tuck Shop
  102
Neutral Bay 140
New Theatre 213, 215
New Year's Eve 31, 37
Newport Arms Hotel 279
Newport Beach 174
Newtown Festival 31
Newtown 131-135
Newtown Social Club 208
Nielsen Park 115
Nomad 81
Nomads Westend 271

North Bondi Fish 108
North End 148
North Fort 149
North Head Quarentine
  Station 149
Northies 162
North Shore 136-145
North Sydney 138
North Sydney Leagues
  Club 211
North Sydney Olympic
  Pool 139
Northern Beaches 146-153
Novotel Brighton Beach
  280
Novotel Sydney Manly
  Pacific 279
Novotel Sydney on Darling
  Harbour 272
NSW National Parks &
  Wildlife Service 180

O

Ocean Planet 232
Oceanworld Manly 149
Old Fitzroy Theatre 215
Old Government House 157
Olsen Irwin Gallery 101
O'Malley's Hotel 275
Open Air Cinema 187
opera 219
Opera Australia 219
Opera Bar 59
Opera on the Harbour 34
Original Backpackers
  Lodge 275
Ormeggio 141
Oscillate Wildly 134
Ovolo Woolloomooloo 274
Oxford Art Factory 79, 208
Oxford Hotel 192
Oxford Tavern 131

P

Paddington 94-98
Paddington Markets 98
Paddington Reservoir
  Gardens 94
Paddy's Markets 74
Palace Norton Street
  Cinemas 184
Palace Verona Cinema 185
Palm Beach 153, 174
Palms on Oxford 194
Pancakes on the Rocks 55
Pantry 150
Papa Gede's 69
Paper2 84
Papi Chuio 150
Park Hyatt Sydney 267
Park8 Hotel 270
Parramasala 31
Parramatta 156-157
Parramatta Ferry 51
Parramatta Riverside
  Theatres 215
Parsley Bay 168
Pelicano 113

Pensione 271
Peppers Anchorage Port
  Stephens 233
Peppers Convent Guest
  House 231
Pepper Tree Wines
  Performance Space
  (Carriageworks) 217
Peter's of Kensington 117
Petersham 129-131
Petersham Charcoal
  Chicken 130
Phounguen 159
Pier One Sydney Harbour
  267
Pilu at Freshwater 152
Pittwater YHA 279
Platform 72 80
Playa Takeria 78
Point Piper 114-117
police 291
Porch & Parlour 108
Porteno 81
Port Stephens 232-234
Port Stephens Motor
  Lodge 233
postal services 292
Podwer Keg 91
Potts Point 88
Powerhouse Museum 75
Press Books 88
Pretty Dog 135
Prince Alfred Park
  Playground 85
Primavera 29
Print Room 95
Pro Dive 162
public holidays 32
public transport 282
Pullman Quay Grand
  Suites Sydney 281
Pylon Lookout 54
Pyrmont 74-76

Q

QT Sydney 269
Quay 59
Quarrymans 76
Queen Victoria Building 69

R

Railway Square YHA 272
Randwick 116-17
Ravesi's 277
Razorhurst 48
Red Rattler 208
Redfern 84-87
Regents Court Hotel 281
religion 292
Retreat at Wisemans 229
Retro on Regent 87
Reuben Hills 81
Revesby Woker's Club 211
Revolver 126
Rino Saffioti's Chocolate
  Shop 128
Ripples Houseboat
  Holidays 229

Ritz Cinema Randwick 181
Riverside Brewing
Company 157
Riverside Theatres 217
Riverview Hotel 121
Rockpool 68
Rocks, The 52-59
Rocks Aroma Festival, The
39
Roosevelt 91
Rose Bay 114-117
Rose Hotel 88
Rose Seidler House 257
Roseberry 163
Roslyn Packer Theatre 217
Rosso Pomadoro 121
Rouse Hill House & Farm
158
Royal 126
Royal Albert Hotel
Royal Botanic Gardens 67
Royal National Park 162
Royal Randwick
Racecourse 117
Rozelle 120-123
Ruby's Diner 102
Rushcutters Bay 111-112
Rushcutters Bay Kiosk 111
Russell 268
Rydges Cronulla 281
Rydges North Sydney 278
Rydges World Square 270

S

safety & security 292
Sagra 78
Saké 56, 113
Salamander Shores 233
Salt Meats Cheeses 141
SAW Bike Tours 49
Scenic World 226
Sculpture by the Sea 30
Sea Life Sydney Aquarium
75
Sean's Panorama 108
Seasonal Concepts 87
Seasons Darling Harbour
281
Sefa Kitchen 108
Seoul Orizin 71
Seymour Centre 217
SH Ervin Gallery 54
Shady Pines Saloon 79
Shangri-La 267
Shark Beach 168
sharks 175
Sheaf 113
Shelly Beach 173
Sheraton on the Park 269
Shift Bar & Club 195
Shop Next Door 151
Showbox Coffee Brewers 150
Side Car 142
Signal 199
Simpsons Hotel Potts
Point 274
Single Origin CBD 68
Sir William Wallace Hotel
131

Skarfe 91
Skyline Drive-In 187
Slide 192
Slyfox 135, 194
Smalltown 152
smoking 292
snakes 291
Sokyo Sushi Bar 76
Sound Lounge 210
South, The 160-163
South Coast 234-237
Southern Highlands
238-239
Spectrum 209
spiders 291
Spit Bridge 140
Spoilt Rotten 142
Spring Street Social 103
St Andrew's Cathedral 62
St Jude 86
St Mary's Cathedral 67
Stables Theatre 217
Standard Bowl 203
Star Bar 211
Star 75
State Library of New
South Wales 67
State Theatre 206, 217
Stillery 114
Stinking Bishops 134
Stonewall Hotel 195
Stowaway Bar 153
Strand Arcade 70
Strickland House 115
Stuffed Beaver 110
Summerhill 127
Sunset Cinema 187
Surly's 82
Surry Hills 80-84
Surveyor General Inn 239
Susannah Place Museum
54
Sydney Beachhouse
YHA 280
Sydney Central YHA 271
Sydney Comedy Festival
36
Sydney Connection 48
Sydney Convicts 198
Sydney Cricket Ground 99
Sydney Culture Walk 48
Sydney Dance Company
218
Sydney Festival 33
Sydney Film Festival 38,
188
Sydney Fish Market 75
Sydney Harbour Bridge 54
Sydney to Hobart Yacht
Race 31
Sydney Jewish Museum
77
Sydney Lyric 218
Sydney Manga & Anime
Show (SMASH) 39
Sydney Observatory 54
Sydney Opera House 58,
59, 206, 210, 218, 221
Sydney Royal Easter Show
35

Sydney Seaplanes 51
Sydney Spokes 198
Sydney Symphony 220
Sydney Theatre Company
213
Sydney Tower Eye 67
Sydney Town Hall 67
Sydney Underground Film
Festival 188
Sydney Underwater
Bushwalking Society
198
Sydney Writers' Festival 36

T

Tallawanta Lodge 231
Tamarama Beach 170
Tappo Osteria 76
Taronga Zoo 180
Taste Cultural Food Tours
48
Taste of Sydney 35
taxis 284
telephones 292
Temperance Society 128
theatre 212-218
This Must Be The Place 79
tickets 293
cheap theatre 216
ticks 291
Tien Hau 159
Thievery 124
Tim Ho Wan 143
Timbah 125
time 293
tipping 293
TITLE 145
toilets 293
Tokyo Sing Song 203
Top 3 by Design 145
tourist information 293
tours 48-51
Traditional Chip Shop 103
travel advice 287
Trekabout Tours 231
Tropfest 188
Tuchuzy 110
Twilight at Taronga 33

U

Ulladulla Guest House 237
Ultimo 74-76
Unbiased Bowling 198
Underbelly Arts Festival
39
Underground Cinema 185
Urban Theatre Projects
214

V

Vanguard 210
Vasco 86
Vaucluse 114-117
Vaucluse House 115
Vaucluse House Tearooms
Cafe 116
Verbrugghen Hall 221

Vibe Rushcutters 275
Victoria Barracks 94
Victor Churchill 101
Victoria Court Hotel 275
views 141
Vintage Record 126
visas & immigration
293
Vivid 38

W

Wake Up! 272
walking 286
Bondi to Coogee
walk 106
Water Polo by the Sea
32
Waterloo 84-87
Watsons Bay 114-117
Watsons Bay Baths 116
Watsons Bay Boutique
Hotel 116
Watsons Bay Ferry 51
Waverly 101-104
weather 293
weights & measures 293
Welcome Hotel 121
Wentworth Park
Greyhound Track 124
West, The 154-159
Westfield Bondi Junction
103
Westfield Sydney 70
Westin Sydney 269
Whale Beach 151, 174
Wharf Theatres 218
Wheels & Doll Baby
84
White Ivy 114
White Rabbit 87
Wilbur's Place 90
Wild Life Sydney Zoo
180
Wild Rover 82
Wilheimina's 122
Wine Library 95
Wolgan Valley Resort
& Spa 226
Woollahra 99-101
Woolloomooloo 88
World Bar 203
World Press Photo
Exhibition 36
World of Women Film
Festival 189
Wyndham Sydney 281

Y

Yellow 90
Yellow Bungalow 110
Y Hotel City South 274
Y Hotel Hyde Park 271

Z

Zimmermann 98
Zoo Emporium 80

INDEX

Maps

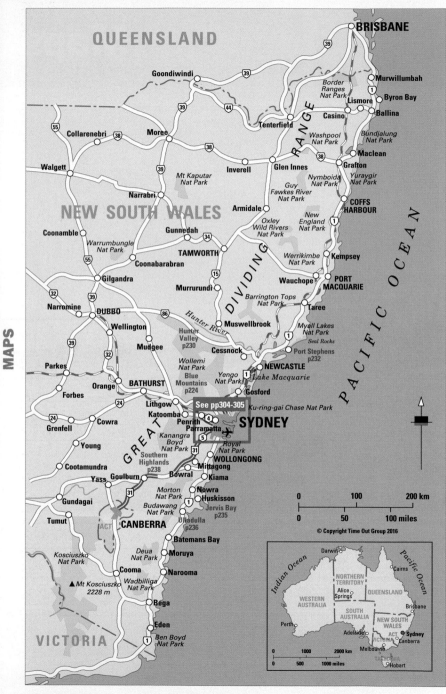

QUEENSLAND

BRISBANE

Goondiwindi

Murwillumbah

Border Ranges Nat Park

Byron Bay

Lismore

Casino

Ballina

Tenterfield

Washpool Nat Park

Bundjalung Nat Park

Collarenebri

Moree

Maclean

Walgett

Inverell

Glen Innes

Grafton

Mt Kaputar Nat Park

Guy Fawkes River Nat Park

Nymboida Nat Park

Yuraygir Nat Park

Narrabri

Armidale

Oxley Wild Rivers Nat Park

New England Nat Park

COFFS HARBOUR

NEW SOUTH WALES

Coonamble

Gunnedah

Warrumbungle Nat Park

TAMWORTH

Werrikimbe Nat Park

Kempsey

Coonabarabran

Gilgandra

Murrurundi

Wauchope

PORT MACQUARIE

Barrington Tops Nat Park

Taree

Narromine

DUBBO

Wellington

Hunter River

Muswellbrook

Myall Lakes Nat Park

Seal Rocks

Parkes

Mudgee

Hunter Valley p230

Cessnock

Port Stephens p232

Wollemi Nat Park

Yengo Nat Park

NEWCASTLE

Orange

BATHURST

Blue Mountains p224

Lake Macquarie

Forbes

Lithgow

Gosford

P A C I F I C   O C E A N

Katoomba

See pp304-305

Ku-ring-gai Chase Nat Park

Cowra

Penrith

SYDNEY

Grenfell

Parramatta

Young

Kanangra Boyd Nat Park

Royal Nat Park

WOLLONGONG

Cootamundra

Southern Highlands p238

Mittagong

Kiama

Yass

Goulburn

Bowral

Morton Nat Park

Nowra

Gundagai

Budawang Nat Park

Huskisson

Jervis Bay p235

Tumut

Ulladulla p236

CANBERRA

Batemans Bay

Deua Nat Park

Moruya

Kosciuszko Nat Park

Cooma

Narooma

▲ Mt Kosciuszko 2228 m

Wadbilliga Nat Park

Bega

Eden

VICTORIA

Ben Boyd Nat Park

MAPS

GREAT DIVIDING RANGE

| 0 | | 100 | | 200 km |
| 0 | 50 | | 100 miles | |

© Copyright Time Out Group 2016

Darwin

Indian Ocean

Pacific Ocean

NORTHERN TERRITORY

Cairns

WESTERN AUSTRALIA

Alice Springs

QUEENSLAND

SOUTH AUSTRALIA

Brisbane

Perth

NEW SOUTH WALES

ACT

Adelaide

Sydney

Canberra

VICTORIA

Melbourne

TASMANIA

Hobart

| 0 | | 1000 | | 2000 km |
| 0 | 500 | | 1000 miles | |

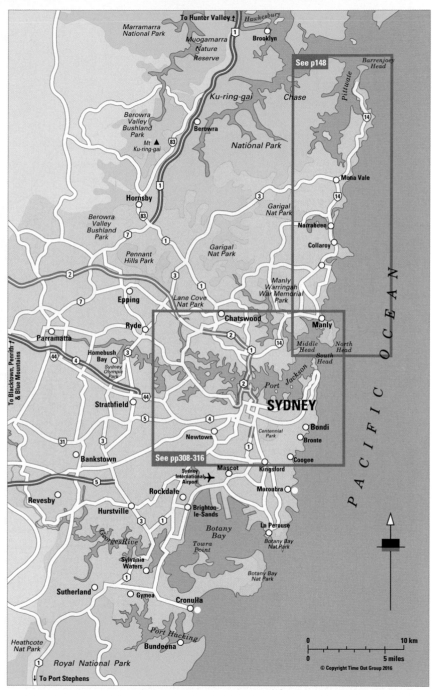

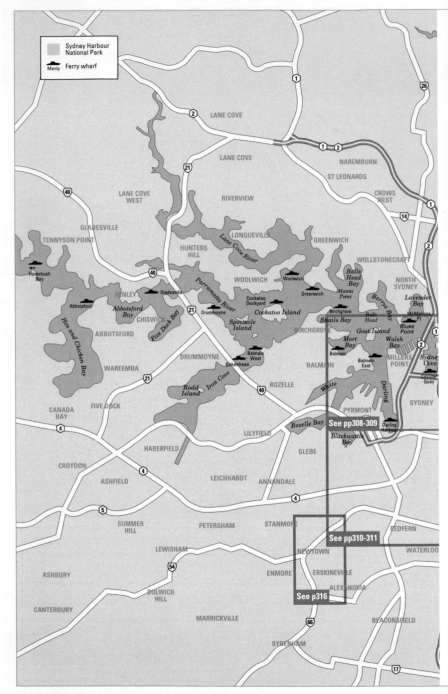

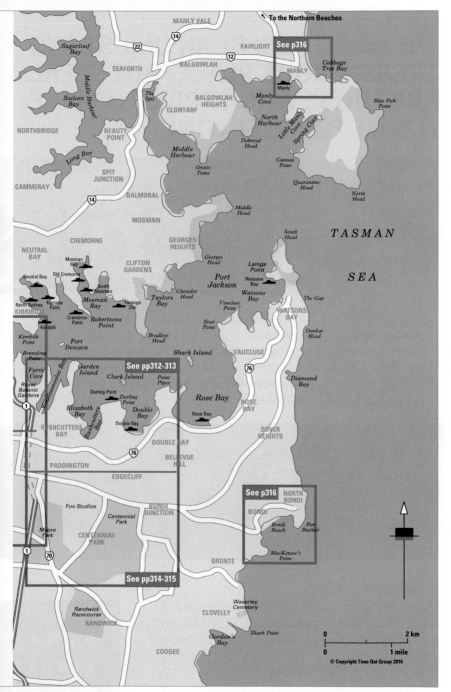

MAPS

THE WORLD CAN BE AN UNJUST AND TREACHEROUS PLACE, BUT THERE ARE THOSE WHO STRIVE TO MAKE IT SAFE FOR EVERYONE.

Operating in some of the world's most dangerous and oppressed countries, **Human Rights Watch** conducts rigorous investigations to bring those who have been targets of abuse to the world's attention. We use strategic advocacy to push people in power to end their repressive practices. And we work for as long as it takes to see that oppressors are held accountable for their crimes.

KNOWLEDGE IS POWER.
LEARN ABOUT LIFE-CHANGING EVENTS IN YOUR WORLD THAT DON'T ALWAYS MAKE THE HEADLINES AND HOW YOU CAN HELP EFFECT POSITIVE CHANGE.

Stay informed, visit HRW.org

HUMAN RIGHTS WATCH

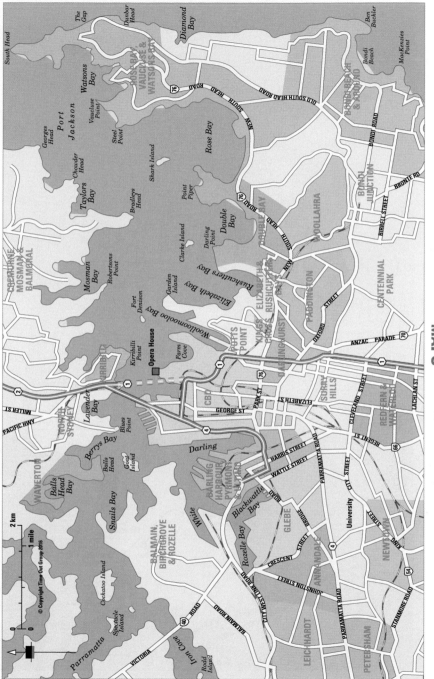

MAPS

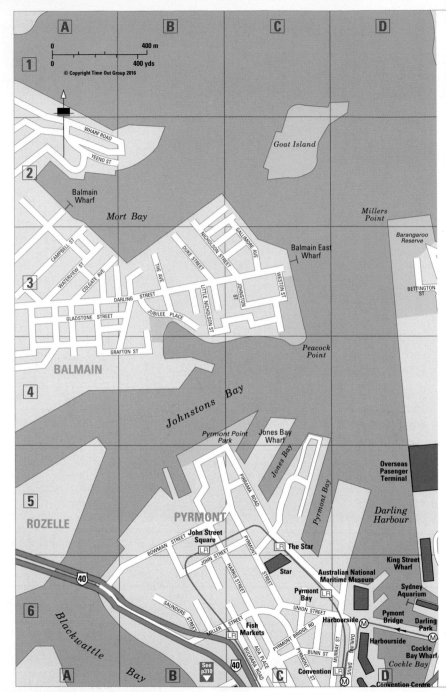

MAPS

A B C D

1
0   400 m
0   400 yds
© Copyright Time Out Group 2016

2
WHARF ROAD
YEEND ST
Balmain Wharf
Mort Bay

Goat Island

Millers Point

3
CAMPBELL ST
WATERVIEW ST
COLGATE AVE
NICHOLSON STREET
GALLIMORE AVE
DUKE STREET
THE AVE
DARLING STREET
LITTLE NICHOLSON ST
JUBILEE PLACE
JOHNSTON ST
WESTON ST
GLADSTONE STREET
Balmain East Wharf

Barangaroo Reserve

BETTINGTON ST

4
GRAFTON ST
BALMAIN
Peacock Point

Johnstons Bay

5
ROZELLE
Pyrmont Point Park
Jones Bay Wharf
Jones Bay
Pyrmont Bay

Overseas Pasenger Terminal

Darling Harbour

6
BOWMAN STREET
PIRRAMA ROAD
PYRMONT
John Street Square
LR
JOHN STREET
PYRMONT STREET
HARRIS STREET
LR **The Star**
Star
Australian National Maritime Museum
Pyrmont Bay
LR
King Street Wharf
Sydney Aquarium

Blackwattle
40
SAUNDERS STREET
MILLER STREET
Fish Markets
UNION STREET
PYRMONT BRIDGE RD
PYRMONT STREET
Harbourside Ⓜ
Pymont Bridge
Darling Park
Harbourside
Ⓜ

A
Bay
B
See p310 ▼
40
BULWARA ROAD
ADA PLACE
BUNN ST
MURRAY ST
DARLING DRIVE
C
Convention LR
Ⓜ
Cockle Bay Wharf
Cockle Bay
D
Convention Centre

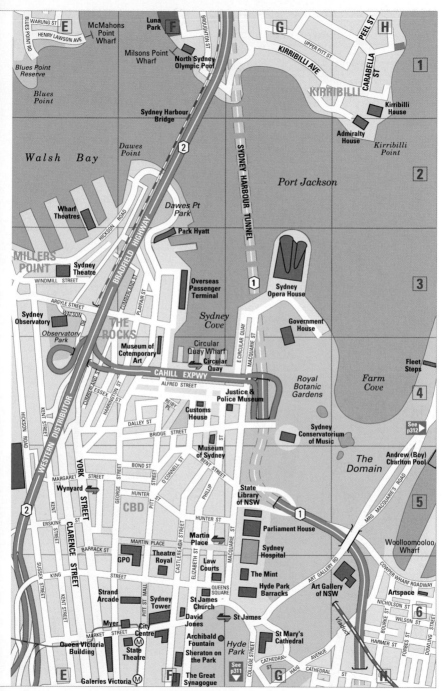

Walsh Bay

Port Jackson

Dawes Point

MILLERS POINT

THE ROCKS

Sydney Cove

Circular Quay

CAHILL EXPWY

CBD

Royal Botanic Gardens

Farm Cove

The Domain

Hyde Park

KIRRIBILLI

Kirribilli Point

E   F   G   H

1

2

3

4

5

6

MAPS

See p312

See p311

Labels on map:

WARUNG ST
BLUES POINT RD
HENRY LAWSON AVE
McMahons Point Wharf
Luna Park
BROUGHTON ST
UPPER PITT ST
KIRRIBILLI AVE
PEEL ST
CARABELLA ST
Blues Point Reserve
Milsons Point Wharf
North Sydney Olympic Pool
Kirribilli House
Blues Point
Sydney Harbour Bridge
Admiralty House
Dawes Point
SYDNEY HARBOUR TUNNEL
Wharf Theatres
Dawes Pt Park
Park Hyatt
HICKSON ROAD
BRADFIELD HIGHWAY
CUMBERLAND STREET
PLAYFAIR ST
Overseas Passenger Terminal
Sydney Opera House
Government House
Sydney Theatre
WINDMILL STREET
ARGYLE STREET
WATSON RD
Sydney Observatory
Observatory Park
Museum of Cotemporary Art
Circular Quay Wharf
Circular Quay
E CIRCULAR QUAY
MACQUARIE ST
Fleet Steps
ALFRED STREET
Customs House
Justice & Police Museum
Royal Botanic Gardens
HICKSON ROAD
KENT STREET
CUMBERLAND ST
ESSEX ST
HARRINGTON ST
REIBY PL
DALLEY ST
BRIDGE STREET
Museum of Sydney
BOND ST
BENT STREET
PHILLIP ST
Sydney Conservatorium of Music
Andrew (Boy) Charlton Pool
MRS MACQUARIES ROAD
WESTERN DISTRIBUTOR
YORK STREET
GEORGE STREET
PITT STREET
O'CONNELL ST
HUNTER
State Library of NSW
Wynyard
MARGARET STREET
Parliament House
HUNTER STREET
Woolloomooloo Wharf
CLARENCE STREET
KENT STREET
ERSKINE STREET
BARRACK ST
MARTIN PLACE
CASTLEREAGH STREET
ELIZABETH STREET
MACQUARIE ST
Sydney Hospital
Theatre Royal
Martin Place
GPO
Law Courts
The Mint
ART GALLERY RD
COWPER WHARF ROADWAY
Art Gallery of NSW
SUSSEX STREET
KING STREET
Strand Arcade
Sydney Tower
QUEENS SQUARE
Hyde Park Barracks
Artspace
NICHOLSON ST
BOURKE ST
WILSON ST
Myer
City Centre
David Jones
St James Church
St James
Viaduct
HARMER ST
FORBES ST
DOWLING STREET
MARKET STREET
Queen Victoria Building
State Theatre
PITT ST MALL
Archibald Fountain
St Mary's Cathedral
Galeries Victoria
The Great Synagogue
Sheraton on the Park
COLLEGE STREET
CATHEDRAL ST
HAIG AVE
CATHEDRAL

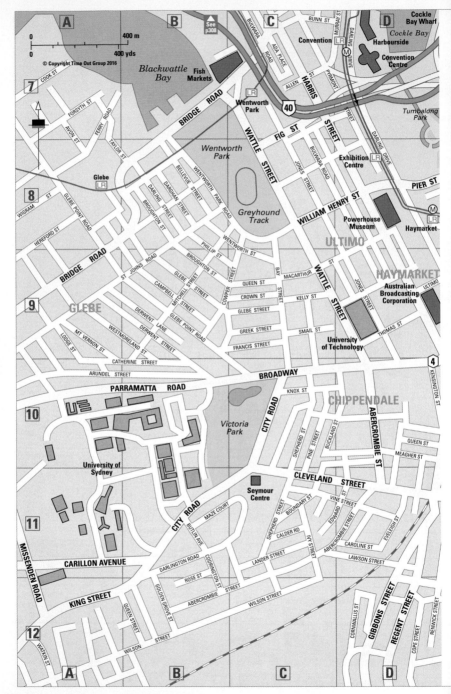

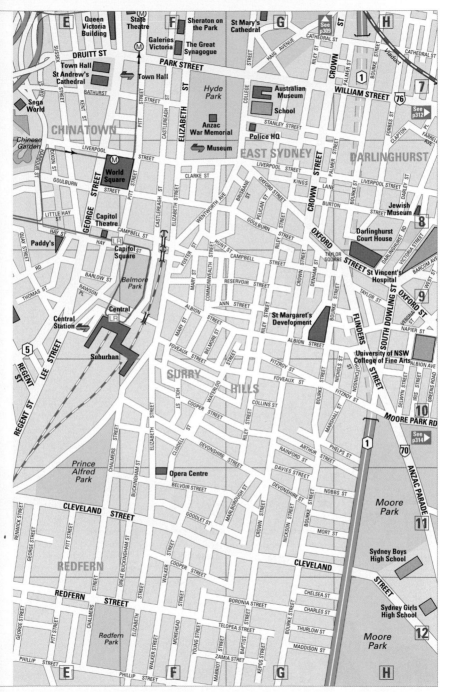

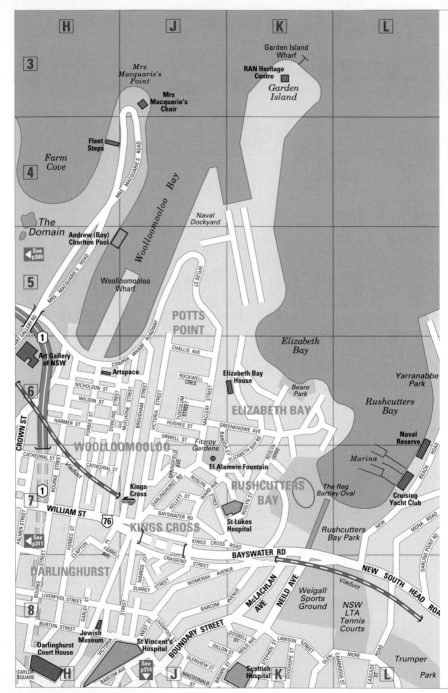

Farm
Cove

The
Domain

See
p309

H 3

J

K

L

Mrs
Macquarie's
Point

Mrs
Macquarie's
Chair

Garden Island
Wharf

RAN Heritage
Centre

Garden
Island

Fleet
Steps

Woolloomooloo Bay

Naval
Dockyard

Andrew (Boy)
Charlton Pool

Woolloomooloo
Wharf

POTTS
POINT

CHALLIS AVE

Elizabeth
Bay

Art Gallery
of NSW

Artspace

COWPER WHARF ROADWAY

NICHOLSON ST

WILSON ST

HARMER ST

WOOLLOOMOOLOO

CATHEDRAL ST

Kings
Cross

ROCKWELL
CRES

Elizabeth Bay
House

Beare
Park

Yarranabbe
Park

Rushcutters
Bay

Naval
Reserve

Marina

ELIZABETH BAY

GREENKNOWE AVE

Fitzroy
Gardens

El Alamein Fountain

RUSHCUTTERS
BAY

The Reg
Bartley Oval

Cruising
Yacht Club

WILLIAM ST

KINGS CROSS

76

BAYSWATER RD

St Lukes
Hospital

Rushcutters
Bay Park

BAYSWATER RD

NEW SOUTH HEAD ROAD

Viaduct

DARLINGHURST

See
p311

CRAIGEND STREET

WOMERAH AVENUE

BARCOM

McLACHLAN AVE

NEILD AVE

Weigall
Sports
Ground

NSW
LTA
Tennis
Courts

Viaduct

MONA ROAD

DARLING POINT RD

Jewish
Museum

St Vincent's
Hospital

BOUNDARY STREET

GOSBELL ST

Scottish
Hospital

Trumper
Park

Darlinghurst
Court House

TAYLOR
SQUARE

See
p314

H

J

K

L

MAPS

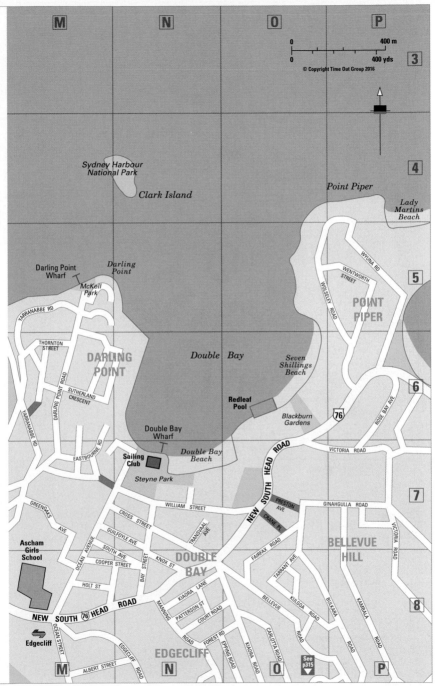

See
p315

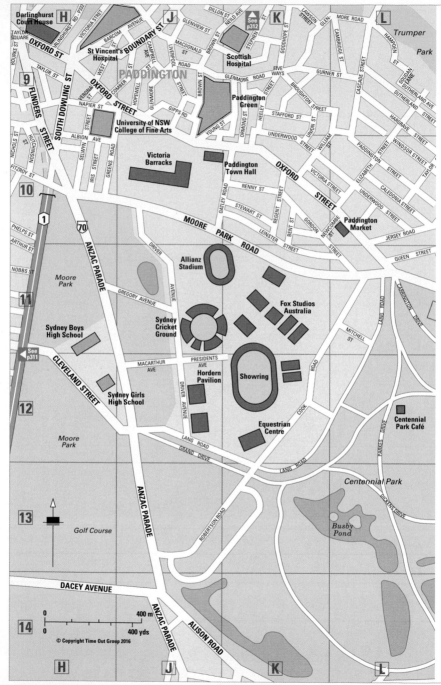

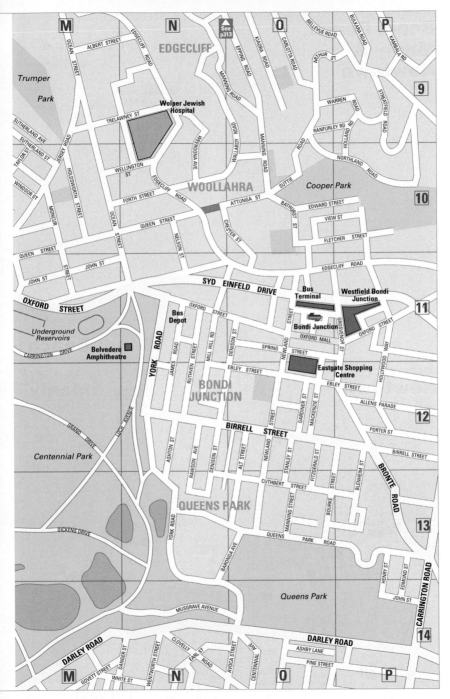

MAPS

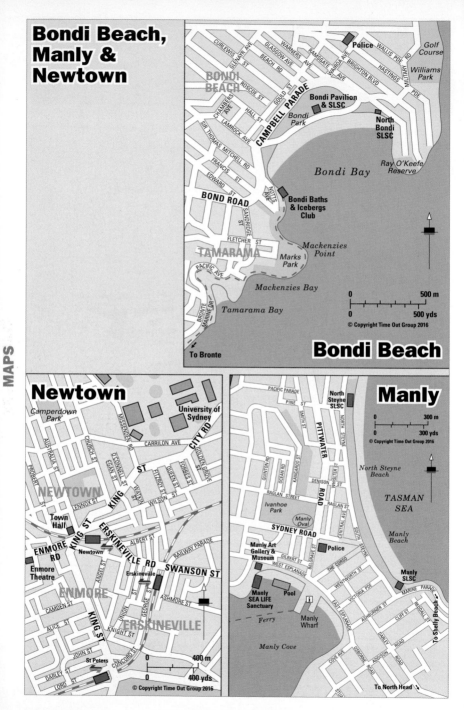

Bondi Beach, Manly & Newtown

Bondi Beach

CURLEWIS ST · WARNERS AVE · RAMSGATE AVE · WALLIS PDE · Golf Course
GLENAYR AVE · GLASGOW AVE · MARINA AVE · BRIGHTON BLVD · HASTINGS · Williams Park
BEACH RD · Police · MILITARY PDE
BONDI BEACH · ROSCOE ST · GOULD ST · CAMPBELL PARADE · Bondi Pavilion & SLSC
CHAMBERS AVE · HALL ST · North Bondi SLSC
LAMROCK AVE · Bondi Park
SIR THOMAS MITCHELL RD · Ray O'Keefe Reserve
FRANCIS ST · Bondi Bay
EDWARD ST · NOTTS AVE
BOND ROAD · Bondi Baths & Icebergs Club
SANDRIDGE ST
FLETCHER ST · Mackenzies Point
TAMARAMA · Marks Park
PACIFIC AVE · Mackenzies Bay
BRONTE MARINE DR · Tamarama Bay

0 · 500 m
0 · 500 yds
© Copyright Time Out Group 2016

To Bronte

Newtown

Camperdown Park · University of Sydney
MISSENDEN RD · CARRILON AVE · CITY RD
AUSTRALIA ST · CHURCH ST · O'CONNELL ST · EGAN ST · KING ST · QUEEN ST · FITZROY ST · FORBES ST · GOLDEN GROVE
PROBERT ST · LENNOX ST · WATKIN ST · WILSON ST
NEWTOWN · KING ST · Town Hall · ERSKINEVILLE RD · ALBERT ST · RAILWAY PARADE
ENMORE RD · Newtown · SWANSON ST
Enmore Theatre · ANGEL ST · Erskineville · ASHMORE ST
ENMORE · GEORGE ST
CAMDEN ST · ERSKINEVILLE · KING ST · KNIGHT ST
ALICE ST
JOHN ST · St Peters · CONCORD RD
DARLEY ST
LORD ST
0 · 400 m
0 · 400 yds
© Copyright Time Out Group 2016

Manly

PACIFIC PARADE · PINE ST · North Steyne SLSC
SMITH ST · PITTWATER ROAD · NORTH STEYNE
QUINTON RD · OCEAN RD · KANGAROO ST · DENISON ST · North Steyne Beach
RAGLAN ST · RAGLAN AVE · TASMAN SEA
Ivanhoe Park · CENTRAL AVE · WHISTLER ST
SYDNEY ROAD · Manly Oval · SOUTH STEYNE · Manly Beach
Manly Art Gallery & Museum · GILBERT ST · Police · BELGRAVE ST
WEST ESPLANADE · THE CORSO
Manly SEA LIFE Sanctuary · Pool · WENTWORTH ST · VICTORIA PDE · Manly SLSC
Ferry · Manly Wharf · EAST ESPLANADE · MARINE PARADE
ASHBURNER ST · DARLEY RD · CLIFF ST · KENDALL ST
Manly Cove · COVE AVE · OSBORNE RD · ADDISON RD · To Shelly Beach
0 · 300 m
0 · 300 yds
© Copyright Time Out Group 2016

To North Head

Street Index

Abercrombie Street – p310 B12/C11/12/D10/11
Ada Place – p308 C6/7, p310 C6/7
Albert Street – p313 M9, p315 M9
Albion Avenue – p311 H9/10, p314 H10
Albion Street – p311 F9/G9/ H9/10
Alfred Street – p309 F3
Alison Road – p314 J14/K14
Allen Street – p310 C7
Allens Parade – p315 P12
Alt Street – p315 O12/13
Ann Street – p311 F9/G9
Anzac Parade – p311 H10/11, p314 H10/11/J12/13/14
Argyle Street – p309 E3/F3
Art Gallery Road – p309 G6/ H5, p312 H5
Arthur Street – p311 G10/ H10/11, p314 H10/111, p315 O9/P9
Arundel Street – p310 A10/ B10
Ashby Lane – p315 O14
Ashton Street – p315 N12
Attunga Street – p315 O10
Avoca Street – p315 N14/ O14
Avon Street – p310 A7/8

Baptist Street – p311 G12
Barcom Avenue – p311 H9, p312 H9/J8/9/K8, p314 H9/J8/9
Barlow Street – p311 E9
Baroda Street – p312 J6/7
Baronga Avenue – p315 N13/ O13
Barrack Street – p309 E5
Bathurst Street – p311 E7/F7
Bathurst Street – p315 O10
Bayswater Road – p312 J7/K7
Bellevue Road – p313 O8, p315 O8
Bellevue Street – p310 B8
Belmore Street – p311 F9
Belvoir Street – p311 F11/ G11
Bent Street – p309 F4
Bent Street – p314 K10
Bettington Street – p308 D3
Birrell Street – p315 N12/ O12/P12
Blenheim Street – p315 P12/13
Blues Point Road – p309 E1
Bond Street – p309 F4
Boronia Street – p311 F12/ G12
Boundary Street – p310 C11
Boundary Street – p312 J8, p314 J9
Bourke Street – p309 H6, p311 G9-12/H7/8/9, p312 H6/7/8, p314 H9, p315 O12/13
Bowman Street – p308 B5
Bridge Road – p310 A8/9/ B7/8
Bridge Street – p309 F3/G3
Brisbane Street – p311 G8
Broadway – p310 C10/D10
Bronte Road – p315 P12/13
Brougham Street – p312 J6/7
Broughton Street – p309 F1
Broughton Street – p310 B8/9
Broughton Street – p314 K9
Brown Place – p312 J9

Brown Street – p314 J9
Buckingham Street – p311 F10/11
Buckland Street – p310 C10/ D10
Bulkara Road – p313 O8/ P8/9, p315 P8/9
Bulwara Road – p308 C6/7, p310 C6/7/8/D8
Bunn Street – p308 C6, p310 C6
Burton Street – p311 G8/H8, p312 H8/J8
Butlin Avenue – p310 B11

Calder Road – p310 C11
Caledonia Street – p314 L10
Cambridge Street – p312 L8/9, p314 L9
Campbell Avenue – p314 J9
Campbell Street – p308 A3
Campbell Street – p310 B9
Campbell Street – p311 E8/ F8/9/G9
Carabella Street – p309 H1
Carillon Avenue – p310 A11/ B11
Carlotta Road – p313 O8/9, p315 O9
Caroline Street – p310 D11
Carrington Drive – p314 L11, p315 M11
Carrington Road – p315 P13/14
Cascade Street – p312 L8/9, p314 L9
Castlereagh Street – p309 F5/6, p311 F7/8/9
Cathedral Street – p309 G6/7/ H7, p311 G7/H7, p312 H7
Catherine Street – p310 A10/ B10
Centennial Avenue – p315 O14
Challis Avenue – p312 J6
Chalmers Street – p311 E10/11/12
Charles Street – p311 G12
Chelsea Street – p311 G12
Chester Street – p315 N10/ O10
City Road – p310 B11/C10/11
Clapton Place – p311 H7, p312 H7
Clarence Street – p309 E5/6
Clarke Street – p311 F8
Cleveland Street – p310 C11/ D11, p311 E11/F11/G11/H11/12, p314 H12
Clisdell Street – p311 F10/11
Clovelly Road – p315 N14
Codrington Street – p310 B11/12
Colgate Avenue – p308 A3
College Street – p309 G6/7, p311 G7/8
Collins Street – p311 G10
Comber Street – p314 H9/ J8/9
Commonwealth Street – p311 F8/9
Cook Road – p314 K11/12/ L11
Cook Street – p310 A7
Cooper Street – p311 F10/ G10, p311 F11/12
Cooper Street – p313 M8/N8
Cope Street – p310 D12
Cornwallis Street – p310 D12
Court Road – p313 N8
Cowper Street – p310 B9/C9

Cowper Wharf Roadway – p309 H6, p312 H6/J5/6
Craigend Street – p312 J8
Crane Place – p313 O7
Cross Street – p313 N7
Crown Street – p309 H6/7, p312 H6
Crown Street – p310 C9
Crown Street – p311 G7-12
Cumberland Street – p309 E4/F3
Cuthbert Street – p315 O13

Dacey Avenue – p314 H14
Dalley Street – p309 F3
Danger Street – p315 M14/ N14
Darghan Street – p310 B8
Darley Road – p315 M14/ N14/O14/P14
Darley Street – p311 H8, p312 H8
Darling Drive – p308 D6, p310 D7/8/9
Darling Point Road – p312 L7/8, p313 M6
Darling Street – p308 A3/B3/ C3, p310 B8
Darlinghurst Road – p311 H7/8, p312 J7/H8
Darlington Road – p310 B11
Davies Street – p311 G10/11
Day Street – p311 E7
Denham Street – p311 G9
Denison Street – p315 N12/13
Derwent Lane – p310 A9/B9
Derwent Street – p310 A9/ B9/10
Devonshire Street – p311 F10/G10/11
Dickens Drive – p314 L13, p315 M13
Dillon Street – p312 J8/K8, p314 J8
Dixon Street – p311 E8
Dowling Street – p309 H6, p312 H6/7
Driver Avenue – p314 J10/11/12
Druitt Street – p311 E7
Duke Street – p308 B3

Earl Street – p315 N14
East Circular Quay – p309 G3/4
Eastbourne Rd – p313 M6/7
Ebley Street – p315 N12/O12/ P12
Edgecliff Road – p313 M8/ N8/9, p315 N9/10/O11/P11
Edmund Street – p315 P13/14
Edward Street – p310 C11/ D11
Edward Street – p315 O10/ P10
Elizabeth Bay Road – p312 K6/7
Elizabeth Street – p309 F5/6, p311 F7-12
Elizabeth Street – p314 L9/10
Epping Road – p313 O8/9, p315 O9
Erskine Street – p309 E5
Essex Street – p309 E4
Eveleigh Street – p310 D11

Fairfax Road – p313 O7/8
Farrell Avenue – p311 H7, p312 H7
Ferry Road – p310 A7/8

Fig Street – p310 C7/8
Fitzgerald Street – p315 O12/13
Fitzroy Street – p311 G10/ H10, p314 H10
Five Ways – p314 K9
Fletcher Street – p315 O10/ P10
Flinders Street – p311 H9/ 10, p314 H9/10
Forbes Street – p309 H6, p311 H7/8, p312 H6/7/8
Forest Road – p313 N8/O8
Forsyth Street – p310 A7
Forth Street – p315 N10
Foster Street – p311 F8/9
Foveaux Street – p311 F9/ 10/G10
Francis Street – p310 C9

Gallimore Avenue – p308 C3
Gardiner Street – p315 O12
George Street – p309 E5/6/ F4/5/6, p311 E7-12
Gibbons Street – p310 D11/12
Ginahgulla Road – p313 O7/P7
Gipps Road – p314 J9
Gladstone Street – p308 A3
Glebe Point Road – p310 A8/ B9
Glebe Street – p310 B9/C9
Glenmore Road – p312 K8/9/ L8, p314 J9/K8/9/L8
Glenview Street – p312 J8/9, p314 J8/9
Golden Grove Street – p310 B12
Goodhope Street – p312 K8/9, p314 K8/9
Goodlet Street – p311 F11/ G11
Gordon Street – p314 K10/ L11
Gosbell Street – p312 K8
Goulburn Street – p311 E8/ F8/G8
Govett Street – p315 M14
Grafton Street – p308 A4/B4
Grand Drive – p314 J12/K13/ L12, p315 M12
Great Buckingham Street – p311 F11/12
Greek Street – p310 C9
Greenknowe Avenue – p312 J6/K6
Greenoaks Avenue – p313 M7
Greens Road – p311 H10, p314 H10
Gregory Avenue – p314 H11/ J11
Grosvenor Street – p315 P11/12
Guilfoyle Avenue – p313 M7/ N7
Gurner Street – p314 K9/L9

Haig Avenue – p309 G6/7, p311 G7
Hampden Street – p314 L9
Harbour Street – p311 E7/8
Hargrave Street – p314 L9/10
Harmer Street – p309 H6, p312 H6
Harrington Street – p309 E4/ F3/4
Harris Street – p308 B5/C6, p310 C6/7/D8/9
Hay Street – p311 E8/9/F10
Heeley Street – p314 K9
Henry Lawson Avenue – p309 E1

Henry Street – p315 P13/14
Hereford Street – p310 A8
Hickson Road – p309
  E34/5/6/F2
Holdsworth Street – p315 M10
Holland Road – p315 P9 /10
Hollywood Way – p315 P11/12
Holt Street – p311 F10
Holt Street – p313 M8
Hopewell Street – p314 J9
Hughes Street – p312 J6
Hunt Street – p311 F8
Hunter Street – p309 F4
Hutchinson Street – p311
  H9/10, p314 H9/10

**Iris Street – p311 H10, p314
H10**
Ivy Street – p310 C11

James Road – p315 N11/12
Jersey Road – p314 L10, p315
  M9/10
John Street – p308 B5/6/C5
John Street – p315 M11
Johnston Street – p308 C3
Jones Street – p310 C7/8/D9
Jubilee Place – p308 B3

**Kambala Road – p313 P8,
p315 P9**
Kellett Street – p312 J7
Kelly Street – p310 C9
Kensington Street – p310 D9
Kent Street – p309 E4/5/6,
  p311 E7
Kepos Street – p311 G12
Kiaora Lane – p313 N8
Kiaora Road – p313 O8/9,
  p315 O9
King Street – p309 E6/F6
King Street – p310 A12
Kings Cross Road – p312j7
Kings Lane – p311 G8/H8
Kirribilli Avenue – p309 G1
Knox Street – p310 C10
Knox Street – p313 N8
Kulgoa Road – p313 O8

Lander Street – p310 C11
Lang Road – p314 J12/
  K12/13/L11/12
Lawson Street – p310 D11
Lawson Street – p312 K8,
  p314 K8
Lee Street – p311 E9/10
Leinster Street – p314 K10/11
Little Hay Street – p311 E8
Little Nicholson Street – p308
  B3
Liverpool Street – p311 E8/
  F9/G9/H8/9, p312 H8/
  J8, p314 J9
Loch Avenue – p315 M12/
  13/N12
Lodge Street – p310 A9

Macarthur Avenue – p314 J12
Macarthur Street – p310 C9/
  D8/9
Macdonald Street – p312 J9,
  p314 J9
Mackenzie Street – p315 O12
Macleay Street – p312 J6/7
Macquarie Street – p309
  G3/4/5/6
Maddison Street – p311 G12
Manning Road – p313 N8,
  p315 N9/O9/10
Manning Street – p315 O12
Margaret Street – p309 E5/F5
Market Street – p309 E6/F6
Marlborough Street – p311
  F11/G11
Marriot Street – p311 F12
Marshall Street – p311 G10
Martin Place – p309 F5
Mary Street – p311 F9
Maze Court – p310 B11/C11

McElhone Street – p312 H7/
  J6/7
McLachlan Avenue – p312 K8
Meagher Street – p310 D10
Mill Hill Road – p315 N11/12
Miller Street – p308 B6/C6
Missenden Road – p310
  A11/12
Mitchell Street – p314 L11
Mona Road – p312 L7
Moncur Street – p315 M10/11
Moore Park Road – p311 H10,
  p314 J10/K10/11
Morehead Street – p311
  F11/12
Mort Street – p311 G11/H11
Mrs Macquarie's Road – p309
  H5, p312 H5/J4
Mt Vernon Street – p310 A9
Murray Street – p308 D6,
  p310 D6/7
Musgrave Avenue – p315 N13

**Napier Street – p311 H9, p314
H9**
Neild Avenue – p312 K8, p314
  K8
Nelson Street – p315 N10/11
New Beach Road – p312 L7
New South Head Road – p312
  L8, p313 M8/N8/O6/7/P6
Newcombe Street – p314 K10/
  L10
Newland Street – p315
  O11/12/13
Nichols Street – p311 H9/10,
  p314 H9/10
Nicholson Street – p308 B3/
  C3
Nicholson Street – p309 H6,
  p312 H6
Nickson Street – p311 G11
Nimrod Street – p312 J8
Nobbs Street – p311 G11/H1,
  p314 H11
Northland Road – p315 P10

Oatley Road – p314 J10/K10
Ocean Avenue – p313 M7/8
Ocean Street – p313 M8/9,
  p315 M9/10
O'Connell Street – p309 F4
Ormond Street – p314 K9
Orwell Street – p312 J6
Oxford Mall – p315 O11
Oxford Street – p313 G8/H8/
  9, p314 H9/J9/10/K10/
  L10/11, p315 M11/N11/
  O11/P11

Paddington Street – p314 L10
Palmer Street – p311 G8/
  H7/8, p312 H7
Park Street – p311 F7/G7
Parkes Drive – p314
  L11/12/13/14
Parramatta Road – p310 A10/
  B10
Patterson Street – p313 N8
Peel Street – p309 H1
Pelican Street – p311 G8
Phelps Street – p311 G10/
  H10, p314 H10
Phillip Street – p309 F3/4,
  p311 E12/F12
Pier Street – p310 D8
Pine Street – p310 C10
Pine Street – p315 O14
Pirrama Road – p308 C5
Pitt Street – p309 F3/4/5/6,
  p311 E11/12, p311 F7
Pitt Street Mall – p309 F6
Porter Street – p315 P12
Presidents Avenue – p314 J12
Preston Avenue – p313 O7
Pyrmont Bridge Road – p308
  C6
Pyrmont Street – p308 C5/
  6/7, p310 C6/7/D7/8

Quay Street – p311 E8/9
Queen Street – p310 C9, p310
  D10
Queen Street – p314 L11,
  p315 M10/N10
Queens Park Road – p315
  O13/P13
Queens Square – p309 F6/
  G6

Rainford Street – p311 G10
Ranfurley Road – p315 O9/P9
Rawson Avenue – p315
  N12/13
Rawson Place – p311 E9
Redfern Street – p311 E12/12
Regent Street – p310 D11/12
Regent Street – p314 K10
Reiby Place – p309 F3
Renny Street – p314 K10
Renwick Street – p310 D12,
  p311 E10
Reservoir Street – p311 F9/G9
Riley Street – p311
  G7/8/9/10
Robertson Road – p314 J13/
  K12/13
Rockwell Crescent – p312 J6
Rose Bay Avenue – p313 P7
Rose Street – p310 B11/12
Roslyn Gardens – p312 K6/7
Roslyn Street – p312 K7/J7
Ruthven Street – p315 N11/12

Saunders Street – p308 B6
Selwyn Street – p311 H9/10,
  p314 H9/10
Shepherd Street – p310
  C10/11
Smail Street – p310 C9
Soudan Lane – p314 L9
South Avenue – p313 M7/N8
South Dowling Street – p311
  H9/10, p314 H9/10
Spring Street – p315 O11
Springfield Avenue – p312 J7
St Johns Road – p310 A9/
  B8/9
Stafford Street – p314 K9
Stanley Street – p311 G7
Stanley Street – p315 O12/13
Stephen Street – p312 K8/9,
  p314 K8/9
Stewart Street – p314 K10
Streatfield Road – p315 P9
Surrey Street – p312 J8
Sussex Street – p309 E5/6,
  p311 E7
Sutherland Avenue – p314 L9,
  p315 M9
Sutherland Crescent – p313
  M6
Sutherland Street – p314 L9,
  p315 M9/10
Suttie Road – p315 O9/10
Syd Einfeld Drive – p315 N11/
  O11/P11
Sydney Harbour Tunnel – p309
  G1/2/3/4

Tarrant Avenue – p313 O8
Taylor Square – p311 H9,
  p312 H9, p314 H9
Taylor Street – p310 A8
Taylor Street – p311 H9,
  p314 H9
Taylor Street – p314 L10,
  p315 M10
Telopea Street – p311 F12/
  G12
The Avenue – p308 B3
Thomas Street – p310 D9,
  p311 E9
Thornton Street – p313 M6
Thurlow Street – p311 G12
Transvaal Avenue – p313 N7
Trelawney Street – p315 M9/
  N9
Tusculum Street – p312 J6

**Ultimo Road – p310 D9,
p311 E9**
Underwood Street – p314
  K9/10/L10
Union Street – p308 C6
Union Street – p314 K9
Upper Pitt Street – p309 G1/
  H1

**Verona Street – p311 H9,
p314 H9**
Victoria Road – p313 P7/8
Victoria Street – p311 H8/9,
  p312 H8/J6/7/8, p314
  H8/9
Victoria Street – p314 K10
Vine Street – p310 C11/D11

Walker Street – p311 F11/12
Wallaroy Road – p315 O9/10
Ward Avenue – p312 J7
Warren Road – p315 O9/P9
Warung Street – p309 E1
Waterloo Street – p311 F10/
  G10
Waterview Street – p308 A3
Watkin Street – p310 A12
Watson Road – p309 E3
Wattle Street – p310 C7/
  8/9/D9
Weeroona Avenue – p315
  N9/10
Wellington Street – p315
  M10/N10
Wentworth Avenue – p311
  F8/G8
Wentworth Park Road – p310
  B8/C8
Wentworth Street – p310 B8/
  C8/9
Wentworth Street – p313 P5
Wentworth Street – p315 N14
West Street – p311 H9, p312
  J8, p314 H9
Westmoreland Street – p310
  A9/B9
Weston Street – p308 C3
Wharf Road – p308 A1/2
White Street – p315 M14/
  N14
Wigram Street – p310 A8
William Henry Street – p310
  C8/D8
William Street – p311 H7,
  p312 H7
William Street – p313 N7
William Street – p314 K10
Wilson Street – p309 H6,
  p312 H6
Wilson Street – p310 A12/
  B12/C12
Windmill Street – p309 E3
Windsor Street – p314 L10,
  p315 M10
Wolseley Road – p313 O5/
  P5
Womerah Avenue – p312
  J8/K8
Wylde Street – p312 J5
Wyuna Road – p313 P5

Yarranabbe Road – p313 M5
Yeend Street – p308 A2
York Road – p315 N11/12/
  13
York Street – p309 E5/6
Young Street – p311 F12
Young Street – p314 J9

Zamia Street – p311 F12/G1

STREET INDEX

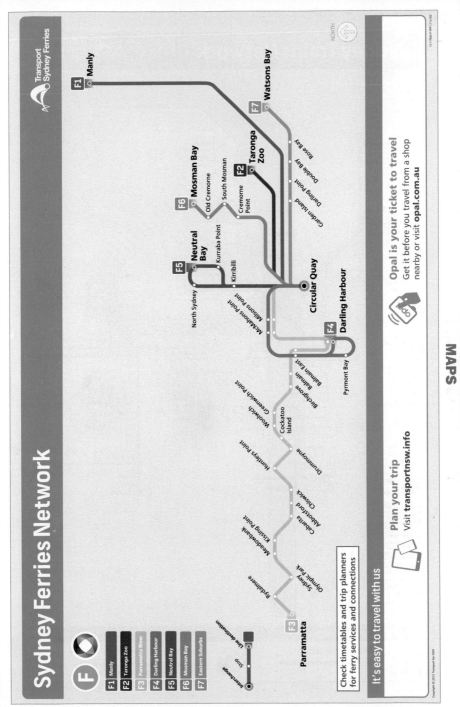

Sydney Ferries Network

Transport Sydney Ferries

F1 Manly
F2 Taronga Zoo
F3 Parramatta River
F4 Darling Harbour
F5 Neutral Bay
F6 Mosman Bay
F7 Eastern Suburbs

Line destination
Stop
Interchange

Check timetables and trip planners for ferry services and connections

It's easy to travel with us

Plan your trip
Visit **transportnsw.info**

Opal is your ticket to travel
Get it before you travel from a shop nearby or visit **opal.com.au**

NORTH

Copyright © 2015 Transport for NSW

151175MA-H1PR (11/15)2

MAPS

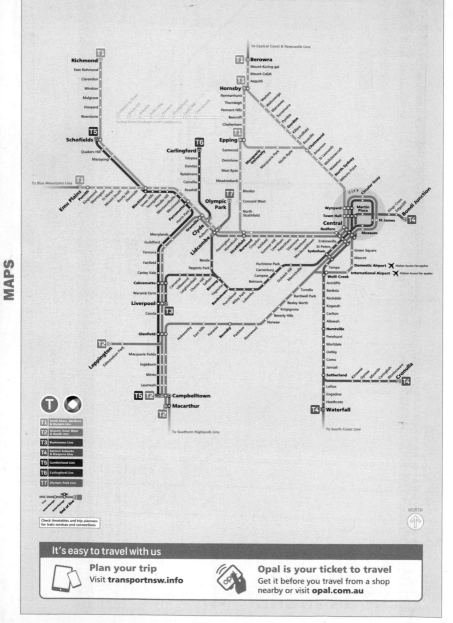

Sydney Trains Network